CALLED TO ARMS

CALLED TO ARMS

ONE FAMILY'S WAR, FROM THE BATTLE OF BRITAIN TO BURMA

EDWARD LAMBAH-STOATE

*To my wife Kitty, and to all those men and women
who understand the meaning of loyalty and duty.*

Author Edward-Lambah-Stoate was educated at Dauntsey's School in Wiltshire, where Lord Tedder was Chairman of the Governors. Having qualifed as a Chartered Surveyor he became a Regional Senior Partner of an international firm of property advisers in Bristol. Having been a CBI County Chairman he now concentrates on his own small family property company. He is the author of a book on advanced motorcycling. He and his wife Kitty have three grown-up children.

Back cover, below: painting of Norman Stoate's ML 909
by Paul Marx.

First published 2011

The History Press
The Mill, Brimscombe Port
Stroud, Gloucestershire, GL5 2QG
www.thehistorypress.co.uk

British Library Cataloguing in Publication Data.
A catalogue record for this book is available from the British Library.

ISBN 978 0 7524 5888 5

Typesetting and origination by The History Press
Printed in Great Britain

CONTENTS

ACKNOWLEDGEMENTS

I would like to thank Jean Roberts who sowed the seed for this book, Rodney Scrase who warmly introduced me to many people who knew and flew with Roy Hussey, and Alistair Donald at the Royal Marines Museum, Eastney. Also all those long suffering and interested people at the National Archives and the Imperial War Museum who were so unfailingly enthusiastic and helpful, Stuart Cruse who produced my maps and David and Geoffrey Stoate who not only gave me material help but moral encouragement as well. Last but not least, many thanks to Angus Mansfield who introduced me to his publishers, and Shaun Barrington at The History Press who encouraged me onward.

THE PRINCIPAL MEMBERS OF THE FAMILY WHO SERVED

Jack (Arthur Donald) Stoate. The author's father. Transferred from the Home Guard to the Royal Marines.

Betty Hussey. The author's mother. Served in the Women's Land Army.

Roy Hussey. Fighter pilot.

Tom Stoate. RAF doctor.

David Stoate. Lieutenant in the Honourable Artillery Company and prisoner of the Japanese.

Norman Stoate. Naval rating and later commander of a fast patrol boat.

Geoffrey Stoate. Royal Observer Corps.

FOREWORD

I met Edward Lambah-Stoate a little while ago now, at a wedding. I recall us having an interesting chat about a little local difficulty that we at the Royal Navy were having at the time – namely, the recovery of one our destroyers that had hit some rocks in the Southern Ocean. It was with pleasure and I might say some surprise that after all these years Tony Mather, a mutual friend, contacted me to say that Edward had written a book about the Second World War and would I consider writing a foreword?

There are of course many books about the Second World War but with the passing of time those actually involved in that struggle become fewer and with a refreshingly light touch Edward has successfully managed to embody many personal reminiscences from those survivors yet maintain an authoritative structure to entertain and educate the reader. At times we are asked to hover above the daily activities of members of the family and at others it is precisely those daily experiences that captivate and enthral. Inevitably, the story is sometimes heartrending but happily it often provides amusement. In all we are provided with a well crafted, almost complete picture of that conflict. The only notable gap in theatres not served in by the family is the North Atlantic.

What marks this work out from most is that although there are many books about individuals or even groups of individuals, this book tracks the war experiences of a single family – or more correctly two families that were joined by marriage. Almost as if it were set up for future readers, the members of the family served in all the services, Royal Navy, Royal Marines, Army and Royal Air Force. We are also let into the workings of the home front, by way of the Home Guard and Women's Land Army, and the invaluable work of the Royal Observer Corps in protecting our island shores.

It must be rare indeed to see a single family so widely represented across the services and across the main theatres of war having a descendant with the enthusiasm and skill to inform and entertain us in the same breath. We move from the Indian Ocean, to the Eastern and Western Mediterranean, Home Waters and D-Day and on to the Baltic, sailing in Capital Ships and what the author calls the Small Ships War. We endure gruesome years of captivity on the Burma–Siam Railway under the Japanese as well as life in the RAF through the eyes of a well decorated fighter pilot ace and contrastingly through those of a frontline doctor in North Africa, Sicily and Italy.

This book is a timely reminder that today's conflicts are vastly different. There is no 'front line' – hardly a visible enemy. Our forces are thin on the ground yet if we get it wrong, the effect could be as far reaching as failure would have been against Nazi oppression. The major difference between then and now is that then every family was touched in one way or another – today we can pretend we are not.

The research that has gone into this book which might otherwise have remain buried has, I am told, been very informative to the surviving members of the family, made more poignant by the intervening death of three veterans of 72 Squadron with whom the author spent some time. It is a sad reminder that first-hand accounts of those days are slipping away from all of us.

From my years of service as a regular officer, I can acknowledge the debt that we all owe those ordinary civilians who became servicemen as volunteers or by conscription; it should never be underestimated, but at the same time we should never undervalue either those regulars whose job it was to train and organise this vast, eclectic mass of individuals to fight for their nation as never before.

Admiral Sir Jonathon Band GCB, DL, ADC

1

ENTRY LEVEL

A birthday celebration opens a window on the past

My uncle, Tim Hussey, was celebrating his 80th birthday in the Black Horse Inn Mangotsfield, near Bristol, just down the road from the Folly Inn where he and his siblings were brought up. During the evening a woman came up to me and said, 'You don't know who I am, do you?' I replied that I knew exactly who she was (and I did) but that I couldn't remember her name. Jean Roberts (that was her name) and I struck up a conversation. Nine months or so later, Jean and her husband Lloyd presented me with several newspaper cuttings, postcards and letters concerning my uncle Roy Hussey, many of these clippings I remember having seen as a small boy in a box of my mother's, but these had been lost after her death in 1972. I was thrilled.

As we got talking, she and he husband Lloyd (who had been at Chipping Sodbury Grammar School with Roy) told me where Roy's grave was located, at Coxley just south of Wells. Close to Armistice Day in November 2005 my wife Kitty and I went down to look at the churchyard and at my wife's suggestion we put a small cross and poppy on the grave with the name Edward Hussey (my mother's maiden name) and my mobile phone number on the back.

Three months later my phone rang and a voice said, 'Is that Edward Hussey?' I replied that it was (knowing that the caller could only have that name from the poppy my wife and I had left at Roy's grave) and so I was introduced to Rodney Scrase, a veteran fighter pilot of the Second World war who had flown in 72 Squadron with my uncle and who still made an annual pilgrimage to Roy's grave from his home in south London.

I had a rough idea of my uncle's and parents' war. Roy I knew to have been a decorated fighter pilot in North Africa and Italy; but now I had a rich source of new information and so the germ of an idea to write this book was sown.

Hubert Hussey and Nellie Herniman were married in early 1920. Nellie was the eldest of seven children of Edwin and Alice Herniman. Edwin must have been an adventurous spirit. Some time before 1900, he took a job as a herdsman for cattle being transported from England to Canada. The herd having been delivered and Ernest paid off, he went in search of gold and found

Hubert and Nellie Hussey. (Author)

Betty aged 12, after her father died. (Author)

Nellie and Roy Hussey. (Author)

Leonard Stoate. (Geoffrey Stoate)

sufficient to buy Littlewell Farm and later Greystones in Coxley just south of Wells, Somerset, and there he fattened beef and sold it in his butcher's shop at 16–18 Queen Street, Wells.

Edwin's sons were Jack and Ted and of his daughters, Nellie was the eldest, followed by Dolly, Ivy, Priscilla, Ethel (Epps) and Edwina. Edwin looked after his children well, Ivy cared for Prissy, who had special needs having fallen out of a loft window we were told. After the Second World War Jack ran a café and a taxi service from the Queen Street premises in Wells and Dolly and her husband Stan were set up at Stream Farm, North Wootton, nearby.

Nellie and Bert took a milk round in the Wells area, run from St Cuthbert Street, but Bert it seems was not a good businessman and ultimately they ended up as landlords of The Beaufort Arms, commonly known as the Folly Inn at Mangotsfield just north of Bristol. There, Nellie had three children, Betty (my mother) born on 10 September 1920, Roy, on 23 March 1923, and John (Tim) on 13 November 1925.

Bert had a keen sense of humour but he suffered from a depressive side also. The story goes that he had rustled a sheep or some such thing that caused a very public family row at the bar and on 12 March 1932 Bert took himself off and swallowed poison in a corner of a nearby field.

The suicide of her father at 12 years old had an understandable effect on my mother, Betty, and the rest of the family. Nellie had trouble coping with three children and the business on her own and Betty left home to live with her grandparents. A couple of years later she moved to London to live with a relative in Hampstead Heath where she worked in the Gown Department of Green and Edwards in Finchley High Street, London.

Betty was a bright pupil at school, but the traumas at home had cut her formal education short. During her life she never stopped educating herself and she became very knowledgeable on many matters – including ancient Middle Eastern history – until her untimely death from cancer aged 52 on 16 May 1972.

Her brother Roy Hussey was educated at Downend School and Chipping Sodbury Grammar school, he also was a bright pupil, good looking, personable and an excellent and competitive sportsman. representing the school at cricket, football and swimming. Lloyd Roberts, several

The Stoate Children. Left to right, Brenda, Tom, Norman, Donald (Jack) David and Geoffrey. (Author)

Temple Mills. (Geoffrey Stoate)

years Roy's junior, described Roy as the schoolboy hero the younger ones looked up to. Roy left grammar school at 17 years old and worked for Parnall and Sons in Bristol for a few months before he lied about his age and was accepted into the Royal Air Force Volunteer Reserve. His younger brother, Tim, and school were not naturally suited, Tim was born to be a farmer and so it transpired.

In 1911, elsewhere in the southwest of England, Leonard Stoate (a staunch Methodist) and Elsie Roberts were also married. Leonard was a shareholder and Managing Director of Stoate and Sons Ltd, his brother William being Chairman. Stoate and Sons was a flour milling business started by Leonard's grandfather, William in 1832, ultimately with interests in Watchet near Minehead, Bristol and Swansea. They ran a few ships which traded in that triangle and that is how the man from Somerset and the girl from Swansea met and fell in love. The Stoates lived at various addresses in Bristol but principally large houses called the Hermitage, in Falcondale Road, Westbury on Trym, and Redrock, Stoke Bishop, where their children, Brenda, Tom, David, Norman, Donald (Jack) and Geoffrey were brought up and privately educated.

In 1911 the Mill in Watchet suffered a disastrous fire, the business relocated and took a new 99-year lease from the Temple Church Ecclesiastical Trustees on a site on the Floating Harbour at Temple Way, Bristol. There it constructed a brand new flour mill, upon the top of which the brand VIGOL Brown bread was prominently advertised until the mill's demolition in the 1980s. In 1933 the business was sold to Spillers Milling and Leonard, although not retiring from his position of Managing Director until 1945, used this capital to invest in farms in Somerset and the Bristol area, thus fulfilling his first wish, to be a farmer. His father had insisted that he went into the family milling business.

One of those farms was called Henfield Farm, it was not far from the Folly Inn and so the scene is set for the family of modest means – publicans – and an altogether more prosperous family of landowners and businessmen to be caught up in a worldwide conflict.

2

A DREAM COME TRUE

Lying in a tin box unnoticed and unremarked upon for the best part of 60 years lay a veritable treasure, the log book, papers, photographs and documents of a Second World War fighter pilot. The pilot was my mother's brother, Roy Hussey.

Roy always wanted to be a pilot, his younger brother Tim recalled – and Tim knew even when they were small boys that all he ever wanted to be was a farmer. His elder brother Roy would tease him, whirling around all the while with his arms stretched out like aeroplane wings. 'You go on and be a farmer on your farm and I'll bomb you from my aeroplane.' So both boys knew exactly what they wanted to do in life.

Roy was 17 when he left Chipping Sodbury Grammar School and found a job at Parnall and Son, a manufacturer and supplier in the aircraft industry. The company was formed in 1820 initially as a weights and measures business, but through its association with the retail industry went on to become a shop fitter. The bronze shop fronts of the Piccadilly Arcade were created by the firm. The business then progressed to fitting out ships. During the First World War it manufactured components for aircraft and seaplanes. During World War II it again concentrated on aircraft components including the wings for the Tiger Moth, wing flaps for the Handley Page Halifax heavy bombers, fuselages for the Short Brothers' Stirling and for the Airspeed HORSA gliders and tail planes for the Bristol Beaufighter, the heavy fighter.

In 1936 the RAF had instigated the RAF Volunteer Reserve in an attempt to attract a wider range of applicants to the service, that is, non public school/officer class. The decree was 'a citizens air force', modern and democratic, attracting 'air-minded' young men from factory, shop and office. With the expansion programme, thousands of young men were now being given a choice of how they would fight the next war. Before war recruitment began the RAF recruited annually about 300 pilots and 1600 airmen but from 1935 to 1938 the average intake rose to 4500 pilots and 4000 airmen and apprentices. Pay in cash and kind was set between £340 and £520 a year. A £300 gratuity was payable after four years service or £500 after six. Roy, who still longed to fly, exaggerated his age a little and applied to the Volunteer Reserve. In 1940, his application was successful.

Pre-war the RAF boasted that no air force in the world set itself a higher standard of training. This included a detailed and exact knowledge of navigation, the theory of flight, the structure

1941, the young Roy Hussey goes to train in America. Most photographs in this chapter were kept in Roy's tin box.

The Link trainer.

Fairchild PT 19 trainer in Canada.

Roy Hussey climbing into the rear cockpit of a Fairchild PT 19 trainer at 3 BFTS Oklahoma.

of an aeroplane, the workings of an aeroengine; of air gunnery, radio, air photography and instruments; fighter tactics, bombing methods and so on. In wartime the need for pilots rose ten-fold – could quality be sacrificed for quantity?

In response to that question the Service developed a four-stage training process, first a posting to an Initial Training Wing, next an Elementary Flying Training School, then a Service Flying Training School and finally to an Operational Training Unit. When the pupil had passed the tests and examinations in the various stages he would reach the ultimate goal – an Operational Squadron.

At the Initial Training Wing, where the posting would last about a month, the pupil would spend half his time in the classroom studying the theoretical side of flying and being given basic information on health, the other half was spent at sports and games, as physical fitness was part of the training. Actual flying was not part of the ITW, but the pupil might be introduced to the workings of joystick and rudder bar in an ingenious piece of equipment called a Link Trainer. The Link Trainers had stubby fuselages and wings and were attached to the floor of a hangar by a set of bellows, which would inflate and deflate themselves in response to the movements of the joystick. It was sophisticated enough even to respond to turns of the rudder bar and manoeuvres to the extent of a spin. In 2010 I met Tony 'Red' Weller, a veteran fighter pilot of 72 Squadron and who, after the War was in the same line of business as another branch of the Stoate family, the Gliddon's of Watchet. Tony was to fly with Roy and he told me the Links were particularly useful for instrument flying training. They had a hood that closed over the 'pilot's' head leaving nothing to 'fly' by except the instruments in front of him.

Once the examinations were passed the student passed to Elementary Flying Training School and would learn to fly. The usual types flown were the Miles Magister monoplane or the Tiger Moth biplane, although in Roy's case, as we will see, he trained in American aircraft. Once again, half the day would be spent in the classroom but now the other half was devoted to practical flying. Fifty hours or more flying time would be recorded in the pupil's logbook before he completed the course. He would have learned to make forced landings, undertake simple aerobatics and short cross-country flights.

At the next stage, the Service Flying Training School, he would fly an aeroplane five or six times more powerful than hitherto, such as the two-motor Airspeed Oxford or the Avro Anson, or the single-engined Miles Master or North American Harvard. The choice was not randomly made, the pupil would have shown whether he was best suited to twins or singles and his allocation was by careful study of his temperament, rather than guesswork.

Practical flying and theory would continue side by side, but the screw tightened with blind approaches and night flying. The training programme was so thoroughly crafted that final examination failures were rare; and so at last our pupil would be proudly entitled to sew the coveted 'wings' on to his tunic.

Roy's flying logbook records his attestation took place in Oxford, he then went to a receiving station at Babbacombe near Torquay in Devon and on to No.3 Initial Training Wing in Torquay for basic training. This was followed by a PRC (Personnel Reception Centre) at Wilmslow, Cheshire and from there to Cruock (on the Clyde) where he embarked on the SS *Stratheden* for Halifax, Canada (his flying logbook was issued by the Royal Canadian Air Force).

The *Stratheden* was one of the P & O 'Strath' sister passenger liners. She was relatively new having been laid down in 1938. On board the same ship was Rodney Scrase. Roy and he were later to fly together, but on the 23,722-ton *Statheden* they were just two of the 1,000 or so passengers the vessel was capable of transportng, and did not meet up.

From Halifax Roy transferred via the Manning Department in Toronto to number 3 BFTS (British Flying Training School) in Miami, Oklahoma.

At this stage of the war many pilots were trained in the US partly because the weather conditions permitted a greater number of flying hours and thus pilots were trained faster, but also because the skies over Britain were fairly busy operationally.

Number 3 BFTS produced a little in-house magazine called *Open Post*. Squadron Leader A.C. Kermode wrote a short history of number 3 BFTS in the first edition. 'It will never be easy to decide when number 3 BFTS first came into being … We say that it was born in the early hours of that Monday morning when the British boys first met representatives of their American hosts.' That is to say 18 June 1941, when number 1 course began in earnest.

Roy's logbook begins on 27 August 1941. His was number 3 course, that is the third intake for the new unit. No.3 course had 51 cadets of which 19, including Roy, were in Fulmar flight. On the inside of the front cover of Roy's copy of *Open Post* the pupils of Fulmar flight have signed their names. Amongst those signatures was one George Longbottom. A pilot of the same name appears again in this story, but more of this later.

By 24 September 1941, the school was up to full strength with 181 cadets, split into units or 'flights' which were competitively set against one another in sports and other activities. The school was inspected on 13 October 1941 by air Marshal Garrod, Air Member for Training and Air Marshal Harris, head of the RAF delegation in Washington (later head of Bomber Command). 3 BFTS combined instruction on the Link Trainers (in which Roy completed stages 1 to 9, marked as average) as well as classroom sessions and practical flying.

On 27 August 1941 in the second seat of a Fairchild PT 19 fitted with a Ranger engine, sits Roy, learning the effect of controls, straight and level flying and medium turns, climbing and gliding. On 10 September 1941 after adding stalls and spins to his second-seat repertoire he undertook his first solo. Before doing so, he certifies in red ink 'That I understand the operation of the fuel system, the brake system, the hydraulic system including the emergency operation of the undercarriage in event of fire of a PT 19 aircraft.' September is taken up with daily flying involving Chandelles, steep turns and loops both solo and with course instructors, Rundle and Tucker. During October, again flying virtually every day, navigation, instrument flying, slow rolls and forced landings were introduced. [Rodney Scrase kindly explained 'Chandelle' – 'French for candle. The term was used in the early days of flying when the French were much involved. It is a reaction out of a steep climb, when approaching the stall you would do a sharp downward turn. Really a question of co-ordination and very often our American instructors would combine it with lazy eights. (flying a figure eight on its side and facing the ground).']

By this time Roy had clocked up nearly 72 hours of flying, about half and half dual and solo including five hours of instruments/cloud flying. On that class of aircraft, the Fairchild PT 19, Wyman P Roger, Flight Commander assessed him 'above average'.

During November he commenced flying instruction in the Voltee BT 13A with a Pratt & Whitney engine and variable pitch propeller and on 8 October 1941 took his first solo in that aeroplane.

December 1941 saw the introduction of the Harvard North American AT6 (curiously enough for a trainer, an aeroplane notoriously difficult to recover from a spin and fickle in cross-wind landing) and on the 9th he undertook his first solo in that marque of aeroplane after, of course, certifying in red ink 'That I understand the brakes, fuel, flaps and hydraulic system of the North American Harvard AT6 and action to take in case of fire in the aircraft.'

Two days prior to that was the attack on Pearl Harbor. Amongst Roy's papers is an extra edition of the *Joplin Globe* dated 6.00 pm 7 December 1941.

JAPS WAR ON U.S.

Tokyo, Dec. 8 (Monday) Japan's Imperial Headquarters announced at 6 a.m. (3 p.m. Sunday Joplin time) today that Japan had entered a state of war with the United States and Britain in the Western Pacific as from dawn today …

… Japan attacked the United States today, striking by air at the great Pearl Harbor naval base at Honolulu, and latest reports indicated that the United States had won the first battle.

Meanwhile back at 3 BFTS advanced coordination and night flying appears in Roy's logbook, with a 1 hour 40 minute cross-country run leaving and returning to Miami via Bartlesville and Chanute.

3 BTFS Roy Hussey looking out of a Voltee BT 13A with variable pitch propeller.

North American Harvard AT–6 trainer at 3 BTFS. Next stop England and Spitfires.

The *Joplin Globe*, 7 December 1941.

On 22 January 1942 he completed the course. The assessment stamp needs a second glance. It seems initially it was stamped 'above average' but subsequently amended by a splotchy ink eradicator to 'average' with a note 'requires supervision!' Whilst he was at Miami Roy compiled a photograph album. It is difficult to glean much from the many photographs as most of them are not annotated. There are, however, a couple of shots of various trainers on their noses. Maybe that had something to do with the change of certification – we will never know. Roy's total flying time is recorded as 168 hours 24 minutes, of which 46 hours and 13 minutes were dual, 50 hours and 16 minutes 30 solo, 15 hours and 50 minutes night dual, 3 hours and 20 minutes night solo and 19 hours and 44 minutes instrument/cloud flying.

On 2 May 1942 Roy returned to England to 17 AFU (Advanced Flying Unit) Watton, in Norfolk, where he flew the Miles Master and Master II aircraft, the former powered by a Bristol Mercury engine and the latter by the American Pratt and Whitney unit, he also put in a couple of sessions on a Link on 3 and 12 May. He emerged from that on 22 May 1942 with total flying time 179 hours 44 minutes, assessed 'average' and under any special faults 'erratic'. Only the Operational Training Unit now lay between him and an operational squadron. Prior to the Second World War pilots learned operational flying in an operational squadron. But wartime conditions made this impractical, it being far too risky for both existing pilots in the Squadron and new entrants. The purpose of the OTU was to introduce the pupil to combat flying without the risks of actual combat. Fighter pilots were taught combat tactics and offensive operations against ground targets. In other words pilots were taken to the edge of war without exposing them or their colleagues to its risks. Nevertheless, there were many casualties in the training units. It was at OTUs that bomber pilots were often teamed up with crews who would stick together in active service.

24 May 1942 saw Roy posted to 53 OTU (Operational Training Unit) at Llandau, near Bridgend in South Wales. It was here that another of his future colleagues in 72 Squadron, Jimmy Corbin, had been posted six months earlier as an instructor. Here the Master II was upgraded to a Spitfire I (he also put two and half hours on the Link trainer here, probably to re-enforce instrument flying training). His first solo in a Spitfire was on on 24 May. Things

become a little more serious now, apart from the usual flying training, we see 'stern attacks' and 'aerobatics'; also in June we see camera guns and drogues (canvas targets behind towing aircraft) in use. It was probably at 53 OTU that Roy was handed a neat little booklet called *Bag the Hun! Estimation of range and angle off.* It is a highly diagrammatic instruction book on deflection shooting and estimation of range. The latter achieved principally by judging the wingspan of the target against the diameter of the ring sight. This was in the days before the introduction of the reflector sight, let alone the giro sight. For example, at 400 yards the wingspan of a Wellington bomber fitted exactly across the ring, at 250 yards the ring was just outboard of the two engines. Roy was a pretty fair hand with a shotgun and rifle, this and his ability on the sportsfield would stand him in good stead later on.

On 17 June 1942, it might have all ended then as the logbook records 'Force landed 800 feet over Llandau due to engine failure – made wheels-down landing on runway – no damage.' All that investment (an estimated £20,000 against the price of a new Spitfire at £5000) and those hours of training had paid off. On 5 July 1942 Roy records 'Sgt Swan and Sgt Pearce killed – dogfighting.'

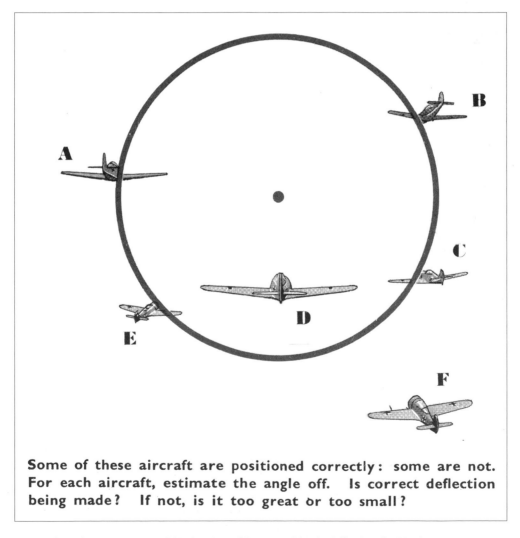

Some of these aircraft are positioned correctly: some are not. For each aircraft, estimate the angle off. Is correct deflection being made? If not, is it too great or too small?

Extract from the training manual; 'Estimation of Range and Angle Off. – Bag the Hun'.

Nellie, Betty, Roy and Tim, taken whilst Roy was at OTU. The inscription on the back in my mother's hand reads, 'Last time we were all together.' (Author)

Fun, nevertheless, seemed to be part and parcel of these fighter boys' prescription. 'Beating up' was a common practice, Roy's friend Barney Barnfather, in the biography written by his grandson Angus Mansfield, describes beating up his home town of Keynsham, near Bristol; Jimmy Corbin did the same and so did Roy. My Uncle Tim well remembers the growl of Roy's Spitfire, waggling its wings and rattling the roof tiles as he screamed at low level over his home, the Folly Inn, and no doubt the nearby Henfield Farm where my father was farm manager. Being 20 years old and in charge of what was effectively the ultimate 'piece of kit' is something of an open invitation to such behaviour.

It is instructive to compare Roy's training programme with that of two of his friends in 72 Squadron, Barney Barnfather and Jimmy Corbin. In *Barney Barnfather – Life on a Spitfire Squadron* by Angus Mansfield, Angus writes

Barney joined the RAFVR in 1940. Upon completion of basic training he was posted to Babbacombe with the Reserve Wing. Later called Initial Training Wing. After square bashing and simple exams were undertaken, flying training was carried out elsewhere in Elementary Flying Training Schools (EFTS). Barney went to 14 EFTS Elmdon Nr. Birmingham in April 1941 where he remained until the end of May. At that time Barney had clocked up approximately 13 hours dual flying and 16 hours solo in a Miles Master, he had covered cross-country flying, instrument flying and at that time was an aspirational pilot. Following some hours in a Hawker Hurricane he was awarded his wings and was posted to 57 OTU where he learned to fly Spitfires. At the time he was posted to an operational squadron he had logged a little over 200 hours flying time.

Jimmy Corbin in his book *Last of the 10 Fighter Boys*, describes how he joined 66 Squadron, his first operational squadron, after 29 hours flying in Spitfires as well as having spent some 13 weeks at the FTS although as he says, it should have been seven weeks, the course was extended due to bad weather. Jimmy notes that he was never taught aerobatics.

In 1938/9 the normal time in an OTU was six weeks. In 1940 at the height of the Battle of Britain it shortened on occasion to two weeks. It was a frequent criticism that some pilots had never fired at an aerial target before going into action. One of those early recruits, Geoffery Wellum in his book *First Light* reveals he had completed a mere 160 hours and had never sat in, let alone flown, a Spitfire when he was posted operational to 92 Squadron. So it is heart-ening to note that in early 1942 Roy's time at OTU at Llandow was twelve weeks. His time there shows him doing air-to-ground, air-to-sea and air-to-air firing practice with and without camera gun, including dogfighting, deflection attacks, aerobatics and formation weaving.

On 3 July 1942, 53 OTU was moved to Rhoose, near Cardiff and ten and half months after starting his training in Oklahoma, on 21 July 1942, Roy passed out, assessed by Squadron Leader A.R Edge as 'above average' with total flying hours of 240 hours 53 minutes under his belt. A sergeant pilot. Next stop an operational posting.

3

A PROPER JOB AT LAST

Roy Hussey takes his newly learned skills to war in North Africa

---

When Roy joined 72 Squadron aged 19 at the beginning of July 1942. He had completed 168 hours and 24 minutes of flying in America, 11½ hours at the Advanced Flying Unit at Watton, Norfolk and 52 hours on Spitfires in 53 Operational Training Unit at Llandau and Rhoose. The investment in him was therefore very considerable. On 2 July 1942 he took his first flight at 72 Squadron of 30 minutes – a reconnaissance flight in a Spitfire 5b – an aeroplane he was to become very familiar with.

72 Squadron was not just any old squadron, it was battle-hardened and Roy was fortunate to be in the company of seasoned pilots such as Brian Kingcome (the CO who between June and October 1940 destroyed seven enemy aircraft) David Cox, Robbie Robertson, Bobby Oxspring, Jimmy Corbin, Danny Daniels and others who had seen action in the Battle of Britain. These people understood the importance of flying and fighting as a unit, trusting in and being trusted by your colleagues.

Jimmy Corbin joined 72 Squadron shortly after Roy, in August 1942. He had experienced combat at the end of the Battle of Britain, had been an instructor at 53 OTU, and was 23 years old – known to some as 'uncle' because of his extreme age! He describes Roy, in *The last of the Few*: 'Roy Hussey was a Sergeant Pilot. He was a nice boy, an excellent pilot who shot down quite a few enemy aircraft.'

During August and September 1942, apart from a one-hour convoy patrol Roy completed some 42 hours of additional training with 72 Squadron including gunnery – ground and air target practice – formation flying and so forth. On 6 and 11 October he undertook 2 hours and 25 minutes convoy patrol and then the Squadron was transferred, via Morpeth, to Ayr in Scotland. On 9 September Roy was transferred again to Londonderry and on 21 October 1942 he departed from Londonderry on HMS *Bideford* en route to Gibraltar and a proper job, now having 284 hours 43 minutes of flying time to his credit. It is worthy of note that the Squadron was split into various ships embarking from different ports, Jimmy Corbin, for example, embarked on SS *Staffordshire,* a merchant cargo vessel starting from the Manchester

The Sergeant Pilot returns. Roy Hussey shortly before overseas posting with 72 Squadron. Found in Roy's tin box.

Ship Canal though Liverpool to the Clyde where the convoy formed up. *Staffordshire* arrived at Gibraltar two days before Roy on board the *Bideford*.

HMS *Bideford* was a Shoreham Class naval sloop, a general-purpose escort vessel, used in convoys to mine sweep and for general convoy duties. She was built in 1931 and broken up by 1949.

In stark contrast to German U-boat failures after the Enigma code was broken in 1943 (after which two in every three U-boat crew perished) in October 1942, German U-boat activity was causing massive attrition to Allied shipping. The Squadron's journey from Belfast to Gibraltar was by no means safe or straightforward; on 6 October Roy records that *Bideford* picked up 36 survivors from a torpedoed liner. The squadron was later to learn that part of their personal luggage and some 20 tons of the Squadron's stores carefully stowed on board a merchant ship were also lost — an event to be repeated later when the Squadron transferred from Tunisia and Malta to Italy, where a ship carrying squadron equipment was sunk in Bari harbour near Brindisi in southern Italy.

Since the entry of the US into the conflict on 8 December 8 1941 her efforts were poured into arresting the Japanese advance through the southern Pacific and halting Rommel's push to Egypt. 72 Squadron was on its way to support an Allied offensive in North Africa that was in effect a plan 'B'. The Americans were all for an immediate offensive in North West Europe, however, Churchill managed to persuade Roosevelt that such an enterprise could not be undertaken with available resources until 1943 at the earliest. On 19 August 1942 the assault at Dieppe failed, where the Canadians took the brunt of the losses, and it was not until June 1944, D-Day, that sufficient troops and equipment were assembled to make an offensive move into North West Europe a practical proposition.

The plan 'B' was Operation *Torch*, an attack upon French West Africa to clear Axis forces completely out of the southern Mediterranean, so this area would be free to create a springboard into Italy, southern France and the Balkans (the so-called soft underbelly of Europe).

The reaction of the French to such an undertaking was by no means a forgone conclusion, particularly if the assault in French-held territories was to be by British troops. Consequently the Americans were to lead the operation under the overall command of General Dwight D. Eisenhower.

The attacking forces were split into three components: the Casablanca Force (the Western Task Force) made up of US troops; the Oran Force (The Central Task Force) made up mainly of US but with some British troops; and the Algiers Force (The Eastern Task Force) mostly British but with some US troops, led by Major-General Ryder. Roy Husssey with 72 Squadron was part of the Algiers Task force.

Air support was to be given by a mixture of new and experienced squadrons and crews, with the majority of bomber capability American, and fighter capability British. Air Marshall Sir Arthur Coningham was head of the North-West African Tactical Airforce. 72 Squadron, part of 324 Wing, was an experienced Battle of Britain unit led by Bobby Oxspring, DFC and Bar. The Wing, at that time, was commanded by Gp. Capt. R.B Ronnie Lees, DFC and Bar and the Wing Leader was Wg Cdr D.A.P. McMullen, DFC and 2 Bars. The Wing fell under 242 Group.

On 12 November 1942, the Squadron landed at Gibraltar. Roy records in his logbook the following pilots under the heading '72 Squadron overseas'.

CO: S/Ldr Oxspring DFC & Bar & Bar

A Flight	Afternotes	B Flight	Afternotes
F/Lt Krohn	posted	F/Lt Forde	DFC
F/O Hardy	NZ DFC	F/O Cox	F/Lt DFC + Bar
P/O Le Cheminant	DFC	P/O Daniels	S/Ld. DFC + Bar
P/O Robertson	DFC (Wounded)	P/O Prytherch	DFM (Missing)
P/O Corbin	DFC	P/O Macdonald	RAAF (missing)
P/O Lowe	(Killed in action)	W/O Charnock	P/O DFM DFC
W/O Gerr	P/O DFC	SGT Fowler	P/O Posted
P/O Lewis	(USA)	SGT Hussey	P/O
P/O Malan	(Killed)	SGT Mottram	(Missing)
SGT Browne	(Missing)	W/O Hunter	P/O RCAF (Missing)
SGT Frampton	P/O (Posted)	SGT Smollet	(Posted)
SGT Pearson	Posted India	F/O Keith	(Killed)
SGT Piggott	Posted India	P/O Stone	(Killed)
		SGT Smith	(Killed)

On 16 November 16 of the Squadron's aircraft were transferred from Gibraltar to Maison Blanche, Algiers. This might sound quite straightforward but the distance required the fitting of long-range fuel tanks. None of the pilots had flown an aircraft with a long-range tank before, they had no idea of how the aircraft would fly or even how to get it off the ground. Undaunted, they removed the armour plating behind the cockpit, stuffed their belongings down the fuselage, refitted the plating, assembled at the end of the runway and waited for Bobby Oxspring, the CO to show how it was done!

The same day French troops in Tunisia joined with American paratroops and attacked German Forces. Not surprisingly Algiers was very busy, packed with every kind of aircraft imaginable, from bombers to light trainers and the landing and dispersal arrangements there were as chaotic as was the departure from Gibraltar.

The squadron remained at Maison Blanche, carrying out its share of airfield patrols until the 18th when they transferred, again using long-range tanks, to Bone, a port about 300 miles to the East. Bone was little more than a single track road (the runway) surrounded by rough ground, full of stones, holes and dust. No sooner had they landed, climbed out of their aircraft and settled down when they were strafed by a Me109. There was nothing to be done but watch it happen. The lesson however was not lost and from then on there was a two-man airfield patrol, flying about 200 yards apart, virtually the whole time during daylight hours, with two other aircraft in readiness. On 19 November F/O Owen Hardy (a New Zealander) bounced a Me109F which was chasing a Spitfire over the harbour at Bone. Hardy opened fire, Glycol

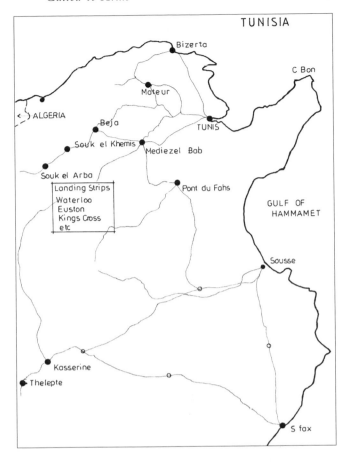

Sketch map of Tunisia.

streamed out of his target, its propeller came free and it crashed into a hillside. This was the Squadron's first victory in North Africa. The squadron was flying Tropical Spitfire Vbs and was now in the thick of the action.

The Spitfire V was the most common type, 6787 were built. It was powered by various incarnations of the Rolls-Royce Merlin engine having a maximum speed of 371 mph at 20,000 feet. It had a service ceiling of 37,500 feet and could climb to 10,000 feet in 4 minutes 18 seconds. Above 20,000 feet it had a climb rate of 2440 feet per minute. The typical armament was four Browning mk. II machine guns and two 20-mm Hispano cannon. The arrangement was such that the outboard gun was a third of the way in from the wing tip which, it was said, could cause some flexing when the guns fired making them less accurate. The tropical version was fitted with a modified air filter. The modifications had, however to be further improved by 72 Squadron's engineer Greggs Farish. He designed, built and fitted another external filter for use on take-off. Once airborne the pilots would release it for re-use.

Jack Lancaster, a former sergeant fitter with 72 Squadron, told me about the thousands and thousands of spark plugs he must have thrown away in the desert. After each sortie all the plugs on Roy's Spitfire (and presumably all other Spitfires) were replaced as the fine desert sand entered the combustion chambers and slowly deposited a glaze on the points that was unbudgeable – no spark, no engine. Jack is sure – taking nothing away from the skill and dedication of the pilots – that part of the reason 72 Squadron was consistently at the top of the score table was the care that the fitters and armourers put into ensuring that 'their' pilot's aeroplanes were as near perfect as possible. When I spoke to Jack in Malta in 2010 there was no mistaking his pride, after 70 years, in his 'ownership' of 'his' pilot's aeroplane.

The Spitfire armament arrangement contrasted with the Hurricane, which some considered a better gun platform, the latter having machine guns arranged in two groups of four as close in to the fuselage as they could be placed consistent with clearing the propeller arc.

On 20 November after a raid on Beja the Squadron was transferred to Souk-el-Arba, an airfield that would be easily recognised because, they were informed, there was a crashed bomber in the middle of it! In any event it was located – and a very rough place it was. The surface was like the moon with mud and potholes. The town of Souk-el-Arba led directly away from the airstrip by way of a road with ditches on either side. Into this ditch they placed the four-gallon fuel tins and ammunition which had been delivered by ground troops, little knowing then that the German pilots ranged their fire along these ditches.

Having scrounged some tents and thin blankets they settled down to a very cold night in the desert. These grim conditions continued for about two weeks, during which time the Squadron was fully operational, flying most days.

On 22 November Roy records 'CO shot down by ground gunners – returned OK later in the day.' Bobby Oxspring was leading eight Spitfires on a sweep over the Mateur-Bizerta road and he had to force-land eight miles from Beja.

The squadron base was being subjected to constant enemy air attacks. On the 22nd it was subjected to three raids with Me109F bombers, Focke Wolfs 190s, Junkers 87s (Stukas) and Macchi 202s. Roy was hit by friendly fire on 23 November. It was on this day also that the airfield was subjected to an intensive attack by a group of Me109s. The squadron was expecting to be joined by another that day and initially thought the group of approaching aeroplanes was the new squadron. When they realised their mistake, there was no chance of getting their aircraft off the ground so they dived for cover as best they could. The petrol and ammunition supplies went up with a mighty whoosh. Remarkably, none of the pilots was hit but this did not apply to the aircrew, some of whom were killed. Roy tried to drag one poor fellow suffering wounds to his stomach to a safer position. Robbie Robertson, to whom Roy was then flying No.2, helped him and they found 'shelter' under a lorry. Fortunately for them, that particular lorry was not targeted.

The aerodrome was being shared with other squadrons, including 152 and 93. 93 was a newly formed squadron led by Sqn Ldr Nelson-Edwards. One of its flight commanders was Flt/Lt Alan Smith DFC, a young New Zealander who had been the wingman of the famous Douglas Bader until the latter's crash and capture as a PoW. The loss of and damage to equipment meant 72 and 93 Squadrons flew as one for a while, being led by either Sqn Ldr Bobby Oxspring or Sqn Ldr Nelson-Edwards.

On 25 November 72 Squadron scored again with 'Chas' Charnock downing an Me109E, 'Danny' Daniel an Me109 and 'Robbie' Robertson an Me109.

Chas, it seems, was quite a character. At 37 he was considerably older than the rest of the pilots, having been commissioned before the war, court-martialled and dismissed the service. When war came he reapplied and was accepted back with the rank of sergeant pilot (later Warrant Officer). By all accounts he was an awesome pilot and an excellent shot. On 27 April 1943 he was re-commissioned and was awarded the DFC. Daniel was also an experienced pilot, a flight commander, later to become Squadron Leader of 72 Squadron. Robbie was as battle experienced and Roy often flew as his number 2 at this stage.

On 26 November 1942, a week after Owen Hardy's 'first kill', Roy had his own, where he fired several bursts at a Me109E in a sweep over Medjez-el-Bab at 3000 feet. Pieces fell off the wings and the aircraft went down vertically. It crashed into a hillside and exploded. This is graphically described in Tom Docherty's book *Swift to Battle*.

The Messerschmitt was at 9000 ft when Hussey attacked from astern, giving it a one-second burst. The Messerschmitt immediately turned and dived away, followed by Hussey who fired more bursts at the fleeing German whose aircraft lost pieces with each burst. Flg.Off. Cox observed Hussey's skill watching the Messerschmitt diving vertically with showers of sparks and emitting white smoke, turning black, before it hit a hillside and exploded.

On the next day Roy recorded a probable Me109F. P/O J Lowe (Johnny) failed to return from this sweep.

All the while the airfield was being attacked. Apart from strafing the Germans used butterfly bombs which, when they hit the ground, spread shrapnel all over the place. Tents were no protection but lying flat on the ground was a good plan. The tents became perforated and more slit trenches were dug; a good night's sleep, however, was not to be expected.

A preoccupation of mine is riding fast motorcycles, I have written a book on the subject. One of my friends in that pursuit, Tony Butler, is a serving Wing Commander in the RAF and he introduced me to the word 'dits'. No doubt service personnel will be familiar with the word but to me it was new. Basically, it is shorthand for a service story that may or may not be true, it is probably based on some sort of fact, but more importantly, it entertains. There is a dit relating to 72 Squadron's time under canvas in North Africa. Sharing Souk-el-Arba with 72 was a Beaufighter squadron. Beaufighters, according to Danny Daniel, produced a particular whistling noise in the air, so one night when a whistling noise was heard Danny advised the company to relax, it was only a Beaufighter coming in; a bloody great explosion followed as the whistle was in fact a bomb. Danny struggled to live that one down.

Sticking with motorbikes, the dispatch rider for 72 Squadron was Daryl Briggs. When I met him in 2010, aged 90, he told me that during the war he mostly rode a BSA M20 girder forked machine. This fully exposed suspension arrangement, he told me, was much better in the dusty but also muddy conditions, as it wore less and was easy to clean and maintain. When I met up with him some of his ex-colleagues let it be known that Daryl had 'lost' his motorbike in France, so I pressed him for the story.

Well, we had disembarked in Marseilles from a landing craft and I along with some others had gone off in search of a drink. Having slaked our thirst I thought I should catch up with the main party only to find there were hundreds of landing craft in the harbour all looking just the same to me, I searched and searched but just couldn't find mine, so I hitched a ride on a lorry. I never did get that bike back!

At the end of November 1942, Roy's operational hours totalled 26 hours and 50 minutes. With 1 destroyed and 1 probable.

Apart from air-to-air combat, the Squadron was very much involved in ground strafing. On 1 December Roy undertook two sorties. On the first he records ' Lew shot up by 4 Macci 200s (returned wounded)' and on the second 'Shot up Djedeida drome, Pranged Ju 87 and light tanks.'

On 2 December Roy records 'Escort to Bisley bombers'. This refers to 614 Squadron who bombed El Aouina that day. Roy notes 'a shaky do. Strafed Hun troops. Chem. Shot down by 5 Fw 190s. Returned OK.' Whether 'shaky do' refers to escorting the Bisleys which were slow flying, vulnerable aircraft, or the sheer unpleasantness of strafing ground troops is not clear. Though my mother Betty Hussey told us as children that Roy was entirely comfortable in air-to-air combat but disliked ground strafing, when the pilots were vulnerable to ground fire, which was usually intense and accurate. It was on this day also that 111 Squadron joined 72 at Souk-el-Arba. Roy's friend, George Longbottom, from 3 BFTS was in 111 Squadron; his story unfolds later.

Reading Roy's flying logbook it is clear that being shot down was by no means a terminal event for the pilot, it seemed quite commonplace (not infrequently by 'friendly' ground fire) and the pilots either force-landed safely or bailed out and returned to their squadrons.

On 3 December he records 'bags of Me109s and FW 190s. George Malan shot down … (returned okay).' This short note refers to a sortie that could have been much worse. The Squadron took off at 1540 to patrol over Tebourra and Djedeida at 14,000 feet, FW 190s were reported below by PO Malan (George Malan was the brother of South African WWII fighter ace Sailor Malan). As the Spitfires went into a dive, American P-38s flying above mistook them for Bf 109s and bounced them. F/O Hardy, PO Robertson and PO Malan still managed to shoot down one Fw between them but PO Malan was hit and had to crash land – luckily amongst American troops.

3 December 1942 was also the day that 72 and 111 Squadrons were told that all of the equipment that had been packed in the UK back in October had been lost at sea, all of the kit bags and 20 tons of engineering stores were gone.

On 4 December Roy records 'bailed out OK' and 'Danny Daniels shot down an Me 109 F/O. Cox 109. Chem [Le Cheminant] 109.'

On the same date he records that Wing Commander Malcom [sic] was awarded the VC. This followed a dreadful day for the Bisleys of 18 and 614 Squadrons; 12 aircraft took off led by Wg Cdr Malcolm to attack an airfield 10 miles North of Chougui without escort. All aircraft were lost, the crews of four, however, survived.

Roy's extremely neat logbook reveals the nature of the man. He is clearly competitive and meticulously notes his victories and those of his colleagues in the Squadron. Not once, however, does he record any promotion, decoration or citation given him, only those going to his colleagues.

Jack Lancaster, one of the ground crew of 72 Squadron who took a particular interest in Roy Hussey and his aircraft told me that on one occasion in Tunisia after Roy had returned to the airfield Jack asked him if he had been checking the oil pressure and temperature gauges. Roy replied on the lines of 'don't know about those buggers, I'm happy just as long that fan thing in the front keeps spinning.' All the surviving people from 72 Squadron that I have spoken to come up with the same judgement of Roy. On the ground he was quiet, calm, unflamboyant, almost reserved at times, but in the air his excellent eyesight came to the fore and it was devil take the hindmost – I'm off. Another clue comes from Gregg Farish's book, *Algiers to Anzio* where he compares Tom Hughes, another pilot, and Roy, whilst describing the exploits of the remarkable Polish ace Horbaczewski.

A vacancy occurred in 43 Squadron in 244 Wing for a Flight Commander and Tom moved to fill it. 43 Squadron's CO was Horbaczewski, one of the leading pilots and personalities of the Polish Air Force. In June 1944, flying Mustangs he led a strafing mission during which two pilots were downed by flak. Horbaczewski saw W/O Tamowicz crash-land in a marsh, then spotted an American Emergency Landing Strip (ELS) under construction nearby. He landed, borrowed a jeep, and drove to the scene of the crash. Wading through hip-deep mud and water, he got to the Mustang and pulled the wounded Tamowicz from the wreck, got him back to the jeep and back to the ELS. Tamowicz climbed into the CO's aeroplane, and Horbaczewski sat on his lap in order to fly them both back to England. A month later, having just destroyed three FWs on the same sortie, he was shot down and killed. His score of 16.5 confirmd kills included 4 V-I rockets. It did not take Tom long to learn from Horbaczewski what had been wrong with his shooting, he was not allowing enough lead, the 'angle-off' referred to in Roy's instructional book *Bag the Hun!* Very shortly Tom's score began to mount and he was awarded the DFC. A vacancy then arose in 72 Squadron and Tom was drafted back. This, Farish considered, meant that 72 Squadron had 3 'dead-eye dicks' leading them: Danny (Daniel) as leader, Tom on the left and Roy on the right. He goes on to write that Roy's reputation amongst the pilots, however, was not as high as Tom's since Tom never forgot his number 2 behind him, whereas Roy would occasionally go for a kill leaving his number 2 exposed.

It seemed to me that this was a good place to put in this glimpse of Roy in the air, although in chronological terms there is a little way to go before he is promoted from Sergeant Pilot to Flight Lieutenant and Flight Commander. We shall see the trait that Farish refers to coming to the fore in Rodney Scrase's account of the action in the citation for Roy's DFC, set down in the next chapter. (Rodney was Roy's number 2 on that freelance).

On 5 December 1942 Roy records 'Pranged Huns and lorry, CO a probable, Brownie and Mo missing.' Jimmy Corbin describes the event:

By that time another 109 had fastened itself on the tail of one of our boys. Between us we tried to drive it away and finally it got the hint and disappeared, but not before it had sprayed the Spitfire with bullets. The aircraft caught fire and I watched anxiously as it hurtled towards the earth. This time it was Sergeant Mottram. In truth it didn't look too good, but maybe he would be able to crash land the aircraft somewhere and make his way back to the Squadron. There was always hope. You couldn't assume anything until a pilot's death was confirmed or it became obvious they were not coming back. Too often I had seen pilots step from the wreckage of an aircraft which should have by rights become their tomb and marvelled at how anyone could survive such an impact.

The Mo whom Roy referred to was Sgt Alan Mottram and amongst Roy's papers are two letters, one from Alan's mother and the other from Alan's father. The one from his mother was posted on 30 March 1944 but according to the administration stamp, probably didn't reach Roy until around June 1944. The restrained but powerful misplaced hope in both is almost unbearable.

Mr and Mrs J Mottram, Oakdene, 39 Hereford Drive, Prestwich, Manchester

Dear Roy,

Now you will wonder why you get a letter from us. We've tried to get in touch with you but didn't know your number. We had a letter today from Harold Payne, he sent it on you see, we wrote him to ask you some details but we see you have left.

I only hope he gave you our congratulations on your promotion and we wish you luck.

Now there are several things we wish to ask you seeing you are the only one to give us same. Is it possible Alan could have got away safely. Why did you think that grave might be his?

Could he have been so far out there, if he has got away what part do you think he could have got to. Is there any possible chance of him being a PoW.

We have had nothing sent back since the few things they sent us from North Africa, we know he had a bank book, we suppose he had that on him, also his keys, he must have had also some letters on him, nothing has been sent to us. Would he have had a number on his clothes or anything to identify him by. It all seems a mystery to us, why we say this is because since you and Harold surmised that grave was Alan's. Jack Mottram got on the track immediately and we have had word from the RAF [to] say such a grave was found it had been buried by the enemy, but there was no indication or any identification to say who it was and they saw no special reason for us to think that it was our son. From the Graves Unit they said also there was this grave at [illegible] but had now been moved to the Beja town cemetery.

They said his body had been buried by the Americans owing to the wording on the cross (how could he have been so far out)?

They say the same has [sic] the RAF has no indication and no identification also found no expanding bangle, which you know he always wore, now read this and what do you think or make of it, the RAF say different to the War Graves Unit.

So now the WGU want us to agree that body is our son Alan, so that they can get the numbers put on the said grave, after telling us there is no identification as to who it is, after all it is only surmise on your part, they are very callous.

I'm so sorry to have to trouble you but, seeing you are the only personal friend and one that was with him on his last [days?]. We would feel so much better if we could get the slightest hope, we haven't given him up.

I had a letter from Ellen, I suppose you know by now she has remarried her husband do you remember the flying jacket she bought Alan, she mentioned it and asked me if I had got it back with his effects, so I told her I had a few filthy things sent and that was all, one thing Roy could you tell me where those <u>large</u> photos of Vera and Ellen got to, they sent a few snaps here that were with the large ones, because I always packed his case, I knew everything that went in.

They told us the case had gone down so you must have all been very unfortunate and lost all your stuff.

Who did the <u>brown</u> woollen gloves belong to I wonder, one thing I would have liked and that [sic] his wings off his coat he was so proud to possess.

He was not well enough after his bus accident and should never have been sent abroad. It was an unlucky move when he joined the 72 squad.

You are supposed to be out there to kill off the <u>Huns</u> but they are over here having good jobs, no fire-watching and looking like robust beings. Oh to be an Alien these days, the Italians here are taken and brought back from their work in motors etc. I must close wishing you all the luck possible, we hope you forgive us writing to you.

Yours sincerely Mr. Mrs. J. Mottram

The reference to 'lost all your stuff' might have referred either to the loss of personal kit and engineering stores on the journey from England, reported on 3 December 1942, or more likely a similar loss in Bari harbour when moving from Tunisia to Malta.

The letter from Alan's father is dated 2 April 1944:

J Mottram, Oakdene, 39 Hereford Drive, Prestwich, Manchester

Dear Roy,

Please excuse the liberty of writing to [you] direct which is arisen through receiving an air-graph from your friend Harold Payne which gave your address but not your number.

The writer is the father of Alan Mottram who was attached to your squadron and who was we understand a friend of yours.

As you are aware Alan was reported missing on December 5, 1942 and since has been officially put forward as presumed killed.

Upon hearing of the grave seen by yourself and Harold Payne we put the matter before the Air Ministry and War Graves Commission for scrutiny, Results of which you have already received from Mrs. Mottram but yesterday a friend of Alan's came along to ask if it was correct that Alan had been brought down over the Mediterranean.

Of course the latter was news to us and we should welcome any help from you verifying same or alternatively give us some idea [where] the engagement took place as the last place we heard of him being in was Algiers.

Any information you can give no matter how slight would help to relieve our present anxiety.

Your assistance in obtaining and informing us of something definite would be greatly appreciated and [we] await your reply with interest and hope.

We hope you are well and wish you best of luck.
From yours sincerely J. Mottram.

Just two words in Roy's logbook – 'Mo missing', represent such despair and anguish.

The second sweep on 5 December was undertaken with 111 and 152 Squadrons and was recorded 'very successful'. 6–9 December 1942 were taken up with escort duties for bombers, including Flying Fortresses and Bisleys. Over Bizerta flak was noted as 'very accurate'.

On 8 December Roy recorded 'Weather u/s.' A reminder that although one thinks of the North African desert as hot and dry, in fact the winter of 1942 was very wet indeed. The condition of Roy's logbook bears this out, it has grains of sand in the binding and mud stains on its cover. The rains came suddenly. The clouds would form and the rain pour down, the airfield becoming a quagmire. The aircraft would sink into it and would literally have to be man-handled out. The Allies, in spite of Somerfeld track mesh, damaged a large number of aircraft taxiing, taking off and landing – particularly Spitfires, which had a propensity to tip on their noses in mud. The Germans, however, had the benefit of established positions with runways, so strafing and bombing attacks were commonplace and apart from answering with ground fire, sometimes there was little more that could be done.

On 17 December Roy records 'Good bombing by the Forts on docks etc which were burning well before. Doggers-ho [dogfighting] with Me109s. Bounced on the deck by FW 190s. Good flak.'

On 20 December 1942 the Squadron undertook two sweeps, on the second of these they intercepted 15 Me109s (Gs, Fs, and Es), Roy recorded 'Robbie [Robertson] shot down (wounded) but OK.' Robertson was blinded in one eye and never flew again. Jimmy Corbin in his book wrote that Robbie blamed Hussey for this but when I met up with Jimmy in November 2009 he had no recollection of the details. In Christopher Shores' excellent work *Fighters over Tunisia* he writes that Roy shot down a Me109 on the 20th and on page 107 there is a photograph showing Roy standing next to what may have been the remains of that aircraft. Roy's logbook however notes no claims for the 20th but 1 Me109G destroyed and 1 Me109F damaged on the 21st.

In January 2010, my friend Angus Mansfield whose Grandfather 'Barney' Barnfield had joined 72 Squadron on 5 May 1943, told me of a website he had found called Pprune. I found my way into it and to my joy and amazement, before he died, Robbie Robertson had dictated his memories of this time and his son had posted them on the site. Robbie's memoirs do not pull punches so we can assume this record is as accurate as we can get.

I didn't fly on 19 December and wasn't due to fly on the 20th, but we had just had a portable gramophone given to us with several records, including Bing Crosby's that Mum and I have copies of at home, and also some Vera Lynns and I was happily listening to a Vera Lynn record of 'Do I Love You, Do I' when the flight commander came over and said that he was due to fly an aeroplane patrol but didn't really feel in the mood and would I mind going? Well there was nothing else to do out there, so said OK. Now I couldn't fly my aircraft so I got in another one. Took off with Sergeant Hussey to do this aerodrome patrol. I'd been up for about 4 minutes and the aircraft decided it was going to fly itself. I'd hold the stick steady and aircraft would fair bump up and down, like a roller coaster. There was obviously something funny somewhere, so I brought it down and landed. I suppose if I'd any sense, I'd have stayed down but I got into another aircraft, took off again and joined Sergeant Hussey for our aerodrome patrol.

Well, we hadn't been up very long when they reported from the ground that there was a 20+ raid coming in from Medjiz el Bab, which was not far up the road from us. Well that seemed great for Hussey and I, in as much as we were high enough to spot a high bunch coming in and we'd probably get a very good bounce on the ones that were coming lower. And lo and behold, in they came. We started to go down on them and it seemed far too easy, because normally the Hun fights in layers and you go down on one lot and the next lot comes down and clobbers you. Well I couldn't see anything above so we continued down and just before we got in range, I looked down and there was one creeping along the deck, coming up underneath Hussey, who was flying about 200 yards from me. So I called up Hussey and told him to break, but he either didn't hear me or else his r/t had gone u/s which wasn't an uncommon occurrence out there at that time. Anyway as the Jerry had started shooting and I could see the flashes all over the place from his guns, I pulled in to try and head him off and with luck have a crack at him, and I'm not sure now whether I hit him or not, but the next thing I knew there was a hell of a bang and I got hit in the head and started bleeding like a stuck pig.

Robbie Robertson managed to crash land and was taken to hospital. The ORB for the day records 'The squadron carried out aerodrome patrols.' Robbie had lost an eye, Roy had lost his mentor.

Two days earlier, on 18 December, there is another good opportunity to examine how different accounts of the same events can be so informative. Roy's logbook saw him on a 35-minute flight as escort to 'Forts' bombing Mature [Mateur] railway. He notes 'Chas [Charnock] shot down again after destroying 2 Me109s. Wounded.' Robbie Robertson's dictation paints a fuller picture:

On 18 December we were told to escort some Bostons to bomb Mateur and I was flying number 3 to Chas and Sollet, a fairly new sergeant as number 2, me as 3 and Roy Hussey as 4. Well just before we got to Mateur, Hussey called up and said his engine was rough and he was going back, so that left me as tailend Charlie of the section. Anyway we were turning right down sun and Chas and I looked up from the port side, where we were flying and saw about 20+ 109s. Despite our shouts on the r/t the squadron continued to turn right but there was no future in that for us. In as much as it would have presented our backs to this wad of enemy aircraft and consequently Chas and I broke left and pulled up into the down-coming enemy aircraft. Now young Sollet, as I said was quite a new lad and we'd impressed upon him that if he ever got into trouble and lost sight of any of us the best thing he could do was not hang around but belt off home as fast as he could, weaving like mad. Anyway, as Chas and I pulled up we were going into the sun, naturally, and I saw Chas get one 109 and I was pulling up to get closer to him and must have gone higher up than I thought, or a worse angle, anyway because the speed suddenly dropped off and I went into a spin. Now there was no future in trying to pull out and climb up again, because I'd have been a sitting duck, so I continued spinning until I got close to the ground and then straightened off and started to belt for home, closely followed by two 109s.

Now the old engine wasn't going too well, it was coughing and spluttering and not going as fast as I'd liked it to go, so I got right down to the deck and I was belting home as fast as possible, weaving like mad, in and out of valleys, frightening the life out of camels and odd bodies I passed over, still pursued by the 109s, who were taking the odd pot shots at me every now and again and all I could do was to keep turning the minute they came within range.

Eventually after one of these turns, I managed to get a fairly good shot in at the leading 109 and he shot straight past me into the deck and I thought by this time the other one would have cleared off, but he was a bit of a keen type and he went on chasing me all the way back to within a few miles of the aerodrome, he finally gave up, but he did manage to put seven bullet holes in the aircraft and when I finally landed at Souk-el-Arba I had no ammunition and very little petrol and I was absolutely drenched in perspiration! Most of it, I must admit due to heaving the aircraft about at low level, and doing all sorts of things that the spit wasn't meant to do and probably quite a percentage due to the fact that I was scared stiff. But anyway, I got back alright.

It's one thing to fight on fairly even terms but when you were having a job keeping the engine going, it does give you food for thought. I spoke to the ground crew afterwards and they showed me one of the petrol filters which was half full of dust and muck and what have you, so I'm not surprised I had trouble with the aircraft. The funny thing was that we told Sollet to go back if he got lost, which he did but he hadn't realized that you were supposed to go down on the deck and weave like mad. He'd climbed up with us to start with, into the sun, and then lost sight of everybody, which wasn't unusual, so doing as he was told he came home. He told me he flew back at 5000 feet, straight and level, no weaving just looking at the countryside and he arrived at Souk-el-Arba without any damage at all, and yet Chas and I, who by this time were, I must say very experienced, were fighting like maniacs and getting shot to pieces – a strange old life.

As for Chas Charnock, In *Fighters over Tunisia* by Christopher Shores, Hans Ring and William N. Hess (1975) it states: 'Down at ground level after his successful combats, Charnock was shot up by Lt. Rudorffer of II/JG2, belly landing at Abiod at 1052 wounded in head and arm; he quickly leaped from his aircraft which burst into flames.' Jimmy Corbin wrote in his diary:

> Hell of a mist at first, but took off at 10.00 am as top cover to Bostons and Fortresses, we were at 17000 ft. They pranged railway sidings at Mateur and aerodrome with 109s on – a very good job by the Yanks. After they had bombed Mateur we were jumped by 109s, about six attacked and eighteen stayed above. I had had no r/t, which made it a bit sticky, and my number 2 went home earlier; two got behind and I had a dogfight; high pressure. So did Chumley. I shook mine off but could not get in a position to fire. On landing Robbie had destroyed one and Chas was missing, he was last seen apparently climbing like hell towards the 109s. We hope he comes back; he should being an expert Hun destroyer, bailer outer etc. A great day – a gramophone has arrived – civilization has come to us at last, will these records be overused.

With regard to Chas Charnock, the ORB has this to say:

> … after these combats when at ground level, W/O Charnock was attacked by four Me109s and a Fw 190. He was wounded by cannon splinters in the head and arm and received burns on the waist and face. He made a successful belly landing without further injury, and ran for cover as his aeroplane went up in flames. He next spoke to an Arab who was reluctant to help him, but on a revolver being shown and shooting the Arab's dog which attacked him, the Arab agreed to take him 18 kilometres to British troops. He was sent to No. 1 field ambulance then to Tabarka and later to No. 5 general hospital Bone.

So out of all of this we learn that the bombers were both Bostons and Fortresses, that the targets were both railway sidings and the aerodrome – and that blocked filters, other engine and r/t troubles were not unusual. One can also glean, given that Chas Charnock crash landed at 10.52 and Jimmy Corbin records taking off at 10.00 hrs, Roy's record of a 35-minute flight would have put his return about 15 minutes into a sortie that lasted in all about one and a half hours, the Spitfire's approximate maximum flying time, allowing for around ten minutes of combat (borne out by Robbie Robertson being virtually out of juice). One can begin to have some sympathy with the Squadron intelligence officers who were supposed to make some sense out of the dreaded 'Form F' post combat reports!

Whilst the machine guns on the Spitfires operated pretty well in desert conditions the cannon (one on each wing) suffered from sand incursion and jamming. On 30 December Roy took up a tropical Spitfire Vb no. H-Z – not a number having been recorded in his logbook as having been flown by him previously – on a 35-minute flight for a cannon test. This seems to have been the only time this machine was flown by him. During December 1942 alone, however, he flew the following 12 numbers: ER-708; ER-HX; H-D; H-T; H-X; H-O; H-Q; H-F; H-N; H-S; H-P; and H-R.

Apart from losses in the air and on ground manoeuvring, the airstrips were under constant attack by enemy bomb and strafing attacks, principally by Ju87s (Stukas) Me109s and FW 190s equipped for that purpose. There would appear, however, to have been a steady supply of new aeroplanes when required.

31 December 1942 logbook:' High cover to Hurri-Divebombers on tank depot. Drome dive bombed by 190s.' So tit for tat. Presumably that sortie was the flight of eight Spitfires from 93 Squadron and twelve from 72 Squadron led by Wg Cdr Gilroy to escort eight Hurribombers from 241 Squadron in an attack upon an MT depot that day.

Roy it may be recalled was in the third batch of trainees at 3 BFTS Miami; also in that batch in Fulmar Flight was George Longbottom. In his logbook on 8 January 1943 Roy notes 'G.

Longbottom shot down (killed).' Sgt G. Longbottom was with 111 Squadron (along with 72 Squadron, part of 324 Wing at Souk-el-Arba). On 8 January 111 Squadron was scrambled at 1330 hrs; firing was heard from above the clouds by ground troops and a Spitfire was seen to hit the ground near Souk El Khemis. This was Longbottom. In Roy's tin box there is a letter dated 3 December 1943, nearly a year after George Longbottom was killed, signed 'Tot'. It was posted on 6 December 1943. At that time Roy was in Italy, but the letter did not reach him until 21 February 1944 when he was stationed at HQ AFDU, Wittering, Northamptonshire. Again, the airmail is not in the best of condition.

Miss E. Eloter[?] North Lodge, [?] Fell, Gateshead, Co. Durham.

3/12/43

Dear Roy,

Just a few lines to say how are you getting along. I've written you one or two letters, but realise you have not time to reply. How are you Roy? Still scaring the daylights out of Jerry? I cut your photo out of the 'Evening Chronicle' after shooting down a transport plane in Sicily. Good work Roy. It mentioned Pilot Officer R H Hussey. But I'll put on your original rank, just to make sure you get the scrawl. We have not received any better news of our dear Fred. But we had a wonderful experience one night at a spiritualist meeting Roy. The medium gave us a wonderful message from George Longbottom, who she explained was a fighter pilot, who was killed in North Africa. Amazing Roy, wasn't it, from a stranger (especially his full name). We are still convinced Fred is alive Roy. Syd our young uncle, 23, is a Beaufighter pilot, and flew to Burma in October. He arrived safely. I sent you a Christmas card Roy, but in case it does not arrive in time may we all wish you all the very best for Xmas, and may you be home next Xmas. Write if you can Roy, we often talk of you and wonder where you are. Best wishes Roy dear and love from us all.

Yours very sincerely Tot
Happy landings always. God bless and protect you Roy

Fred may have been a friend of Roy's from 3BFTS as there are a number of photographs annotated 'Fred' in Roy's album.

At the back of Roy's logbook he records the airstrips where the Squadron was based. In the 14 months from November 1942 to January 1943 it reads as follows:

Date	Strip
November 1942	Gibraltar
November 1942	Algiers
November 1942	Bone
November 1942	Souk-el-Arba
January 1943	Waterloo
January 1943	Euston
April 1943	Telepte
May 1943	La Sebala I
May 1943	La Sebala II
May 1943	Mateur
June 1943	Malta (Hal-Far)
July 1943	Comiso (Sicily)
July 1943	Pachino (South)
August 1943	Pandebeanco

September 1943	Cassala
September 1943	Falconie
September 1943	Tusciano (Italy)
October 1943	Naples
January 1944	Lago

For the most part in Africa at least, the strips, as Peter Olver recalls in Steve Darlow's book *Five of the Few* 'were sandy strips with an oil drum each end. When the squadrons left them you would never have known they had been there.'

It is a recurring theme in comments by other 72 Squadron pilots how fortunate the Squadron was in its ground personnel. Everyone was under canvas and the conditions seemed to be either wet and muddy or hot and dusty, neither conducive to mechanical reliability, yet rarely were pilots frustrated by lack of aeroplanes, parts or mechanical failures.

The conditions for personnel were pretty primitive. For the most part they were sleeping under canvas. Baked during the day (when it was not raining), cold at night. Rations were tinned bully or salted fish and 'hard tack' biscuits.

The airstrips were often placed amongst the indigenous rural population. Souk-el-Khemis, where they were shortly to go, adjoined a pig farm and the pigs would root around the camp looking for something to eat. On one occasion Jimmy Corbin had returned from a successful sortie and was with Danny Daniel who was sitting on his bed filling out his logbook when a pig bumped the door and lumbered in. Danny picked up his revolver and aimed. There was a loud bang and the pig lay twitching on the floor. Jimmy Corbin:

'Bloody hell Dan, you've shot it. What did you go and do that for?'
Word quickly spread around the base of the pig's assassination … There was a knock on the door … to reveal an airman I had not seen before.
'What do you want, we're a bit busy at the moment' Daniel said.
'I thought I might be able to help you boys out. I used to be a butcher.'
In no time the airman had skinned the animal and cut it up into a range of joints.

As they sat down to pork that evening, Danny was missing but in a short while he re-appeared with the farmer and his wife, whom he showed to two empty seats. Jimmy:

He piled two clean plates with the cooked pork and placed them in front of the farmer and his wife. If they knew they were eating their own livestock they didn't show it … Dan came and sat down near me and Hussey, who was staring open mouthed at what had taken place. But Daniel just shrugged and grinned at us.
'Well it just seemed the decent thing to do. It's their pig after all.'

The beginning of January 1943 proved to be a headache for Roy and Jimmy Corbin. At some stage Chas Charnock, making his way back to the base after having been shot down, had stumbled upon a monastery which had a spectacular supply of wine. Upon his return to the Squadron he had purloined a lorry and filled a number of old petrol tins with the nectar. The only drinking vessels were large tin mugs and Roy and Jimmy had overreached themselves and had landed up in hospital – not with an excess of alcohol but with 'dysentery' due to petrol poisoning (or so it was diagnosed) and who were they to contradict medical science? In any event Roy has no reports of flying from 3–7 January. On the 6th the Squadron had been informed that it was the top scoring squadron in North Africa.

On Roy's list of the pilots of 72 Squadron upon his arrival at Gibraltar in November 1942 at the bottom of Flight B are PO Stone and Sgt Smith both noted killed. On 26 January 1943, Roy records 'Tac – R (Tactical reconnaissance) 1 hours 10 minutes' and 'Smithy and Stone killed in collision near Jeffna.' A sad loss on a day without combat.

72 Squadron under canvas in North Africa. (Tony 'Red' Weller)

On 15 January 1943 the Squadron moved from Souk-el-Arba to Souk-el-Khemis. Souk-el-Khemis was a much larger, flatter area, better drained and in relative terms with better accommodation, that is to say only eight to a tent, put up in an orange grove removed from the airfield. The improved drainage was a double-edged sword in that the surfaces were extremely dusty, particularly when there were aircraft movements – which there were! There were problems with the air filters becoming choked with dust so, as mentioned earlier, Greggs Farish developed his own additional filter that the pilots jettisoned for re-use as soon as they were airborne.

With the American 11 Corps having been lured into a disastrous trap in the Atlas Mountains, in January 1943 the arrival of the Eighth Army at Tripoli and the withdrawal of the Africa Korps to the Mareth Line brought an end to the second phase of the Tunisian Campaign. The US commander was replaced by General George Patton and in northern Tunisia the British V Corps kept the pressure on through January but every attempt to advance had been repelled. The Axis forces, however, were in trouble as essential supplies were not getting through in sufficient quantities from Sicily owing to Allied action over and on the sea.

The crucial battle took place on 23 January 1943 at Kasserine Pass. As luck would have it the weather improved and the Allies had the best of the skies, giving the re-invigorated ground troops the support they desperately needed. 72 Squadron moved down to Telepte, near the Kasserine Pass in March 1943.

Rommel's bold offensive had failed on the point of success to a large extent through command and supply difficulties. In particular, Rommel was not his old self but a sick and dispirited man. Von Arnim, with whom he did not get on, had been obstructive and unhelpful particularly over the use and deployment of the 10th Panzer Division equipped with the awesome Tiger tanks.

By contrast, Allied command difficulties had been overcome by Eisenhower. On 16 January he appointed General Sir Howard Alexander as his second in command to take charge of all Allied ground forces. The previous refusal of General Juin to allow French troops to be placed under British command was overruled, and the British American and French armies fought as one.

Good work was still coming through from 72 Squadron. On 28 January 1943, on a TAC-R flight Roy records 'shot up 1 B ... great tank. Then after note '1 Valentine confirmed!' The Allied blockade of the Mediterranean was biting at this time. The Allies had a 6:1 advantage in troops and a 15:1 superiority in tanks. It was not uncommon for enemy equipment to be used and as he was over German-occupied territory one can only hope that either the British Valentine was not occupied by an Allied crew, or that it was standing empty.

It was on this day also that Pilot Officer Rodney Scrase and Flying Officer Tom Hughes, Sergeant AE (Sammy) Passmore and Sergeant J B King turned up again. Tom Hughes and Rodney Scrase had, for a short while, been engaged in ferrying duties to and from Gibraltar. Sgt Passmore was killed only one month later coming into land in very difficult conditions.

On 31 January 1943 Roy records ' Escort Hurri-reco.' On the same day 72 Squadron sent up 12 Spitfires and 111 Squadron six Spitfires to escort nine Hurribombers of 225 Squadron to attack lorries west of Pont du Fahs. This was the last action of 72 Squadron for a couple of weeks as on 1 February they were sent to Constantine for a rest before proceeding to Gibraltar, where they would be the second squadron to be re-equipped with the new Spitfire mark IX. The mark IX was a considerable improvement over the mark V and could out-perform both the Me109G and the FW 190.

For reasons that will become clear later, when meeting with Rodney Scrase and Jimmy Corbin I asked both whether they knew if Roy was a virgin – quickly adding that if they did not wish to reply that was perfectly alright, but that I would explain why I asked the question in due course. Rodney replied that he simply did not know. Jimmy was rather more positive 'I can confirm that he was not; I remember our being given a few days leave taking very little else than our personal equipment (looking down to his trouser belt) and a 303 rifle ...'

The reason I asked was that I remember when I was probably 10 or 11 years old asking my mother, Betty Hussey, whether Uncle Roy was ever married. She replied that he was not. I responded by offering that that was a good thing as he did not leave a widow behind. She told me never to say that, as he wouldn't have experienced the joys of marriage. This would probably have been her code for sex to her small son. Well, I feel pleased that Jimmy confirmed Roy didn't totally miss out.

Roy's logbook although as neat as ever, is not as precise on dates at this time. Maybe his R&R had something to do with it. Whilst he records the flying activities during the first three weeks of February 1943, such as 'Algiers to Gibraltar (in a Dakota)' and 'Spitfire IX exper. on type' and 'Gibraltar to Algiers' and 'Practice flying' it is not until 25 February that a date is inserted. He records 'Maison Blanche to Euston' (the airfields around Souk-el-Khemis were named after London mainline railway stations) and 'Force landed nr. Calle. S Passmore Killed.' Again this short note covers a bad day for 72 Squadron, although a good day for the campaign, as the Allies reoccupied the Kasserine Pass, Sbeitla and Sidi bou Zid, regaining all the previously lost territory.

On 25 February 72 Squadron returned to the front with its 17 new Spitfire Mark IXs. It was disastrous; on the way to the Euston strip at Souk-el-Khemis they ran into a very heavy rain/hail storm; two of the aircraft landed at Tingley (a good plan since a month before that airstrip had received a new American matting material) one wheels up and one standing on its nose. Roy managed to make a very good wheels-down forced landing on a flat piece of ground at La Calle, damaging the airscrew in the process. At Souk-el-Khemis where there were hailstones the size of golf balls, rain and six inches of standing water, Sgt Passmore spun in and was killed and two others crash landed. So the strength was immediately down to 11 aircraft.

On 27 February 1943 72 Squadron flew its first mission with its Mark IXs. Roy's logbook for the 27th and 28th records two cannon tests and one very local sweep to 28,000 feet (presumably checking out the faster rate of climb and higher ceiling offered by the Mark IX).

As compared with the Mark V the Mark IX Spitfire was a considerable improvement. Whilst it continued to be powered by the Rolls-Royce Merlin engine and weighed 800 lbs more than the Mark V it had a service ceiling of 43,000 feet (as against the Mark V's 37,500 feet), it could climb to 20,000 feet in 5 minutes 42 seconds (the Mark V could only manage 10,000 feet in 4 minutes 18 seconds) and at 20,000 feet could climb at 3950 feet per minute as against 2440 for the Mark V. Its armament was the same as the Mark V, four Browning .303 machine guns and two 20 mm Hispano cannon. Most importantly it was more than a match for the Me109G and fearsome FW 190. The disappointment of the pilots about the disastrous delivery of these new aircraft can therefore be imagined.

Roy's cannon tests lasted 25 and 15 minutes respectively and the sweep 1 hour 10 minutes. Each sortie was in a different Mark IX.

By March 1943 the Allies were pressing upon Tunis. The squadron continued to be employed on a virtually daily basis on air-to-air combat, ground strafing and providing cover for bombers, some of which were Hurricanes converted to dive bombers (Hurribombers, though 'diving' exaggerates the actual angle of attack) and some heavy B26s (Martin Marauders), Flying Fortresses, Mitchells and Bostons.

From 1–7 March, Roy flew most days as high cover to Hurries and Fortresses bombing Tunis and Bizerta. On 1 March on returning to base a group of Bf 109s were seen bouncing some Spitfires on airfield patrol. These 109s were in turn bounced by the returning aircraft. Sqn Ldr Oxspring and W/O Hunter chased one fighter, which tried to escape. This was easily overtaken by the new Mark IXs and was destroyed. Roy's logbook records 'CO and Red [Warrant Officer Hunter RCAF] 109 destroyed. 4 damaged.'

On 2 March Roy records 'Half Me109G2 destroyed shared with Jupp. Chem [le Cheminant] 109 destroyed. The first note refers to a sweep where Roy was one of eight Mark IXs, flying at 28,000 ft. escorting B-17s. The British fighters outclimbed 20 German fighters to 34,000 ft. who broke off to attempt an attack on the bombers below. The Spitfires then descended to 18,000 ft and saw three Me109s over Medjez el Bab. These tried to outclimb the British fighters and when this failed they dived away. F/O Jupp and Roy gave chase and shot one down west of Pont du Fahs at ground level with three long bursts. Le Cheminant's victory was later on the same day at 1650 when 72 Squadron was providing top cover to Hurribombers of 225 Squadron attacking tanks northeast of Beja. The *Bristol Evening Post* of Tuesday April 27th 1943:

> Surprise for MEs
> A Bristol man is one of a squadron of fighter pilots who shot up a number of Messerschmitts over Pont du Fahs during Easter.
>   He is Sgt-Pilot R J H Hussey (20) whose home is the Beaufort Arms, Mangotsfield.
>   'Good work!' exclaimed his mother when told of the feat by the *Evening Post*. 'I am glad. We heard unofficially that he shot down another plane some time ago.'
>   Denis Martin, a Reuters correspondent in Tunisia, cabled this story of the Easter success:
>   'The RAF had good hunting over Pont du Fahs at the weekend. Wing-Comdr. Gilroy of Edinburgh who was leading a squadron met 12 Messerschmitts over the town, dived in to the attack and was the first to score. Three Messerschmitts crashed down in flames and a fourth was damaged in both wings. The remainder fled.'

F/O Tom Hughes had joined the Squadron in early 1943, and it was on this last sortie on 2 March that he forced-landed after a throttle linkage fault and was posted missing. Two days later, however, on 4 March, he turned up having found his way back to the strip mostly on foot, after walking for 20 hours. Roy was something of a doodler and on that day his logbook notes 'Hughes returned after forced landing' after which there is a doodle of a boot with an RAF wing emerging from the top!

324 Wing comprised some heavy hitting squadrons, not least of which was 111 Squadron. However, since its arrival in Africa on 17 November 1942 the top scorer was 72 Squadron. Roy was an excellent shot and was to become amongst the Squadron's big hitters. By the end of the Africa campaign he had 5½ victories, finishing with a total of 13½ by the time he was posted back to England from Italy in January 1944. At the time of his posting he was second highest scorer in the Squadron after Danny Daniel.

The remainder of March continued to be exceptionally busy for 72 Squadron. Roy (flying in eight different Mark IXs) either provided top cover for bombers or was being scrambled.

His one liner on the 23rd reads 'Scrambled – shot at by own flak' On the 26th Roy records two separate sorties, for the second one he noted 'Withdraw cover for B.26 [Martin Marauder] from Gabes;' and 'Jumped 16+ Me109s and Fw 190. Dan 109 des. Hardy 109 des.' This must refer to the sweep on 26 March 1943 when 12 Mark IXs set off to provide withdrawal cover to the Douglas A-20 Havocs of the 47th bombing Group which had been attacking airfields at Djebel Tebaga in the South. While at 23,000 ft the bombers' close escort was seen at 17,000 ft in combat with 15 Bf 109s and FW 190s and two sections of 72 Squadron went down to bounce these, F/Lt Daniel and F/O Hardy each claiming a 109 and F/Lt Cox one damaged.

Up until March 1943 the Axis air forces had inflicted substantial losses on Allied forces. April, however, saw the return to the front of experienced troops and pilots, putting Axis forces under increasing pressure and ultimately into a defensive decline.

Roy was commissioned as Pilot Officer on 27 March 1943 (although the Squadron was not formally notified until 12 June). For 72 Squadron April 1943 opened with more of the same, Roy was flying most days.

By late summer 1940 just under a third of pilots were sergeants, many of them products of the RAFVR. Their duties were indistinguishable from those of officers: to fly and fight. The decision whether or not to award a commission to a pilot on completing Initial Training was based on obscure criteria. One consideration was leadership potential. The practice seems to have been to commission those who most easily fitted into the pre-war concept of what constituted an officer and gentlemen. That meant public schoolboys and those who fitted into the upper or middle classes. Essentially however, the system was a meritocracy.

In spite of the duties being the same NCO and Officer pilots messed separately, in the officers mess there were mess bills, in the NCOs mess everything was provided. It must have been quite strange for an NCO pilot to be commissioned and stay with the same squadron but move from one mess to another. In Roy's case it would have been made much easier because of the unconventionally relaxed conditions in which the Squadron was living.

On 10 April Roy records 'high cover to Spit bombers <u>Damaged Me109</u>. Guns Jammed.' The underlining is in a lighter blue ink, as if to emphasise his frustration in having failed to destroy it.

The 11th was again a busy day, 72 Squadron took off at 0745 with 111 Squadron to escort 12 Hurribombers from 241 Squadron, on return the Squadron was directed to fly top cover over Medjez el Bab to Flying Fortresses when ten 109s were seen below. The 109s were bounced and the Squadron claimed its 150th victory. On the first sortie Roy returned early after only 10 minutes with an oil leak, on the second he remained with the Squadron for the full 1 hour 30 minutes, noting 'Bombed railway yards. CO Dan. George. 3 109s destroyed' (meaning Bobby Oxspring, Danny Daniel and George Malan each destroyed a Me109).

On 16 April, in a flight over Medjez el Bab, Roy records 'Bags of 109s. Damaged 2 109s.' The note omits to record that the flight had already been detailed top cover to six A-20s (Douglas Havocs) over Djebel el Rass, and immediately on return to base had been sent out again to Medjez el Bab. Tom Docherty describes the sortie:

Mid-morning on the 16th saw the squadron escorting A-20s to bomb Djebel el Rass. Returning from the bombing it was diverted to Medjez el Bab, where it encountered nine Messerchmitts. Sgt Hussey (EN291) tore into the formation attacking five all together and damaging two …

19 April saw a scrap over Tunis with 48 Spitfires led by Wg Cdr Gilroy. The result was one 109 destroyed by Danny Daniels and three others damaged by Cox, Corbin and Hardy. Danny Daniels collided with another 109 and crash landed, returning later to the base on foot.

Lest it should be construed that it was all going the Allies' way, Roy records on the 20th 'Bloody good flak' and on the 21st 'Flak again – Cox hit but OK.' 22 April saw the loss of

Warhawks; with British roundels they were known as Kittyhawks.

W/O 'Red' Hunter who was last seen chasing a 109 with two more on his tail on a freelance sweep over Tunis. Roy records 'Fired at 109. Dam.' On 24 April Roy, in a 12 Spitfire group led by Wg Cdr Gilroy, scored another 109G destroyed but again records ' Bags of flak over land battle'. On the same sweep F/O Le Cheminant blew another Bf 109 in half and F/O Scrase and Sgt Griffiths each claimed a damaged 109. On the 25th on a 45-minute flight Roy records 'O2 trouble.' He flew aircraft number RN–S from 17–30 April, except for the 24th when he shot down the 109G, so the oxygen trouble was clearly a temporary difficulty. Easter Monday 26 April 1943 was the day George Malan killed, brought down by flak at about 1000 feet over Pont du Fahs.

The Services had an ingenious system for post. Letters received by the overseas postal services were reduced to microfilm. One microfilm could hold thousands of letters resulting in weight savings for the transport planes carrying them. At the destination, the film was developed. The recreated letters known as airgraphs, looking like photocopies of the original, were then delivered. An airgraph postmarked 25 April 1943 by Roy to his Aunty Epps, c/o Queen Street, Wells, Somerset gives some idea of Roy's interests and personality and how busy the Squadron had been.

Dear A. Epps,

Thanks a lot for your airmail letter, also the greetings. I have meant to write for a long time but I suppose I am too lazy, so I don't work that hard. I hope everyone in Wells are [sic] in good health and spirit. Tell Grandad not to work too hard. I cannot tell you what I am doing out here, but I am very well and happy, and that the squadron is the top scoring sqd. out here. Tony Watson [?] is not doing bad, DFC and DSO, he was lucky to get to Malta when it was good for fighter boys there. I hope Michael [Roy's cousin] is doing OK at school, I suppose he has grown quite a bit lately, give him my best wishes. Tell Edwina [Epp's younger sister] I will write to her soon, I have no excuses to offer for not writing; I wonder if you could get any films for my camera, the size is 6.16 as it is impossible to get any out here, I would be very grateful if you could. Well I have to go now.

Love to all
Roy

As a Sergeant Pilot Roy had been recommended for the Distinguished Flying Medal and the Squadron was notified of the award on 18 May 1943.

DFM Citation
London Gazette 1 June 1943
Hussey, Roy Jack Hubert 1312369, Sergeant, RAFVR

In operations in North Africa, this airman took part in a very large number of sorties, including attacks on airfields and road transport. He has invariably displayed fine leadership and great tenacity and has destroyed at least four enemy aircraft in combat.

The following is a report from the local Wells press:

DFM for former Wells man
Four Nazi 'planes destroyed

The Distinguished Flying Medal has been awarded to a Wells airman who attacked enemy airfields and transport in North Africa.

He is 21 years old R J H Hussey, son of the late Bert Hussey who carried on a milk retailing business in St Cuthbert Street and grandson of Mr J Herniman, purveyor of Queen Street. He was born at Wells and lives at Mangotsfield.

Shortly after this on 15 June the *Bristol Evening Post* reported his award of the Conspicuous Gallantry Medal:

Local Airman's Distinction
Award of CGM in N. Africa

The CGM goes to Pilot Office R J H Hussey (20) who was born in Bristol.

Before January this year the medal was awarded only to RAF men serving with the fleet and Pilot-Officer Hussey is one of the first to win it since it has been open to all RAF men.

The citation says: 'Pilot Officer Hussey has done all his operational flying in the North African Theatre. He has carried out determined attacks on ground targets, and has proved himself a fearless fighter in the air, even when opposed by superior numbers of enemy fighters.'

In April the squadron of which he was a member shot down a number of Me109s over Pont du Fahs. He destroyed one of them.

In March of this year he gained his commission but before this was awarded the DFM.

27 April 1943 was an interesting day for 72 Squadron, after a sweep lasting 1 hour and 25 minutes, Roy records ' Sweep Pont du Fahs area. Jimmy dam. Warhawk. Thousands of transports and tanks.' Such cryptic notes cannot adequately describe the events so we must turn to Jimmy Corbin to provide more detail.

Jimmy's logbook records 'Freelance patrol Lake area. Bumped into P-40s. Pooped at yanks who asked for trouble.' Asking for trouble was correct! The flight had seen a group of aircraft bombing well behind Allied lines. The group was American so Jimmy's burst no doubt encouraged them to do some damage elsewhere!

On 28 April Roy was again in the air over Tunis in a Spitfire IX sortie of 12 led by Sqn Ldr Daniel. Daniel claimed a damaged 109 and Sgt H.B. Smith was seen in a dive with glycol streaming from his aircraft, and crashed south of Teboura. Roy records 'Fired at 109 Nr. Tunis. No Luck. Smithy (Aussi) Missing'; a later note in different ink records 'PoW'.

On the 29th and 30th he records 'large tank battle SE Medjez' and 'Battle for heights Nr. Medjez.' Allied ground forces were pushing their way forward to Tunis.

Again the little details in Roy's logbook hide a drama. The March entries are counter-signed: 'Bobby Oxspring S/Ldr DFC = OC 72 Squadron', but the April entries are confirmed by

SINGLE-ENGINE AIRCRAFT				MULTI-ENGINE AIRCRAFT						PASS-ENGER	INSTR/CLOUD FLYING [Incl. in cols. (1) to (10)]		LINK TRAINER
DAY		NIGHT		DAY			NIGHT						OPS.
DUAL (1)	PILOT (2)	DUAL (3)	PILOT (4)	DUAL (5)	1ST PILOT (6)	2ND PILOT (7)	DUAL (8)	1ST PILOT (9)	2ND PILOT (10)	(11)	DUAL (12)	PILOT (13)	(14)
62:35	333:35	5:16	4:15							10:55	80:34	:35	133:20
	1:10		Y:1	DOGGERS. HO WITH 109s FIRED NO RESULTS. DAN SHOT DOWN. OK.									
	1:15		B:3	BLOODY GOOD FLAK.									
	1:20		B:3	FLAK AGAIN. COX HIT BUT OK.									
	:50		B:1	FIRED AT 109. DAM. SEX DEST 109. RED MISSING.									
	1:35		B:3										
	1:20		B:4	LAND BATTLE NR MEDJEZ.									
	1:10		B:3	109s OVER LAKES									
	1:15		B:1	109 G DESTROYED. BAGS OF FLAK OVER LAND BATTLE.									
	:45		B:3	O₂ TROUBLE.									
	1:15		B:1	BOMBING HUN TANKS. GEORGE MALAN MISSING (KILLED).									
	1:35		B:3	JIMMY DAM WARHAWK. THOUSANDS OF TRANSPORTS + TANKS SEEN N OF LAKES (BRITISH) FLAK TOO.									
	1:15		B:1	FIRED AT 109 NR TUNIS NO LUCK. SMITHY (AUSS) MISSING.									
	1:30		B:3	LARGE TANK BATTLE S.E. OF MEDJEZ.									
	:30			BATTLE FOR HEIGHTS NR MEDJEZ									
			89										
							TOTAL	36:50					
							OPS.	35:35					
							NON-OPS	1:15					
F/O D.F.M. O.C. B FLIGHT.						*J.D. Daniel*		S/Ldr D.F.C OC 72 Sqund.					
82:35	351:50	5:16	4:15							10:55	80:34	:35	147
(1)	(2)	(3)	(4)	(5)	(6)	(7)	(8)	(9)	(10)	(11)	(12)	(13)	(14)

Roy Hussey's logbook for April 1943. (Tim Hussey)

'S.W. Daniel S/Ldr DFC OC 72 Squadron'. It was during April that Bobby Oxspring DFC and 2 bars, a Battle of Britain veteran (Jimmy Corbin told me he hero-worshipped him) froze on take off and could not leave the ground. He was rested on 23 April and posted to HQ 242 Wing for duties in the war room, and F/Lt Danny Daniel, flight Commander of B Flight, took over as CO. 72 was a close-knit community. Wg Cdr Gilroy apparently was minded to report Bobby as LMF (Lack of Moral Fibre) but the rumblings from the Squadron were considerable and so the putative charges were shelved and the internal promotion of Danny Daniel to CO took place. As a result of the reshuffle A. Prytherch (pronounced Pritherick) took over as OC 'B' Flight. A wise decision as 72 Squadron continued to be the highest scoring squadron until at least May 1942 when the war in Tunisia ended. Later Prytherch was to lose his life over Sicily.

Saturday 1 May saw 72 Squadron toppled as top scoring squadron in 324 Wing by 111 Squadron, the latter having 48 ⅝ th and 72 Squadron 48 ⅛ th, since arrival in Africa.

On 5 May 1943 Wg Cdr Gilroy led 12 Spitfires in a freelance sweep over Tunis at 25,000 ft where they encountered eight Bf 109s at 15,000 ft over Mateur. Roy records 'Bounced 7 109s. No luck. Jake hit but OK.'

On the 6th Roy undertook two sweeps, one of 1 hour 20 minutes and the other 1 hour 35 minutes. The first of these was uneventful: '1st Army advancing – burning tanks and transports.' The second, however, was not. 'Doggers with 4 109s fired no results – 1st Army in Tunis.' This skirmish is almost certainly the one led by Wg Cdr Gilroy where bad weather prevented much being seen over Tunis but North of Bizerta 16 Bf 109s were spotted, four at 10,000 ft, eight at 16,000 ft and four at 15,000 ft. Those at 10,000 were chased off by one section, led by Gilroy, whilst the other climbed and got inside the 109s and began a terrific battle with F/Lt Hagger claiming one, PO Keith two and a probable and F/Lt Pyrtherch and PO Shaw one each.

On 11 May 1943 Roy flew three sorties; the first from Euston to Sebala records 'Moved into captured Jerry 'drome,' the second was a 1 hour 20 minutes convoy patrol off Bizerta and the last one, 1 hour and 10 minutes back to Euston. After the final sweep of the day he noted: 'War in Tunisia ends.'

It may have been because the Squadron now had sensible airfields to fly from and also that raids on their airfields had more or less ceased that throughout May and June Roy flew seven machines: RN-S, BN-F, RN-Z, N-347, RN-P, RN-X, RN-N. Plenty of variety yes, but not as much as five months earlier, where he flew 12 different machines in one month alone. For the whole of May, except on two occasions, he flew RN-S.

On 26 May 1943 Roy asks: 'What now?' Since arriving at Gibraltar in November 1942, Roy had logged 178 hours, 90% of which was operational, had 5½ victories, a DFM and CGM and a commission to Pilot Officer.

So ended the Tunisian campaign and with it the long battle for North Africa. Peter Olver, (the father of Michael Olver who was later become my best man), another veteran of the North Africa Campaign, told me he considered the North African campaign to be tougher than the Battle of Britain. There was, however, one stark difference.

In the summer of 1940, the Battle of Britain was fought against overwhelming air superiority in aircraft and personnel. The Germans had 769 serviceable bombers, 656 Me109s, 168 Me110s, 316 Ju 87s plus 100 reconnaissance aircraft. The RAF had 504 Hurricanes and Spitfires and 27 Boulton Paul Defiants. The Defiants were pretty well death traps until they were found a role as night fighters. Around 1050 pilots were available, 50 of whom had been 'borrowed' from the Fleet Air Arm. Many of the German crews were battle seasoned, having seen action over Spain, Czechoslovakia and Poland.

In North Africa the Allies outnumbered Axis forces in the air and on the ground. They had more men and more equipment. The Germans tended to leave experienced pilots in the front line until wounds, capture or death enforced a rest, for the simple reason that against superior numbers they needed the best and most experienced staying operational in order to achieve the best results. The British system of resting experienced pilots to train new ones, however, bore fruit, by producing an ever increasing number of well trained crew.

On 31 May 1943, the ORB records:

53 and one-sixth des. 12 and two-thirds prob. 50 dam. Experiment and improvisation, pleasing to look back and see that our efforts have been crowned with success.

Signed. D. Daniel

4

ITALY AND HOME

Roy Hussey with 72 Squadron move to Malta and then to Sicily in preparation for the long slog up Italy where the targets increasingly become ground rather than air.

It was not long before Roy's 'What now?' question was answered. On 9/10 June 1943 the Squadron was moved, on board LST (landing ship tank) 403, to Malta – Sicily next stop.

Before leaving North Africa for Malta the Squadron had deposited a large amount of equipment for storage at Souk-el-Khemis. During a heavy air aid on the harbour at Bari on the ankle of Italy, on 2/3 December 1943 when that area was in Allied hands, the ship transporting it was sunk. Roy took many photographs and one assumes his shots of his time in North Africa were lost in the sinking.

Operation *Torch* having opened in November 1942 was successfully concluded with the end of hostilities in Tunisia in May 1943. The Allies now turned to Operation *Husky*, the invasion of Sicily. The decision to invade Sicily in July 1943 fulfilled a number of strategic objectives. It provided a means of drawing German divisions away from the Russian front to appease Stalin, it forestalled American demands for a cross-Channel invasion in 1943 and it satisfied Churchill's ambitions in the region. As we shall see later, however, it also had the effect of starving other theatres of men and equipment. It took 38 days for Sicily to fall, which it did on 17 August 1943, and along with it Mussolini's government.

On a more domestic level, the North African Tactical Air Force was disbanded and 324 Wing became part of the Desert Air Force. 324 Wing comprised 43, 72, 93, 111, and 243 Squadrons flying Spitfires. The Wing was tasked with establishing air superiority over Sicily prior to and during a seaborne invasion.

For the first time in seven months the Squadron was not under canvas. They were now stationed at Hal Far, Malta, and billeted in the small coastal village of Birzebbuga. By 11 June 1943 the Squadron was back flying although Roy did not get airborne until the 14th when he records 'Sector reco – air test'.

Stationed on Malta at this time were six wings of aircraft, twenty-three fighter squadrons, over 400 aircraft, numerically superior to Axis forces though the Spitfire Mark V remained notably inferior to the 109G. The end of June 1943 once again saw 72 Squadron top scorer.

Some R& R on Malta.

On 16 June Roy was over Sicily for the first time: 'Similar to N. Africa – some flak.' On 18 June after another sweep over Sicily, Roy records '109s Pryth bailed out – in sea 10 miles off coast (Sicily) Missing.' In spite of the accurate fix and searches by air-sea rescue launches no sign of Prytherch (pronounced Pritherick) could be found. Rodney Scrase recalls Prycherch radioing that he was having to ditch due to engine failure, he was last seen being dragged along the sea by his parachute, and was presumed drowned. Prytherch was Flight Commander of B Flight, he had been with the Squadron for two years and was Roy's flight commander. A sad loss both for him and the Squadron. As a result F/Lt M Johnston took over as 'B' Flight Commander.

On 20 June Roy records 'HM the King visits Malta.' A sign one might think of the Allies' confidence in their air supremacy. However, the Squadron was scrambled five times on that day, Roy flew two sweeps; the first was a 30-minute air test when he notes 'Keith got 1st 109 for the squadron at Malta.' The second lasted 1 hour and he notes 'N.D. [no dice?] Sex [Sexton] des. 109 recco. Sharpe missing believed killed.' One of the five sweeps took off at 1830 hrs. With Wg Cdr Dundas leading three Spitfires, flown by F/O C.C. Sharp, W/O Alan Gear and Sgt Keith Clarkson Climbing to 26,000 ft and flying towards the Sicilian coast two enemy aircraft were spotted. Dundas split his flight into two, Sharpe and Gear, and himself and Clarkson. One of the enemy aircraft shot down Sharp, with the attacker then being picked off by Gear.

In one of the few complaints about equipment, 20 June also saw a retrograde step so far as the Squadron was concerned. They were ordered to surrender six of their Mark IXs for 'Clapped out Mark Vs'. The more experienced pilots kept the altogether better Mark IXs. Roy, now being one of the latter, continued to fly RN-S.

On 27 and 28 June on two sweeps one lasting an hour and the other 1 hour 40 minutes he recorded 'FA for each. One assumes the shorthand refers to Fanny Adams!!

July was an immensely busy month for 72 Squadron and Roy. Apart from freelance sweeps the Squadron was also providing top cover for the mostly B-17 bombers of the Strategic Air Force. Roy flew most days with three sweeps on the 10th, five on the 12th, three on the 13th, two on the 15th and 23rd, three on the 25th, two on the 27th, three on the 28th and two on the 31st.

On 8 July his logbook records 'Shot up Comiso Airdrome. Ju52 destroyed – Hein. Dam and Me109 (wheels down) shot down in circuit. Quite a party.'

This may describe an action that other sources indicate as having taken place on 6 July, where PO Hussey leading Blue Section reported three enemy aircraft circling to land at Comiso. He dived down and attacked one white-wing-tipped 109G, which had one wheel down, offering

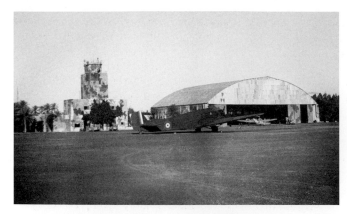

Captured JU 52 similar to the one Roy Hussey destroyed over Comiso on 8 July 1943.

Roy features in the *Daily Sketch*, August 7 1943.

Sketch map of Sicily.

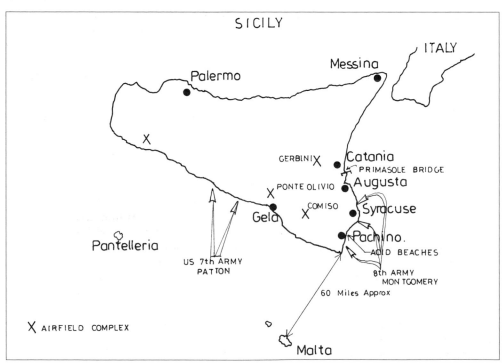

an easy target. Sqn Ldr Daniel shot down another at short range with his cannon and Sgt Scott and F/Sgt Hermiston shared another 109 destroyed and damaged two others. As if that was not sufficient they set about strafing runs damaging a Ju52, an Fw 190, and a Henschel Hs 129, various administration buildings and a radio station. As Roy puts it – 'quite a party'.

During the early stages of the air war, pilots, particularly new ones, were often criticised for their failure to recognize friendly aircraft. Indeed, George Malan's famous brother 'Sailor' was involved in the destruction of an RAF Hurricane, but was absolved after an inquiry. During Roy's training, aircraft recognition features pretty highly, as in his 'tin box' are various classroom books from his pupillage days, two of these are loose-leaf files filled with recognition tips for German and Allied aircraft. Amongst these is a Junkers 52. Extracts from its description include:

> Germany's chief transport plane employed for the carrying of parachute troops, Air-borne infantry and equipment. The Ju 52/3m (3m stands for 3 motors) has 3 770 hp BMW 132 motors capable of approx 189 mph. It is an angular low wing monoplane of all metal construction with a fixed spatted under carriage.
>
> The chief qualities of the Ju 52 are its robustness, the ease with which it can be handled, the short take off and alighting run and its weight carrying powers. A machine of this type can be flown from and set down in a field only 200 yards long provided it has no high obstacles around it.

The Allies were bombing military installations and airfields not only as a means of attack upon the island but also to frustrate a German withdrawal. The Ju52 would have been an essential tool in shifting troops and equipment and one can be sure all those wise words from his text book would have been ringing in Roy's ears as he attacked the aircraft on the deck!

On 9 July Roy notes 'Large convoy S. Malta – invasion fleet?' His surmise was accurate, as on the 10th he records 'Sicily invaded in the early hours of today.'

The Sicily land battle sounded relatively straightforward: break through the rocky bits on the coast, get a good foothold, then launch a two-pronged attack north towards the airfields and naval facilities of Catania, Sicily's second largest city, north-west to cut the hub of roads climbing east-west through Enna and Leonforte, in the island's heart. The Germans however, pivoted their defences around the impregnable Mount Etna in the north-east corner of Sicily. They fought hard, inflicting considerable casualties on British troops of the Eighth Army, before their inevitable withdrawal to the mainland.

The Americans fared better through western Sicily, advancing at a breakneck pace. Their 7th Army under Patton was winning battles and showing its fighting colours.

Eisenhower remained the Supreme Commander, with Montgomery head of British Eighth Army and Patton the American 7th Army. Following attacks by the RAF and USAAF, British and American Airborne troops landed. The troops were highly trained but not battle experienced and casualties, some 27 per cent of the Americans and 23 per cent of the British, were very high. What made it all the more tragic was that many of the transport aircraft were shot down by 'friendly fire' and the troops drowned when the transports ditched in the sea. Lessons from this were learned and at D-Day Allied aircraft were painted with 'Invasion Stripes' to assist in aircraft recognition.

The airborne landings, however, did succeed in taking some of the heat out of the American beach landings at the Gulf of Gela and the British at Syracuse. Patton advanced on Palermo taking it on 22 July. Mongomery, hindered by the Sicilian terrain as much as stubborn resistance by German forces, took Messina on 17 August. Too late, unfortunately, to prevent the brilliant withdrawal by the Germans of some 100,000 German and Italian troops and equipment across the two-and-a-half-mile Messina Straits to the Italian mainland.

Still flying from Malta over Sicily on 11 July 1943 Roy records 'Damaged Macci 200 (Bloody poor show) Keith 2 E/A, CO 1 E/A des.' It is to be presumed that the reference to 'bloody poor show' was in respect of his failure to have destroyed the Macci. Roy was a noted fine shot.

Bombed out hangar at Catania.

The squadron was still hitting hard. On 12 July 1943 when Roy flew five separate sweeps, the longest of which was 2 hours and 8 minutes, he records 'Doggers with 109s, self 1 destroyed, 1 damaged.' Roy also notes 'The squadron destroyed 14 E/A [enemy aircraft]. Malta record.'

The following day, the 13th, was lucky for him at least, he records 'Very lucky – cannon hits in the tail unit – Griff. [Alan Griffiths] hit also.' The next day, Roy flew the same machine as the previous day on three sweeps and he notes '3 109G's destroyed shared with Griff. Macci 200 destroyed, shared 109 with Keith strafed Jerry Drome with Griff. – destroyed two 109s and blew up ammo truck with soldiers – also 109 damaged in the air.'

The pounding of Catania continued but it was not one way; on 15 July 'Bags of flak' and on 20 July 'Flak!' is noted down. Between these dates on the 17th Roy records 'Griff. Missing – crashed into 109 – believed bailed out.' A note added later reads 'Killed – shute caught in tail plane – buried at Melini.' It later transpired that Alan Griffiths had shot down an Me109 at close range line astern, the 109 had exploded and fragments had brought down Alan's machine.

The 18th saw another victory, Me110 shared with 'Pip' Piper. Roy records 'Des. Me110 (Pip. Piper) crashed near Mt. Etna.' His third sortie on 28 July notes 'A.S.R (air-sea rescue) escort to Walrus [a sea plane] 1 hour 30 minutes. Saw empty dinghy.'

On the first sortie on 31 July he was flying escort to Mitchell bombers in a raid over the Sicilian hills between Enna and Messina at Adrano. He notes 'Good work by bombers. Bombed 'Adrano.' The second sortie was a 1 hour and 55 minute patrol over 'Acid.' Acid beaches was the name given to British amphibious landing beaches between Noto and Sortino south-west of Syracuse.

The squadron's successes were not without cost. Morris, an Australian, was shot down but later picked up by the Navy. Johnny King was posted missing, and his close friend Griff. Alan Griffiths had been killed. Slid into the rear pages of his logbook is a slip of paper with the following (not in Roy's handwriting) written upon it:

Mr. Wm. George Griffiths
Stourcliffe,
Carmarthen
Wales

Maybe this was Alan's home address where Roy might have sent a letter.

In his logbook flying hours collection box at the end of July 1943 Roy records:

Total Spitfire	340 hrs
Operational (July)	41:50 hrs
Non-Ops	7:45 hrs
Total Ops	238:30 hrs

On a lighter note, having moved from Hal Far, Malta to Comiso aerodrome on 15 July 1943, a prize of war was an Italian Caprione 200 light trainer (a bit like a Tiger Moth biplane). Farish managed to get it going and Danny Daniel had tested it. On 28 July Sgt Scott (Scottie) and Roy flew over to Lentini as they wanted to try and find Sgt Griffiths' grave. On the 29th with Scott in the front seat and Roy in the rear they returned to Comiso. Scottie did not want to attempt a landing as conditions were difficult, so he handed over to Roy. Farish picks up the story.

> Then one day it had its first prang. Roy Hussey and Scottie, two pilots, took it over to Lentini across country to try and find Griff's grave, During the trip they got shot at by ack-ack fire and saw the 'orrid sight of two Me109s pass them about 500 yards away. However when they came back, Scottie who had never flown it before, was in the front cockpit and, finding the cross-wind a little awkward at Comiso, asked Roy to try and bring her in. This Roy did in typical fighter pilot fashion, touched down fast right across the runway, not even choosing to run on a grass taxi track, found himself driving straight for a bomb hole and a pile of rubble, reached for the brakes and found they were in the front cockpit. Scottie, sitting there quite obliviously until they hit something, broke the undercarriage and collapsed undignifiedly on the ground.

Roy Hussey (seated) in the Caprioni 'Pisser'. (Tim Hussey)

The 'piano' party.

All that is recorded in Roy's logbook about the incident is 'Pranged u/c (undercarriage) on landing (bomb hole).'

I have mentioned before the admiration with which the pilots held Greggs Farish, the engineering officer for 72 and 111 Squadrons. In his book *Algiers to Anzio*, Greggs Farish describes how he was hunting high and low for a 20-ton engineering press to change the sleeves on the Thornycroft lorry's engine. Coupled with this prize he had promised the boys that somehow or another he would also source a piano. On both endeavours he had had many false starts. However, eventually they were crowned with success. The foraging party included F/Sgt Mann, Sgt North, W/O Weedon, W/O Norton, D/O King, and pilots F/O Roy Hussey, F/Sgt Morris and Sgt Scott, the latter two being Aussies. Farrish was no fool and the inclusion of some pilots was part of his plan.

On the way driving in the Thornycroft, they took a detour to Melilli to look for Sgt Griffith's grave for Roy. They eventually found it in a row of about ten little mounds of soldier's graves. There was a rough wooden cross; lop-sided on it written; 'Sgt Grifiths, RAF died in air collision' They added '72 Squadron' and 'Killed in action' and 'Pilot' in ink. The rest was written in pencil and Greggs promised he would get a proper cross made out of prop blades.

The expedition eventually found its way – having ground past 239 Wing (where Tom Stoate, another of my uncles would shortly be serving), 244 Wing and 322 Wings – to Catania. The town had been pretty heavily damaged and some shops looted, but Roy struck lucky and found about a hundred camera films, size 120 – a marvellous find.

That night they slept rough in the middle of an artillery barrage. The following morning they drove on to Augusta on the hunt for a piano. Augusta was a looter's paradise but a provost Marshall had been appointed who decreed that looters would be shot. Greggs reckoned with three pilots on board they would take their chances, so he left the ground crews on the edge of town and proceeded on with Roy, Scottie and Morris.

Now I had left the others by the wagon and went to reconnoitre. While inspecting the house there was noise from opposite in the otherwise deserted street. I was horrified to see two MPs looking out of an upstairs window, but then realized that it was me who had caught them doing a bit of quiet pilfering on their own. That fixed them. Everything else seemed clear … The deed was swiftly done … The pilots got the piano downstairs with great shushes, bumps and curses. Quickly we had the piano out of the front door, on its back altogether with super-human strength we lifted it onto the wagon, tent over, tail board up and away before anyone else saw us – except the two MPs opposite laughing.

One of the interesting things about these stories is that it matters where you get them. That was Farrish's version. When I was speaking to Jack Lancaster, a sergeant fitter who looked after Roy's aeroplane, he had a different twist. Namely that he was in the party, went up to see what the MPs were up to with his service revolver in his hand and from them found out where they might find a piano and he had then helped to get it down the stairs and into the lorry.

None of this really matters – it is a dit and is supposed to amuse.

On the way back they picked up a couple of Italian girls, resulting in a pair of pink knickers on the dashboard, but that is a different story; or is it also a dit?

August opens mostly with bomber escort duties and on the 4th another ASR (air sea rescue). On 4 August 1943 F/O George Keith was hit by flak had bailed out over the sea, hitting his leg on the tail plane as he left the aircraft. George Keith, the first pilot of 72 Squadron to destroy an enemy aircraft in Malta six weeks earlier and with whom Roy 14 days earlier had shared a 109, was taken to 25 Mobile Field Hospital where he died in the night.

News of George Keith's DFC and bar came through shortly after he was killed. On 14 August 1943, Roy notes 'Keith & Sex DFC.' On 17 August 1943 Roy records 'Campaign in Sicily ends.'

Alan ' Griff' Griffiths' grave. He was buried by the enemy after he collided with the remains of a Me109 he had shot down over Sicily in 1943. (Tony 'Red' Weller)

Unidentified members of 72 Squadron, 1943, kept in Roy's tin box.

The squadron however continued the offensive on to Italy. Roy flew three patrols on the 19th, three on 26 and 28 August. On the middle patrol on the 26th he records 'Patrol Locri (Italy) Bombing road – railway junction – poor bombing.'

The last flight on 26 August recorded the Squadron's move from Agnone to Pachino, and on the 28th Roy records 'Pachino to Gerbini 7 (Pandebeanco).' Not for long however as on 2 September 1943 they moved on again from Pandebeanco to Cassala. On the 3rd after a patrol over Augusta he records '<u>Italy invaded</u>' and 'Eighth Army enters Italy from landing craft.' This would be the so-called 'Baytown Landings' into Calabria, the toe of the Italian boot. 3 September also saw the Italian government signing a secret armistice with the Allies.

The shift in base for 72 Squadron was on 6 September. When they flew in to Falcone on the north coast of Sicily. Roy records 'Wiz place.' On 8 September 1943 he records: 'Italy surrenders.'

The squadron was now undertaking a different type of operation, the air threat was reduced and the Squadron was mainly providing air support to the ground forces. He notes on 9 September 'Avalanche Operation'.

Operation *Avalanche* was the invasion proper of Italy. It was originally proposed to mount an assault on Naples, this however would have stretched supply lines too far particularly in terms of fighter aircraft cover, so the beaches (the so-called Peaches Beaches) at Salerno 50 miles to the south were settled upon. Together with this there was to be a further landing on the 'sole' of Italy at Taranto, this was undertaken by 3,600 men of the British 1st Paratroop Division and was virtually unopposed.

The Salerno landing was mainly an American 5th Army operation, under the command of General Mark Clark. The 5th Army comprised the VI Corps, the British X Corps and the US 82nd Airborne Division, some nine divisions in all. The assault craft totalled some 450 vessels. These had been assembled from Sicily, Tripoli, Oran, and Bizerte in North Africa. To achieve surprise (a lesson learned from the disastrous Dieppe landing in 1942) there was no preliminary bombardment either naval or by air. The landings commenced at 0310 hrs. Luftwaffe attacks on the beachhead were driven off at dawn as Allied aircraft from Sicily and supporting carriers appeared.

The British Eighth Army, in the south, was again becoming bogged down, German forces under the supreme command of Generalfeldmarschall Kesselring were defending fiercely, trying at all costs to prevent the link-up between the 5th and Eighth Armies. At one time the 5th Army was attempting to control a front some 35 miles long, so Allied heavy bombers were diverted to Italy from strategic targets in Germany and their efforts together with heavy naval bombardments finally prevented the Germans from pushing the invading troops back into the sea. By 15 September, the Germans began an orderly withdrawal, the 5th and Eighth Armies linked up and the airfield at Foggia was captured. Naples fell on 1 October and southern Italy was in Allied hands by 6 October.

Back to 72 Squadron, now based at Casala in Sicily. Following the surrender of Italy the detail of prisoner logistics should not be overlooked; on 9 September Roy notes 'escorted S.M 79 Wops Crew [Italian aircraft] from Stromboli to San Antonio.'

Most of the remainder of September was taken up in providing air cover to the landing forces around Naples and 'Peaches Beaches'. On 13 September the Squadron moved again, he records 'Falcone to Tusciano' and '4 miles from the Huns. Plenty of noise and dust'. Tusciano was on the Italian mainland, on the river of the same name. The airfields adjoined a British artillery unit which, along with the Navy, was bombarding the Germans with their heavy guns, hence 'plenty of noise and dust'.

On 15 September he notes 'Squadron's 200th E/A des. by Jack Pearson.' The 16th saw a very short 10-minute flight! He notes 'Broke 18ins off prop. blades on take off – Lucky B___.' On the same day 'Pip' Piper had a forced landing behind enemy lines but six days later on the 21st Roy records 'Pip walked back with Yank paratroops.'

In between times, on the 17th, Roy records 'Destroyed two Do.217s. Seven bailed out. One fell out of shute – Believed to be radio bombers [glider bombers] – Navy pranged – [*Warspite*].'

The Royal Naval name *Warspite* was a name (given to a good number of ships) that carried the highest number of battle honours, ranging from Cadiz in 1596 to Biscay in 1944. Roy's reference to HMS *Warspite* refers to a First World War battleship, which in May 1941, took part took part in the battle of Crete, where she sustained damage by a heavy bomb. On 16 September during the Landings at Salerno, she was hit by a German Glider bomb (Fritz-X bomb). She was towed to Gibraltar for temporary repairs and fully repaired at Rosyth in March 1944. In June she was deployed at Normandy with only three functioning main turrets and as such may have been useful to Norman Stoate, one of my father's brothers, and again at Walcharen when it fell to the Canadians and the Royal Marines to clear the approaches to Antwerp, as we shall see later.

Rodney Scrase was flying as Roy's wingman on this sweep. Rodney wrote of his experiences in the December 2001 issue of the magazine *Swift Reply*. The account very clearly echoes the comments made by Greggs Farish about Roy's 'get on with it' personality. This action is referred to again in Roy's DFC Citation.

September 16th was a day I shall always remember. Flying as number 2 to Roy we were vectored onto enemy plots over the Bay of Salerno where British and American warships were providing maximum possible support to our ground troops, who only two days after the landings were having a tough time. We were at 20,000 feet and heading towards two Do 217s. At that moment I had trouble with my second stage supercharger (this gave more power above a pre-selected altitude) which kept cutting in and out. Roy flew on ahead and shot down the first Dornier. By the time I had sorted out my problems, he had caught up with the second aircraft and got that one too. As I came up alongside, the crew were bailing out and today almost 60 years after the event I can still see the enemy, the last of whom was in too much of a hurry to pull his rip-cord and sadly went down with his plane se-sawing up and down the tail plane. These aircraft were using a new form of bomb – a 3000lb Henschel 293 released by one aircraft and then guided by the second plane by the 'bomb aimer' who used radio control to make adjustments to its flight. Over the next two days the Dorniers were able to inflict considerable damage on our ships – sinking a US cruiser and damaging several of their ships as well as severely damaging our own battleship HMS *Warspite*.

Later, on 29 January 1944, the Luftwaffe scored a major success when Fritz-X bombs sank the cruiser *Spartan* and the cargo ship *Samuel Huntington* with heavy loss of life.

The 3000-pound Fritz X – it looked like a normal freefall bomb but for the stabilizing stub wings midway along its body – relied on simply accelerating under gravity to penetrate large warship armour. The missile was released using the normal bombsite, after which the pilot put his Dornier 217 into a climb to drag the speed back from 290 mph to 165 mph to keep the bomb aimer lined up with both missile and target. The observer used this to help him radio-control the missile in its final 10 to 15 seconds to impact.

Fritz-X came as a nasty surprise to the Allies. To pit a handful of Dornier 217s against a host of Seafires (the naval version of the Spitfire) was a poor hand to play. Far better to threaten air-craft carriers themselves, especially as the Royal Navy was still scarred by the loss of the *Prince of Wales* and *Repulse* to Japanese air attack. The tactic worked: the day after the *Philadelphia*, *Savannah* and *Uganda* were hit, the Royal Navy withdrew all five carriers from the fray. As it happened, the carrier-based fighters had enjoyed limited success, in part because the FW 190 could outrun the Seafire but also because the Germans were able to jam the three controlling radio frequencies. So Roy's attack may have been more than usually valuable.

For the remainder of September and the first half of October Roy flew almost daily patrols over 'Peaches Beaches', North Salerno or the North Naples area.

On 13 October 72 Squadron and Roy Hussey moved again, this time to Tusciano, a forward airfield in Italy that was within range of enemy artillery but covered also by Allied guns behind, so it too was a particularly noisy location.

Nothing further is recorded until 28 October, when he is in a USAAF Dakota on leave. A pretty busy leave, in terms of logistics, it would seem, as his flying logbook continues to be filled in:

October	
28th	Pomigliano to Foggia
28th	Foggia to Catania
29th	Catania to Tripoli
30th	Tripoli to Benina
30th	Benina to Cairo West
November	
9th	Cairo West to Marble Arch
9th	Marble Arch to Catania
10th	Catania to Capopichiano

On each trip he was being transported in a Dakota, either RAF or USAAF except the final one where he was 2nd pilot to W/O Fenner in a Boston.

In his logbook in the collection of flying hours summary at the end of October 1943 he signs always as R.J. Hussey. The Operations Record Book notes him as being Flight Commander A flight on 28 October, during October he had also been promoted to F/Lt so this time he also signs as F/Lt 'O.C.' A. Flight.

Although the fall of Naples and capture of Foggia Airfield on 1 and 6 October 1943 respectively signalled the end of Operation *Avalanche,* the battle for Italy was no means finished. The Germans staged a fighting withdrawal and settled into a strong defensive position on the 'Winter line', a series of defensive bunkers along the 'Gustav line' at Italy's narrowest point that

R & R; a friend in Naples Bay, 1943.

effectively sealed off southern Italy. Both the west coast route and the central mountain routes were blocked. The stalemate would not be broken until the bloody battles of Monte Cassino and the breakout from Anzio.

12 November saw him back in a Spitfire flying three sorties on bombline patrol. The 13th proved to be a good day for the Squadron, Roy notes 'CO 109 Des. Morris Mac. 109s des. Tom [Larlee] 2 des'.

On 19 November Roy notes 'strafed (damaged) two lorries – soldiers and donkey cart.' And again on the 19th just to remind us that it was not all plain sailing, 'hit by flak in starb. aileron.' On 28 November 'Strafed two lorries & staff car (all flamers) also damaged tank carriers & and tanks. Also 1 house wooden – flamer.'

It must be time for another dit, this one again from Jack Lancaster, I am sure Jack will not mind me recording that in 2010 when I spent a week with him and some other veterans from those days with 72 Squadron, all pushing or beyond 90 years old, neither his eyesight nor hearing were in prime condition, but everything else including his brain and humour were were certainly intact. We were talking about Roy and his manner and Jack was reminded of a conversation he had with Roy just after he had returned from one of these strafing missions in Italy.

> I saw that Roy had fired his guns so I asked if he had hit anything, in his south Gloucestershire accent, he replied in the negative so I asked why he fired, 'Oh' he said 'I was flying along this mountain road when it turned a sharp corner so as I rounded the corner I opened up – you never know what's around the corner Jack!'

The November collection summary was countersigned by Danny Daniel DFC and Bar signifying that Danny had, during November, been awarded that bar.

Again December 1943 saw 72 Squadron and Roy flying most days. To give an idea of the scale of some of the bombing raids, on 1 December he records a 1 hour 30 minute flight 'Cover for 200+ bombers, bombing gun positions – prelude to push on Rome?'

On the 7th he notes 'Escort to B25 [Mitchell bombers] Rome area, plastered target.'

In reading Roy's logbook from November 1942 I had been noting – but not understanding – tiny, seemingly random numbers, mostly in pencil. Now, on 3 December 1943, like cracking

Roy Hussey flew this Mk IX
Spitfire in December 1943.

a code it all becomes clear, they are his private totals of operational sorties flown, the total at 3 December 1943, being 236 separate sorties. The normal number of operational hours before being rested was 200; by the end of December 1943 Roy had recorded 376.

The loss of Prytherch had meant there was a vacancy for a flight commander for B Flight and Danny Daniel asked for and got back Tom Hughes, who returned on 17 November from his brief stay at 43 Squadron. Returning to Roy's flying hours collection box, at the end of November 1943 Roy had completed 350 operational hours and flown over 230 sorties. Greggs Farish summed matters up quite succinctly:

> … the most remarkable thing about Roy Hussey was his ability to survive. The normal tour of duty for a pilot was officially 200 hours, but the CO could always extend this some. Indeed Bobby [Oxspring] extended his own tour of duty too long … that was when Danny had to take over the squadron … To come back to Roy Hussey, he never showed the normal signs of fatigue and kept shooting down enemy aircraft as well as ever, so his tour of duty was extended from 200 hours firstly to 400 hours, and then on to 450 hours as Flight Commander … I never heard of anyone else doing 450 continuous hours of operational flying.

On 9 December 1944 '4 transport destroyed. Jack and Tom missing.' This referred to F/Lt Jack Pearson and W/O Tom Larlee. Tom Larlee evaded capture and returned to the Squadron in May 1944, after Roy had left. On the 15th ' Chased 5 Fw 190s. Joe Me109 Des' On 18 December' Tom (Hughes) missing, crashed in flames Nr. Casino– Burnt. PoW. Mac – Con – Coles 3 Me109s Des on previous show' and on the next day after an engagement with 15+ fw190s '1 Fw destroyed. Boucher missing believed killed.'

Amongst Roy's papers in the tin box was another letter, this time from Tom Hughes' mother. It is dated 18 January 1944. Roy was still in Italy but by the time the letter reached him three months later on 25 March 1944 he was back in England. It had chased him from 53 OTU Llandow, to Kirton in Lindsay, in Lincolnshire. The letter has had water damage and is not easily legible.

6 Garth Drive Mosely Hill, Liverpool 18

18 January 1944

Dear Mr Hussey

I am Tom Hughes' mother. I wonder if you know anything at all about the journey Tom made on 18 December 1943 when he was lost. If you were with him & could give us any information at all – as to whether you saw him turn back – or crash –or bail out – whether it was light or dark – where Santa Maria La Fanza is – (We have a World Gazetteer but can't find La Santa Maria La Fanza marked) or any tiny bit of news about him on that fateful journey – we shall be terribly grateful.

We have suffered such anguish & suspense in waiting that do not hesitate to give us the plain unvarnished truth if you know anything.

If you were not with him on that flight could you possibly pass this on to some member of his squadron who was with him. – you would do us a great service if you would and we should be so very thankful of any news of any kind.

We are waiting to hear if he is a prisoner of war but that news is not through yet. I am so sorry to trouble you – & good luck to you & all those brave fellows in the 72nd squadron.
Yours most sincerely

Mrs. Adelade Hughes.

This calm, courageous letter did not arrive with Roy until nearly three months after its posting. It is to be hoped that Tom's mother had the news that Tom was a PoW well before then. Although the Squadron Operations Record Book shows Tom being reported a PoW on 17 April 1944, Roy's logbook records that Tom was PoW in ink and in writing that seems to have been put down at the same time as he recorded him missing. In January 1944 a month to the day after Tom was shot down his mother was still waiting news of his fate. When I wrote to Tom in 2010 about this and to give him the contents of his mother's letter, he wrote back.

Dear Mr Lambah-Stoate,

I was delighted to get your letter yesterday with the copied letter that Roy had received from my mother in 1944.

Our family lost two aged uncles in an air-raid on Liverpool and then my brother and I were missing in the Royal Marines and RAF so Mum had much to worry about and she died of polio in 1948.

I am so glad to hear you are writing something about Roy Hussey; I still have very warm memories of our short friendship in 1943.

With best wishes
Yours sincerely

Tom Hughes

It is often good value to look at an ORB for Christmas. With 72 Squadron Roy Hussey's colleague Tony 'Red' Weller was shot down by flak on Christmas day 1943 and happily found his way back to the Squadron unscathed. I met Tony in Malta in 2010. There remained a sharp mind, a twinkle in the eye and humour lines round his mouth – accentuated when I asked him what he was doing on Christmas Day 1943. I then showed him the entry in Roy Hussey's logbook 'Flak – Red Weller hit. Bailed out O.K. our side.'

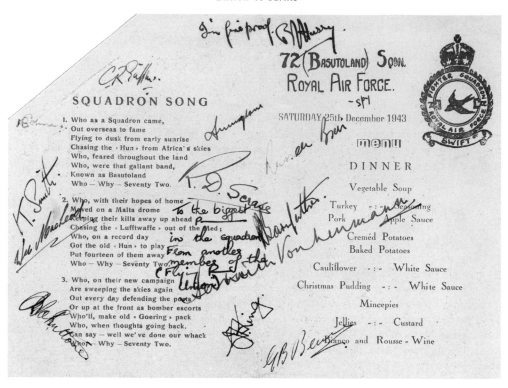

SQUADRON SONG

72 (BASUTOLAND) Sqdn.
ROYAL AIR FORCE.

SATURDAY 25th December 1943

menu

DINNER

1. Who as a Squadron came,
   Out overseas to fame
   Flying to dusk from early sunrise
   Chasing the ‹ Hun › from Africa's skies
   Who, feared throughout the land
   Who, were that gallant band,
   Known as Basutoland
   Who — Why — Seventy Two.

2. Who, with their hopes of home
   Moved on a Malta drome
   Keeping their kills away up ahead
   Chasing the ‹ Lufftwaffe › out of the Med;
   Who, on a record day
   Got the old ‹ Hun › to play
   Put fourteen of them away
   Who — Why — Seventy Two.

3. Who, on their new campaign
   Are sweeping the skies again
   Out every day defending the ports
   Or up at the front as bomber escorts
   Who'll, make old ‹ Goering › pack
   Who, when thoughts going back,
   Can say — well we've done our whack
   Who — Why — Seventy Two.

Vegetable Soup

Turkey -:- Seasoning
Pork -:- Apple Sauce

Cremed Potatoes
Baked Potatoes

Cauliflower -:- White Sauce

Christmas Pudding -:- White Sauce

Mincepies

Jellies -:- Custard

Branco and Rousse - Wine

Christmas dinner menu. Tony ‘Red’ Weller returned in time for this having been shot down earlier in the day. Note Roy Hussey's comment ‘I'm fireproof!’ at the top.

Roy's copy of the Christmas dinner menu survives, signed by Barney Barnfather and Rodney Scrase to name but two. Roy's signature is accompanied by his words 'I'm fireproof!' Folklore in the mess taught one that acceptance of the likelihood of one's death was often a precursor to the chop. If one doubted that one was going to survive then the way downhill was pretty quick. Roy was obviously having none of that.

On 30 December '1 Fw damaged [E/A dive bombing our troops.] On the 31st he recorded 'Top cover to Mustangs' an aeroplane that nine months later he was to become very familiar with.

The New Year started as the old one finished; Roy flew most days, carrying out bomb line patrols, escorting Martin Marauders and Bostons in large formations of up to 200 aircraft. He even managed to put pen to paper writing an airgraph to his auntie Epps with a censor's date of 1 January 1944 and postmarked 10 January.

Dear A Epps

Sorry I haven't replied to your letter before but as you can guess we have had a busy Christmas. We had plenty of turkeys wine and food and managed to organize a dance and party with some English Sisters. Of course I put up a black by getting slightly under the weather and spent all of Christmas Eve in a car in a bomb-hole. Well I must thank you very much for your parcel, all of it was very useful as soap is very hard to get and the Italians do not forget to charge for anything you buy the b__s. Give Michael my love. I don't think I will recognize him <u>when</u> I come home. I hope you all at Wells had a very merry Xmas and I wish you all a very prosperous New Year. Give my love to all.

Roy

On 13 January 1944, the Squadron records note Roy's award of the DFC.

DFC Citation – Roy Hussey

An outstanding pilot, this officer combines courage and accurate shooting with cool judgement and fine leadership. Since being awarded the D.F.M. he has taken part in the Sicilian and Italian operations with conspicuous success, destroying a further five enemy aircraft bringing his total to victories to at least 10 hostile aircraft destroyed and others damaged. On one occasion in September 1943, Flight Lieutenant Hussey shot down two Do 217s within the space of two minutes. At all times his fine fighting spirit, courage and devotion to duty have worthy of the highest praise.

Although the Allies had mastery of the skies by now, the enemy still shot back. On 14 January 1944 he records the following cryptic note 'Ju 88? Where. Hit in cockpit'; seemingly meaning he had missed one that had damaged his aircraft. Not too seriously it seems, as he was back flying the same aircraft number again two days later. It was on this day also that he was gazetted as Mentioned in Dispatches. The citation is now lost. This was recorded in the ORB on 16 February 1944, after Roy had left.

On 19 January 1944, the day his sister (my mother) was getting married to my father he flew two sorties, one a bombline patrol and the other a sweep over Viterbo and Rome, which included 200 + B25 bombers.

On the 21st he notes 'Scotty bailed out in sea 300 ft. – OK.' Sgt Scottie Scott, it may be recalled, was with Roy when they took The 'Pisser' (the Caprione 200 light trainer) to Lentini to find Alan Griffith's grave at Lentini and Roy managed to take the undercarriage off landing in a bomb crater. 300ft is very low indeed to bail out and Scottie was lucky to survive.

On the 24th he notes 'FW 190 destroyed. Shared with 'Furgie' King. On the next day 'Halliday missing – believed bailed out in sea.'

Rodney 'Boy' Scrase (later DFC) emerges from his tent near Naples 1943.

It was not all work. Rodney Scrase:

January was a month when in company with Roy Hussey and ably conducted by an Italian guide we climbed Mount Vesuvius. At 4200 feet it was not a great height but one needed a guide to be able to get there and back safely, this at a time when the volcano was not quiescent.

At the end of January 1944 Roy's summary read as follows:

Monthly Total	41:45 Hrs
Non-Ops	40 Hrs
Operational	41:05 Hrs
Total Ops	417:45 Hrs

On 23 and 24 January 1944 Roy had been flying patrols over the Anzio invasion area, based at Lago pretty well mid-way between Rome and Florence, but on the 29th he was on his way to Tunis via Palermo. He had been posted away from 72 Squadron, tour expired. Tom Stoate, another of my uncles, an RAF doctor, remained very nearly until the end of the Italian Campaign, as recounted later.

Since arriving in the Mediterranean theatre one year and two months earlier Roy had flown 296 sorties, nearly 420 operational hours and had destroyed 13½ aircraft as well as many ground transport and fixed targets damaged or destroyed. It was time for a rest. Unusually, there seems to be no record of his leaving 72 Squadron but on 29 January he was on two USAAF Dakotas from Naples to Palermo and from Palermo to Tunis. On 30 January he records flying a Fairchild for 45 minutes, recording 'exp.on type'. Did this man like flying?

5

THE FINAL JOURNEY

Roy Hussey's love of flying is given ample scope at the Airfighting Development Unit following which he is posted to 19 Squadron flying Mustangs escorting bombers attacking Germany. Boredom sets in – and then tragedy.

In early 1942 Roy had been a pupil at 53 OTU, now two years later, in March 1944 after some leave, Roy was posted there as an instructor. The Unit had been transferred from Llandow to Kirton in Lindsey, Lincolnshire, and it was to there he flew from Wittering, Nothamptonshire on 10 March in a Proctor with F/Lt. Lane as second pilot. Chasing Roy about was the letter from Tom Hughes' mother of 18 January, first directed to Llandow and then forwarded to Kirton, Lindsey, postmarked 3 March 1944.

March was taken up with relatively short-duration familiarisation flights in various Spitfire mark Is, including a squadron Balbo (RAF slang for a large formation of aircraft first developed by Douglas Bader's Duxford big Wing) of 1 hr 45 minutes on the 18th. There is nothing recorded for 23 March 1944, Roy's 21st birthday, so perhaps he had a day off.

The early part of April was similarly uneventful with instructional formation flying in a variety of Spitfire Mark IIs. On 11 April he was posted to AFDU (Air Fighting Development Unit) Wittering, arriving on 14 April in an Airspeed Oxford with Roy as second pilot. His time at 53 OTU was very short and given that he flew there from Wittering where the AFDU was stationed, it seems almost as if his posting to the AFDU was already in hand but he needed to be parked somewhere for a month.

The remainder of April was taken up by large numbers of relatively short duration flights in aircraft ranging from Spitfire marks IX, I, II, III, V and Vc, Mustang I, Oxford, Typhoon III and Hurricanes. (The 'c' in 'Vc' refers to the type of wing, one which could incorporate a variation of armament, the so-called 'universal' wing.) The flights included two height climbs, one on 14 April lasting 2 hours 10 minutes with a 90-gallon overload, a speed run on the 18th in a Spitfire Vc, a tank drop on the 19th, gyro sight attacks on the 28th and on the 29th to 30th, a series of 15 and 30 degree RP (Rocket Projectile) attacks in Hurricanes of no specified variant.

Apart from the wide variety of aircraft that he flew at AFDU it was home to several others, including an Me109, a Ju88, an American 'Billy' Mitchell, a Flying Fortress, a P38 Lightning

Remains of an Airspeed Oxford at AFDU 1944.

and many others. His interest in aircraft was such that his photographs of many of the unusual ones are left for us to pore over, some of them reproduced here.

The Hawker Hurricane was arguably the RAF's most versatile aircraft, its wide undercarriage which opened outwards planting the aeroplane firmly on the ground made it very forgiving, in contrast to the Spitfire, which had a very narrow undercarriage and as we have seen was also nose-heavy on the ground. In the air, the Hurricane was a very stable gun platform; it was, however, slower than the Spit.

The Hurricane started life as a 1930s construction Hawker Fury biplane, using wire braced tubular steel and a good deal of fabric covering. It performed well in the Battle of Britain in 1940, being able to turn more tightly than a Spitfire. Its golden period had probably been in North Africa and Italy. The Hurricane was continually modified in terms of armament and wing design, the 'E' wing being designed not for fighter combat but as a platform for a wide range of ground attack weapons, such as 250 and 500 lb bombs, anti-tank cannon or up to eight 60-lb RPs (Rocket Projectiles). It was also capable of being fitted with 44- or 90-gallon long range tanks, the former being combat tanks and the latter for ferry purposes.

Spitfires, Mustangs and Typhoons with their exposed cooling systems were particularly vulnerable to ground fire. The Mark IV Hurricane, however, was very heavily armoured and capable of sustaining considerable punishment. Peter Olver, whom I have mentioned earlier, when CO of 213 Squadron based behind German lines in Cyrenaica hit a telegraph pole when returning to his airstrip after a mission. I had read about this and when talking to him one day said he had a lucky escape when he lost part of his tail plane. 'Tail plane be buggered' he responded 'I hit the main wing just outside the propeller arc, spun round the pole and with great luck managed to keep the aircraft in the air and made it back.'

The development of RPs was seen as particularly important. The lessons of air superiority had been learned in the First World War but then it was still an adjunct to ground battles. In the Second World War the importance of air battles was really understood as they could decide everything. RPs were primarily used in ground attacks against targets such as trains, tanks, motor transport, buildings and slow-moving targets such as shipping and surfaced submarines. No doubt Roy's records of firing RPs day after day were part of the AFDU's contribution to the development of the weapon and its delivery.

Rocket projectiles were an effective means of delivering a large warhead capable of destroying or disabling heavy tanks. The rocket body was a steel tube 3 inches (76 mm) in diameter, hence the name, RP-3. The tube was filled with 11 pounds (5 kg) of cordite, which was the propellant; this was fired electrically. A warhead was screwed into the forward end, initially a solid 25-lb (11-kg), 3.44-inch armour piercing shell which was quickly supplemented by a 6-inch diameter, 60-lb (27-kg) high explosive head. Another type of head was a 25-lb (11-kg) mild steel (later concrete) practice head.

Four small tailfins gave enough spin to stabilize the rocket, it was unguided and targeting was a matter of judgment and experience. In time the Giro sight became sufficiently sophisticated to carry out the necessary calculations. The approach to the target needed to be precise, with no sideslip or yaw, which could throw the RP off line. Aircraft speed also had to be precise at the moment of launch, and because the launch rails were a fixture, the angle of attack also required precision. Trajectory drop was another problem, especially at longer ranges.

Junkers JU88-A4, the fighter bomber considered by many as the Luftwaffe's equivalent of the Mosquito. Used on all fronts as a bomber, dive bomber, torpedo bomber, recon, fighter and as a radar-equipped night fighter. Also used at the end of the war as a pilotless bomb strapped to a BF 109, which flew the JU88 to its target before releasing. Powered by Junkers Jumo 211 engines with annular radiators. This one landed unexpectedly at RAF Chivenor in 1941, the pilot got lost! It was taken to RAE Farnborough for evaluation in 1942. Later it went to the US where after further evaluation it became a museum exhibit. The picture and the following aircraft are from Roy's tin box.

On the plus side the rocket was less complicated and more reliable than a gun firing a shell and there was no recoil on firing. It was found to be a demoralising form of attack against ground troops, and the 60-lb warhead could be devastating. The rocket installations were light enough to be carried by single-seat fighters. Against slow-moving large targets like shipping and U-boats, or buildings, the rocket was a formidable weapon.

Tactics had to be developed for the individual aircraft types which were to be armed with the RPs. And this presumably was the reason for Roy flying so many different types of aircraft at AFDU. Aiming was through a standard GM.II reflector gunsight. A later modification enabled the reflector to be tilted with the aid of a graduated scale, depressing the line of sight, the GM.IIL.

The first operational use of the RP was in the Western Desert as a 'tank-busting' weapon mounted on Hurricane Mk. IIEs and IVs. The 25-lb armour-piercing heads were found to be ineffective against the Panzer VI (Tiger) tanks so a new 60-pound semi-armour-piercing (SAP) head capable of knocking turrets off tanks was developed. Roy would certainly have seen these in action in Italy, if not Africa.

May saw further use of the Mustang Mark III in speed runs, a useful experience, as Mustangs were where Roy was headed. Between 8–10 May, Roy flew eight times, with each flight averaging an hour, in a Spitfire Mark IX carrying out dive bombing runs at 45 and 60 degrees. These tests were continued on the 12th, 13th and 14th. A significant number of flights were to other airfields including Sutton Bridge in Lincolnshire, Duxford, Newmarket and Northholt, but there is no clue as to the reasons for the journeys. The final flight in May took place on the 17th when he was flown in an Oxford to attend 48 Course CGS (Central Gunnery School) Catfoss.

The course, which lasted for a month until 21 June 1944, was an assessment course in air gunnery and instruction on how to be an air gunnery instructor. The attendees were graded as exceptional, above average, good average, average or below average. The areas for assessments were:

i)	As a marksman	Air to Ground
		On Drogue
ii)	As a marksman	Fighter Combat
		Bomber Combat
iii)	As an instructor	

Roy passed out as 'above average' on (i) (drogue only scored) and (ii) fighter combat, and 'good average' on (ii) bomber combat and (iii) as instructor.

On a separate certificate it is noted that on the 20-ft towed sleeve of the drogue he scored 15 per cent hits. This was not exceptional. The average was reckoned to be around 20 per cent. However, what really counted was being able to destroy enemy aircraft in action rather than hit a drogue in non-combat conditions.

Shooting a smallish nimble object moving at a similar speed while turning, rolling and diving was quite a task. G forces turned muscles and blood into molten lead. The reflector sight which replaced the old ring sight projected a dot of red light on the angled underside of the Perspex windscreen. It was bracketed by a set of range bars which could be adjusted to the size of bombers or fighters. This was helpful in assessing range and the red dot told you of the line of bullet flight, if both you and the target were stationary. Unfortunately it did not help too much when everything was moving about. Practice and judgment were the only way to hone these skills. Many bases, including Tangmere, had clay pigeon ranges to help.

On 28 April 1944 Roy recorded the use of a gyro-sight. The Gyro-sight was first introduced in 1941, being fitted to certain Spitfires and the Bolton Paul Defiant. The Mark I however, was not a success. It had a number of drawbacks, including requiring the pilot/gunner to look through a small aperture. Production was postponed and work started on an improved sight,

Hawker Tempest V. A very refined development of the Typhoon with Laminar flow wing, lengthened fuselage and tear drop canopy. It was used successfully to chase V1s, also in ground attack and fighter roles. The introduction of the Focke Wulfe 190 by the Luftwaffe greatly influenced its design. Succeeded by the Tempest II with Bristol Centaurus radial engine. Invasion stripes are correct on this one shown. Again, 4 cannons, bombs or 8 rockets were standard armaments.

which would incorporate a normal reflector system instead. This new sight became the Mark II Gyro Sight, first tested in late 1943 with production examples available later in the same year.

The gyro gunsight calculated automatically target lead (the amount of aim-off in front of a moving target) and bullet drop. The sight incorporated a gyroscopic mechanism that computed the necessary deflection required to ensure a hit on the target. It worked by having both a fixed and a moving aiming point or graticule, the fixed one signifying the direction the guns are pointing (in effect, the same as a 'normal', non-gyro, sight), the moving one the corrected aiming point. Providing the pilot/gunner used the correct moving graticule then a hit on the target was likely.

On 21 June 1944, having completed that brief interlude at the Central Gunnery School, which included leaving behind for us to see today 859 ft of gun camera cinefilm demonstrating various angles of attack on Wellingtons and Spitfires, it was back to Wittering, and the Air Fighting Development Unit. There for the remainder of the month he was primarily flying various Spitfire Mark IXs for flights of about 30 minutes each, doing dive-bombing runs.

July saw him flying a total of 47 hours in Spitfires, Typhoons, Tempests, Hurricanes as well as a Proctor and an Oxford. A few of the flights lasted just over an hour but most were around 30 minutes doing Rocket Projectile tests, air tests, machine gun tests with camera, one leaflet drop and an escort to Lancasters with the New Zealand 485 Squadron where he notes '(Buzz bombs)' meaning Doodle Bugs or V1 rockets.

On 30 July 1944 he had a speed run in the Spitfire XIV with its yet more powerful Griffon engine. This model was a genuine development from previous marks. It was 16 inches longer than the Mark IX, heavier, but with the new Rolls-Royce Griffon 65, 37-litre liquid-cooled

Hawker Typhoon 1A. This photo is possibly of the first prototype for evaluation. In a tight turn or pull out from a dive the rear fuselage failed ahead of the tailplane. This was solved in production versions by the addition of fish plates around the weak point of the fuselage in all operational versions that followed. The 1B was the major version, which had the same canopy as above with 'car door' entrance to the cockpit. The later 1Bs were fitted with an all round vision hood (bubble) but still retained the car door entry. Final versions were armed with 4 cannon and could carry bombs or 8 rockets. The Typhoon achieved major success at the Falaise gap destroying German armour.

V12 engine developed 2035 horsepower compared with 1475–1650 hp for the Mark IX. It has been said that this mark looked too much like the American P-51 Mustang to be a 'Real Spitfire'. Nearly 1000 models were produced nevertheless, between July 1943 and February 1945 – and it was capable of 439 mph at 24,500 ft (the Mark IX produced 408 mph) just 2 mph less than the Mark III Mustang.

More of the same routine followed in August where on the 3rd Roy notes when flying Typhoon No.290, 'RP (Double clusters 16).' A typical RP-3 installation was four projectiles on launching rails under each wing. A selector switch was fitted to allow the pilot to fire them singly, in pairs, or as a full salvo. Towards the end of the war Typhoons had their installation adapted to carry an additional four rockets doubled up under the eight already fitted, so it is assumed that this 16 double cluster form was experimental – it must have delivered a hell of a punch on receipt!

Roy's logbook has many references to angle of attack, this has considerable importance as it was discovered that if the rockets were fired at a shallow angle in water, near misses resulted in the rocket heads curving upwards and piercing shipping below the waterline.

Whilst Roy and the AFDU were experimenting with RPs in August 1944, possibly the best known action involving RP-3s was actually taking place in the Failaise Pocket in Normandy, against a stubborn German defence post D-Day.

On 28 August he added both the US Navy's Grumman Wildcat and Hellcat to his flying repertoire. The Wildcat was mostly seen in the Pacific theatre. Known as the stubby, it was underpowered and could be outclimbed and out-turned by the Japanese Zero fighter. The Hellcat was the Wildcat's successor, a complete redesign that took into account lessons learned in combat with the Zero. The time for test flying however was drawing to an end and in a fine example of combined operations (with the Navy) there was obviously a bit of a do on 31 August 1944, as recorded in a letter to Roy by 'Pat' from the Wrens Quarters.

Wrens Quarters, Dawnsmere House, Dawnsmere, Nr Spalding Lincs

3/9/44

My Dear Roy,

This letter will probably be a surprise to you, but when I say I will write, I write! So here I am feeling half asleep and waiting for you or somebody else to come over and shoot us up. Expect you're all in bed still!

Well, Roy, I really did enjoy myself on Thursday – hope you did too. Cleaning up after you'd all gone wasn't so good though – there seemed to be broken glass and food all over the place – especially down the passage where somebody seemed to have chucked an empty bottle – remember?!

We're working at last – I've had to paddle out to one of these wretched yellow huts as the tide is pretty high – see what we do for you?!

You'll have to excuse this short letter, but I had rather a good time in Kings Lynn last night & don't feel like doing anything at all this morning – except sleep of course. And mind you write back Roy, or I'll cook all your results!

Love Pat

Messerschmitt BF109E with missing canopy. This one landed in a UK airfield after the pilot believed he was back over France after crossing the Bristol Channel thinking it was the English Channel. Taken to Boscombe Down for evaluation against both the Spitfire and Hurricane, tests highlighted the advantage of the 109's Daimler Benz fuel injected engine against the carburettor-fitted British Rolls-Royce Merlin engines, which caused engine cut-off in a parabolic dive or inverted flight. All Rolls-Royce engines were subsequently fitted with fuel injection systems based on the Daimler Benz design. This aircraft crashed later killing its English test pilot.

North American P51A Mustang, designed and flown within a 12-month period to meet British specifications issued by the UK to North American Aviation Corp. Originally, it was known as the A36A Invader by North American and the USAAF. This early version was fitted with a V12 Allison engine. The RAF evaluated the A36A and found unsatisfactory performance issues at medium to high altitudes; they used them for low level recce only and Army co-operation roles. The MOD issued a request for N.A. to try the Rolls-Royce Merlin engine to improve performance. So successful were the results that the Merlin was then built under licence by the US Packard factory. The version shown was fitted with a Packard-built Rolls-Royce Merlin engine (a copy of the Spitfire powerplant) and renamed by the British as the 'Mustang 1'. Later versions were re-designated P51B, followed by the P51D with the famous teardrop hood that was used extensively on bomber escort long range missions.

On 3 September 1944 flying in a Spitfire he was escort to a captured FW 190 to Hatfield, later on the same day he added the Anson to his aircraft flown and on the 5th, again in a Spitfire, he acted as escort to a Me110 being flown to Shorham. His last flight at AFDU was on 9 September when he flew a Proctor to Biggin Hill, his first station with 72 Squadron two years earlier.

A few days leave is assumed as the next entry is on 16 September 1944 when he is posted to TEU (Tactical Exercise Unit) Chedworth near Aston-Down. Chedworth airfield comprised 2 blister hangars, a large number of support buildings and two runways. The site was home to the Radar Counter Measures (radar jamming flights) and Night Leaflet (propaganda leaflet drops) squadrons flying B-24s and B-17s.

Roy's posting however was to convert to the P-51 Mustang. Roy had flown escort to Mustangs in December 1943 from near Naples. His first flight in one had been recorded on 14 April 1944 at AFDU (a Mk1). On 11 May at AFDU he flew twice in Mustang No. 857. Mustangs were built by the North American Aviation Inc., the same company that produced the Harvard Trainer that Roy flew as a pupil. The early Mustangs were powered by Allison engines but the successful installation of a Rolls-Royce Merlin 60-series engine (built under licence by Packard) along with a variable pitch four-blade propeller created an entirely different aircraft from the earlier units. The Merlin engine provided the high-altitude performance which was so lacking in the earlier Allison-engined versions. Mustang III was the British name for the Merlin-powered P-51B and P-51C, the difference between the two being their place of manufacture.

The Mustang III was virtually identical to the American version, apart from the canopy. The British version featured the Malcolm hood, a Plexiglas bubble canopy, familiar from the Spitfire. This improved visibility to the sides, and increased headroom somewhat, slightly improving rear visibility.

Some American pilots are said to have preferred the Malcolm hood to the bubble canopy the Americans adopted for the later P-51D, perhaps because the Malcolm hood retained the original rear fuselage of the Mustang, which contributed to the aircraft's stability in flight.

The first RAF squadron to receive the Mustang III was 65 Squadron based at Gravesend, which received its aircraft in December 1943. 19 (where Roy was soon to go) and 65 Squadrons were the first to go operational with the type, in February 1944, escorting US heavy bombers as well as both US and RAF medium bombers.

The Mustang III operated in an entirely different role to the earlier Mustang I and IIs, its early service was as a fighter-bomber and reconnaissance aircraft, and it was to these that Roy had provided escort cover in December 1943, in Italy.

Many pilots regarded the Malcolm-hooded P-51B/C as the best Mustang of the entire series. It was lighter, faster, and had crisper handling (although care was needed to maintain its trim) than the later bubble-hooded P-51D and actually had a better all-round view. Its primary

Pilot's handbook for the Mustang III.

weakness, however, was in its armament – only four rather than six guns – which proved prone to jamming. This was solved towards the end of the production run, and was unlikely to have been a problem for the later versions, which Roy would have flown.

Early in the B/C production run, a new fuel tank was added behind the pilot. Along with external drop tanks, this conferred on the Mustang enormous range – up to 2300 miles or six hours – which was to prove so important. The tank was rarely filled to capacity though, as it introduced directional instability – I remember Betty Hussey, my mother mentioning to me as a boy that Roy had told her about this instability. Indeed the manufacturer's *Pilots Notes for the Mustang III* describes in considerable detail the effects of a stall or spin with the fuselage tank full or half full.

From 16 September 1944 to 20 September at Chedworth Roy flew 10 hours 20 minutes in various Mustang IIIs, flying local, formation and cross-country flights, but no gunnery practice. Interestingly his certificate of proficiency in this mark was signed on 16 September, his first day at the conversion course, perhaps not too surprising as he had already had a little experience with this aeroplane at the AFDU.

Making up for the lack of gunnery practice, the next port of call was 83 GSU (Group Support Unit) Bognor Regis, where on 26 September he flew 1 hour 10 minutes in a Mustang III with air to ground firing. The 26th must have been an inconvenient moment for the Unit as this was that day that it was to move to another base. In any event, later on the same day Roy was flown as second pilot in an Anson to Matlask in Scotland back to operational flying to join 19 Squadron.

19 Squadron is a squadron of firsts, it was based at Duxford on 4 August 1938 when it was the first squadron to be issued with Spitfire Mk.Is in place of its Gauntlet biplanes, and it was one of the first squadrons to take operational delivery of the Mustang III, in February 1944. His logbook with 19 Squadron opens on 6 October 1944, with a 2 hour 45 minute flight escorting Halifaxes to Gelsenkirchen where he records 'bags of flak three bombers down in flames.' On 15 October he flew on a 3 hour 15 minute mission as escort to 18 Lancasters which bombed the dam at Soest. The 22nd saw him escorting 100 Lancasters bombing Neus and on the 28th 650 Lancasters bombing Cologne.

November opened with the big formation bomber runs over Germany. On the 4th and 16th, 19 Squadron were escorting 1000 Lancasters over Solingen and Hamburg respectively. On 2 December over Dortmund he notes 'Very heavy flak' and on 12 December when escorting Lancaster's over Bittein, he records 'Me109s got 3 Lancs' and 'Jimmy Patton Missing.'

During the many times I read his logbook I became increasing struck by the sense – and it was nothing more than that – of how for the most part it now loses its former colour. It is pretty well confined to recording destination and duration of flights. The weather during this period was seasonally poor as he often records 10/10ths or DNCO (Duty Not Carried Out), but nevertheless that sparkle, it seemed to me, had gone. When I looked up 19 Squadron's Operations Record Book for this period, however, I was in a sense gratified; gratified that my senses had not been deceiving me and gratified that Roy was not alone.

Immediately before Roy joined it, 19 Squadron had been on the European mainland, post D-Day supporting land forces – principally strafing ground targets – destroying locomotives and barges in Belgium and Holland. It had left for Matlask on 29 September 1944, three days after Roy had completed his gunnery practice at the Group Support Unit. The ORB states 'The Wing took off for Matlask, and we were very disappointed when the full realisation of what life was like on a RAF station struck them.' And again on 29 September, 'No flying, everyone brassed.'; on the 30th 'Uneventful patrol of the Rhur'; again on 1 October ' No operational activity. Everybody still brassed. Sortie to Norwich aborted'; on 6 October 'Yet another escort of Lancs. to the Ruhr'; and finally on 13 October 1944 ' Squadron's last day at Matlask – loud cheers!!' The ORB continues:

14 October
Andrews field, though not quite Utopia seems to be a great improvement on Matlask. Larger mess, better billets, magnificent airfield, WAAFS (not yet in evidence) but darned awful food.

21 October
No operational activity but lovely weather so the powers that be decided to see how fast the Wing could land, and practice flying was the order of the day. Masses of aircraft were observed belting at the runway at the same time and flying control very nearly produced foreign bodies on several occasions. However, all our aircraft returned safely and retired to the bar to recover shaken nerves.

28 October
Sqd. airborne on a Lanc. escort to Cologne, led by W/c Loud. Very cold and dreary.

30 November
Today a fighter sweep Munster Dummer Lake area. Very very dull 10/10 cloud all the way.

18 December
F/Lt RJ Hussey takes over as Flt Cdr B flight.

He filled the place of Jimmy Patton who had been reported missing a fortnight earlier.

Boring though it might have seemed, fighter escort operational flying, or come to that, flying of any nature, always had its dangers. On 15 January 1945 he records 'Mac missing. Collision with another A/C.'

Flying for long periods at 25–30,000 ft in an unheated unpressurised cockpit meant new discomforts. Pilots experienced the illusion that their stomachs were inflating grotesquely. They felt intense pain in their elbows, knees and shoulders caused by tiny bubbles of gas in their blood. The prolonged inhalation of oxygen created a burning sensation when they breathed and the skin round their mouths became raw and tender. An oxygen failure even at great heights, when there might be a chance of recovery as the aircraft descended, could be fatal and maybe this is what happened to 'Mac'.

The squadron had not forgotten how to enjoy itself on the ground. 27 January 1945:

Duff weather so aircraft had to stay at Bradwell [Bradwell Bay was a satellite to Andrews field]. However there was big mess dance at Andrews Field so we managed to get transport back. The station band was in its usual fine form and a fine time was had by all. Bob Haywood with his usual hospitality kept open house [the White Swan] to warm us up before the party. We hope he and Kay will get over the loss of the banisters.

By the end of January 1945 Roy had completed 494 operational hours of flying.

3 February
The Wing was briefed for a fighter sweep of the Frankfurt area, with permission to strafe East of the Rhine, the Wing split up owing to bad weather and the squadron found two small marshalling yards which were truly shot up, though without any definite results. However we had at least fired our guns in anger again after an all too long lapse.

The Wing comprising 19 and 65 Squadrons was transferred back to Scotland on 13 February 1945, this time to Peterhead. They were replaced at Andrews Field, near Gravesend, Essex, by 316, a Polish squadron.

February 1945 continues in the same vein, on the 6th the Squadron flew escort to 18 Lancasters where he notes 'Lancs led by W/Co Tait bombing special target. DNCO weather

After two-and-a-half short years the boy is now very much a man. Flt. Lieut. Roy Hussey shortly before he was killed.

u/s.' Wing Commander Tait was CO Flying of 617, the renowned Dambuster squadron. (Guy Gibson VC. DSO and bar DFC and bar, its first CO having been rested and then killed flying a Mosquito in a raid on Rheydt over Holland on 19 September 1944, five months earlier). Tait led 617 Squadron on three separate attacks on the *Tirpitz*. The first attack, on September 11, 1944 comprised 27 Lancasters of 9 and 617 Squadrons flown from North Russia and caused significant damage but failed to sink her. The Germans decided that it was not practical to make *Tirpitz* fully seaworthy again and she was moved to Tromso, further south in Norway, but only for use as a semi-static, heavy artillery battery.

The British were not aware of the extent of the damage and the *Tirpitz* was attacked again on 29 October. 37 Lancasters were dispatched from Lossiemouth, Scotland. With the removal of the Lancaster's mid-upper gun turrets and the installation of extra fuel tanks, the *Tirpitz* could now be reached directly from Britain, although it required a 2250 mile operation.

The weather was ideal for the attack until an unexpected wind shift covered the *Tirpitz* with cloud just thirty seconds before the first Lancaster was ready to bomb. No direct hits were scored. The Germans responded by basing a fighter wing at a nearby airfield; however, on the third and final attack not a single fighter seems to have taken off.

The final assault took place on 12 November 1944. 30 Lancasters from 9 Squadron led by S/L A.G. Williams DFC and 617 Squadron led by Wg Cdr J.B. 'Willie' Tait DSO DFC took off from Scotland. The weather was clear as the bombers flew at 1,000 feet to avoid early detection by enemy radar prior to rendezvousing at a lake 100 miles southeast of Tromso. The attacking force then climbed to bombing height – between 12,000 and 16,000 feet – and the warship was sighted from about 20 miles away.

The first bombs narrowly missed the target, but then a great yellow flash burst on the deck. It then suffered a tremendous explosion as the ammunition store magazines went up, The *Tirpitz* rolled over and sank.

With the range of the Mustang III, 19 Squadron, based at Peterhead, was able to fly fighter escort for the Beaufighters and Mosquitos of Coastal Command on their strikes against Norway. This almost-forgotten war was one of the most dangerous for aircrew, with strike aircraft and their escorts making long over-water flights at low level to face a well armed enemy when they arrived at the target, then returning the same way; no aircrew ditching in the cold North Sea on these operations – other than those who could make it to the Scottish coast – was ever likely to be rescued before they succumbed to exposure.

On Tuesday 20 February 1945, at about 1400 hours, Roy was flying Mustang KH440 (one of the 274 P-51Bs and 626 P-51Cs received by the RAF). 19 Squadron Operational Record book notes:

> Good weather and in the afternoon as there was no show on, it was decided that the squadron should do some practice flying, and then land at Dallachy the Beaufighter station [RNZAF 489] for tea, and a talk with them. A most unfortunate accident occurred there, as we were coming to land F/Lt. Hussey DFC DFM 'B' Flight Commander spun in on approach and was killed. His loss will be very deeply felt on the squadron.

Nellie Hussey had lost her son. My mother Betty and my Uncle Tim had lost their brother. Roy was 21 years old.

The dates from 9 February to his last flight on the 20th in his log have been filled out in a hand not dissimilar to his own but not in his familiar blue/black ink and with a broader nib. The operational hours recorded in February total a further 14 hours 35 minutes bringing his operational total to 511 hours and 35 minutes.

In his short life he was credited with 13½ enemy aircraft confirmed destroyed, as well as many probables and damaged and numerous successful ground attacks. He was decorated with a DFC, DFM, CGM and a Mention in Dispatches. Starting as Sergeant Pilot he had been promoted to Pilot Officer, Flying Officer and Flight Lieutenant/Flight Commnader. As we learned in the opening chapter, all Roy ever wanted to do was fly. This he achieved, piloting fifteen different types excluding type variations.

His remains were interred on Saturday 10 March 1945 at Coxley church near Wells, Somerset, three days before his 22nd birthday. Both my parents were present, as was my elder brother, Tony, aged three months.

The funeral arrangements were taken care of and paid for by Nellie's sister Epps. Amongst some papers given to me by Epps' niece, my mother's bridesmaid, Jean Roberts (nee Crokes), is a letter addressed to Epps and her husband Roly.

Beaufort Arms Mangotsfield
April 28th '45

Dear Epps and Roly,

Thank you very much to seeing to my [?] it was a great help I am very grateful to you both.

    I have put in a cheque £8-10-0 and have sent to Mr Wicks [funeral Director]. I hope you are keeping well. Madge Jefferies [Roy's girlfriend] was very pleased and quite enjoyed her visit to Queen Street. I hope to come down soon, but at present I don't think I could stand it. Betty [my mother] is not too well but now she has heard from Jack [my father] she will feel brighter. John [my uncle Tim] is working very hard at the farm and great comfort to me, he is very kind. I don't think we shall ever be the same again, we carry on – but there is always the awful loss – nothing to look forward to – before it was we must do this or that and hope for a safe return – but now it's terrible. I feel so sorry for John. The news is good & I hope it will soon finish & people will get back to work again. I am still in a hurry and rush. No help. I had a very nice letter from Nellie Candy, she saw Roy's death in the Buckingham paper & wrote me. I thought it was very kind of her. Give my love to Dad and all the rest.

Yours lovingly
Nell

Still attached to the letter is the cheque drawn on Lloyds bank, Staple Hill, Bristol, for £8-10-0, which Epps never cashed.

6

SINGAPORE AND SURVIVAL ON THE BURMA–SIAM RAILWAY

David Stoate joins the army and volunteers for an overseas posting that carries with it officer training. He is in the heat of battle in Singapore, then 'celebrates' four birthdays as a Japanese PoW, a severe test of physical and mental stamina – and luck.

David Stoate, third of the six children born to Leonard and Elsie Stoate, was born on 22 August 1916. Educated at Clifton College, Bristol, he was a non-academic enjoying sports including being selected as cox for the first rowing IV. Later he played squash for Northumberland and Gloucestershire counties.

Having left Clifton in 1933, on 1 January 1934 he joined the flour milling firm of Stoate and sons Ltd and served an apprenticeship in flour milling technology under the guidance of his father whilst also attending Bristol College of Technology. In 1937 he passed out with a First Class City and Guilds. The family business had been sold to Spillers in 1933 and David remained with Spillers, apart from military service during the Second World War, until he retired in 1979. In 1981 he published *The Millers Manual,* a technical aid for mill management.

David was Assistant Works Manager but within three months of the outbreak of war his call up papers arrived, and on 29 December 1939 he attended a centre at Edgware, London, to complete his attestation and swear his Loyal Oath.

Attestation forms are constructed in a careful way, particularly so far as age is concerned; for example they record 'apparent age' rather than 'age' and 'Date of Birth' is written as 'DoB as declared on attestation.' In other words if someone wanted to enter false details here, as did Roy Hussey, as long as you looked over 18 the authorities were not going to enquire further.

So at the age of 23 David was drafted to the 11th Regiment Honourable Artillery Company, Royal Horse Artillery based at Elstree. David describes his call-up and early training:

The HAC (Honorable Artillery Company) was based at Elstree when I joined up and, as a gunner, I first had to deal with square bashing. I have already said I am a slow learner and trying to keep in step and sloping arms did not come easy! I did a lot of driving of Army vehicles, one such was the Quad which was a covered wagon and held the gun crew and also hauled a 12-pounder gun and ammunition trailer. I also spent quite a bit of time in the vehicle maintenance department. Later I was to become a tank driver. Captain Armstrong was the

Bombardier David Stoate. (Geoffrey Stoate)

David Stoate on his way to India.
(David Stoate)

2nd Lieutenant David Stoate. (David Stoate)

Commander and there was a wireless operator but no armaments. It was purely a reconnaissance vehicle.

Once the bombing started, Elstree was considered too dangerous and we moved near Cranleigh in Surrey. I was promoted to Lance Bombardier and later to Bombardier.

During these few months David attended an MT Course at Rhyl, as well as postings to Swanage, Newmarket and finally the Mobilisation Centre at Williams Barracks, Aldershot.

Life consisted of various exercises, I think we were waiting for an invasion. Anyway a lot of us were getting very bored and, in February 1941, a notice came up on the board asking for volunteers to go to a cadet school in Deolali, near Bombay in India, to be trained as officers. It is said that one should never volunteer but I, and many others, did.

I was accepted and on 4 January 1941 we sailed in the *Highland Chieftain* to Bombay. The ship was a converted meat carrier and we, Other Ranks, were literally herded into the large hold, sleeping in hammocks. Fortunately we arrived at Durban safely having had an escort of destroyers and probably something bigger. We stayed there for a couple of days and were allowed ashore. The reception was terrific with invitations to tea, and everyone most welcoming. Going up the Indian Ocean, there was a scare of being torpedoed and we put in to Mombassa for four days.

This part of the Indian Ocean was quite heavily populated with Stoate brothers at this time. As we shall see, another brother, Norman, was returning to England having served on the aircraft carrier HMS *Eagle* to train for his commission; and David's elder brother Tom was arriving at East London near Durban in South Africa as an RAF doctor.

We were not allowed ashore at Mombassa and it was very hot – I suppose it was better than being torpedoed! Eventually we got the all clear and arrived at Bombay safely. During the voyage, I spent a great deal of time learning how to play bridge. I had never played before although I had played whist. We played for quite low stakes and I lost a total of about £5 which was quite a lot of money then, but it was well worth it as I learnt the rudiments, which were to come in useful later.

The *Highland Chieftain* docked in early March 1941 and David proceeded to Deolali about 100 miles north east of Bombay. David's camp at Deolali had long been a base, during the nineteenth century it was a rest camp where British soldiers who had completed their tour of duty were sent to wait for transportation home. The wait was often many months before they were picked up and taken back to England. Boredom and heat drove many a soldier crazy – hence the word doolally.

On 5 March 1941 David underwent his medical and dentistry examination and was passed A1 fit so on 6 March he commenced his officer training course. This was completed on 2 August, David was discharged as a 2nd Lieutenant. This was gazetted on either 22 or 26 August 1941 – the records conflict on this. Later, on 1 October 1942, he was retrospectively promoted to the honorary rank of full Lieutenant – for reasons which will unfold this was not gazetted.

I find it very hard to describe my reaction to our arrival at Deolali. We had left very sparse living in England as there was strict rationing of practically everything. We now fed at a long mess table beautifully laid out with white tablecloth, glass and cutlery and were served by Indian waiters. The food was excellent.

We each were allotted a bearer. He was responsible for looking after our every need including sending our clothes to the laundry (dhobi wallah). It was returned clean and ironed the same day. He also made sure our footwear was highly polished each day together with our Sam Browne.

I teamed up with four guys also from the HAC, Peter Densham, Dennis Heritage, Slush Salusbury and Norman (known to us as Podge) Cadel. We went to Bombay several weekends taking our bearers with us and renting a room in a block of flats. I cannot remember what we did but I know we had a great time.

So far as the white residents were concerned, I don't think they knew there was a war on, after all it was happening a long way away. I know we went to a dance hall one evening but the girls were there with their parents and were reluctant to have anything to do with anyone in uniform.

There were some horses stabled within our barracks and I had several rides, we also frequently took a tonga [two-wheel horse-drawn vehicle with driver] to Deolali village which was about a mile away.

We were at Deolali for six months and it was essential that we learnt Urdu as we were going to be posted, as officers, to the Indian Army. I am sure the Indian teacher did his best but, at the end of six months, I could order a cup of tea, get a shave with a cutthroat for one anna and knew a few more words and sentences, but then I am a slow learner.

In the HAC we had 12-pounder guns and were trained not only to fire them but take them to bits and put them back again. We had the same guns at Deolali, in other words we were trained in field artillery. On becoming a 2nd Lieutenant in September 1942, aged 24, I was posted to the 1st Indian Heavy AA which was an anti-aircraft unit with Bofors guns, about which I knew nothing.

We left Bombay, probably early October 1941 and, sailing out of Bombay, we knew we had to turn either right to go to the Middle East or left to Singapore. We turned east and arrived at Singapore where we joined an encampment somewhere around the middle of the Island. When we got our commission, nobody knew to which regiment we were going to be posted. All my friends went off in different directions but none went the same way as I did, except for Podge Cadel who was on the railway with me. I met up with all the others after the war. Sadly none of them survive now.

Had David's ship turned right he might have ended up in Libya, where part of the 2nd Indian Field Regiment played an important role in countering Rommel's right hook round the southern flank of the Allies' position at Bir Hakeim in May 1942. After four hours ferocious fighting the regiment's losses were numbered in hundreds, one brigade was virtually wiped out, but Rommel lost more than a third of his tanks on a single day and received a sharp check to his ambitions.

The campaign for the defence of Singapore, 15 miles by 20 miles, an island about the same size as The Isle of Wight – the major British military base and anchor for the combined operations of the American/British/Dutch/Australian Command – lasted a short time only. It started on 8 December 1941 when the Japanese invaded Thailand (prior to June 1939 called Siam) and finished on 15 February 1942 when Singapore fell to the Japanese.

Singapore is connected in the north to the Malaysian mainland by a causeway leading to Johor. The Malaysian peninsula was covered in dense jungle but rich in resources, notably rubber. The Japanese economy was growing but the nation lacked natural resources; their options were to trade for them or to conquer nations who had them. They chose the latter, attacking China. The US and Britain imposed trade sanctions on oil, rubber and tin. To the Japanese therefore, there was a huge strategic benefit in gaining control of both the mainland and the island fortress of Singapore itself. Their intention to end European domination of southeast Asia in toto would have been less apparent.

Given that intent, Japan had to attack the European strongest points first. Singapore was a port that could be used as a launch pad against other Allied interests in the area.

Subsidiary to this principal strategic aim, the Japanese also sought to eliminate those in Singapore who were supporting China in the Second Sino-Japanese War. The ethnic Han

Jiksha Station, Singapore. (Norman Stoate)

Chinese in Malaya and Singapore had financially and materially aided the Chinese defence against the Japanese. Such aid had contributed to the stalling of the Japanese advance in China.

All of this had been understood by the British military prior to the Second World War and a strategic plan known as *Matador* had been approved by the Cabinet and Whitehall. Contrary to common belief, the British military in Malaya and Singapore were not caught napping by the Japanese. British military planners had anticipated an assault from the rear, that is, down the Malay Peninsula.

Matador included a detailed battle plan to stop the invaders, who were expected to land along Thailand's eastern coastline at the Isthmus of Kra and in north-eastern Malaya. The counter measure envisaged entering southern Thailand to forestall Japanese landings on the eastern coastline. The essence of the concept was that in order to ensure the landward security of Singapore, the whole of the Malayan mainland must be held. As circumstances changed, the forward defence line was extended to Thailand.

Operation *Matador* was endorsed by Whitehall in 1941, but the resources for its implementation – aeroplanes crucially, and other reinforcements – were never provided. Over 400 of the 500 aircraft required were diverted to Russia.

The battle for Malaya and Singapore, therefore, was lost in the corridors of Whitehall before the first shot was fired, when the political leadership failed to provide resources. The strength of the British fortress of Singapore was overestimated and the Japanese threat underestimated. What went wrong on the ground was not the strategic and tactical planning but the political decision-making.

The fall has been dubbed the worst disaster in British military history. It was and remains the largest largest British capitulation. About 80,000 British, Australian and Indian troops became prisoners of war, the overall figure some 130,000 when these were added to the 50,000 taken by the Japanese in the earlier fighting in Malaya.

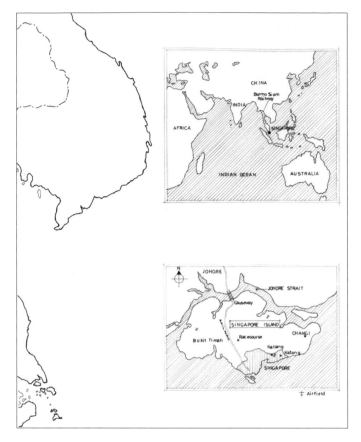

Sketch map of Singapore.

While David's elder brother Tom, Roy Hussey and for a period his younger brother Norman Stoate were in the Mediterranian theatre, having the benefit of relatively adequate supplies, it was in Singapore that David Stoate spent his short operational service career as a young subaltern.

Singapore has been called the 'Gibraltar of the East', as it had a similar strategic importance. The purpose of the fortified base was to provide a stronghold to protect British interests in the East and act as a staging post to Australia and New Zealand. David remembers it as it was in October 1941:

> Visiting Singapore City, you would not know there was a war on. People generally were not a bit receptive. I went to the main squash club and was told I could not play after 5 pm as the courts were reserved for members after then.
>
> At that time, it was anticipated that Japan would attack Singapore but they were expected to come by sea since the dense Malayan jungle in the north would act as a natural barrier. HMS *Prince of Wales* and HMS *Repulse*, two fine battleships, were dispatched and they were to have been accompanied by HMS *Indomitable*, an aircraft carrier, but unfortunately it had earlier run aground with disastrous consequences.

The Japanese 25th Army's invasion of Malaya from Indochina commenced on 8 December 1941. They moved into northern Malaya and Thailand by sea.

When the Japanese attacked Pearl Harbor on 7 December 1941 Roy Hussey had barely started his war service at 3 British Flying Training School in Miami, Oklahoma. David Stoate, however, was about to be in the thick of action. The Pearl Harbor attack should be seen as integral to the Malayan campaign. The sinking of the American Pacific Fleet was meant to deter the United States from intervening in Southeast Asia. As we know, it had the reverse effect, awakening the sleeping giant.

Japanese troops in Thailand 'persuaded' the Thai government to let them use their military bases for the expansion in Southeast Asia. They then proceeded overland across the Thai-Malayan border to attack Malaya.

Having established land bases on the mainland, the Japanese began the strategic bombing of sites all over Singapore, although anti-aircraft fire, for which David and his men were partly responsible, kept most of the Japanese bombers from totally devastating the island so long as ammunition was available. David recalls the start of the campaign.

On 8 December 1941, Japanese forces landed at Kota Bharu in North Malaya.

As soon as the Japanese invaded Malaya, the regiment was dispersed to the various aerodromes (I think there were four) on the island. Our unit comprised four Bofors guns and we were dispatched to Seletar aerodrome, the largest.

While there I never saw a Jap plane! Later, when the RAF pulled out of Seletar, we moved to a large house, which was requisitioned, on the outskirts of Singapore. I was in charge of a gun, which we surrounded with sand bags, set up in the garden. While there we did have some success and also came under mortar fire. During our final encounter, our gun failed to fire and as I did not know how to put it right and mortar fire was around, I ordered 'Sub addmi neechay', which meant, 'all men flat on your backsides.' I think this was the only time my Urdu came in useful!

Before returing to David's personal reminiscences and military part in the fall of Singapore it seems a good moment to look at the context militarialy and politically in which he and his men found themselves.

The Japanese Army was resisted by the Indian Army and several battalions of the British Army in Malaya. The Japanese 25th Army was outnumbered by Allied forces in both Malaya and Singapore, Japanese commanders, however, had the advantage of knowing where they intended to strike and concentrated their forces accordingly. This contrasted with the Allied armies which were lamentably underequipped in aircraft and artillery and with a complete absence of armoured units, and which were attempting to provide defensive positions over a huge area.

The Imperial Japanese Air Force had greater numbers of aircraft and better trained pilots than the assortment of largely untrained crew and inferior Allied equipment remaining in Malaya, Borneo and Singapore. The Mitsubishi A6M Zero helped the Japanese to gain superiority in the air. The Allies had no tanks or armoured vehicles to speak of. The Japanese troops were already experienced from the Indo-China conflict and tactically, mentally and physically they pursued a different style of combat, which valued their own lives at naught.

At sea, a deterrent force (Force Z) of the battleships HMS *Prince of Wales* and HMS *Repulse* and four destroyers reached Malaya before the Japanese began their air assaults. It was intended that an Illustrious class aircraft carrier, HMS *Indomitable* would provide air cover to Force Z. *Indomitable* had been launched in March 1941 and commissioned in October that year. On her maiden voyage on 3 November 1941 she hit a coral reef in the West Indies and although little damage was sustained she was not able to reach Singapore in time to serve her role. Such was the Japanese air superiority that the two capital ships, The *Prince of Wales* and the *Repulse* were sunk, leaving the east coast of Tampa exposed and allowing the Japanese to continue their landings. (For the full story see *In the Highest Traditions of the Royal Navy: The Life of Captain John Leach* by Matthew Wills.)

Japanese forces quickly isolated, surrounded, and forced the surrender of Indian units defending the Malayan coast. They advanced down the peninsula overwhelming the defences.

Although more Allied units, including some from the Australian 8th Division, joined the campaign, the Japanese prevented the Allied forces from regrouping, overran cities, and rapidly advanced towards Singapore, sometimes using commandeered bicycles to move infantry through the jungle.

On 11 January 1942 Kuala Lumpur fell and on 31 January (only seven weeks since the Japanese invasion commenced) the last Allied forces left Malaya and Allied engineers blew up the Causeway linking Johor on the mainland and the island of Singapore. This act only delayed Japanese landfall for a week to 8 February 1942 and did nothing to prevent Japanese infiltrators, often diguised as Singaporean civilians, crossing the Straits of Johor by boat.

Montgomery wrote: 'A sure way to victory is to concentrate great force at the selected place at the right time and to smash the enemy' and that is pretty well what the Japanese had contrived.

The garrison of Singapore had some 85,000 soldiers, the equivalent on paper of just over four divisions. There were about 70,000 front-line troops in 38 infantry battalions, 13 British, 6 Australian, 17 Indian and 2 Malayan, plus 3 machine-gun battalions. The newly arrived British 18th Infantry Division, whilst at full strength, lacked experience and appropriate training; most of the other units were under strength, a few having been amalgamated after heavy casualties as a result of the mainland campaign. The local battalions had no experience and in some cases no training.

Against the Allied forces of 85,000 men, of which David and his men formed a tiny part, the Japanese had just over 30,000 men from three divisions, including the elite Imperial Guards Division, which included a light tank brigade.

Churchill had replaced the Far East Commander-in-Chief, Air Chief Marshal Sir Robert Brooke-Popham in November 1941 with the younger more 'up-to-date' Lieutenant-General Arthur Percival. During the weeks before the invasion, there was a series of increasingly disruptive disagreements amongst senior Allied commanders, as well as pressure from the Australian Prime Minister Robert Menzies. Brooke-Popham was aware of the deficiencies of British and Allied forces in Singapore and Malaya and had sent a stream of telegrams to Whitehall to petition and plead for air and land reinforcements. As he told the Australian Advisory War Council, he had made 'all representations short of resigning'. The die, however, was cast in terms of troops and materiel for the defence of Singapore.

The Australian 8th Division, commanded by Major-General Gordon Bennett, had responsibility for the western side of Singapore, including the prime invasion points in the north-west of the island. This was mostly mangrove swamp and jungle, broken by rivers and creeks. In the heart of the 'Western Area' was RAF Tengah, Singapore's largest airfield. The Australian 22nd Brigade was assigned a 10-mile wide sector in the west, and the 27th Brigade had responsibility for a 4,000-yard zone just west of the Causeway. The infantry positions were reinforced by a recently arrived Australian Machine-Gun Battalion. Also under Bennett's command was the 44th Indian Infantry Brigade.

The Indian III Corps under Lientenant-General Sir Lewis-Heath, including the Indian 11th Infantry Division, the British 18th Division and the 15th Indian Infantry Brigade, was assigned the north-eastern sector, known as the 'Northern Area'. This included the naval base at Sembawang.

The 'Southern Area', including the main urban areas in the south-east, was commanded by Major-General Frank Keith Simmons. His forces comprised about 18 battalions, including the Malayan Ist Infantry Division, the Straits Settlements Volunteer Force Brigade and the Indian 12th Infantry Brigade.

During December 1941, 51 Hurricane Mk II fighters were sent to Singapore, with 24 pilots, the nuclei of five squadrons. They arrived on 3 January 1942, by which stage the squadrons, equipped with the American-built Buffalo fighters, had been overwhelmed. 232 Squadron was formed and 488 Squadron RNZAF, a Buffalo squadron converted from Buffalos to Hurricanes. 232 Squadron became operational on 20 January and destroyed three Ki-43s that day, for the loss of three Hurricanes. 232 Squadron did very well as the the Ki-43, the Hayabusa Peregrine, known to the Americans as 'Oscars' were similar to the A6M Zero but more common.

However, like the Buffalos before them, the Hurricanes were outclassed and began to suffer severe losses in intense dogfights.

During the period 27–30 January, another 48 Hurricanes (Mk IIA) arrived with 226 Group comprising four squadrons, deployed to airfields code-named P1 and P2, near Palambang, Sumatra, in the Dutch East Indies. The staggered arrival of the Hurricanes, along with inadequate early warning systems, meant that Japanese air raids were able to destroy a large proportion of the Hurricanes on the ground in both Sumatra and Singapore.

By 8 February 1942 air cover was provided by only ten Hawker Hurricane fighters of RAF 232 Squadron. They were based at Kallang airfield, it being the only operational airstrip left. The surviving squadrons had withdrawn by January to reinforce the Dutch East Indies. This fighter force performed extremely well, but was outnumbered and outmatched by the Japanese Zeros and suffered severe losses.

Malaya and Singapore is full of all sorts of races – Malays, Indians, Chinese and others and British troops knew little about them. As well as using using aerial reconnaissance, the Japanese also used fifth columnists, often the future members of the Japanese Free Indian Army – scouts, infiltrators and snipers wearing Malay dress. By these various means and by using the high ground across the straits such as the Sultan of Johor's Palace, the Japanese had gained accurate knowledge of the Allied positions. From 3 February those positions were shelled by Japanese artillery. Their scouts fired Very light pistols to reveal Allied positions. Japanese air and artillery bombardment attacks on Singapore intensified over the next five days, severely disrupting communications between Allied units and their commanders and preparations for the defence of the island.

There has been much talk of the heavy guns of Singapore facing seaward and thus being useless in against a landward attack. I, of course am no expert but it seems this might not stand scrutiny. There was no direct naval attack which might illustrate that they were successful in their mission and perhaps earned their keep. An escape by civilians and military personnel was possible by sea because of them, indeed the Australian General Gordon Bennett did exactly that. The evidence suggests that only two of the 15-inch naval guns (similar to the pair outside the Imperial War Museum in London) were fixed and facing out to sea.

Although placed to fire on enemy ships to the south, most of the guns could turn northwards and they did fire at the invaders. It seems what really made the difference was the type of ammunition and the type of gun supplied. Shells were primarily the armour piercing rather than High Explosive (HE) type, designed to penetrate the hulls of heavily armoured warships. These were ineffective against personnel. For ground defence/attack HE ammunition is required. The lack of high explosive ammunition was, presumably, the result of the confused belief that an invading army could not come from the north. Military analysts later estimated that if the guns had been well supplied with High Explosive shells the Japanese attackers would have suffered heavy casualties, but concluded the invasion would not have been prevented by this means alone. The second point regarding the type of guns is that for the most part they were naval guns designed to fire a flat trajectory, whereas field artillery is designed to throw a parabalic trajectory, which is more effective against ground targets. (The difference between High Explosive and Armour Piercing ammunition is one that my father Jack Stoate learned later in the war with 30 Battalion Royal Marines, moving through the Low Countries in northern Europe.)

The Japanese had moved down through Malaya, finally arriving at the Straits of Johor on 31 January. They then had to cross the Straits. The Causeway linking the mainland to Singapore island was therefore blown up. On 8 February they attacked, using rubber boats to get across the water. British Hurricanes engaged the Japanese and a number of aerial dogfights took place over Sarimbun beach and other western areas. In the first encounter, the last ten Hurricanes were scrambled from Kallang Airfield to intercept a Japanese formation of about 84 planes flying from Johor to provide air cover for their invasion force. In the prelude to the invasion of the island on 8 February, airfields at Tengah, Seletar where David had been stationed and

Sembawang, in range of Japanese artillery at Johor Bahru, had been subjected to heavy bombardment and were no longer operational; the only surviving airfield was at Kallang.

In two sorties the Hurricanes shot down six Japanese aircraft for the loss of one of their own. They flew back to Kallang halfway through the battle, hurriedly re-fuelled, then returned to it. Air battles went on over the island for the rest of the day, and by nightfall it was clear that with the few machines Percival had left, Kallang could no longer be used as a base. With his assent the remaining Hurricanes were withdrawn to Palembang, Sumatra, and Kallang became merely an advanced landing ground. No Allied aircraft were seen again over Singapore, and the Japanese had full control of the skies.

Blowing up the causeway had delayed the Japanese attack. At 8.30pm on 8 February, however, Australian machine gunners opened fire on vessels carrying a first wave of 4,000 Japanese troops from the 5th and 18th Divisions towards Singapore island. The Japanese assaulted Sarimbun Beach, in the sector controlled by the Australian 22nd Brigade.

Fierce fighting raged, but eventually the increasing Japanese numbers and the superiority of their artillery, aircraft and military intelligence began to take its toll. In the northwest of the island they exploited gaps in the thinly spread Allied lines such as rivers and creeks. By midnight the two Australian brigades had lost communication with each other and the 22nd Brigade was forced to retreat.

The Australian 27th Brigade, to the north, did not face Japanese assaults until the Imperial Guards landed at 10pm on 9 February. At last some cheer for the defenders, this assault went very badly for the Japanese. They suffered severe casualties from Australian mortars and machine guns, and from burning oil which had been pumped into the water. Nevertheless a small number of Guards reached the shore and maintained a tenuous beachhead.

By the evening of 10 February, all remaining Allied Air Force personnel were ordered to transfer to the Dutch East Indies as Kallang Airfield was so pitted with bomb craters that even for the stable Hurricanes, it was no longer usable.

Command and control problems caused further cracks in the Allied defence and ultimately the Allies lost control of the beaches adjoining the west side of the Causeway enabling the Imperial Guards armoured units to land unopposed there. Tanks with flotation equipment attached were towed across the strait.

The 22nd Brigade were outflanked on the Jurong Line, and the 11th Indian Division bypassed at the naval base. However, the Imperial Guards failed to seize an opportunity to advance into the city centre itself.

On that same evening of 10 February, Winston Churchill cabled Wavell (Allied Supreme Commander South East Asia):

> I think you ought to realise the way we view the situation in Singapore. It was reported to Cabinet by the CIGS [Chief of the Imperial General Staff, General Alan Brooke] that Percival has over 100,000 men, of whom 33,000 are British and 17,000 Australian. It is doubtful whether the Japanese have as many in the whole Malay Peninsula … In these circumstances the defenders must greatly outnumber Japanese forces who have crossed the straits, and in a well-contested battle they should destroy them. There must at this stage be no thought of saving the troops or sparing the population. The battle must be fought to the bitter end at all costs. The 18th Division has a chance to make its name in history. Commanders and senior officers should die with their troops. The honour of the British Empire and of the British Army is at stake. I rely on you to show no mercy to weakness in any form … It is expected that every unit will be brought into close contact with the enemy and fight it out …

Wavell passed on the message in almost identical terms to Percival:

> It will be disgraceful if we yield our boasted Fortress of Singapore to inferior forces. There must be no thought of sparing the troops or civil population and no mercy must be shown to

any weakness in any shape or form. Commanders and senior officers must lead their troops and if necessary die with them. There must be no question or thought of surrender. Every unit must fight it out to the end in close contact with the enemy.

The importance of Singapore was clearly not lost on Churchill but there were conflicting claims upon available resources. It is unlikely, nevertheless, that he could have foreseen how a British surrender to the Japanese would have repercussions beyond the battlefield during the coming hellish years suffered by David and tens of thousands of others under Japanese rule.

The British surrender punctured the myth of white invincibility and made a deep impression on the people of South-east Asia, the colonialists – the British and Dutch – and on the Japanese. It signalled the beginning of the end of the British Empire and the rise of nationalism in the colonies.

By 11 February 1942, Japanese supplies were running low, but they called on Percival to 'give up this meaningless and desperate resistance'. By this stage the fighting strength of the 22nd Brigade, which had borne the brunt of the Japanese attacks, had been reduced to a few hundred men. The Japanese had captured the Bukit Timah area, including most of the Allied ammunition and fuel and control of the main water supplies.

The battle for Bukit Timah was the main battle for Singapore. It raged for six days on an arc that withdrew from the race course and forest reserve area, taking up a last position around about Adam and the golf course, a mile nearer to the city. The following day, the Allied lines stabilised around a small area in the south-east of the island and fought off determined Japanese assaults.

A Malayan platoon, led by Lt Adnan bin Saidi, held off the Japanese for two days. His unit defended Buket Chandu, an area which included a major allied ammunition store. Adnan was executed by the Japanese after his unit was overrun.

On 13 February, with the Allies still losing ground, senior officers advised Percival to surrender in the interests of minimising civilian casualties. Percival refused, but behind the scenes unsuccessfully sought authority to surrender from his superiors. David describes those two days:

> I won't say much about the nightmare days prior to the fall of Singapore, we were amongst the last to leave Seletar aerodrome on 12 February. We were ordered to move back to the outskirts of Singapore City. We spent Friday the 13th on a sports ground and had a very uncomfortable day with bombing, shelling and mortar fire. That night we moved back another mile or so to a Chinaman's house with our four guns in the front of surrounding houses. Here again we were singled out for some intense mortar fire but fortunately the Chinese had two very good air raid shelters in his garden and we were able to take refuge in these when there were no aircraft about.

Civilian casualties mounted as one million people crowded into the area still held by the Allies and bombing and artillery fire intensified. Civilian authorities began to fear that the water supply would give out.

> After the RAF left Seletar I acquired an Austin 10, a considerable amount of food and drink and we took a large portion of this back with us on our withdrawal and supplemented it with what we found in the Chinaman's larder.
>
> On the 14th we shot down our first plane and nobody was more surprised than the pilot I feel sure, as two of them came right over us at about 500ft, which of course was very foolish.

By the morning of 15 February, the Japanese had broken through the last line of defence and the Allies were running out of food and ammunition. The anti-aircraft guns had also run out of ammunition and were unable to repel any further Japanese air attacks, which threatened to cause heavy casualties in the city centre. Looting and desertion by Allied troops further added to the chaos in the city centre.

Percival held a conference with his senior commanders. He posed two alternatives. Either launch an immediate counter-attack to regain the reservoirs and the military food depots in the Buket Timah region and drive the enemy's artillery off its commanding heights outside the town, or capitulate. All present agreed that no counter-attack was possible. Percival opted for surrender.

Earlier that day Percival had issued orders to destroy before 4 pm all secret and technical equipment, ciphers, codes, secret documents and heavy guns. The Japanese commander, General Yamashita, accepted his assurance that no ships or planes remained in Singapore. He also accepted full responsibility for the lives of British and Australian troops, as well as British civilians remaining in Singapore and ordered that all British and Australian PoWs were to proceed to Changi. Percival formally surrendered shortly after 5.15 pm.

For David and the other Allied service men and women it was a desperate end to a desperate battle. Many of the British and Australian soldiers taken prisoner who went to Singapore's Changi prison would never return home. Thousands of others were shipped on prisoner transports to other parts of Asia, including Japan, to be used as forced labour. Many of those aboard the ships perished. David spent eight months in Changi after which, in October 1942, along with a great many others, he was transferred to the Burma railway where he spent the rest of the war in captivity moving to various camps along the route.

On the morning of the 15th, we were all just about whacked having had no sleep for days when we saw a staff car go past us with a white flag. I can honestly say that up to that moment, the thought of capitulation had not occurred to any of us, but naturally it set us wondering from then on, and in many ways, the strain of those last few hours was worse than all the rest, as one felt the game was up and all one had to do was not to stop a bullet from then on. At 4.00 pm we received the cease-fire order and were told to unload our guns. At 5.00 pm this order was cancelled and we were told to carry on. At 6.00 pm the cease-fire was given again and timed for 8.00 pm. And this proved to be the time of the final surrender of Singapore.

That night we turned on all the lights and did away with the blackout, had a stiff whisky and slept as we had never slept before. We fully realised the position but were far too tired either to worry about it or the future. For two days we stayed where we were and hardly saw a Jap. On the afternoon of the 17th we were ordered to march out to Changi Camp, about 15 miles from Singapore City with whatever possessions we could carry. A 15-mile march with all my kit did not appear to me the best of propositions and I managed to wangle my way onto a truck which was carrying some stores out to the camp. We spent the night on the floor of some large barrack block and moved in to our quarters on the following day.

We were living as a regiment in former Officers' quarters, consisting of two small two-storey houses. There were 41 officers in the regiment and we had five Other Ranks who cooked for us. I was living in the smallest room with five other officers but a better bunch of fellows it would be hard to find. I spent some eight months there on a meagre diet awaiting developments. Whilst there, I was in charge of the bakery, an oven erected in a bank in the garden, and my fellow officers ground rice each day and I made them into a kind of scone – I believe there were two each, each day! On 26 October 1942, half of us were moved by cattle truck from Singapore Island to Bampong in Thailand. The other half were shipped to Japan and I believe their ship was torpedoed on the way and that there were no survivors.

The Japanese swiftly sought vengeance against the Chinese and to eliminate anyone who appeared to harbour anti-Japanese sentiment. The other races of Singapore, such as the Malays and the Indians, were not spared. The residents would suffer great hardships under Japanese rule over the following three-and-a-half years.

The Japanese also successfully recruited many Indian soldiers taken prisoner. From a total of about 40,000 Indian personnel in Singapore in February 1942, about 30,000 joined the

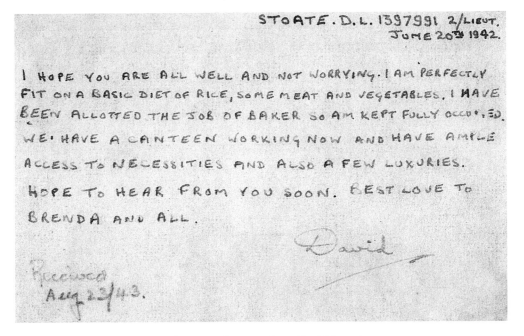

STOATE. D.L. 1397991 2/LIEUT.
JUNE 20th 1942.

I HOPE YOU ARE ALL WELL AND NOT WORRYING. I AM PERFECTLY
FIT ON A BASIC DIET OF RICE, SOME MEAT AND VEGETABLES. I HAVE
BEEN ALLOTTED THE JOB OF BAKER SO AM KEPT FULLY OCCUPIED.
WE HAVE A CANTEEN WORKING NOW AND HAVE AMPLE
ACCESS TO NECESSITIES AND ALSO A FEW LUXURIES.
HOPE TO HEAR FROM YOU SOON. BEST LOVE TO
BRENDA AND ALL.

David

Received
Aug 23/43.

'Letter' home from Changi. It took 14 months to get there. (David Stoate)

pro-Japanese 'Indian National Army' which fought against the Allies in Burma. Others became PoW camp guards at Changi. However, many Indian Army personnel resisted recruitment and remained PoWs and an unknown number were taken to Japanese-occupied areas in the South Pacific as forced labour to suffer the same severe hardships and brutality as that experienced by other prisoners of Japan. Of the 10,000 that did not join with the Japanese, about 6,000 survived to be liberated by Australian and US forces.

The vanquished have no idea how long their conquerors might remain. The Romans stayed in Britain for 500 years. The French resistance was in reality two movements politically divided. In the Low Countries, there was anger and recrimination after the Germans had been rolled back. The grisly evidence of this was witnessed by my father Jack Stoate at close quarters in 1945.

Could *Matador* have stopped the Japanese – and, in doing so, change the course of history dramatically? Holding the Peninsula in northern Johor or beyond would have slowed the Japanese advance but would not have stopped it. To succeed, the Allied forces at that time would have needed the support of American reinforcements. Churchill placed Malaya below the Middle East and Russia in terms of priorities. Who can say that he was wrong? Keeping Hitler occupied on the Russian front was key, certainly militarily and perhaps politically. The Middle East and Russia absorbed all energies and resources. The war in the Middle East, which was the world's oil pipeline and gateway to India, was not going well. Russian vulnerability added to the complexities of the situation. In 1941, Churchill delivered 440 aircraft to Russia despite the comment by the Chiefs of Staff that, on purely military grounds, they would 'pay a better dividend' if sent to the Far East or the Middle East.

So far as Singapore was concerned, the reality was that all the guns and fortifications in the world probably would not have ensured its landward defence. So whilst Churchill may be accused of making a major tactical blunder, in the wider strategic and political sense he took a gamble that in the specific did not pay off but which in a wider context clearly did.

All this of course would not have been uppermost in Second Lieutenant David Stoate's mind. Events at Alexandra Barracks Hospital on 14 February 1942 were more relevant to his particular circumstances than military world strategy.

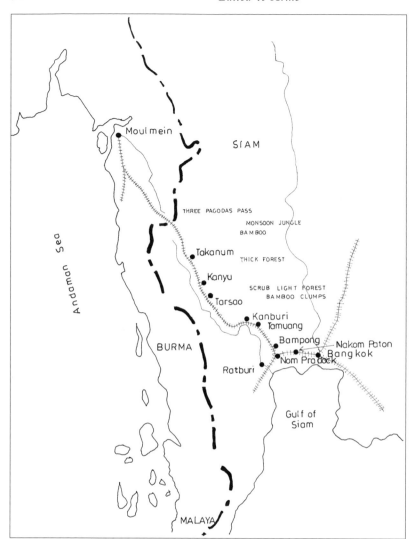

SIAM

THREE PAGODAS PASS

MONSOON JUNGLE
BAMBOO

THICK FOREST

SCRUB LIGHT FOREST
BAMBOO CLUMPS

Moulmein

Takanum

Kanyu

Tarsao

Kanburi
Tamuang

Bampong

Nakom Paton
Bangkok
Nom Pradock

Ratburi

BURMA

Andaman Sea

Gulf of
Siam

MALAYA

Sketch map of
the Railway.

As Japanese soldiers advanced towards the hospital at about 1 pm, a British Lieutenant acting as an envoy with a white flag approached the Japanese forces but was bayoneted and killed. After the Japanese troops entered the hospital, a number of patients, including those undergoing surgery at the time, were killed along with doctors and members of nursing staff. The following day about 200 male staff members and patients who had been assembled and bound the previous day, many of them walking wounded, were ordered to walk about 400 metres to an industrial area. Anyone who fell on the way was bayoneted. The men were forced into a series of small, badly ventilated rooms and were imprisoned overnight without water. Some died during the night as a result of their treatment. The remainder were bayoneted the following morning; there were only five survivors.

At first the Japanese carried all before them; in the Philippines, Hong Kong, Singapore, and against the Dutch East Indies. Island groups were taken, Burma invaded, India threatened, northern Australia raided, in six months the eastern Pacific was in Japanese hands. There seemed little to halt the onrush. Though the sheer scope of the task undertaken was immense – to acquire the largest empire yet known in the Orient, disguised under the name of 'the Co-Prosperity Sphere'.

The invasion of Burma from Thailand in late 1941 and early 1942 gave the Japanese a logistical problem. To maintain their forces in Burma, the Japanese had to bring supplies and troops to Burma by sea, through the Straits of Malacca and the Andaman Sea. This route was vulnerable to attack by Allied submarines and a different means of transport was needed. The obvious alternative was a railway. The Japanese started construction at BamPong at the south (Thailand) end and Thanbyuzayat at the Burma end more or less simultaneously, in June 1942. The base materials were produced by the forced labour of Allied PoWs and civilian populations. Most of the tracks and sleepers, however, were brought from dismantled branches of railways in Malaya and the Dutch East Indies. On 17 October 1943, the two sections of the line met at the Three Pagodas Pass on the Thai/Burmese border.

The Burma–Siam Railway is not simply a route connecting Siam (Thailand) with Burma, that would be shorter and more direct. It runs along the River Kwai, following a much longer route, more or less parallel to the border between Burma and Siam, for over 260 miles. It was constructed to connect the pre-existing railways in Burma and Thailand to the Pacific Ocean at Bangkok and the Indian Ocean at Thanbyuzayat, Burma.

David suggested that to get an account of what his next four birthdays as a PoW of the Japanese was like I should look to other chroniclers as well as his own memories. Two books were of particular importance. The first is *The Burma-Siam Railway – The Secret Diary of Dr Robert Hardie*. Robert Hardie was a Scottish doctor of Medicine, a partner in a medical practice in Kuala Lumpur. In 1939 he was commissioned as a medical officer in the Malayan Volunteer Field Ambulance and became a prisoner of war on the fall of Singapore. He ran what passed for hospitals in a number of camps including BamPong and Kanburi, where David was also a PoW, although at different times. The second book, lent to me by David, is called *Railroad of Death* by John Coast. Both of these men kept diaries during their captivity, an offence that would certainly have been punished by a severe beating and even death – the former could very likely lead to the latter.

A point that is made clear by both authors and confirmed to me by David is that for the most part, officers were not engaged on the building of the railway itself. As we shall see they had other duties. The brunt of the building fell upon the Other Ranks, who had a much worse time than the officers – but everything is relative.

Article 49 of the Geneva Convention stated that officers 'may in no circumstances be compelled to work'. Japan signed the Convention but never ratified it. After the outbreak of war the Japanese Government gave an assurance that, though not legally bound by the Geneva Convention, it would in general respect its terms. In practice it flagrantly and cynically contravened it.

Ranks above Lieutenant Colonel were shipped to Japan. The highest rank in camps, therefore, was Lieutenant Colonel. Many senior officers were of the prewar Sandhurst variety who were pretty useless in negotiating with the Japanese as they could not cope with the enemy's mindset. In any event, the last point of appeal in a camp was the camp commander, so it was pretty well inevitable that the captors could do what they pleased. This is starkly illustrated by the following description by Hardie:

12 July 1943; today also a party of 20 helpless Dutch sick came into camp from up-river – one lad, a Javanese, on the point of death with tuberculosis, another dying of dysentery and so nearly dead that his filthy blanket was already a mass of flies and bluebottles attracted by the stink of putrefaction and death. That the sick have to reach such a desperate condition before they qualify for evacuation shows the extent of the Nipponese recognition of humanitarian principles. The whole party of just-living skeletons, collapsed and exhausted, made a ghastly picture: bearded, filthy, those that could stand staggering with matchstick legs and wasted faces, their eyes glazed with anguish and despair. No protest to the Jap authorities against this inhuman treatment of the sick, and the barbarous brutalities being inflicted by the engineers and guards on the railway workers, seems to have any effect.

… In return for 'certain concessions' from the Japs the Battalion COs had unanimously agreed that officers should do certain work about the camp for our own health.

David recalls that some time during this period, he

… got a job as odd job man with the cottage industries which were organised by ourselves for doing boot repairs, cup covers, messtin repairs, rebuilding cards and general repairs of that nature. It suited me down to the ground as I found time went much quicker when I was really busy.

Robert Hardie:

The officers were more fortunate. The younger ones had been out with the working parties for upwards of a year where they constantly had to bear the responsibility of mediating between the Nips and the troops and where they had frequently had been hit for their pains. Many of them had been doing full coolie work of the hardest type in an officers' working party, 300-strong for the last six months. Their health was better than the troops, though nearly all of them had been several times ill or in hospital; their food too was more supplemented, although no Thai would have dreamt of eating such stuff.

Officers' working duties included duties on road maintenance parties, the felling of trees and bamboo. Bamboos were not the small horticultural stalks we are familiar with in the UK, they grew to 60 feet and were as thick as a man's thigh at their base. This material had to be manhandled for distances up to two-and-a-half miles to the railway construction site or to the camp where it was used to construct buildings and shelter roofed with 'Atap'. The effect of the diet was such that to walk half a kilometre was a real effort, knee joints were 'unaccountably weak and flabby'. Targets were handed down by the Japanese and 'if the target was 40 trees you would be lucky to get away with 70.' Officers also created kitchen gardens to supplement the food. These gardens, Robert Hardie writes, were 'quite the most valuable source of food, we had ladies finger, ginger, spinach, chilli bushes, pineapples, guavas, papaya.' Unfortunately these invaluable supplements were not always to be had. David recalls one of the gruelling marches moving from one camp to another.

A quick cup of tea and then away on a 28-mile march with all our kit. By 9 am we had about 10 miles behind us and stopped for breakfast on the wayside, a truck from the camp we were making for bringing it out to us. In case breakfast conjures up an idea of eggs, bacon, fried bread, tomatoes and post toasties, let me say that it was merely rice, ½ pint of vegetable stew and a pint of tepid tea. I was carrying a full pack, water bottle and a kitbag ¾ full.

David recalls another trip, this time by rail but no less demanding:

We set off on yet another of those memorable journeys for which the Nips proved themselves to be the worst organisers in the world. The whole trip was unbelievably uncomfortable. We left Kanburi camp at 3.30pm and marched with all the kit we possessed in the world to a level crossing about 300 yards from the camp. Open metal goods trucks then arrived on the scene and we were bundled into these at the rate of 28 men to a truck. We stayed on the railway line in the hot sun until 8 pm when we finally moved off. We arrived at Non Pradok (where I had previously spent a day on the way up to Kanburi) at about midnight. We were pushed into a siding and were not allowed out of the trucks until morning – totally unnecessary and very unpleasant as you cannot lie down with so many to a truck.

Having had to hurredly detrain following an air raid they entrained again sitting on top of petrol drums.

The difficulty at this stage of the journey was to stay awake. One of the worst parts was the tremendous thirst one gets as drinking water was non-existent, all water having either to be boiled or sterilised with chlorinating tablets. Can you imagine a truck load of petrol drums, piled on with stores, on top of that our own kit and finally 28 weary men peering into the darkness and wondering what the dickens was going to happen next? Anyone falling asleep would certainly have fallen off, the result being a further addition to the already colossal casualty figure. However the thought of this kept us awake and we arrived at a sub-station of Bangkok around midnight. We were able to make out bombed buildings and sidings on the way and the station itself was lit by large wood fires. During the latter part of the journey we had travelled with a large number of Jap sick, recently evacuated from Burma. They were in an appalling condition, as bad as our own troops up country, the stench coming from metal-covered trucks in the hot sun, filled with men with dysentery, being unbelievable. They had waited 108 days to be evacuated and two died at the bridge station while we were there. Nobody seemed to take any interest in them whatever and the general principle that sick men do not need food appeared to have been practised on them too. Every party except one saw the same sight as we did, so there must have been a considerable number of them.

Malaysians and Chinese prisoners and volunteers, the latter mostly Malaysian, were treated even worse that the Allied Other Ranks.

The advent of Asiatic labour brought up to die in thousands is perhaps the blackest and foullest blot on the record of the IJA. These simple and happy people lived 50 men to one tent, no latrines, diet of pure rice and dried fish. One MO for 300 Asiatics. The Nips regarded their Asiatics as machines pure and simple and utterly failed to regard them as human beings. Cholera meant no treatment as they were going to die anyway – concentrate on the ones able to work. In Asiatic camps women and children had been allowed to come too.

It was, if anything, even worse for occupying Japanese soldiers who were no longer any use to the Japanese army. They were pretty well abandoned without shelter, food or medical help. David recalled he and others giving them food and water in acts of humanitarianism that were in total contrast to how the Allied prisoners were treated by their Japanese captors. Although common sentiments of the time ran along the lines of a slow death would be too good and a swift bullet certainly too kindly. John Coast describes one particular aspect of the suffering:

On about 22 May during the night, the monsoon broke out on us. From now on for four and a half solid months the monsoon was with us. As this history unfolds you must always see and hear and feel rain, rain, rain. You worked in the rain, you ate in the rain and it rained through your leaky tent at night; never were you dry. And mud! the camp slope was as slippery as a brown ice rink; the journey to cookhouse or latrine, particularly at night, meant falling into a pool of water or slipping up on your way and coming back to the tent with 2 inches of mud and muck on your boots and an inch of it coated on the seat of your shorts.

Ancient tents began to arrive but most of the men lived in their shacks for at least a month; these shacks didn't keep out more than half the rain, and it always showered through the roof in a fine spray, so that they slept on sodden sacks in near nudity, night after night. The floors of the shacks were inches deep in slimy mud. For such accommodation officers were theoretically paying $42 a month.

As the weather got fouler the work of digging and making the railway became infinitely harder and bloodier; but this only infuriated the higher-up Nips, who simply gave the order that the same amount of work would be got through as before – the monsoon was to be ignored. And that started the grand 'speedo' that was to last until the railway was finished. It

meant longer hours of work for the men; and it meant railway work again for all spare officers; and eventually all 'yasme' (rest days) were abolished. The officers, thanks to Ino, who only
wanted to be able honestly to sign his chit that all officers were working, were once again
fortunate; they paraded with the men in the morning, drew some blunt old axes and saws, and
sludged off into the jungle just outside Takanun village to fell small trees suitable for use in
bridge building. We felled the trees marked and dragged out and trimmed the trunks, and had
the job clear after an hour or two.

The worst thing about it was the number of mosquitoes. Some people went out with their
bare backs and came in with their entire torsos pink under a rash of bites; others nearly suf-
focated themselves in wet strips of mosquito netting they tore off to make a sort of 'bernous'
under which or through which the mosquitoes bit just the same. When the trees were ready
we had to stay out in the jungle all morning and avoid all Nips for fear of them realising how
little we did. We generally found shelter from the rain underneath some Thai house, where we
sat and swatted mosquitoes and tried to buy fruit until it was nearly 1 o'clock and safe to wend
our way back to camp.

John Coast described the beginning of the working day. After a slow and sodden visit to the
cookhouse for meagre rations,

… as the first light of dawn breaks through the clouds it is time to get on parade. The troops
go out first, and we follow immediately to check the numbers. They stand there in fives, filthy
old hats on their heads; some with bare feet, some with old, broken up boots; every man wears
a Jap-Happy stained with mud and sweat, his mess-tin and spoon stuck in the string belt.
Some put their mess-tins in a haversack. Nearly everybody has three or four days growth of
beard, and many are fully bearded. Most of them are very thin, with big, swollen 'rice-bellies'
and there are various sorts of skin diseases, dermatitis and ringworm, in huge patches on every
part of their bodies

While we wait in the drizzle for the Nip engineers to arrive in their cheap mackintoshes,
we look around us once again. Everything is grey-green. A thick mist rises slowly each morning out of the jungle on either side of us, looking as if the trees were cloud topped; during the
course of the morning it slowly vanishes. On all sides we hear the Wak Waks whistling like
plaintive banshees and; the optimists say that that means the rain will soon stop.

Now our administrative Nips move forward from where they have been chatting to meet
the engineers who are walking in from their camp, a kilo up the road. The engineers are led
as usual by the old gunso [sgt.] with the squint, and he wastes little time. He goes round with
a stub of pencil and a board and details the parties for embankment, cutting, bridging, and
timber collecting, and off we shamble with our respective Nip engineer privates in charge. We
pass the tool tent on our way, drawing out all the tools that Taramoto has said he would teach
us to love, which we'd cheerfully bury in the head of any and every Nip we could.

John Coast describes the process of building an embankment or cutting:

The technique of making a cutting was very simple. One party picked and dug the clinging
earth at the bottom and loaded it on to stretchers, the other party staggered away through the
slush up some crude steps in the bank and dumped the load clear away. Then came back for
the next load. And so on and so on hundreds of times a day. The bridging engineers are beating up so many people a day that we take no real notice of anything less than a broken limb.

Bridge-building:

Today is our turn for the big bridge, a bloody awful job. So far they've got the founda-
tion secure, after they've fallen down once; and the upright baulks are in for the first 40 m,

covering four large bays. We're now having to haul up the first cross-pieces with primitive hand tackle and our own strength. They are always about six Nips on the bridge, all giving different and contradictory orders; and they invariably go completely mad when a certain, dumb Nip officer comes along and stands there silently watching us. As long as he stays, there is chaotic work and no rest at all.

The men dump their kit under logs out of the rain, and are once at work. Some are hauling on the ropes, some are up on the bridge trying to haul the baulks upright, some are sorting out the next timbers. Two fortunates – worked on strict rotation, and curiously enough never queried by Nips who take it as an old British Army custom – are brewing some hot concoction jokingly referred to as tea.

For the officer there is perpetual nervous strain, trying to interpret, mediate, procure 'yasmes' and so on. For the men there is physical and nervous strain. The whole morning is a maze of growled Kurrahs! (here you!) and buggairos (Fool!) and Kanayaros! (look at this idiot). The Nips have no proper abuse in their language, but the sound of a sudden bellowed Kurrah! Was one of the usual introductions to a bloody good clip over the ear or some especially dirty job to do.

Well the work goes on for a couple of hours, and nothing out of the ordinary happens. The tea is boiling, it seems. ' Nippon – small 'yasme' OK, Cha? (tea) 'More ten minutes,' mumbles the Nip, the expected reply, and after about a quarter of an hour we break off and sit under some big tree where the rain can't bother us so much; drops on a bare back aren't noticed. Our ten minutes are soon up, and back at work one of the Nips finds his shift is one short.

Immediately a flood of snarls in Japanese and: Shoko! (officer!) 'Kurrah Kurrah!' I go over and listen to the stream of ape-like words; we'd never learn their bloody language, but they always expect us to understand them, and hit us if we don't. The troops often understood marvellously accurately from two or three words picked out plus a little instinct. 'Yes, Nippon, but one man benjo (latrine) jungle.' I point to the jungle. The Nip understands but continues to shout. 'OK! Nippon he be back soon!' 'Buggario' the little beauty bellows, 'No OK!' I'll be bloody lucky if I can get this chap off a beating when he comes back.

After two minutes the man appears, still fastening his Jap-Happy. The Nip shouts, 'Kurrah!' at him and he knows there is trouble ahead. He walks up fast, but warily. 'I Benjo Nippon,' he says ready to receive a bang. 'Benjo no good,' says the Nip 'yasme benjo! Shoko no good.' 'But this man dysentery, Nippon; stomach no good, Nippon.' I demonstrate in gesture language. But we are wasting time. Suddenly the Nip flashes up with his hand and we both get a swipe in the face, and ten seconds later everyone is working again and the Nips have forgotten all about it … and so the morning drags on.

John Coast has thoughtfully translated some of the Japanese words but elsewhere he gives greater descriptions of some key words; for example 'speedo' has the sense of work very fast or I will hit you very hard with a bamboo – or crowbar, whichever is nearest.

A Jap-happy was a G-string, a rectangular piece of cheap cloth with a tape at one end. The string went around the waist, the strip of cloth hung down behind and was tucked up between the legs and stuck inside the string around the waist in front, so that a small flap hung over the front. It was a very simple loincloth.

The men were doing hard coolie work in tropical weather, on insufficient rations with little or no medical attention. There was hardly a man, David included, who had not already been in hospital, and most of them were already familiar with malaria, dysentery, and vitamin deficiency diseases. They were on average one to two stone under weight, and in a very poor state of resistance. Already the total kit of the average troop might be an old hat, a pair of boots with leaky soles, no socks, a Jap-happy in which he worked, perhaps a patched pair of shorts, his only 'smart garment' – no other clothes at all. Then there would be a water bottle with a worn-out cork; a mess tin and spoon, a ground sheet with the water proofing gone and which was dirty and leaky, two sacks or perhaps an old blanket, a pack to carry this in and possibly a share in a mosquito net. Many had less. Discipline could be very brutal. David:

We had one major incident when I was in the camp. It started by one of the water pump parties failing to see a Nip warrant officer who was waiting for a salute. Also previously the same pump party had failed to do coolie work for a couple of Nip medical orderlies who were great friends of the warrant officer. The final outcome was that one of our interpreters told the Nip commander that he had met a few Japanese gentlemen in peacetime but none since he had been taken PoW. The result was that he was involved in a brawl with the commander and was then beaten up very severely and locked in a small cell. He was kept there on a very slender diet for over two months and the last we heard of him he was going mental as well as being very weak physically. In addition, we were all taken off all jobs, including cookhouse and canteen and a skeleton staff of Other Ranks replaced us. We were confined to our huts for 14 days, not being allowed to lie down or play games during working hours.

Incredible as it is, a sense of humour was not entirely destroyed.

We were put on heavy work involving walking over 15 miles in a day carrying bamboos, clearing virgin jungle, cutting grass which stood 4 feet high that cut your arms and legs, and hut building. Reveille was at 7am, work parade at 8am, finish morning work at 1.30pm, start again at 3.30 and finish at 7.00pm if you were lucky. This meant you got up in the dark and finished in the dark.

We had to have a parade and headcount twice a day when we had to number ourselves off, one to twenty; I can still count up to twenty in Japanese! We saluted whoever took it and came to attention, the command being ki-oski. I was good at getting my knees together but not my heels! Although I was shouted at, I was lucky never to get bashed. It became a joke amongst some in the camp and Major Stibie presented me with a drawing which clearly represented my predicament!

In the camps desease was an ever-present fact of life, some camps were quite large housing up to 10,000 prisoners, living conditions were crude and sanitary arrangements likewise, typically a trench with a pole running across it to rest against.

Diseases included dysentery, a potentially fatal inflammatory disorder of the intestine manifesting itself in extreme diarrhoea with blood and mucus present in the faeces. Both amoebic and bacillary form were present, the latter lacerated the bowels and was the more extreme form. Treatment is by antibiotic (of which there was virtually none) and or by rehydration, aided by the addition of salt or carbohydrate.

Prisoners also suffered from jaundice, a symptom of a bodily failure, usually kidney or liver dysfunction resulting in problems with red blood cell production. It can be brought on by malaria, and manifests itself by the skin and eyes taking on a yellowish hue often accompanied by high fever.

Scabies was also present, a rash and skin infection caused by mites that burrow beneath the skin and lay their eggs, this causes itchiness, a rash and bumps between the fingers and, on the underside of the wrists, elbows and knees. The remedy is to wash clothes in hot water and detergent, neither of which was available.

Scabies was highly contagious and was always complicated by some vicious secondary infection which in turn ended up as ulceration. The usual way of getting the infection was by lice bites. Treatment two ways: 1 Maguires, looked like engine oil and was very hot. Or 2 blue stone or copper sulphate which bit into your flesh and stung like hell for hours afterwards but which did ultimately cure you. The MI room had queues full of men having great craters in their backsides touched up by crude 'Blue stone' and all over their mottled bodies they were daubed black and blue. As regards the ulcer cases who had been compelled to go on working, for many of them the only thing was amputation if they could stand it. What could doctors do with a great pink and green ulcer taking in the ankle and stretching right up to the knee,

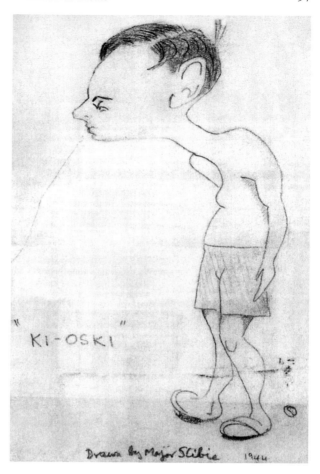

David Stoate's predicament when it came to standing to attention, as illustrated by Major Stibie. (David Stoate)

exuding a vile stench and bared literally to the bone? It is amazing to learn that there were many successful amputations.

Ulcers were generally the knock-on effect of one or other of the diseases listed – an irritation scratched would almost certainly turn ulcerous, as described by Hardie:

In addition to the normal diseases brought on by the hard work, pellagra and other horrible deficiency diseases were reducing the men to skeletons, and more than half of them had tropical deceases. These ulcers were evil things. You scratch yourself on a bamboo without knowing it, and because the bamboo is very sharp the infection is carried deeply in. Next day there is the beginning of a sore that you didn't notice, but scratch absent mindedly with dirty finger nails. The following morning there is an open ulcer the size of a red-raw sixpence. You can't go sick with that, and there's no known cure for it. The medical orderly patches you up with a wad of disinfectant and you make your own bandage with a bit of a strip torn off an old Jap-happy. Next day though the thing's a big as a shilling and two days later it's a vile looking open sore with a stinking suppurating yellow and red carbuncular centre the size of a half crown. To stand up and walk at all hurts like hell but it's a matter of luck whether the Nip medical orderly will let you go sick or not. If he does the bloody thing will stop getting bigger so fast – possibly; but if he makes you work again you can expect a wicked hole the size of a tennis ball by the end of the week and perhaps if they ever do evacuate you you'll have to lose a leg.

Typhus was rampant, spread by body lice. The symptoms are chills, a cough, a very high temperature, sensitivity to light, a severe headache, stupor, a red spot rash on arms, back and chest.

Cholera, a highly contagious gastro-enteritis infection contracted from contaminated food
and water, is characterised by extreme diarrhoea. Death can come within three hours. The
remedy is rehydration augmented by homemade additives such as sugar, salt, baking soda or
fruit juices, preventative measures being sterilisation, care in sewage engineering and water
purification. Cholera was a real killer. Bodies had to be burned as soon as possible after death
and sanctions for carelessness around food were severe:

> Cholera vaccine was good for four weeks only. We had to be fanatical about flies. Any man
> seen throwing even a grain of rice on the ground was disciplined. The thing that shakes me is
> that you are talking to a man in the afternoon and by night he is dead and so altered that you
> literally can't recognize him.
>
> Saline solution needed to pump into the veins of dehydrated patients was only produced
> by the Nips for one case in case ten. At the back end of the camp blue spirals of smoke rise
> continually, that was the crematorium and beside it the ever increasing cemetery.

Mosquito-transmitted diseases were also present. Dengue fever presented with severe headache,
muscular and joint pains, a bright red rash on lower limbs and chest, abdominal pain, nausea,
vomiting and diarrhoea.

> Cerebral malaria. Another brute of a disease. This brand of malaria occurs when the infection
> goes to the brain. The patient loses consciousness. He groans and raves until he either dies or
> the miracle happens and he recovers consciousness. The giving of intravenous quinine was
> frowned upon as extreme and very dangerous medically, but the camp MOs made their own
> solutions and pumped it in and eventually saved some 60% of cases. It is said that never have so
> few medics saved so many lives against such colossal odds.

Prisoners of course suffered from vitamin deficiency diseases. Pellagra results from a deficiency
in niacin, B3. The symptoms are 'the four Ds,' diarrhoea, dermatitis, dementia and death. Beri-
beri is due to a deficiency in thiamine, B1. It attacks the nervous system, manifesting itself as
two types: wet, which affects the heart and vascular/respiratory systems, and dry which is a
wasting disease, ultimately causing paralysis, attacking the nervous system. The symptoms for
the wet form are waking at night short of breath, increased heart rate, swelling of the lower legs
and shortness of breath during activity. The dry form manifests itself by symptoms such as difficulty in walking, loss of sensation in the hands and feet, mental confusion.

It is self evident that the conditions for these diseases to thrive were just about perfectly
provided in the crowded and primitive living conditions in the jungle. Both prophylactic and
curative drugs were available at the time but not provided. No one knew in the morning when
he woke up, whether he would be alive that night.

> Amoebic dysentery was a slow and less deadly business, all the patients together isolated from
> the rest of the camp, many of them were fit enough to administer and look after themselves.
> Cure was by emetin but it didn't exist in any quantity to be noticeably effective.
>
> Bacillary Dysentery lacerated bowels internally, it could get you in days, treatment was by
> Magnesium Sulphide. Amoebic dysentery might get you in the end … Dengue Fever was
> short lived … carried by the Tiger mosquito. Avitamenosis or vitamin deficiency diseases
> were of two types, one that makes your joints swell and ache till life was an absolute misery
> and the other brought on all sorts of dermatitis to the body and private parts causing horrible
> glandular swellings and maddening irritation that when scratched went rotten. There were so
> many of these diseases about, plus normal beri-beri, that it was insufficient to enter hospital
> with Diphtheria.

Diphtheria is a disease recognised by thickening of the neck transmitted by close human contact. The symptoms are breathing difficulty, ultimately asphyxiation and/or heart failure.

Inevitably, David was not immune from contagion; his service records contain notes of his medical inspection carried out back in Bristol in November 1945 where it records some of his bouts including dysentery – amoebic and bacillary – malaria BT (15 times), jaundice and tropical ulcers.

> While at the various camps I spent some part of the time being ill, which meant I did not have to work. I had numerous attacks of dysentery for which there was no medicine, just trudging day and night in all weathers, from the hut to the latrine which consisted of a pole across a pit. Also endless doses of malaria: you just sweated and shivered under a blanket for a few days and hoped it would pass. If it got really bad, you were given a powdered dose of quinine. It really was ghastly to take and we wrapped it in paper and tried to swallow it. Apart from that, there were jaundice and leg ulcers. I was one of the lucky ones as I had quite mild ones but some had sores right down to the bone. The worst thing was cholera, which hit one of the camps I was in, I think it was Tarso. At one time we were burying 17 men a day. All mess tins and cutlery were sterilised in boiling water before use and this undoubtedly saved a lot of lives. In July 1944 when I moved from Tamuang to Nakhon Pathom, a hospital camp, I was able to get treatment for all my ills and when I moved back to Kanburi I was underweight but comparatively fit and remained so for the rest of my internment.

The hardship, dreariness and isolation of this existence was relieved to some extent by the occasional delivery of letters from home, by contact with the natives of the region, and extraordinarily, by radio. Man's ingenuity never fails to astonish but Coast, Hardie and David Stoate all confirm that in their respective camps there was occasional radio contact. Quite how those responsible were able to construct let alone run a radio seems little short of miraculous. Putting that miracle aside it was also extraordinarily brave as discovery would have meant certain death. Hardie describes the absolute secrecy surrounding the provenance of the occasional snippet of news, one officer was less than discreet in this regard and was soundly beaten by his own comrades, no doubt 'pour encourager les autres'. David applauded their courage:

> The risks attached to running a set were enormous and I hope that the fellows that have provided us with such a magnificent service will get decorated. At Kanburi in August 1943 a sudden search was made of the huts and three sets were found in one of the huts. Two of the people concerned were literally beaten to death and several others who were implicated had broken arms, jaws and thigh bones, so you can see, it required a lot of courage to go on working a set, knowing what to expect if you were caught.

In at least one camp the news of the invasion of Italy was known, as was the news of the tremendous Allied success in Libya in November 1942, where David's elder brother Tom was serving with the RAF.

In addition to radio, news letters from home were of immense importance and a great comfort. Coast wrote that '… everyone's spirits were improved by the receipt of mail from home. Somewhere on the same earth there were people who did seem to mind what happened to you.'

This was understood by the Japanese, as Coast explains; 'The Japs in charge withheld the letters from men who were sick and unable to work – they would get them if they worked – otherwise they would be burned.'

Letters home were permitted, that is to say it was permitted to fill out cards of a pre-printed form that might or might not reach their destination. Even Red Cross parcels rarely reached their destination; some were found stockpiled in a warehouse at the end of hostilities, others were shamelessly plundered by the Japanese.

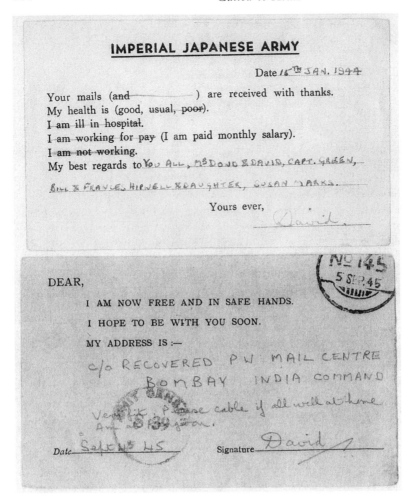

'Letters' home.
(David Stoate)

The importance of letters to all serving men and women must not be underestimated. From the capitulation of Singapore to the capitulation of Japan David received 115 letters or cards spread over 15 deliveries – well above the average. In composing a form of letter/report to his parents, after Japan had capitulated but before he had been repatriated, David wrote:

August 19th 1945. Looking back over the past five and a half years, the most outstanding comfort has been the arrival of a spasmodic bunch of mail, for which I can never thank you both enough. While at Kanburi, I received two lots, one in May and the other in July, which informed me that all was well at home up to August 1944. Yesterday a large amount of mail was released and I now know that everything was all right up to the end of January 1945 so reckon we should all come through this war all right with a bit of luck.

The huts would house up to a hundred men. Sleeping arrangements were continuous stages built of bamboo, some 200 yards long. They harboured mites and bed bugs that not only made sleeping very difficult but also spread disease. The temperature was 80–90 degrees. In the monsoon season the camps were often flooded and the floods caused the effluent in the latrines to flow around the camps, again with disastrous effects on hygiene and health. Hardie described the existence as a 'dull but tolerable regime handicapped mainly by perpetual food shortage and lack of drugs for the hospital'. In his account he makes it plain that his position as MO entitled him to rather more comfort than others, but as I wrote earlier, everything is relative. On the subject of relative 'comfort', David recalls some better moments at the Officer's camp at Kanburi:

Generally speaking we had quite a good time in the camp though there were numerous restrictions. Work did not start until 10 am, finished at 1 pm, afternoon 3 pm to 6 pm. You were not allowed to lie down on your bed, read or play any games during working hours, unless you were very sick and had a special label. Smoking outside the huts was prohibited except for one area on the parade ground after 8 pm. No concerts were allowed for the first six weeks I was there and after that we were allowed one a week. These were first class as we had a lot of dresses and feminine apparel which was apparently intended for some women from Singapore who were to be transferred to Thailand but never came. The result was we had some gorgeous beauties in bright evening dresses, doing dances and turns which really made you think you were at home. No talking was allowed on the stage, so any performance was confined to dancing and singing but we had plenty of talent and most of the shows were excellent. We also had classical and jazz concerts by the band. There was also an excellent canteen which, in time of plenty, kept us without hunger pains but unfortunately the supply was very limited, hence good feeding was spasmodic.

In every account that I have read there is a continuous thread – entertainment. It is difficult to conceive how it was accomplished, but in spite of speech being banned on the stage, musical instruments were somehow transported, maintained and indeed even constructed; concerts and singsongs were regular features. In addition to this 'universities' were often set up to expand or even keep in working order the minds of those who wished to participate.

The rations were mainly rice, supplemented with a small amount of dried fish or vegetable, at one stage Coast's ration was increased from 3–5 to 5–8 ounces but he was still ravenously hungry, hardly surprising as 5 to 8 ounces of rice is still less than a cupful. The language of both authors is consistent, in that 'feeding' rather 'eating' is the term employed.

In spite of these conditions it is rare that the PoWs turned their minds to escape, the principal reason being that there was nowhere to escape to. This was quite unlike Europe. India or Australia was 2000 miles away over dense jungle or ocean respectively. Rewards were offered to natives for the return of escaping prisoners, the odds against success were very long indeed and failure meant certain death. Yet the odd attempt was made. John Coast:

There was one famous story of a gallant but futile attempt to escape, led by a senior major, soon after they arrived near the Burma border and saw what was in store for them. They made up a party of nine men, including an Indian and a Burmese cook who acted as their guide. Between them they raised 500 dollars, the Burmese cook had increased that to 1000 dollars. Their plan was to make for the Ye river, float on a raft down to the coast and there attempt to find a boat which they could sail to India. But they had reckoned without the jungle. They found their route lay through such dense country that it was only possible to hack their way through a few kilometres of it a day. Their compass bearings took them over river and mountain alike and sometimes they had to crawl up the faces of gorges and waterfalls – all this carrying heavy kit.

They did at length reach their river, however, and made their raft, loaded their kit and on it and started down stream. After a short distance they came upon some rapids and the raft broke up and they were thrown into the water. The Burmese cook saved one Englishman from drowning and their only casualties were some kit and 500 dollars lost. They rebuilt the raft on the banks of this fast flowing river and set off for a second time but when they reached a long series of rapids and waterfalls they had to abandon the idea of a raft and try to reach the sea on foot.

Then their journey really began and in more difficult country than they had ever seen before. Several of them had malaria and as was inevitable the bamboo scratches started ulcers which they had to walk with and could not treat. The leader of the party, a very powerful fellow was the first to succumb under a burden of some 70 tropical ulcers. In truly heroic spirit he refused to burden his companions and insisted that they should go on and so he lay down quietly in the jungle to die.

After a week there were six of them left alive in a Burmese village. After letting then stay there for some time and realising that their future progress was impossible the village headman apologised and said that if he kept them there much longer a Nip patrol would be certain to find them and then he himself would be shot and his village punished. If they really could not go on in he would have to inform the nearest Japanese. As this was the case the Japanese were informed and the six men were picked up in a condition too feeble to walk, one of them dying of dysentery almost at once.

The five survivors who still included the Indian and the Burmese were brought back to their camp and sentenced to death; The British commander was ordered to attend the execution; this he refused to do protesting as a representative of the British government at the illegality and inhumanity of the sentence.

For some unexplained reason the men were reprieved – at least for a while. What ultimately happened to them has been lost in the mists of time.

Given that the Japanese determined that the railway was to be built by PoWs, its line following the river Kwai was something of a benefit to the prisoners. The river itself was already a transport route. During the engineering of the railway it was a means of transport for the men involved as well as a place where they could on occasion bathe, and where natives would ply their wares. Trade with the natives was a way of supplementing the meagre diet. Bartering watches and pens was popular and David traded his travelling clock and Tissot watch. John Coast remarked that 'the chief thing that made it pleasant was the Thai traders.'

Naturally, the railway did not slavishly follow one side of the river or the other but as the river meandered the line was made to cross it by bridges, including the bridge made famous by the film *The Bridge over the River Kwai*. As the war progressed and the Allied air forces were able to regain the skies, several attempts were made to destroy these bridges by bombing runs. One such bombing run killed 100 PoWs and wounded 400 at Non Pradok, a railside camp where David had stayed for most of one day, when moving from the hospital camp at Nakhon Pathom to the officer's camp at Kanburi.

I remember we had a few members of the band with us, including a violin, guitar, clarinet and a mess tin as a drum and formed a choir and brought the house down with bawdy songs. We arrived at Kanburi camp in the middle of the night (you always arrive at every camp in the middle of the night under Nip supervision) had a cup of tea and a spot of rice and stew and so to bed on an earth floor. The following day I was moved on to a bamboo slat bed (which soon harboured bed bugs) it is really a continuous platform made of split bamboo and running the entire length of the hut some 200ft long – and was able to take stock of the new circumstances in which I was about to live. There were about 3000 officers, including a few Other Ranks in the camp, which was very small covering about 500 yards by 200 yards, at least that was the area to which we were confined.

On 17 October 1944, some sixteen months after its commencement, the railway was finished. Some tens of thousands of European, and some hundreds of thousands of Asians had completed a railway over 400 kilometres long through jungle and mountains. (A previous assessment, carried out by British Engineers, had suggested it would take five years.)

One bridge had to be constructed stretching a good 400 yards apparently clinging to a cliff face 20–30 feet above the river. An observer remarked: 'Three weeks ago there was nothing, now there is not only this vast bridge but steam engines limping slowly across it. Two thousand pre-dynastic slaves of Wan Po had built the entire thing in 17 days.'

John Coast writes that his camp at that time was ordered to hold a thanksgiving service. The following is a rough tranlsation of the speech read out by the camp commandant Colonel Yanagida:

> You prisoners of 2 Group started to build this railway in Chungkai. You then went on to Wan Po, where you blasted your way through rocks and where you made a great bridge. You then came further up with me to Takanun where you completed the sector allotted to you in a satisfactory manner. For one month it was difficult to get vegetable rations in your camp, owing to the bad road and the ration was reduced. Some of you were sick and some of you died. But you must acknowledge that you have always been fairly and justly treated by the Imperial Japanese Army. It is now your stern duty to improve your health in order to able to carry out any further task which may be allocated to your Group.

Coast suggests that 'any comment on such a staggeringly insolent, hypocritical speech is superfluous.' The total labour force consisted of about 68,000 Allied PoWs and 200,000 Asian labourers. The combined death toll as a direct result of the project was around 106,000, of which 16,000 were Allied PoWs and 90,000 Asian labourers. The dead PoWs included 6,318 British personnel, 2,815 Australians 2,490 Dutch, about 356 Americans and a smaller number of Canadians.

During the three-year period from October 1942 to October 1945, David summarises his movements:

Oct. 26th 1942	Moved by train from Singapore to Bampong Thailand
Oct. 28th	By truck to Kanburi
Oct.30th	By barge to Tarso and on to Kanyu
Apr. 3rd 1943	Moved to Upper Kanyu
Aug.8th	Moved back to Lower Kanyu
Aug.17th	Moved back to Tarso
May 24th 1944	Moved to Tamuang
July	Evacuated to main hospital camp at Nakhon Pathom
Apr. 3rd 1945	Moved back to Kanburi
July 31st	On the move to a new camp
Aug. 1st	Overnight in cattle truck at Non Pradok
Aug. 2nd	Arrived at Bangkok Sub-station Bangkok and towed down river in barges to wharf near the sea
Aug. 3rd	Rested
Aug. 5th	Back on train 35 men to a cattle truck
Aug. 6th	Arrived at unknown destination to start a trek of 28 miles to a new camp about 100 miles NE of Bangkok
Aug 15th	Japan capitulated
Aug. 22nd	4th birthday in captivity, still in jungle
Sept. 1st	Boarded lorries bound for Bangkok airport
Sept. 3rd	Boarded Dakota for Rangoon
Oct. 4th	Sailed via Suez canal to Liverpool

I have tried to portray an idea of the horrors of the treatment of prisoners on the railway. Every day was a gamble of life or death. It is difficult to find anything positive that could possibly have emerged from these events; however, David and others maintain that the sense of comradeship and the concern of those prisoners for their fellow man survived all the time through the four birthdays that David spent as a PoW. The war against Japan ended on 15 August 1945. David describes that day.

On 16 August, I was on what was called the long bamboo party, carrying those bloody bamboos from a dump two-and-a-half miles from the camp. We then got our first indication that something was amiss. A large number of Other Ranks were building a camp next to ours and they were recalled in the morning and sent back to their camp. The Nips were very amiable and some were drinking heavily. In the afternoon we usually did two trips but we only had to do one, a very strange occurrence. One or two Thais on the roadside had indicated that Tokyo had capitulated but we were not prepared to believe them. By the time we got back to camp, rumour was absolutely rife but nobody knew. Later on, in the evening, it was officially given out by our own Senior Officers that Japan had capitulated but that they still had no official information from the Nips themselves. Reveille was still at 7 am. The following day on August 17th, normal work was resumed but all outside work parties were recalled in the middle of the morning and we were now awaiting further developments. A large quantity of Red Cross goods had been issued to us that morning and we hoped to get our teeth into them some time that afternoon. In three-and-a-half years of PoW life we had each had 1/6th of a parcel, intended for one man (apart from an issue in Changi in September). This no doubt infuriated the authorities when they found out, as I have not the least doubt they were under the impression that we had done well.

But even the end of hostilities was not a straightforward matter of release and home. There were thousands of men to be documented, checked over and repatriated, in the meantime their locations had to be identified and they had to be fed, housed and transported to clearing centres. In David's case this involved a train journey to Bangkok and flight to Ragoon, still perversely escorted by Japanese guards.

It was very difficult to realise that one was a free man at this time, as we still had armed Nips in the camp and we were still doing coolie work carrying vegetables and canteen goods down a one-and-a-half mile track from the main road to the camp.

David flew out of Bangkok on 3 September 1945 to Rangoon, leaving there on 4 October arriving in England on 15 October.

It is impossible to set down one's reactions to coming out of three-and-a-half years of a world filled with misery, disease, malnutrition and harsh treatment to one of civilisation as we knew it in the days of peace, and I will not attempt to try. It seemed as though we had crashed, all been killed and suddenly found ourselves in paradise.

When I visited David to have a chat and ask if I might have his permission to obtain his service records, he was quite happy for me to do so but added 'There won't be much in them as I was a PoW for virtually the whole war.' Surprisingly, it turned out that David's records were the most voluminous and complete of any I obtained – particularly during the period of re-settlement after he had returned to England on 15 October 1945.

David is a very practical individual; upon his return he was 29 years old, Spillers had kept his job open for him, and it seemed to be a matter of 'That was then, let's get on with the now.' How did the 'now' turn out?

All returning servicemen were required to complete a form regarding resettlement. Section A was compulsory and David completed his on Guy Fawkes Day 1945: 'I have considered the scheme for Civil Resettlement and I have decided that if I am eligible I will not avail myself of the opportunities offered by the scheme.'

David was advised that he should attend a Medical Board and that one would be convened at the earliest opportunity. The instructing letter to the Medical Board states:

NOTE; whatever category in which he is placed by the Medical Board, HE WILL ON NO ACCOUNT BE ORDERED TO REPORT FOR DUTY.

The medical examination was ordered for 22 November 1945 at Horfield in Bristol where the report notes that David was a PoW in Malaya from February 1942 to October 1942 and from October 1942 to August 1945 in Thailand ('worked on railway while in Thailand').

His weight in shoes and trousers was noted as 148 lbs (having put on half a stone in the last three months). At attestation David weighed in at 153 lbs so thankfully he had recovered most of his natural weight by the time the Board was put in session. Perhaps some chickens after the Japanese surrender had helped:

Work had been cut down to an absolute minimum and food was now comparatively plentiful with lashings of meat. Three of us shared a chicken and had an amusing time knocking it over the head and trying to dress it, a thing which none of us had done before. We slit it open and I dived in as though it were a bran tub and pulled out all sorts of weird pipes and things, some of which we kept and some we threw away. Having tunnelled our way through it from tip to toe, we pushed a large stick through it and grilled it over a log fire. It must have been one of the oldest chickens in Thailand as it was pretty tough and its toughness definitely was not due to a lack of cooking. However it went down very well and we had another one the next day, which we boiled with sweet potatoes and onions.

According to the medical, his eyesight and hearing, it seemed, were not impaired. E-Coli bacteria in his intestine were found but he was assessed as being fit for duty.

In a letter dated 21 December 1945 he was ordered to attend No. 6 Military Dispersal Unit, Sherford Camp, Taunton on 4 January to be released. This he duly did. There then followed a series of correspondence with dates of release varying from 21 April 1946 to to 13 August 1946. There was an ongoing debate about David's overseas and release leave entitlement, with queries being dispatched to India as to the embarkation date of the *Highland Chieftain* and the date that David was dismissed Other Ranks to take up his commission etc.

In May, working for Spillers and writing from Calgary, Alberta, David provided them with the information they were hunting for, including the embarkation date of 4 January 1941 and sailing date of 11 January – but even that required him to supply evidence.

The upshot was that his initial leave entitlement of 113 days was increased to 278 days commencing on 4 January 1946, so hopefully he would have received a nice little cheque for that.

But that does not conclude the whole 'getting back to civilian life' operation. On 1 August 1950 David was sent Army Form D.406, the object of which was to consider the availability for recall of officers on the unemployed list or a reservist. Amazingly, David – now a Mill Manager responsible for the control of a flour milling plant and supervision of some 400 employees – returned it completed!

7

THE BRIDGE

Norman Stoate's call up papers arrive and he takes the train through France to Marseilles, where he joins HMS Eagle under Admiral Cunningham's fine leadership in the Far East and eastern Mediterranean.

Norman Stoate was number four of the Stoate siblings, born on 14 February 1919 after David and ahead of Donald. He was tall with fair hair and startlingly blue eyes, he was my godfather and I am certainly biased, but to me he was dashing, sporty and tremendous fun. I am sure there must have been something of the Nordic invader in there somewhere. At the service of thanksgiving for his life, Geoffrey Stoate, the youngest of the brothers remembered how 'things seemed to revolve around Norman,' he was a kind of hub in the family. When his wife Jean allowed me to look through his documents and photos it became plain that it was not only family matters that revolved around him, there were many photographs and a mass of correspondence generated by him to friends and former war comrades that could be the subject of a separate study altogether. His war service saw him in the East, the Mediterranean, home waters and the Baltic Sea and he was a natural fit for the Royal Navy; so this chapter title chose itself quite naturally.

Norman was educated at Clifton College, Bristol and on leaving in 1936 he followed David, his elder brother and studied milling at Bristol College of Technology in Unity Street Bristol and from there, again like his brother David, worked at Stoate & Sons Ltd.

Norman Stoate's war service started in November 1939, three months after war was declared on Germany. His time in the Mediterranean was split into two parts, the first as an Ordinary and later Able Seaman in the Eastern Mediterranean Fleet, the second after he was commissioned where he served in the Western Mediterranean based in Gibraltar. From 1941 until April 1946, when he was demobbed, he served in the Channel, North Sea and Baltic Sea.

Norman left behind a mixture of a log, notes and a diary of his war years that we will use to tell his story. Some parts are sparse and some are supplemented by the notes of a comrade. These I have moulded in, more or less as Norman did. Before going to his chronicle however I would like to set the scene of his first theatre of active service.

In the Second World War, the Royal Navy called upon nearly 800,000 officers and men, together with 74,000 in the Women's Royal Naval Service (WRENS). Norman's active service

Rating Norman Stoate.
(Geoffrey Stoate)

commenced on the aircraft carrier HMS *Eagle*. In the Second World War aircraft carriers, rather than battleships, became the capital ships around which task forces were built.

The first part of Norman's Mediterranean service from mid 1940 to early 1941 started just before Italy joined the Nazi forces, after the fall of France in June 1940. As we shall see he saw plenty of action against the Italian Navy, the principal opposing fleet in the Mediterraean. Our Eastern Mediterranean Fleet was commanded by Admiral Sir Andrew Cunningham ('ABC'). Norman as a humble Ordinary Seaman had the dubious honour of being stood to attention before ABC for a dressing down, not once but twice!

Despite this or perhaps because of it, Norman clearly held the C-in-C in considerable regard. He was not alone; long after Norman had left the Eastern Mediterranean Fleet for other duties, in the autumn of 1943 Cunningham succeeded Sir Dudley Pound as First Sea Lord. He was one of the few commanders on either side who retained the confidence of the government he served for the duration.

The Mediterranean saw the second largest conventional naval warfare (after the Pacific) of the war. The British Fleet was large but in good part obsolete. By agreement with Britain the larger part of the French Fleet was concentrated in the Mediterranean to help protect British and French interests in North Africa and the Middle East. Although considerably smaller than that of Great Britain the French Fleet was, after a scheme of investment and modernization dating from 1937, well equipped and the fourth largest fleet in the world. Part of it was attached to the British Eastern Mediterranean Fleet under the command of Cunningham.

After France fell on 24 June 1940 a settlement was struck between France and Germany whereby Germany agreed not to occupy the southern part of France – Vichy France.

Cunningham and the French Admiral Rene Godfroy enjoyed a close relationship and when France capitulated, the part of the French Fleet serving in the eastern Mediterranean was neutralized by negotiation. But Norman describes how *Eagle* along with the rest of the British Fleet had her guns trained on the French ships in the harbour nevertheless.

Ships yielded to Vichy France became neutral. Intense political negotiations commenced on how to ensure the neutrality of the Vichy Fleet based in Toulon and Mers el Kabbir (Oran) in Algeria. The British demanded that it should be scuttled and the Vichy government (Admiral Darlan) refused but stated 'on their honour' that they would not let it fall under German command.

Churchill was not prepared to take the risk of the ships being used against Britain and the Commonwealth and on 3 July 1940, made the decision for their destruction. Only two weeks earlier French and British matelots had been drinking together in Gibraltar, now the British were firing on their comrades. It was a scene of utter devastation; 1300 French sailors died in the bombardment. It was said that Churchill's face streamed with tears when he reported to the House of Commons.

In 1942, when the Germans occupied Vichy France, their intention to capture the remainder of the French Fleet was thwarted by the French who fulfilled their earlier promise by scuttling the bulk of what remained of their fleet at anchor in Toulon Harbour.

Italian superiority in the Mediterranean was on paper immense but Cunningham took the offensive and achieved a series of victories with slender forces. On 11 November 1940 the Navy Fleet Air arm made fine use of specialist training in a raid on Taranto, which resulted in serious Italian losses. Four months later, off Cape Matapan, Italy lost three heavy cruisers in a night action that bore the stamp of Cunningham's aggressive genius. (For the full story, see *The Battle of Matapan: The Trafalgar of the Mediterranean* by Mark Simmons.)

The reaction of the Axis forces was swift. Their supply chain to North Africa was under huge pressure and Hitler sent the Luftwaffe to the aid of the Italians, the result being a concentrated attack on the aircraft carrier *Illustrious*. The ship survived due in no small part to the armour plating of her flight deck, and she was patched up in Malta. The use of steel on the flight decks of British aircraft carriers paid off handsomely and contrasted with the American construction, which used timber. American carriers suffered very badly indeed in the Pacific under Japanese bombing.

A more protracted trial was endured by the British Navy when the Germans supported the Italian Army which had invaded Greece. German forces came in such strength that a British contingent, helping the Greeks, had to be withdrawn by sea under conditions of extreme difficulty. Demands on the Navy increased when the Germans captured Crete by airborne assault in May 1941. The result: a further withdrawal of troops by a fleet whose endurance and resources were already stretched to the limit. Losses mounted daily, for the ships had to operate without air cover. After three cruisers and six destroyers had been sunk and two battleships, seven destroyers and over thirty transports and fleet auxiliaries severely damaged, Cunningham's staff suggested that enough had been done and that any remaining troops would have to surrender. Cunningham gave his memorable reply: 'The fleet will continue, it takes three years to build a ship. It takes three hundred years to build a tradition.' Cunningham did not intend that faith in the Navy should be broken.

Admiral Cunningham's trials in the Mediterranean continued, supplies had somehow to be got through to Malta, the base from which British submarines maintained a continuous threat to Italian shipping supplying the Italian and German Armies in North Africa. 1941 ended with the temporary elimination of the entire British battle squadron. The battleship, HMS *Barham* was torpedoed and the flag ship *Queen Elizabeth,* together with the *Valiant,* were badly damaged by Italian frogmen in Alexandria harbour where HMS *Eagle* and Norman were based. The Italians were expert in this type of underwater commando operation and Norman's later Mediterranean duties put him in the forefront of counteractive measures.

Later again, Norman was in the thick of the supreme Anglo-American effort in Europe, designed to thrust into the heart of Germany. It began on 6 June 1944 with Operation *Neptune,*

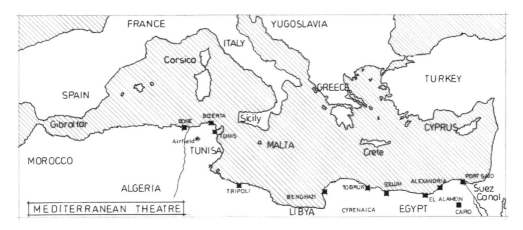

Sketch map of the Mediterranean.

the assault phase on Normandy – D-Day. The Normandy landings would involve 125,000 officers and men, some 5,000 ships including 6 battleships, 23 cruisers, 104 destroyers, more than 4000 Landing Craft of various kinds together with attendant minesweepers and auxiliaries, of which Norman commanded one, ML 909. But for now we must go back four years.

When Norman joined his first ship, the old aircraft carrier HMS *Eagle*, in February 1940, the land route to the Mediterranean was still available through France and it was by train to Marseilles that he journeyed south to join his ship in Alexandria, a main naval base in the eastern Mediterraean.

The Mediterranean formed a vital link in the trade route for Great Britain, connecting via the Suez Canal and Red Sea to the dominions in the Middle East, Far East and Antipodes. As we have seen, at the outbreak of war the Mediterranean was controlled by the Allied fleets of Britain and France. During the first part of Norman's service on HMS *Eagle* the Italian Fleet was not an immediate threat to British interests, however, after Mussolini joined Italy to the German fascist cause on 10 June 1940, the situation in the Mediterranean was transformed. The Mediterranean Sea had long been a focus of British maritime power – the defence of Gibraltar, Malta and the Suez Canal was central. Malta was the lynch-pin of the whole strategy as it provided a stop-off for Allied convoys heading east and a base from which to attack the Axis supply routes across the Mediterranean to Africa. In the event, Malta, noted as the most bombed place on earth, held on by her fingernails until the Allies had reasonable control over the skies in late 1942, but for a time the fleet was confined to the smaller port at Alexandria in British-controlled Egypt.

Each side in the battle of the Mediterranean had three principal aims: to attack the supply lines of the other side; to keep open the supply lines to their own armies in North Africa; and to destroy the ability of the other side to wage war at sea. We have seen earlier in Roy Hussey's story that the *Regia Aeronautica*, the Italian air force, was not considered a serious threat to Allied aircraft. The same did not apply to the Italian navy. The Italian vessels, which outnumbered the British Fleet, were well founded, modern and well armed and with better and more sophisticated range-finding devices, although it is said that some of her cruisers were not well armoured. They were in home waters. The Italian Fleet however lacked radar, and that coupled perhaps with the command chain of the Italian Navy, which was precisely and closely controlled by Italian Naval Headquarters, was a constraint, particularly when faced with Cunningham who, as Norman records in his notes, was a bold and aggressive leader who took the fight to the enemy. And at Matapan, the British had a hidden, huge advantage – the work of the code breakers at Bletchley Park.

HMS *Eagle*. (Norman Stoate)

Returning for a moment to those three tenets of the Battle for the Mediterranean and in particular the supply chains to North Africa. Rommel and his armies were not only dependent upon the Italian Navy to deliver supplies but also on the harbour arrangements for debarkation. The largest port was Tripoli in Axis-held Libya, the next largest was Tobruk followed closely by Bardia. The capacity of these ports was insufficient to supply the Axis armies fully, let alone taking into consideration Allied attrition of Axis shipping, which was severe, due in no small part to signal interception, code breaking and radar. This is the struggle into which Norman was to be pitched, pretty much at the beginning of hostilities.

After call-up, Ordinary Seaman N R Stoate went through initial training and was drafted to the aircraft carrier HMS *Eagle*. HMS *Eagle,* like many in the British Fleet in the Mediterranean at that time, was an old ship. Her history went back to 1911, when the Chilean Navy ordered two 28,000-ton displacement super-dreadnought battleships, each to be armed with ten 14 inch (356mm) and sixteen 6 inch (152mm) guns, to be named *Almirante Latorre* and *Almirante Cochrane*. *Latorre* was laid down in November 1911, with *Almirante Cochrane* being laid down at the Armstrong yards at Newcastle upon Tyne on 20 February 1913. At the outbreak of the First World War, construction of the two ships was suspended. As *Almirante Latorre* was almost complete, she was purchased for the Royal Navy, entering service as HMS *Canada* in 1915. Construction of her sister ship *Almirante Cochrane* was much less advanced, and no work was carried out until 1917, when the British decided to complete her as an aircraft carrier for the Royal Navy. She was therefore purchased from Chile, to be converted into the carrier HMS *Eagle*. She was the fourteenth ship to bear that name. Many of her forebears were awarded Battle Honours and this current ship continued that proud tradition being awarded Honours in the Mediterranean in 1940 when Norman was on board and again for the Malta convoys in 1942. It was on Operation *Pedestal,* probably the most signifcant of the many Malta convoys, that she was sunk. Her motto was 'Arduus ad solem' – 'Striving (or labouring) towards the sun'.

Initially her redesign was as a base for seaplane operations. After trials with other ships, however, the design was changed to a proper fleet carrier with a full flight deck and 'island'. She was launched on 8 June 1918 but delays meant that *Eagle* remained unfinished at the end of the First World War.

Progress was slowed again by industrial action following the end of the Great War, and was suspended altogether in October 1919 when Chile wanted to repurchase the ship and have it re-converted to a battleship. The Royal Navy, however, had a need to carry out trials with a through-deck carrier fitted with an island and construction to that end was resumed in November 1919. Sea trials and initial flying trials were carried out in February 1920. She was then sent to Devonport dockyard for completion, with her machinery being converted from part-coal burning to all oil burning, a much longer island being fitted and anti-torpedo bulges added. She was finally commissioned on 26 February 1924.

HMS *Eagle* was the first large through-deck aircraft carrier to join the Royal Navy. She was sent to serve in the Mediterranean Fleet from 1924 until 1931, when she was returned to the United Kingdom for a major refit, including being fitted with new boilers as well as arrester gear and improved anti-aircraft armament.

Pirates operating around Java are not a new phenomenon and following the refit, in 1933 *Eagle* was sent to the Far East, serving on the China Station throughout 1934, with her aircraft being deployed against against pirate ships and their bases before returning to the Mediterranean in 1935.

In September 1939, at the outbreak of the Second World War, *Eagle* was based at Singapore, where she had been since 1937, with an air Wing consisting of two squadrons (813 and 823 Naval Air Squadrons) equipped with a total of eighteen Fairey Swordfish Torpedo Bombers. Shortly thereafter she was transferred to the East Indies Squadron based at Colombo, Ceylon (now Sri Lanka) where she was principally engaged in mercantile escort duties. Her first offensive action of the war, in December 1939, was as part of the hunt for the *Admiral Graf Spee* and *Admiral Scheer*. In January 1940 shortly before Norman joined her she was nominated as escort to convoy US1, a convoy of 12 large ocean liners which were carrying ANZAC troops to Egypt. When Norman was drafted to her on 17 February 1940 she had just completed this task, having docked in Aden on 8 February. At this time she was still looking eastwards to her trade defence role in the Indian Ocean. However, after repairs following an accidental explosion on board killing 13, she joined the battleships *Malaya, Ramillies, Royal Sovereign* and *Warspite* in the eastern Mediterranean at Alexandria in May 1940. *Warspite* was the battleship that Roy Hussey may have saved off Sicily by shooting down the two guided bomb Dornier 217s menacing the East Mediterranean Fleet in 1943.

When Norman, aged 21, joined her in early 1940, the war was about to take a terrible downturn for Britain and her Allies. The year saw the fall of France, the withdrawal of the 300,000-strong British Expeditionary Force at Dunkirk, Italy enter the war and the desperately close-fought Battle of Britain. His journey was perhaps not as one might expect by sea but by by rail through France to the Mediterranean Sea, where he boarded a transport ship from the port of Marseilles. Norman describes these first few months of his call up and service:

NOVEMBER 1939

Call up papers for the Services, told to nominate which Service we wanted to go into, nominated the Navy but when I came before the Board I was asked to give my second choice, told them that there really wasn't one, also that I had built my own boat, did not tell them the name 'Iva Leak', also that I had done Sharpy racing on the Hamble, all in all it seemed to sway them so got into the Navy. Went for Medical in building opposite Colston Hall, Bristol, unable to supply urine sample so had to go out and have a pint!

Reported to HMS *Royal Arthur*, Skegness, Butlins old holiday camp. Took my 2-seater Morris 8 with me but not allowed to keep it in the establishment, so kept it in a farmer's barn. Battery not too good so always took a few other matelots with me to push start it. Very hard winter, slept in un-heated chalets, blankets ringing wet with condensation, some got pneumonia, lots of square bashing and naval training.

JANUARY 1940

Moved to Portsmouth, billeted in 'H' block, air raids, barracks pretty primitive. Took a portable wireless, which was popular with all, although reception not too good, too much metal around I think. Gunnery training at HMS *Excellent* (Whale Island) reckoned to be the toughest for discipline in the country. Very cold, rifle drill on parade ground, most of us dropped our rifles at one time or other due to hands being so cold. Made to run around the parade ground at the double.

FEBRUARY 1940

3rd   Taken to Portsmouth by Mum and Pop, had tea in hotel and then saw me aboard the *Amsterdam* to cross the Channel to the unknown...

5th   Arrived Cherbourg about 0800. Were given morning and part afternoon leave, walked around Cherbourg. Left by train about 2000hrs.

6th   Spent whole day travelling through France. Poor countryside. Travelled in 3rd class compartment, slept on luggage rack. Fun and frolic at stations and en route.

7th   Arrived at Marseilles about 0800 and boarded the S.S. *Andes,* a very large and modern ship. The only time it had sailed before, it was to bring Canadian troops across the Atlantic. Spent the day on the ship. Left Marseilles at 1730 and anchored outside in the Bay...

12th   Clocks advanced 30 mins. Reached Port Said 1000hrs, docked just outside the town. First thing sighted off Port Said was sailing boats. Small boats soon came around to sell things, a lot of bargaining. Boys diving for pennies. Afternoon leave, went into P.S. hired a taxi which showed us the sights. The surroundings of P.S. quite good but inside filthy and smelly. Bought large fountain pen for 1/6d, were pestered by small boys selling things. Were searched at the gate, not allowed to take my camera.

13th   Left Port Said 1500hrs. Sailed down the Suez Canal passing Australian troops on another ship.[very likely part of the convoy just escorted by HMS *Eagle*] Plenty of camels seen. Speed through Canal 5 knots. Very unfertile and deserty land each side. Peasants live in extremely small houses. Boy amused the ship on his bicycle. Were followed through the canal by Italian and other ships. Most of canal navigated by night by searchlights. Won 11/6 on Housie Housie.

14th   Left Suez canal in the morning. Town at the exit. About 16 ships anchored, ready to go through canal. Entered the Red Sea, able to see land each side, very rugged and high, sandy in colour. Wore sun helmets for the first time. Saw a shark. Clocks advanced 30 mins...

17th   Saturday arrived in Aden 0930. Sellers soon around the ship. No shore leave given. Aden scattered and dirty town surrounded by earthy cliffs. People chiefly black. In afternoon was drafted to HMS *Eagle* aircraft carrier, 100 of us altogether. Carries 18 Swordfish built end of last war. Bought 50 cigars Havanas 3/-.

In order to pick up the thread of the Stoate and Hussey boys and the progress of the war, it is as well to reconfirm that we are still in February 1940, Roy Hussey has not yet been accepted into the RAFVR and David is still at Elstree, the Battle of Britain is six months away and the expeditionary Force to France is still in position, with the withdrawal at Dunkirk four months distant.

Although Ordinary Seaman Norman Stoate would not have been aware of it, *Eagle* was in need of repairs and was shortly to be nominated to return to England for this purpose. Such was the shortage of aircraft carriers, however, this was to be cancelled as she was needed to escort US2, another troopship convoy. *Eagle* was was being used very hard indeed. Norman continues with the record of his first 'shakedown' voyage.

18th   Duck suits worn for first time. Sat about and explored ship. Set sail 1630. P.Vs [patrol vessels] put out, duty watch on 6" Starboard forward gun 1800-2000hrs and 0001-0400hrs.

20th   Indian Ocean. Usual routine which consists of watch keeping. Out brooms and squeegees i.e. washing down the decks, holy stoning the deck, on hands and knees rubbing a white brick like stone on the decks [*Eagle* had a timber deck]. Washing paintwork. Painting, rope splicing and knots, games on mess deck, sleeping. Noticed more flying fish, larger than the Red Sea fish. Star shells fired...

25th   Arrive Colombo about 0930. Shore leave in the afternoon. Went to the Lord Nelson (pub). Toured around in a taxi for an hour for 2 Rupees 50 cents. Ate and drank at the B.S.S.I.

26th   Provisioned ship. Took in flour from Runtons Mills, N.S.W. Other ships at Colombo, HMS *Ramillies, Kent, Hobart, Sussex* and *Lucia*.

Colombo not a very up-to-date town. Very tropical with a large number of good houses with large estates. People very keen on cricket. Tremendous number of rickshaws about. Some of the streets very wide and good. Harbour, situated in front of town, very full of boats and ships. Native living quarters very poor, dark room with a bamboo mat as a door. Their alcoholic drink is Toddy, fermented coconut milk.

27th   At Colombo. Afternoon and evening shore leave. Went to the Galle Face Hotel and had a good swim. Saw Mr Ridley, an Australian staying at the Bristol Hotel, about flour mills, he gave me an address. Changed £1 for 12 Rupees 95 cents...

29th   Shore leave. Went in a Rickshaw to the Realstorf Milling Co., very long way through poor streets, caused some amusement to the locals, I am sure, never seen a sailor out in those parts. Saw the Manager, who looked a bit surprised, and was shown over the premises. First was the flour mill about three years old. Wheat used there was nearly always 100% Australian with sometimes a little Karachi. Wheat is not washed or whizzed but is cleaned by sieves and indented reels. Wheat is damped and cold conditioned, it is then fed to four Maxima Midget Roller Mills where it is rolled and sieved until the resulting bran, weatings and flour is made. Also making stone milled wholemeal. One Nitrogen peroxide bleacher is used. As an experiment they put some flour in a 10 gallon drum and then blew in some Co^2 to kill any livestock and quickly sealed the drum up, resulting flour was reported to be better for baking. Main pest was weevil, no trouble with moth. Mill and warehouse had to be rat proof by law. Firm also make coconut oil, metal drums, soap, coconut cake and fibre, with a large repair shop.

Norman, like his brother David, will always be the miller.

March was to see *Eagle* detached from Force 1 in preparation for its escort duties with US2. She was to proceed to Trincomalee, pretty well diagonally across Ceylon from Colombo on its north east side and from thence to Singapore. It was on that passage that one of the 250lb bombs exploded on board with Norman recording fifteen deaths.

MARCH 1940

4th   Harbour routine. Called 0530, cleaned decks 0600-0700. Breakfast, fall-in 0900, odd jobs, stand easy 1030, 1045-1230 instruction or jobs, afternoon free, divisions 1600. Duty every 4th day, stand by duty every 4th day.

5th   Left Colombo 0730. Gun practice, our gun broke down after firing one round. Swordfish had torpedo practice, torpedoes picked up afterwards.

6th   Arrive Trincomalee 1030. A quiet naval base surrounded by dense forest with plenty of coconut and banana trees. Trinco. a very small village, shops all open. Naval canteen and billiard room.

7th   Harbour routine. Saw sharks swimming around ship at night…

12th   Left Trincomalee

Life seems quite tranquil but we are about to be reminded that war conditions exist and life is by no means without risk. Norman describes the events of 14 March when a bomb accidentally and fatally exploded with a defective fuse. After repairs caused by the explosion, in May 1940 *Eagle* will join the other battleships in the eastern Mediterranean at Alexandria.

14th   250lbs bomb exploded in the ship as ammunition was being hoisted on deck. 15 killed and about 13 injured. Swordfish caught fire and a certain amount of damage done to the ship. I was reading in the 'nets' at the time, quite near the explosion.

15th   Bodies sewn into weighted canvas bags. Funeral for the dead at sea as bodies were slid over stern. Swordfish crashed into Pom-poms on landing and went over the side, crew of three saved, aircraft lost. Good sunrises and sunsets.

16th   Arrived at Singapore. Anchored near dockyard. Singapore dollar 2/4d.

17th   Sunday. De-ammunition ship…

22nd   Friday treated as a Sunday, everybody knackered.

23rd   Evacuated from the ship for the day while the 13 dangerous bombs were being removed. Played soccer and slept. *Eagle* moored alongside the dock…

27th   Move into barracks about one mile from the *Eagle*. Start dropping anchor into dry dock. *Eagle* went into floating dock. Barracks very modern, in fact not yet finished. Very airy rooms with fans in ceiling. 62 beds in a long dormitory, beds fitted with mosquito nets. Outlook over river and dense jungle. Swimming pool. Went to dock on buses every morning.

The bomb damage caused *Eagle* to miss her rendezvous with US2 and April saw her in dock having a partial refit – including the provision of a homing device so that her returning aircraft could find her more easily. Norman seemed to be doing a fair amount of painting.

APRIL 1940
1st 2nd 3rd 4th 5th

        Painting or wash paint on *Eagle*. Films shown in barracks. Union Pacific, Alexander's Ragtime Band, High Flyers, Pygmalion, Only Angels have Wings.

6th   Weekend leave from 1300 hrs, poured with rain to begin with but cleared up later. Went to Singapore about 15 miles away. Interesting journey through rubber estates, coconut groves and banana trees with bananas on them. Passed a few villages which consisted of a few wooden huts and shops thatched with coconut palms.

7th   Went for a walk round the station and golf club in the morning. Union Jack club in afternoon. Swam in the evening at Fort Canning. Union Jack Club 30 cents for a bed, 20 cents for a lie down. Singapore itself consists chiefly of native quarters and coloured houses. Quite a good sea front round the harbour which was full of sampans. Saw the 'Marx Bros at the Circus' at the Capital.

A Fairy Swordfish crashes on *Eagle*'s deck. (Norman Stoate)

8th   Painting and swimming.

9th   War declared on Norway, Denmark overrun [In 1945 Norman would be part of
           British forces sent forward to Lubec to secure Denmark from the Russian advance
           across north west Europe]…

19th   Painted Viscount Manderville's cabin with enamel paint, made a bit of a mess of it,
           running like mad, curtains everywhere. [Manderville was amongst those killed when
           Eagle was sunk by torpedo in August 1942]

20th   Weekend leave. Hired a taxi with O/S Morley and went looking for a boat to hire.
           Hired a sampan plus one crew for 6 cents and sailed and paddled around the islands,
           landed on one, children scattered like rabbits. Saw rubber running from trees, pineap-
           ples growing, and tremendous parade of ants going along the ground to the top of a
           tree.

21st   Picked a coconut and had quite a job to get the outer shell off, drank the milk,
           persuaded small boy to climb tree. Went back to U.J.C. Played billiards and saw 'The
           Invisible Man Returns.'…

25th   Painting. New draft arrives from England, amongst them was Peter Rowland from
           Bristol. [whom Norman knew]

26th   Painting, finished cabin.

27 April – 2 May
           Painting mess deck.

28th   Prepare to leave Fleet Shore accommodation to go back to *Eagle*.

In Europe the German forces were shortly to overwhelm the British Expeditionary Forces,
The Allied Armies were retreating to Dunkirk and the modest RAF involvement insisted on
by Churchill and greatly resented by Dowding, who was correctly wanting to keep the greatest
number of aeroplanes and pilots available for defence of home shores, was in trouble. Meanwhile
Eagle was about to leave Singapore. She was headed for the eastern Mediterranean to replace
Glorious who had been recalled to home waters after the German invasion of Norway.
    We begin to see Norman's taste for smaller craft in the shape of the pinnace and jolly boat.
The jolly boat was a general purpose ship's boat. Commonly employed for bringing fresh meat
aboard larger ships, it was popularly called a 'blood boat'. Historically, jolly boats could be sailed
using either a lug or spritsail, and could also be pulled with oars. Norman's however had a
petrol engine and screw.

MAY 1940
4th   Return to live on *Eagle*, provision ship.

6th–7th
           Ammunition ship, from 0600-1845.

8th   Joined 1st Pinnace's crew. Out and back all day until 0030 hours. Brought 2nd Punjab
           Regiment from shore to play the Retreat on the flight deck.

9th   Prepared for sea. Left Singapore 1400 hours.

10th At sea, worked on Pinnace. Sea pretty rough, strong wind at night.

11th About 0115 hrs ship sighted fairly close (2000 yds) Alarm signal was given, all guns loaded and directed on ship, turned out to be British Merchant ship painted grey. Strong sea and wind.

12th – 13th
 At sea. Action Stations, collision and abandon ship practice. Rough weather.

14th Arrived Columbo in morning. A good collection of Danish and Dutch merchantmen in harbour. One sloop (a troopship). Harbour very choppy, weather strong. Left Pinnace's crew to become coxwain of the jolly boat (Starboard watch).

15th Driving jolly boat all day, to other ships and ashore…

17th Left Colombo for Aden.

18th At sea. Fairly rough and windy. Alarm signals sounded at night. Loaded guns ready for action. Planes were ready for take off. After some time ship turned out to be friendly…

22nd Arrived at Aden about 0700 hrs. Harbour fairly choppy. Jolly boat lowered, took officers to *Gloucester* and a sloop just outside barrier, and *Prince of Wales* steps, fairly difficult to get alongside. Left Aden 1630 along with *Gloucester* and *Sydney*.

23rd At sea. Joined the Mediterranean Fleet

East Mediterranean Fleet consisted of:

<u>Battleships</u>
Warspite, Royal Sovereign, Malaya, Ramillies (Refitting).

<u>Aircraft Carriers</u>
Eagle

<u>Cruisers</u>
Calypso (torpedoed 12/6/40) *Sydney, Orion, Gloucester, Neptune, Liverpool, Stuart, Caledon, Capetown.*

<u>Destroyers</u>
Hostile, Hyoperon, Hasty, Nubian, Mohawk, Hereward, Decoy, Dainty, Ilex, Havock

<u>Submarine Depot Ship</u>
Medway

Submarines
Minesweepers

In a handwritten later note Norman records that *Neptune* struck four mines, there was only one survivor; and *Gloucester* was hit by bombs off Crete – few survivors.

It will be seen that in May 1940 the Eastern Mediterranean Fleet had only HMS *Eagle*, a relatively small and old aircraft carrier to provide air cover in contrast to the Axis forces, who had airfields in Sicily, Italy and later Rhodes. We will see later, again and again, particularly in Sicily and Italy, the strategic importance of denying Axis forces the use of these airfields and taking them when possible.

In August 1940 *Eagle* was joined by the more modern carrier *Illustrious*, with a displacement of 28,000 tons and a 52-aircraft capability, as opposed to *Eagle's* 18. *Illustrious* was lead ship of the Illustrious class and sister ship to the *Indomitable* who, as we saw with David Stoate was unable to make her rendezvous with Force Z when the Japanese made their attack on Thailand and Malaya in December 1941.

27th   *Eagle* sailed 0330, duty Port Watch, two destroyers with us. Rig of the day change from Tropical rig to Duck suits. Arrived at Alexandria in evening, waited outside for a time while two other ships came out. Moored to a buoy.

28th   Harbour routine. Jolly boat lowered – 24 hrs off. Other ships in harbour, *Royal Sovereign, Gloucester, Sidney, Orion, Neptune, Leander, Medway, Malaya,* French battleship *Lorraine, Warspite, Liverpool* besides 3–4 flotillas of destroyers and submarines. Sunderland bombers and Imperial Air Liners taking off from harbour, all the time.

29th   Jolly boat broke down, engine boiled up, just reached Ras el Tin pier, towed back to *Eagle* by one of *Malaya's* boats.

30th   Jolly boat engine de-coked. Tried her out in the evening but she failed half way to shore by only firing on two cylinders, got a tow back by our pinnace after waiting for 1½ hrs. We then worked on it until 0200 hrs, porpoises in harbour.

31st   Still the same trouble. Jolly boat hoisted and reconditioned engine put in. Tried to start her in evening but timing was wrong.

The withdrawal of the BEF from France at Dunkirk had begun on 24 May. Once Italy thought she could see the way the wind was blowing, in June she threw her lot in with Germany and declared war on Britain. Norman Stoate was about to see some action. Meanwhile, life for an Ordinary Seaman remained relatively domestic, although we have a timely reminder that not everyone can cope with the noise of war. The fleet loses one of its cruisers, *Calypso*, to an Italian submarine with the loss of 38 lives. Norman gets a dressing down for disturbing the fleet's radar screen when back in Alexandria.

JUNE 1940
3rd   Put to sea for a shoot. Each gun in Port battery 6ins guns, fired 24 rounds, we fired (starboard) 12 rounds. After first round one of gun's crew missing. I was told to go and find him. Found him white and shivering and in quite a state, was terrified of the noise and flash of the gun. Poor boy was drafted off the ship. Most were sympathetic, of course some took the micky. Arrived back in the evening.

4th   Put to sea again for A.A. [anti-aircraft] shooting, back in evening.

5th   Jolly boat still not working properly, distributor trouble and clutch. Danish boat enters harbour with a bad list to port due to her cargo of timber slipping. Bathing over side.

6th   Worked on jolly boat.

7th   Harbour routine, Divisions every day, National anthem of all ships in harbour played at divisions, all standing smartly to attention, sometimes as many as 5-6 anthems.

8th   Jolly boat repaired by the evening. Very busy evening and night. Ran into Prohibited area over chains, engine stopped but was alright, area was Sunderland bombers' moorings.

9th   Sunday routine. Church service always held on flight deck.

10th   Did a few trips in jolly boat, harbour fairly rough. *Eagle* set out for a night shoot but we heard that Italy had entered the war so returned to harbour immediately.

Norman makes an explanatory note in his records and then goes on to describe the first clash between the British and Italian fleets at Calabria, which took place on 9 July four weeks after Italy allied itself with Germany.

France and neighbouring countries had been overrun by the Germans which left North Africa, Middle East and the Suez Canal open as easy prey. Our army in Egypt was negligible, we relied on the French for this, and equipment was out of date. So it was up to the Med. Fleet under the command of Andrew Cunningham to keep the seas open, against all odds. The Italian navy in the Med was far superior both in numbers and speed and had vast aircraft support near at hand. ABC's immediate plan was to seek out and attack, which we did, starting with the battle of 'Calabria' 9 July, followed by action off Cape Spada 19 July, when the *Sydney* stopped the cruiser *Bartolomeo Colleoni* which was then finished off with torpedoes by *Ilex*. The main destruction of Italian ships was the raid on Taranto where three Italian battleships were put out of commission – one permanently. Both *Illustrious* and *Eagle* were to take part but owing to bomb damage by near misses on the *Eagle* she was not fit enough so some of her planes landed on *Illustrious* and carried out the raid from there. Great damage was done.

11th   Set sail with most of the fleet at 0300 hrs. Remained on look out all day, first degree of readiness at night.

12th   Action Stations sounded 0315, thought shot or explosion was heard, false alarm, no action, remained closed up on guns all day and night.

13th   At sea with the fleet consisting of *Warspite*, *Malaya*, and about 14 destroyers. About 20 miles ahead was another force of cruisers and destroyers, our Swordfish up and down all day doing reconnaissance. We swept east and central Med to N Italy to seek out the enemy, nothing sighted.

14th   At sea. Closed up all day and night in shifts. Lost the cruiser *Calypso* torpedoed S.W. Crete 0200 hrs one officer 38 ratings dead.

15th   Arrived back at Alex. Destroyers leading the way with F.Vs out followed by battle-ships, cruisers and ourselves all in a line. One submarine attacked by destroyer and Sunderland flying boat. Mines had been laid.

16th   In harbour. Air raid siren went. Instruction for all boats to leave *Eagle* with all possible haste on hearing siren. Left at full speed with jolly boat to Water Port. Sir Andrew Cunningham sent his Flag Officer for me. Brought before the Commander, off caps and charged with upsetting the whole radar of Alexandria by the roar of my engine, informed their lordships that I was only carrying out instructions, did not hear any more.

17th   In harbour, went ashore, bought photos and watchstrap. Went to the flicks and round native quarter, very narrow, smelly and dirty streets.

18th   Duty in jolly boat, took shelter on *Orion* during air raid alarm. Three alarms today…

22nd   Went to sea in the evening, 4 gladiator fighters landed on flight deck, two action alarms during the night…

25th   Harbour routine. French give in, French flags at half-mast. Painted J.B. [jolly boat]

26th   J.B. lowered, D.S.B. duty i.e. taking mail and signals round to all ships. drew alongside ships' gangway and duty seaman would take the bag.

27th   About 6 cruisers left harbour. Swimming test in harbour – passed.

28th   Harbour routine. In jolly boat.

29th   Put to sea about 2400 hrs, 2 battleships and a flotilla of destroyers with us.

Norman describes *Eagle*'s and his part in the neutralisation of the French Fleet at Alexandria. The sinking of another part of the French Fleet based in Algeria in 1940 had perhaps one unforeseen effect. The Americans, who were not to enter the war for 18 months and who, in 1940, expected Britain to crumble beneath the German might, now saw the determination with which Britain was prepared to fight and were more forthcoming in providing aid. This included the loan of *Wasp*, an aircraft carrier which, after America had entered the war, would play a key role in the defence of Malta and in Operation *Pedestal*.

Norman's record continues with July 1940, where the action hots up considerably. *Eagle* narrowly escapes being hit by sustained but unsuccessful bombing attacks by Italian aircraft:

JULY 1940
1st   At sea

2nd   Return to harbour in forenoon.

3rd   In harbour. Trouble with French ships over making them unfit for going to sea. 3 French cruisers give in. Battleship *Lorraine* however would not let anybody go on board or take her oil off. Armed landing party left ship to stand by. Closed up at action stations, was sent aft to Marines six inch gun which was trained on *Lorraine* who was said to have machine guns at gangway.

4th   Air raid by five Italian bombers. Bombs dropped in harbour, one on the coal dump. At Action Stations all day. French fleet give in at Alexandria in the evening.

5th   Painted the 'Island'

6th   Ditto

7th   Put to sea with the *Malaya* and flotilla of destroyers. Large Italian fleet at sea.

HMS *Eagle* in action – some near misses. (Norman Stoate)

8th   Three severe bombing attacks all concentrated on *Eagle*. First attack 5 bombers, 2nd
            9 bombers, 3rd 5 bombers. Bombs dropped very near ship, was closed up at S2 gun.
            Bombers came over in set formation, bombs coming down in straight line often
            chained together. Bombing action took place off Crete. The bridge of the *Gloucester*
            was hit, Captain Carside killed and about 17 injured.

With hindsight it seems strange that given the general understanding of the importance of
air superiority and given that our fleet in the eastern Mediterranean was virtually solely
reliant upon the 18 'Stringbag' Swordfish torpedo bombers of HMS *Eagle* and the 50 or so
of *Illustrious*, that the Italans did not make much greater use of their landbased air force. As
Norman describes however, unlike the divebombers favoured by the Germans, Italian bombers
operated in formations at high altitudes during the first stages of the war. Usually dropping
their bombs together at about 12,000 feet.

At Calabria, the Italians carried out the ultimate test of the claims of pre-war air-power
theorists concerning massed bombers being able to sink modern warships. Fast-moving ships,
however, proved to be a far more difficult target than anticipated. Captains waited until the
bombers released their sticks of bombs and in the remaining moments took evasive action.
While hundreds of bombs were dropped by the Italians, on 8 July, the single hit on the *Gloucester*
represented the outcome of the air attacks. Notwithstanding *Gloucester's* Captain being killed
she remained at sea and was back in action on the following day to take part in the first fleet
against fleet sea battle of the war, the battle of Calabria. Ultimately, she wold be lost.

The Italians were escorting a merchant fleet to Bengazi in Lybia and the British were similarly escorting a merchant fleet from Alexandria to Malta. The two fleets converged at Calabria,
about 65 miles from the Punta Stilo, the toe of Italy, on 9 July 1940. On paper the Italian Fleet
outclassed the British, particularly with regard to air cover. They launched 126 aircraft into
battle and inflicted damage on *Eagle, Warspite* and *Malaya*. The British had the limited cover of
Eagle's 18 Swordfish, one of which severely damaged the Italian destroyer *Leone Pancaldo*. The
Italian cruiser *Bolzano* was hit three times and the battleship *Guilio Cesare* was damaged. The
battle should have been a decisive victory for the Italians but history has called it a draw, with
the propaganda battle going to the Allies.

Norman describes the action:

9th   Major battle of Calabria took place against the Italian Fleet which consisted of 2
            battleships, 10 cruisers and about 19 destroyers. Ours 3 battleships, 9 cruisers, 15
            destroyers and *Eagle*. No damage to our force. *Eagle* flew off Swordfish to attack
            Italians with torpedoes, the first time in history that an aircraft carrier had cooper-
            ated with the fleet in action. Swordfish scored a hit on a cruiser, *Warspite* hit a Cesare
            battleship at 15-mile range (a naval record that still stands) 1 submarine and destroyer
            also sunk, enemy scattered behind smoke screen and ran for home. Action lasted
            about 3 hours.

10th   At sea. 9 Swords took off to torpedo Augusta, nothing worth torpedoing so returned
            5 with torpedoes. their reports suggest the Italian destroyer *Leone Pancallo* was sunk
            on this mission [later to be salvaged and returned to service, only to be sunk again].

11th   From 1100 hrs we were subjected to severe bombing attacks. Bombers in waves of
            5 appearing every half hour to an hour. All bombs dropped very near to ship, one
            tremendous explosion in front of our bows causing shrapnel to fall on the decks.
            Both our fighters (Gladiators) went up. Cmdr Keighley-Peach got shot in the leg but
            2 planes brought down, from one of them five parachutists jumped, saw four land in
            the sea, 2 reported picked up by one of our destroyers. Was closed up at S.2 gun, gas
            mask worn some of the time.

12th   At sea off Libyan coast. Air raid in the morning. One 1000lb bomb dropped just in front of our bows sending a terrific spray of water over the ship. Our fighter got one bomber down.

13th   At sea. More severe bombing attacks, no damage done, fighter got two bombers down. Our firing was so intense that we ran out of ack ack ammunition, believe some other ships did as well.

14th   Entered harbour. Busy day with jolly boat. Convoy from Malta arrived.

15th   In harbour. Ammunition ship etc. All ships had a list on so that their bottoms could be scraped. Convoy arrived from Suez.

16th   Duty jolly boat. Air raid alarm at 2330. Took J.B. to breakwater, could hear bombs whistling very close and see them explode. Tremendous flashes when AA guns opened up. Two planes in the raid, about 20 bombs dropped…

19th   Stages lowered over the side to paint ship but told we were off to sea after some cruisers. In stages, sailed at 1200 hrs. One Italian cruiser sunk by HMS *Sydney* Capt. Collins, cruiser was the *Bartolemeo Colleonie*, others got away. Our Swordfish attacked Tobruk harbour, 3 ships sunk.

20th   Back in harbour. Three destroyers and HMS *Sydney* came in about mid-day, all hands cleared lower deck to cheer her…

5th   Air raid, one small ship near us was hit and set on fire, was later towed away afloat.

26th   In harbour.

27th   Put to sea 0200 hrs, were bombed later in the day, no damage done. HMS *Sydney* seemed to be the target.

28th   At sea, one air raid, very few bombs dropped.

29th   At sea. Convoy which we were escorting repeatedly bombed, no damage done. One of *Eagle*'s fighters brought down a bomber but later it had to make a forced landing in the sea, pilot picked up.

30th   Arrived back in harbour 0530, fuelled etc.

31st   Put to sea again in afternoon. Practice 6″ gun shoot at night with the *Malaya* and *Royal Sovereign*, also used star shells and tracers.

Back in the UK the Battle of Britain was in full swing and Norman's eldest brother Tom, then stationed at Filton, Bristol, was to experience a full-on German bomber raid three weeks later. On 30 August 1940 *Illustrious* joined the East Mediterranean Fleet to support *Eagle*. But Norman was looking for something more.

AUGUST 1940

1st   Back in harbour. Put in request for a commission…

7th   Started dazzle painting or camouflaging the ship.

8th	Continued painting.
9th	Put to sea in evening for night flying tests…
13th	HMS *Kent* enters harbour. Air raid at night. A few bombs and mines dropped, Italian planes fly low. Lay off in jolly boat, look for mines after the raid, 0100 hrs.
14th	In harbour.
15th	Fleet put to sea for bombarding. [In a later note Norman writes 'Swordfish from *Eagle* attacked and sank 4 ships with 3 torpedoes.']
16th	Fleet bombard African ports…
21st	All ships start flying kites with special wire attached against low flying aircraft. [A similar defensive device to the Holman projectiles as described in the next chapter.]
22nd	In harbour.
23rd	Air raid, 3 aircraft caught in searchlight. Fleet opened fire but planes disappeared behind a cloud.
24th	In harbour. Heard that HMS *Hostile* H55 [a destroyer that ran into a minefield] had been sunk.
25th	Air raid. Lt. Young crashed in gladiator and was killed.
26th	In harbour.
27th	Air raid at night, 2 killed 5 injured. J.B. hoisted.
28th	Put to sea about 0800 hrs, returned 1500 hrs. Practice flying on and off. Very few spots of rain fall.
29th	In harbour.
30th	Cmdr. Keighley-Peach awarded D.S.C., brought down an Italian seaplane bomber.

That month the Mediteranean Fleet was split into two. Admiral Cunningham's Eastern Mediterranean Fleet was reinforced by the newly commissioned carrier *Illustrious*, the modernised battleship *Valiant* and the *Coventry* and *Calcutta*, both anti-aircraft cruisers. It was also soon to be expanded by cruisers *Liverpool, Kent* and *Gloucester* and much needed supplies including AA guns, Bofors ammunition and Bren guns as well as predictors and height finders to support the existing amament.

Britain was determined to ensure the survival of Malta as a base and therefore strengthened the naval protection for the merchant supply fleets. In addition to supplying Malta, a number of Italian targets were to be attacked, amongst them Cagliari and Rhodes.

On 1 September 1940 Cunningham left Alexandria with the battleships *Warspite* and *Malaya*, carrier *Eagle*, the cruisers *Sydney* and *Orion* and nine destroyers. Norman notes for September 1940:

| 1st | At sea with most of the fleet except *Ramillies*. |

2nd   Were joined off Malta by the *Illustrious*, battleships and 2 A.A. ships *Coventry* and *Calcutta*. 3 of *Illustrious*' Fulmar low winged monoplanes landed on *Eagle* in the evening. Turned back with the *Malaya*, *Coventry*, cruisers and destroyers. One dive bomber attack, one bomb falling near S2 gun [Norman's station]. Earlier in the day action stations false alarm, flock of birds flying in formation.

3rd   No air raids, off Crete in the evening. Fulmar planes took off.

4th   About 0300 hrs 13 of our Swordfish took off to bomb aerodrome at Rhodes, quite a bit of damage done. *Illustrious* also bombed airfield the other side of Rhodes. Returned to harbour in evening. [Other reports indicate that the take off was delayed owing to air attacks on the 4th and that *Eagle* lost four of her aircraft on the raid.]

5th   Entered dry dock to have bottom scraped and painted to try and get a bit more speed out of the old girl. [*Eagle* also needed a dry dock inspection to see what damage she might have sustained from the recent near miss.]

6th   In dock. Slept in jolly boat because dock was being flooded, grounded on some rocks.

7th   Left dock in morning.

8th   Air raid at night. Lay off in J.B. saw 3 Italian bombers in searchlights, big A.A. barrage by fleet no aircraft brought down.

9th   In harbour.

10th   Air raid alarm at night. Left *Eagle* in J.B. as usual, had to report to Admiral Cunningham on quarter deck of *Warspite* for running engine in an air raid, said those were my instructions and had been doing it for months, no action taken.

11th–17th
       In harbour.

18th   HMS *Kent* torpedoed in the stern.

19th   *Kent* towed into harbour, put in floating dock…

27th   HMS *York* joins the fleet.

29th   HMS *Ajax* joins the fleet.

30th   Italian submarine sunk a few miles from harbour. HMAS *Stuart* brought back some survivors.

Earlier in the year Germany had successfully invaded Albania, but had neglected to inform Mussolini beforehand. Not to be upstaged Il Duce ordered the Italian invasion of Greece on 28 October 1940, the Italian army invading from Albania. The Greeks, dragged into the war, defeated the invaders, pushing Mussolini's forces back into Albania. The Germans were bounced into sending their own forces to support their allies and took Greece in April 1941. Crete, however, did not fall until after 20 May 1941. This diversion delayed the German invasion of the Soviet Union by six weeks. The delay proved disastrous to the German cause, with

HMS *Liverpool* hit in the stern. (Norman Stoate)

the onset of the Russian winter and the strong resistance of the Soviet armed forces halting it before the gates of Moscow. The Germans by this time realised that the fighting capability and spirit of their ally was not of the highest calibre and sent in the Luftwaffe in greater strength to pound Malta, amongst other targets.

Norman witnesses the sinking of the Italian destroyer *Artiglieri* by HMS *York*, having been previously damaged by HMS *Ajax* and the results of HMS *Liverpool* being torpedoed and seriously damaged. He takes part in Operation *Barbarity*, the setting up of a forward position at Suda Bay, Crete.

OCTOBER 1940

7th   In harbour. Passed out in torpedoes exam.

8th   Put to sea. Fired 10 rounds on all guns was No. 5 on SI 6″ gun. Carried on West with the rest of the fleet. [The fleet was escorting Convoy MF3 during its passage to Malta. Code named MB6.]

9th   At sea. Quiet day.

10th   2 torpedoes fired at us by submarine, both missed.

11th   2 subs almost certainly sunk by planes and destroyers. Very heavy rain, visibility poor. Lie off Malta all day. HMS *Imperial* hit by mine but proceeded to Malta harbour under own steam. Convoy also enters harbour.

Sinking of the Italian ship *Artiglieri*
attacking Convoy MF3 supplying Malta.
(Norman Stoate)

HMS *Eagle* in Suda Bay, Crete. Note the camouflage paint. (Norman Stoate)

12th   HMS *Ajax* sinks 2 MTBs, one gets away. Engages a destroyer but gets a hole in the bows, 13 killed, 22 injured. The damaged destroyer *Artiglieri* later found abandoned and was blown up by HMS *York*, one mass of smoke hovered in the air. 3 floating mines seen, 2 bombing raids on the fleet, one bomber brought down by our fighter.

13th   Turn back to Alex: Weather windy and very rainy. Couple of bombings and many subs around. *Illustrious'* planes bomb Leros [Greece], 15 planes take part. Action stations, calcium flares fired.

14th   Off Crete in the morning, lots of depth charging, very wet. *Liverpool* badly hit by torpedo taken in tow.

15th   In harbour, paint jolly boat.

17th   HMS *Liverpool* towed into harbour, whole of forecastle blown off, was towed in stern first.

18th   Air raid, saw three planes in searchlight, one was firing tracers at our fighter, terrific barrage put up but no plane brought down.

19th   Air raid, no damage done.

20th   Put to sea for night flying and landing practice…

27th   8 of our bombers made an attack, scoring hits on barracks, munition dumps etc. Good day.

28th   Return to harbour in afternoon, fuel and leave again at night. Greece and Italy are at war with each other from 0600 hrs.

29th   Shadow convoy to Suda Bay, Crete, whole fleet is at sea except *Ajax*, *Kent* and *Liverpool*. [This refers to Operation *Barbarity*.]

30th   Proceed on way to Greece, no sight of planes or enemy craft.

31st   Off West coast of Greece. Greek destroyer carries out bombardment of [German-occupied] South Albania.

Following the near misses sustained in the previous two months, significant damage to *Eagle's* plating was revealed resulting in contamination of her aviation fuel system. November 1940 sees her nominated for a refit, but looking at Norman's diary it seems to have been more of a ten-day paint job, from the 5th to 15 November. In any event she puts to sea on the 16th and sees plenty of action between Suda Bay (Crete) and Alexandria, providing cover to the Malta relief convoy MB9, which in turn was part of Operation *Collar*. On the return trip to Alexandria whilst escorting Convoy MF4 she detaches herself on 26 November to launch an air attack on the Axis-controlled harbour at Tripoli, in Lybia.

Also during November 1940, Admiral Cunningham launched a daring attack against the Italian fleet at Taranto with the battleship *Barham,* two cruisers (HMS *Berwick* and *Glasgow*), two destroyers and aircraft based on the carrier HMS *Illustrious*. *Eagle* was unable to take a full part in the attack owing to damage, however some of her aircraft flew from *Illustrious,* which became the first carrier in history to launch a major strike against an enemy fleet; an act to be repeated 13 months later by Japan at Pearl Harbor. Twenty-one aircraft from numbers 813, 815, 819, and 824 Squadrons based on *Illustrious* attacked the Italian fleet at night. The Italians were caught off guard; this action decisively altered the balance of naval power in the Mediterranean. One battleship was sunk and two were heavily damaged. Half of the Italian battle fleet was disabled for six months.

NOVEMBER 1940

1st   Returning to Alex. After hanging around most of the day off Greece. Still hoping to meet some of the Italian fleet, however we did not even see a plane. Sea and weather very rough for last few days.

2nd   Pass Crete in early morning, air raid alarm but no bombs dropped. Torpedo attack on us by 4 planes, in afternoon. Saw two torpedoes dropped at I should say about 3 miles away – missed. Closed up at action stations again at night, planes hovering about.

3rd   Return to Alex in morning.

4th   In harbour, paint ship side…

11th   Fleet air arm torpedo ships in Taranto harbour. Badly damaged 2 battleships, 2 cruisers, 2 auxiliary craft and battleship damaged. 5 Swordfish from *Eagle* took part flying off *Illustrious*. Fleet intercepted convoy, sunk 3 ships.

12th   Joined diving party, removed asdic dome from ship, also freed a wire from the ship's screw.

13th   Harbour. Air raid at night.

14th   HMS *Glasgow* joins the fleet, enters harbour in the morning. HMS *Berwick* enters
            in evening. Rest of fleet return. HMS *Decoy* hit by bomb on the stern in Alex. 6
            reported killed.

15th   HMS *Barham* joins fleet. Jolly boat lowered. Air raids all this week.

16th   Put to sea at 0300 hrs with *Valiant, Barham* and destroyers, go through Kaso Straits
            [off Greece] action stations all night.

17th   At sea. Enter Suda Bay, jolly boat lowered and I take the Captain [Capt. Bridge]
            through the submarine defences in the harbour to landing steps, and wait for the
            return trip. Ship sails in afternoon...

22nd   Rated Able Seaman. Saw Lt-Cmdr Attfield, Lt. Thorpe and Capt. Bridge re commission.

23rd   Put to sea about 0200 hrs with *Malaya* and *Ramillies* etc.

24th   At sea. Arrive in Suda Bay, Crete about 100 hrs. Destroyers refuel, leave in afternoon.

25th   At sea shadowing convoy. Action stations all night, HMS *Newcastle* joins us off Malta.

26th   Our Swordfish carry out bombing attack on Tripoli, hit ships, quay and warehouses.
            Berwick, Newcastle, Ramillies leave us for Western Med. Hang around Malta till dark.
            Ark Royal raids Sardinia. *Illustrious* raids Dodecanese [The Greek Island group that
            includes Kos and Rhodes] and Leros.

27th   Hear that Western Med fleet have met up with Italian ships. *Ark Royal* sends off
            striking force of torpedo aircraft, hit battleship and destroyer, another cruiser set on
            fire by ships gunfire others believed damaged. *Berwick* receives two hits, 6 ratings one
            officer killed.

28th   Return to Alex. No air raids this trip.

29th   Return to harbour about 1000 hrs.

30th   HMS *Manchester* and *Southampton* enter Alex, rest of fleet return in evening.

At the end of November and during December 1940 *Eagle* required work to defective stern
glands. Her squadrons, 812 and 824, were disembarked for operations based ashore (as had happened on quite a few occasions over that past few months). *Eagle* was nominated for future
deployment for ocean interception and trade defence duties when available for release, which
effectively meant when she was replaced by HMS *Formidable*.

So ends 1940, Norman's first year of service. His brother David had joined the Honourable
Artillery Company in December 1939 and was about to embark to India to train for his
commission. His eldest brother Tom, an RAF doctor, had left his station at Filton and was
on his way to South Africa. Unknown to them in 1941, fate was about to put three of the
five Stoate brothers in close proximity in the Indian Ocean off East Africa. Roy Hussey
started his flying training in America, which was to lead to his being posted to North Africa
after Montgomery's Eighth Army had broken out of El Alamein. This was the beginning
of the chase that by May 1943 would see the driving of the Axis forces from North Africa.

Norman's notes for December are sparse: '1st, Sunday divisions. RAA inspection.' But there is another later note where he explains that *Eagle* did not undertake further trips to Malta whilst he was serving on her as the Germans had brought up Stuka dive bombers and *Eagle's* deck was not armoured.

In December Japan started the invasion that ended in the fall of Singapore. Tobruk was under siege from April until November 1941 and Crete fell to the Germans on 20 May. The latter was not without sacrifice by German paratroops who lost 7500 of their number (not least because they became separated from their equipment in the drop). This was to be the last time Hitler deployed these troops in this way, quite possibly saving Malta, Cyprus and perhaps even Gibraltar from airborne assault. Later, in 1944, Norman was to record observing the airborne troops heading for Arnhem, another example of airborne troops suffering badly. But not before the Allies lost large numbers of airborne troops in attacking and taking Sicily. On 22 June Hitler commenced his delayed invasion of Russia – Operation *Barbarossa*.

Eagle puts to sea again but her proposed operations with Force H to Malta are cancelled as the fleet loses much of its cover when *Illustrious* is badly damaged. *Eagle* is diverted to Alexandria where she picks up RAF personnel who are disembarked at Suda Bay, Crete, en route for Malta. Even her proposed operation to bomb Rhodes on her return journey to Alexandria is frustrated by exceptionally bad weather.

Early 1941 also sees Norman's service with *Eagle* in the Eastern Mediterranean drawing to a close.

JANUARY 1941

6th   *Eagle* put to sea for daylight deck landings. One sea Gladiator crashed on deck, pilot unhurt.

11th   Sailed again with *Barham* and destroyer for Suda Bay. Stuka dive bombers attacked and hit *Illustrious*, serious damage. Took on board two Blackburn Skua dive bombers – no good.

13th   Sailed from Suda Bay, Crete, to carry out air raids against Rhodes, full gale blowing, operation cancelled along with later planned raids on Benghazi. One of the roughest nights since *Eagle* joined the Med fleet.

16th   Arrived Alexandria 0200, had to hang around outside owing to suspected mines. Entered harbour 0730.

23rd   Left HMS *Eagle* for shore accommodation HMS *Canopus*.

30th   Left Alexandria for Port Said.

31st   Under canvas at Port Said.

Norman was headed back to England to train for his commission. But his early service in the obsolete and slow HMS *Eagle* valiantly supporting the island fortress of Malta and harrassing the Axis supply lines to North Africa suggests we should pause to look briefly at the remainder of *Eagle's* life and ultimate demise.

As Norman left her in February 1941 the first Fulmar aircraft embarked and four Swordfish were transferred to shore. On the 19th a first (unsuccessful) attempt was made at a deck landing of a Brewster Buffalo aircraft. *Eagle* was attacked while joining convoy MC8 but repelled attacks with her own aircraft. During the following month there were three successful Brewster Buffalo landings. *Eagle* was transferred to Port Sudan to counter an Italian threat in the Red

February 1941. *Agnio Georgios* after hitting a mine in the Suez Canal. (Norman Stoate)

Sea – Operation *Atmosphere.* April was a good month for *Eagle,* launching three successful attacks on six Italian destroyers which were either sunk directly or scuttled after being seriously damaged. On the 8th, HMS *Formidable* arrived and *Eagle* was released from Mediterranean service and embarked for Aden, then to Mombassa. On 13 April Cunningham sent a message to *Eagle* as she sailed through the Suez Canal.

> I very much regret not having the opportunity to come aboard and saying goodbye to you all. We are very sad to see *Eagle* leaving the Med fleet where at the outset of the Italian war she bore the brunt of the enemy air raids on the fleet and replied with such good effect. The best wishes of the whole fleet go with her and we all know that wherever she is stationed her work will be of the same high standard that we have come to expect from her. My grateful thanks for all your good work go with you.

In May *Eagle's* intended nomination for service with the Indian Ocean Hunting Group was cancelled and she was nominated instead for service at Gibraltar.

Having diverted to chase a German commerce raider *Pinguin* in the Indian Ocean, *Eagle* docked at Durban and then on to Cape Town. She then unsuccessfully chased German commerce raider *Atlantis* in the South Atlantic. The following month she pursued a German supply ship supporting *Bismarck.* For this task she was controlled directly by the Admiralty relying on decryption of German Enigma signals. In July, based on St Helena, she was on South Atlantic patrols. *Eagle* returned to Freetown in August for rest and recuperation and a boiler clean. The Commander-in-Chief South Atlantic requested that she remain in the South Atlantic notwithstanding the Admiralty requirement for her to return to the UK. She was now in a very fragile condition, starkly illustrated when a bridge guardrail collapsed killing one of the ship's company. The C-in-C South Atlantic had his way and, during September, *Eagle* continued service in South Atlantic in very poor weather conditions. A fire broke out in the hangar leaving only four Swordfish available, She lost her sea Walrus, fortunately without loss of life. Her evaporators were becoming ineffective resulting in loss of speed. *Eagle* was becoming increasingly tired. She returned to Freetown in October and from thence to Gibraltar and onward to Liverpool for a refit at Cammel Laird's shipyard. Following the loss of HMS *Ark Royal* and the implications of war with Japan the refit was reconsidered. In another change of plan the refit proceeded, including improved radar for fire control and surface warning. Improved armament was also fitted.

In January 1942 she commenced her refit trials and prepared for service in the Mediterranean as a replacement for *Ark Royal*. In February she was nominated ocean escort of military convoy WS16 across the Atlantic and then detached for Mediterranean service based in Gibraltar.

The next months saw her used relentlessly for convoy escort duties; 1942 was the year that so nearly saw the loss of Malta, as much by starvation as by direct enemy action against the island itself. On 6 March along with aircraft carrier *Argus* she delivered aircraft to Malta. On the 25th she made another Malta delivery, then returned to Gibraltar for repair during April. By this time the US had entered the War and in May *Eagle* carried out a Malta delivery with USS *Wasp*. The following month she carried out further Malta deliveries and survived intensive air attacks. By this time Malta was nearly starved into submission; it was calculated that without further supplies she would have to capitulate at the end of July. This was extended to the end of August when Malta's sister island Gozo offered to pool its food supplies with Malta. Again *Eagle* formed part of a convoy and on the 14th survived an attack by an Italian submarine. Undaunted, on the 20th she undertook a further Malta delivery as part of Operation *Insect*.

August saw the end of HMS *Eagle*. She joined aircraft carriers *Victorious, Indomitable, Furious,* and *Argus* in the Atlantic for a series of exercises to improve Fighter Direction and multicarrier operating techniques prior to the planned Malta convoy, Operation *Pedestal*. On 11 August 1942, just five days after *Pedestal* had set out, *Eagle* was attacked by German submarine U73, which had penetrated the destroyer screen. She was hit by four torpedoes and sunk south of Majorca in eight minutes. Two officers and 158 ratings were killed but 927 of the ship's company, including Captain Mackintosh, who by this time had replaced Captain Bridge under whom Norman had served, were picked up by British destroyers *Laforey* and *Lookout* and the British tug *Jaunty*.

By the end of October 1942 Malta had received 367 Spitfires, mostly from the decks of *Wasp* and *Eagle*. *Eagle's* achievments reflect magnificently on the men who served in her, particularly of course, her Captain.

Norman's celebrated his 22nd birthday in the Red Sea on his way back to Britain to train for his commission. *Eagle* was so sorry to see him go that she chased him right round the east coast of Africa to Cape Town.

FEBRUARY 1941

1st   Embarked on HMS *Christian Huygens*. [Norman might well have seen the *Christian Huygens* again later in the war as she was finally lost to a mine in 1945 in the Scheldt Estuary, off Antwerp, where Norman was later to find himself.]

2nd   Sailed through Suez Canal but stopped by wreck which had hit a mine. [A later note reads] '*Agnos Georgios*. The first ship to hit a mine in the Canal. We were about two ships behind it! This delayed big ships for some considerable time including HMS *Eagle*, which passed through the Canal on 12 April 1941.

11th   Reached Port Suez.

14th   Left Suez, convoyed by *Carthage*.

22nd   Arrived Aden

28th   Crossed the line (Equator).

As Norman was returning to Britain for training in preparation for his commission via Mombassa, Durban, Capetown and Freetown, his brother David was doing precisely the same thing at the same time but in David's case he was en route to India via Mombassa and Durban. Perhaps the two brothers were on ships that literally passed in the night Tom Stoate their eldest brother had one month earlier sailed over the same part of the Indian Ocean to his first overseas posting near Durban, South Africa.

MAY 1941
13th–21st
     Home on leave, and so endeth the life of Able Seaman Stoate.

8

THE SMALL SHIPS WAR

Norman Stoate is commissioned and returns to the Med, defending Gibraltar with his own command. He returns to home waters for the D-Day landings and is in the middle of the Ostend tragedy when a massive accidental explosion takes many lives.

It is now mid 1941, Norman is about to train through the Royal Navy Volunteer Reserve (RNVR) for his commission and then join the 'Small Ships' of the Royal Navy.

The RNVR was instituted during the First World War as means of inducting personnel into the Royal Navy without their committing to full-time service. During the Second World War no more ratings were accepted into the RNVR, which then became the main route for accelerated wartime officer entry. The service was colloquially called the 'Wavy Navy', after the 3/8-inch wavy sleeve 'rings' that RNVR officers wore to differentiate them from RN/RNR officers. Those who became officers during the war were considered to have joined the RNVR and wore that service's uniform. Most of the officers in Landing Craft, Coastal Forces and the Atlantic Convoys were RNVR. A significant number achieved command of corvettes and even frigates. Quite a few also went into the submarine branch of the service and some achieved command there. Norman was to become commander of an ML (Motor Launch – a type of fast patrol boat).

RNVR officers trained through HMS *King Alfred,* a shore-based establishment the location of which has changed over the years. During the Second World War *King Alfred* was located in various buildings in Brighton and Hove including the newly built (but not yet opened) Hove Marina complex. This building and the adjacent Royal Navy Reserve were commissioned as HMS *King Alfred* on 11 September 1938.

In May 1941 Roedean School for Girls was requisitioned to house the Navy's Torpedo and Mine training school, HMS *Vernon*, which was evacuated from Portsmouth. Norman was there during his torpedo course in 1941. April 1942 saw the opening of the RN W/T Training School in Queens Road and West House, this was followed in July 1942 by a Combined Operations Landing Craft base, HMS *Lizard*, opened at Aldrington Basin to act as the training and re-supply depot for Royal Navy and Royal Marine landing craft flotillas.

Norman told me of some of the training they undertook at *King Alfred*, some of which may seem quite ridiculous now. For navigation and flotilla movements, for example, they laid out some playing fields with white boundary paint to denote navigational hazards such as light houses, rocks, buoys etc and then in teams of two they were mounted on ice cream vendor's tricycles, fitted out with a 'chart' and compass, one doing the pedalling and the other the navigation, to learn pilotage and coastal navigation. These exercises could be made more complicated by setting four or five tricycles on the field together and requiring them to perform as a flotilla, with a 'Flotilla Commander' signalling course direction changes. One can laugh, but it was cheap and apparently effective, as witnessed by the 22,500 officers who passed out from *King Alfred* and who were to form the backbone of the Royal Navy's officer strength.

Over the five years of war, HMS *King Alfred* trained men from a variety of Commonwealth and Allied nations including Australia, Belgium, Canada, China, Holland, New Zealand, Norway, South Africa, and the US.

JUNE 1941
Entered HMS *King Alfred* for a Naval Officer's course. Squad drill, Navigation, Signalling, boat handling etc.

JULY 1941
30th   Passed out as Sub Lieutenant. Went before a board of Top Brass. Condensed
           conversation:

'Name?'
'Stoate, Sir.'
'Looks a bit like a weasel doesn't he, Ha ha ha.'
I obviously had to go along with the merriment.
'What branch of the Navy do you wish to enter?'
'Coastal Forces please Sir.'
'Everybody wants that, we don't think there is much chance, what's your next choice?'
'The next smallest ship, please Sir.'

I got what I wanted, Coastal Forces.

So while Roy Hussey is shortly to set sail for the US as a pupil pilot, Norman's brother David is training in India and his eldest brother Tom, as an RAF Medical Officer, is in Port Said, Cairo, Norman is studying for his torpedo exams. These presumably were not too hard to pass as he had already been tested for that branch in October 1940 on board HMS *Eagle*.

AUGUST 1941
Took Torpedo course at Lancing, stayed and slept at Roedean Girls School, notice still over bed. 'If you want a Mistress in the night ring the bell' – No luck!

OCTOBER/NOVEMBER 1941 (approx)
Boarded 1st class sleeper to Glasgow and then on to Fort William and Ardrishaig for Asdic, boat handing and navigation courses.

Amongst the small ships at Ardrishaig were the Fairmile Motor Launches MLs. MLs were of the same little ship class as the racier MTBs (Motor Torpedo Boats) and MGBs (Motor Gun Boats) but were larger, more numerous and more versatile, albeit slower. It was aboard an ML that Norman was shortly to serve.

MLs owed their being to the British industrialist Noel Macklin. Shortly before the Second World War Macklin, designer and manufacturer of the Railton and Invicta sports and racing car, submitted to the Admiralty at his own expense an innovative plan and prototype for a KD (knock down) motor launch. The launch design used prefabricated parts, which allowed

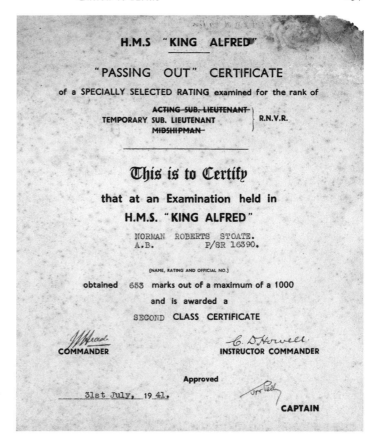

'Passing Out' Certificate of
Temporary Sub Lieutenant
Stoate. (Norman Stoate)

various small manufacturers, such as furniture makers (Parker Knoll amongst others) and piano manufacturers, to produce the individual components. These components could then be assembled in separate shipyards. The hull was made of double diagonal mahogany planking with plywood frames divided into nine watertight compartments. In July 1939, two months before the outbreak of war, the Admiralty awarded Macklin a contract to build twelve Type A Fairmiles. These had three engines and were capable of 20 knots.

The design of the Fairmile A was unsatisfactory in a number of ways, mainly related to their hard chine hull form. Within the Admiralty, however, a design existed for a similar sized vessel with round bilges based on the lines of a destroyer hull. This vessel became the Fairmile wooden kit boat assembled locally. The new boat became known as the Fairmile B Type Motor Launch of which, at close of hostilities, some 650 had been built.

Each kit was made up of six packages, and each package was designed to fit in a standard 15-ton lorry. The planners at the Fairmile yard at Cobham, Surrey, staggered delivery of packages to the boatyards to make sure that production was not interrupted by late arrival, and conversely to make sure that a backlog of parts did not build up. Today, this approach forms the basis of many manufacturing processes, where 'just in time' delivery keeps costs to a minimum and makes maximum use of resources.

In contrast to the MTB – which was an aggressively offensive vessel – the B type ML was intended as a submarine chaser (to protect coastal convoys, port approaches and coastal waters against submarines, essentially a defensive role), and so all the boats were fitted with Asdic (sonar) as standard. Initially, their main armament reflected their anti-submarine focus, with 12 depth charges, a single 3-lb gun aft, and one set of twin 0.303-in machine guns. The initial design of the B Type called for three engines, following the specification of the A type. It was

Called to Arms

Sub Lieutenant Norman Stoate, 1941.
(Author)

soon realized, however, that the American Hall-Scott petrol engines could not be produced quickly enough to satisfy demand, and so they were reduced to two, capable of producing 18 knots. Despite disappointment at the loss of speed, it was recognised that the reduction in power did not materially affect the boat's ability to perform its designated role of protection against submarines. The vessel in all its guises provided good service, escorting coastal shipping and patrolling waterways looking for submarine threats and covering the approaches to ports.

Pre-war searches for suppliers of high-powered diesel engines suitable for marine use had proved fruitless, so petrol engines were settled upon. As we shall see from an incident in April 1945 which Norman was in the thick of, shortly before the end of hostilities, petrol engines were a much greater fire hazard than diesel engines. As a consequence MLs were fitted with Methol Bromide appliances which could be operated from either the bridge or the engine room. These were very effective in putting out a petrol fire by introducing gas to stifle flames. The gas, however, was lethal if inhaled, so the area concerned had first to be evacuated and the ship thoroughly vented after their use.

MLs had a fuel capacity of 2305 gallons, which was sufficient for a range of 1500 miles at 12 knots. On occasion, extra fuel tanks fitted to the deck significantly extended their range, when they carried out long sea passages.

The Germans did not really have an equivalent, the nearest was their S-Boot (Schnell boot) or E boat – they were the same craft. These were highly aggressive craft, larger than the Motor Torpedo Boats but slightly shorter than the MLs. They were powered by three very efficient Daimler Benz diesel engines, but with a range of only 700 miles.

MLs proved themselves to have excellent qualities in most weather conditions, although there was a tendency towards broaching in conditions of Force Eight or above from the stern or stern quarters. Once the seas got up to Force Ten the boats had to heave to, by steering just off the wind at minimum speed. In such weather conditions the boats showed themselves to be more durable than their crews, who suffered badly as the small boats were thrown about by the sea and covered continually in spray.

As the war moved on adaptations were made for roles other than anti-submarine and the armament was modified and upgraded, such as the replacement of the 3 pounder with one or more 20mm Oerlikon cannon. Britain had spare torpedo tubes (taken from the 50 American lend-lease destroyers transferred to Britain), and some MLs including one that Norman served on, had two of these these fixed to the deck.

A far-sighted specification was that the boats should be capable of being reconfigured for different roles with 48 hours notice. To meet this requirement the boats were fitted with steel deck strips with pre-tapped holes. Armament was bolted to the strips, and to change roles the unwanted armament had simply to be unbolted and new armament fitted in its place. In this way the boats could be fitted with different equipment with minimum fuss, including torpedo tubes, mines, depth charges, various guns and other specialist gear.

The Fairmile B Type Motor Launches were a great success. Although they lacked the speed of the Motor Torpedo Boats and Motor Gun Boats, they proved their worth again and again with their versatility and ability to operate in heavy weather. Their speed limited them primarily to less glamorous defensive operations, with the faster MTBs and MGBs conducting the offensive sweeps, nevertheless many Fairmiles were upgunned and the number of depth charges reduced. Although they lacked the speed to deal decisively with the faster S-boote, the Fairmiles packed heavy firepower and provided a significant deterrent to the German convoy raiders. They were also were pressed in to service in a number of roles, which properly

Gibraltar 1942. ML 170 as part of 9th Flotilla sporting a 21-inch torpedo tube removed from an obsolete American destroyer on lend lease, with the object of sinking the Vichy French fleet if it tried to break out of the Mediterranean through the Straits of Gibraltar. Norman had been commissioned for just over year and was 1st Lieutenant ('Jimmy-the-one') on ML 174. (Norman Stoate)

demanded much faster vessels. For example, they were used in clandestine operations, working with the Special Operations Executive to insert and remove agents.

When the time came to invade France on 6 June 1944, Norman's ML 909 rounded up many assault craft which were powerless or rudderless (often through the coxwain having been killed) 'rafted up' to them and drove them on to Juno beach, performing a vital but largely unheralded function. On the following 3 days, 7–9 June, Norman was also pretty busy.

MLs also acted as minesweepers. That variant provided especially good service in Malta and 36 MLs swept in the British and American forces during the invasion of Normandy. Several boats were modified to sweep acoustic mines, and others specialised in magnetic minesweeping. Five months after D–Day, the Royal Marines and the Canadians were heavily involved in clearing German resistance from Walcheren Island in the Estuary off Antwerp in Holland. One of Norman's ship's company had a friend on board an ML a little after this time who was lost when his ML was blown up sweeping the heavily mined waters.

Yet further variants included ambulance, rescue boats and minelayers. Their mines, around 6 foot in length and about 18 inches in diameter, of which each ML carried six, were laid in a set pattern and on being released from the ML sank to the bottom of the sea. A soluble pellet would dissolve and release the timer on a time clock which was set for a pre-determined date after the mine was laid. German mine sweepers might sweep the channel and declare the area safe, but the mines might well have not been ready for detonation until after the channel had been swept. MLs could also lay conventional pimple mines, each ML carrying eight mines. These were released from the MLs and would sink to the bottom of the sea where the mine was released from its mooring to float up several feet below the sea surface suspended on its wire from the mooring. These mines were contact mines and a vessel running into them would cause them to detonate.

In early 1942, Norman, now 23 years old and fully trained, was about to join 9th Flotilla, an operational ML flotilla back in the Mediterranean, but this time in the western Mediterranean, on the Rock.

Gibraltar was a strongly protected naval station and ML Flotilla 9 had a large part of the task of protecting her. Norman's old ship, HMS *Eagle* was now part of the Western Mediterranean Fleet and he was to be on Gibraltar when she was sunk. It was as part of Operation *Pedestal* that the damaged oil tanker *Ohio* was 'strapped' between the two destroyers, HMS *Penn* and HMS *Bramham* and more or less lifted into Grand Harbour Malta to provide fuel for the beleaguered island.

The Western Mediterranean Fleet had the task of maintaining Allied Naval superiority and providing a strong escort for the convoys which had to be pushed through to Malta. The integrity of Gibraltar was essential to the safety of Malta and Malta was essential to the strategy of Allied attrition on Axis supply lines to Africa. The fleet, which operated in both the Atlantic and the Mediterranean, was under the command of Vice-Admiral Somerville and based on Gibraltar.

In January 1941 9th ML Flotilla comprising MLs 169, 170, 172, 173-176 and 178 had been based in Ardrossan on the west coast of Scotland more or less opposite the Isle of Arran. It had made its own (escorted) passage to Gibraltar during that summer, presumably with the extra petrol tanks bolted to the deck for the long passage. Just before Norman joined the flotilla, on 15 February 1942, ML 169 was lost by fire and subsequent explosion.

The 9th flotilla was responsible for anti-submarine operations in the straits between Cape Spartel and Ceuta. The ships would operate close in shore on both sides of the straits using hydrophones. Occasionally they undertook escort duties to Algiers or Casablanca. The work was often monotonous and unspectacular but important nevertheless.

Trawlers (MFVs) fitted for anti-submarine work played a big part in the defence of the straits. Spanish territorial waters to the north and south made it difficult to maintain an efficient block against enemy U boats. A number did get through by creeping close inshore in those territorial waters. At night a number of MLs would keep up a hydrophone watch off-shore with engines stopped to pick up any U-boat trying to slip in.

Foredeck of ML 174 showing the 3 pounder and twin Lewis .303 machine guns. The First World War Lewis gun was taken out of mothballs following the fall of France; nearly 60,000 were refitted, repaired and issued during the War. It was purportedly the most successful AA weapon of the conflict in bringing down low-flying enemy aircraft.

Gibraltar 1942. Norman Stoate was CO of MFV 89, sister ship to this vessel before taking command of HDML 1235. (Norman Stoate)

Enemy agents had a complete view of Gibraltar Bay from Algeciras and of the straits from the Spanish shore or Tangiers, it was therefore necessary for convoys to move at night. This greatly added to the difficulty of keeping a good A/S (Audio Signal) watch as the trawlers could not safely steam across the straits with the convoy entering. Near misses were frequent.

Along with their smaller cousins the HDMLs (Harbour Defence Motor Launches) MLs also had a hand in combating the two-man submarines and limpeteers, who were pretty successful in sinking Allied shipping, their last notable success being in August 1943 when three ships in the outer harbour were sunk or beached.

'Joined ML 174 as 1st Lieutenant, based on the Costal Forces base HMS Iskra.' *Iskra* was not a shore establishment as implied but a 1917 Polish-built three master sailing training ship. At the outbreak of hostilities she was based in North Africa and was acquired by France. When France surrendered in June 1940 she was seized by the Royal Navy and was based in Gibraltar.

> All personnel in Base and Flotilla were a grand lot. Duties on M.L. 174 daily running of ships crew, discipline etc. under CO Lieutenant Bobby Mayhew. Crew numbered about 16. Duties of Flotilla; Straits of Gibraltar anti submarine patrol guarding the Rock from the sea and occasionally convoy escort. We were later fitted with old US 21-inch torpedo tubes, one of the ideas was to torpedo submarines that were driven to the surface by our depth charges ... never happened. On one occasion we had to hide ourselves in small bays in the South Spanish coast and torpedo any Vichy French ship if they made a dash for it through the Straits of Gibraltar to a German port, probably fortunately for us they did not try, although we were all keyed up ready for them. All in all quite hard work with many night time watches but a bit on the boring side, not enough action.

The form was for the MLs to work in pairs so that one would be loaded with torpedoes and two depth charges and the other would have a full set of depth charges and no torpedoes.

The latter would drop depth charges on a suspected submarine whilst the other would use its torpedoes as it surfaced. The 3-pounder gun fitted to the MLs would be no match for the 4- or 5-inch guns carried by submarines. The MLs were timber, the submarines were not.

After Norman had left ML 174 it was converted to a minesweeper, at which time the forward Oerlikon was replaced with a Bofors. The boat went on with the 9th Flotilla to see action in Italy, then Greece, where it landed British troops who were tasked with the containment of ELAS, the communist movement, at a small village near Patras in January 1945. The flotilla eventually left Trieste for pay-off in October 1945.

Back to Gibraltar and the closing months of 1942. In November General Eisenhower had set up his headquarters in Gibraltar prior to Operation *Torch*, the plan to invade French North Africa and join up with Montgomery's army, clearing the Germans and the Italians from the African continent. At this moment 'the Rock' was home to both Norman and Roy Hussey.

At the beginning of 1943 Norman was about to assume his first command.

March 1943 (approx) was given command of M.F.V.89, an ex fishing boat, crew of about five. Single screw with quite a bit of freeboard, difficult to handle in bad, windy weather but an enjoyable challenge. Duties mainly harbour patrol, dropping charges chiefly at night against Italian frogmen who were apt to fix mines and warheads on the keel of ships. No mines fitted during my period with M.F.V.89 or frogmen sighted, but on 7–8 December 1942 Italian frogmen Visinti and Magro who were going to attack two aircraft carriers and two battleships in Gibraltar were killed by these small charges and two others were captured, so we felt we were doing a worthwhile job, if a very noisy one. The routine was to take the charge with its fuse in your hand, light it and throw it smartly over the stern when in a matter of seconds there would be an almighty crack, not particularly pleasant for those trying to sleep below or the surrounding ships. Sometimes we took an English frogman on board to dive and inspect the keel of a suspected ship. The frogmen were Lieutenants Bill Bailey and Lionel Crabb [the famous 'Buster' Crabb, commander of the Underwater Bomb Disposal Unit who would (probably) die in mysterious circumstances in 1956 whilst working for MI6].

Gibraltar 1942. Norman Stoate's second command, HDML 1235. (Norman Stoate)

In June 1943 Norman was to be given command of a Harbour Defence Motor Launch (HDML). These vessels were originally intended for the defence of estuarial and local waters, but they proved such a sea-tolerant and versatile design that they were used in every theatre of operation as the war progressed. They were to be found escorting convoys off the west coast of Africa (where Roy Hussey's uncle Jack Herniman was based serving with the RAF) carrying out covert activities in the Mediterranean and undertaking anti-submarine patrols off Iceland.

To this end they were commonly fitted with a 2-pounder on the foredeck, an Oerlikon 20mm HA/LA Cannon (High Angle/Low Angle) on the stern cabin (this could also be used for anti-aircraft defence) and like the MLs, a 0.303 Vickers machine gun on each side of the bridge, for the purpose of repelling boarding parties. They carried 10 depth charges, on the aft decks. The 2-pounder guns were not particularly accurate, possibly in view of the boats' tendency to roll, and many were replaced by another Oerlikon HA/LA gun.

They were normally manned by RNVR officers with temporary commissions, and 'hostilities only' ratings. However the crews gained an enviable reputation for their skill and expertise in handling and fighting with their vessels.

There were 486 HDMLs built, mainly by UK yacht builders. They had a displacement hull 72 feet (22m) long with a beam of 16 feet (4.9m) and a loaded draught of 5 feet (1.5m). The loaded displacement was 54 tons. The hull, built of mahogany in earlier models and later (the more leaky ones) in larch, they had a pronounced flare forward to throw the bow wave clear, and provided considerable lift to prevent all but the heaviest seas from coming aboard. Although sturdy at sea, they had a considerable tendency to roll, especially when taking seas at anything other than right angles. The cause was their considerable reserve of stability, the effect of which was to impart a powerful righting moment if the ship was pushed over in a seaway. This, coupled with the round bilged hull and lack of bilge keels, would set up a rapid and violent rolling.

One of the design criteria was that HDMLs had to be capable of turning within the turning circle of a submerged submarine. To achieve this, they were fitted with two very large rudders and, to improve the ability to turn even more, the keel ended 13 feet from the stern. A side effect of this was that the hull lacked directional stability, and was extremely difficult to hold on a straight course.

The hull was very strong, constucted with frames or 'timbers' riveted perpendicularly from the keel to the gunwhale on the inside of the planking. The planking itself was two diagonally opposed skins with a layer of oiled calico between them – known as 'double-diagonal' construction. Aft above the waterline they were fitted with deep-section rubbing strakes, their purpose being to roll depth charges (kept and delivered from a rack on the side decks) clear of the hull and propellers. The hull was divided into six watertight compartments. Provided the bulkheads were not damaged, the ship could remain afloat with any one compartment flooded.

HDMLs were designed to accommodate a crew of 10. There were berths for six ratings in the fore cabin, The two commissioned officers were berthed in comparatively roomy accommodation in the after end of the ship; the two petty officers being in a cabin on the port side just aft of the engine room. The main steering position was on the open bridge where the two engine room telegraphs were fitted. There were also voice pipes connected to the inside steering position, the engine room, the radio room and the wardroom.

In Gibraltar they were mostly employed in protecting the anchorage against midget submarines and limpeteeers. They would stop engines use hydrophones and then if anything was picked up or movement detected on the surface they would start engines to get underway and drop explosive charges over the side.

Of course at night time things could get tricky, when a convoy was assembling, a merchant ship might be seen bearing down to make a crash start. On very dark nights searchlights on the harbour moles were switched on to help with the detection of swimmers. Their beams were set on the horizontal so the harbour was lit up like daylight. Just as suddenly the lights would be switched off and the ship's look-outs would be unsighted. Norman takes up the narrative for June 1943.

Left MFV 89 to take Command of HDML 1235. Length 72 ft Beam 15ft 10in Draft 4ft 9in, 46 tons, two Gardner diesel engines 160 H.P. each. Stuart Turner for lighting. Speed 11–12 knots. Guns, 3 pdr. Oerliken, Vickers or Lewis, 8 depth charges. Crew 12.

8th   Big alert in Gibraltar Bay. Took some of the six frogman including Syd Know to dive
        on 60 ships. *Pat Harrison, Mahsud* and *Cameratan* [American Liberty ship of 5000 tons,
        and British freighters of 7500 and 4875 tons respectively] holed by limpet mine or
        warheads. After the attack Italian agents placed diving equipment on Spanish shore to
        make British think divers had come from a submarine when they really came from
        the Olterra in Algeciras harbour, which Crabb and Bailey had suspected for some
        time but were not allowed to investigate.

Norman adds a later note:

When Italy came into the war the *Olterra* [5000 ton Italian tanker] scuttled herself in Gibraltar Bay, in the Spanish section. She was later refloated and towed into Alteciras harbour and secured to the breakwater near the harbour mouth. Italy sent a frogman crew to live aboard, headed by Visinti. They cut out a hole in the hull 6ft below the water line which led into the bow compartment and by a process of watertight doors and pumping out launched them-selves and torpedoes with warheads to attack ships in the bay.

HDML 1235 very busy on Bay patrol. All ships arriving from Spain had to be searched for limpet mines. Dropping small charges all the time, sweeping search lights on sea looking for Italian frogmen. If any ship in the Bay wanted us to help they hoisted a flag signal from the yard arm so that we would visit them and arrange a diver or deal with other matters. Also had to keep Spanish rowing boats away from the ships in case they were fifth columnist and out to sabotage the ships. They were really there to sell goods, chiefly wine to the ships' crews, but we would not take the risk. This brought about many clashes, see separate report, and in another incident I made one throw all his bottles of wine over the side, he said he would cut my throat next time I came to La Linea … went the next day … no scars! In another incident I was chasing one of the boats for a search but went too near the shore and knocked my Asdic dome off the bottom of 1235. Reasons in writing! But I was by no means the first. Usually however, we let them off with a warning. They often tried to bribe us – probably seemed quite natural to them.

On one occasion we took Crabb out to dive on a ship and found a limpet mine attached to the keel, he managed to take it off and we towed it across the Bay to Rosia Bay for the experts to have a look at it. Occasionally we escorted iron ore ships. As the ships went to Malaga we had to keep outside Spanish territorial waters and wait for the loaded ships to appear for the return journey. On one occasion the sea got exceedingly rough, in fact dangerously rough, I could not put into Malaga otherwise we would all be interned so I rigged a sea anchor [a long length of warp with a canvas bag or similar at the end trailed over the bow] to keep our head to wind and sea but we still drifted towards the Spanish coast. The iron ore ship duly loaded appeared for her return journey so we had to turn about, a very dangerous manoeuvre, so everybody on deck with lifejackets on. Fortunately the manoeuvre was successful, but still a very dangerous situation with a following sea, so although I do not profess that I could do any better than the Cox'n I felt that I could not leave him with the responsibility so took the wheel myself until we arrived at Gibraltar, knackered and thankful to get in the shelter of the Rock.

Three days after his 25th birthday, on 17 February 1944 Norman was promoted to full Lieutenant RNVR and soon afterwards left Gibraltar for England.

In a way I was glad to leave Gibraltar after about 2¼ years. Although the work was inter-esting and there was a very good social life. I had rather a reputation of working hard and playing hard, sports, squash, six-a-side, hockey, shooting, social parties on board, ashore, in the Wrennery, dances, dinners, trips over the border to La Linea, Algeciras.

At one time I had a half share in a sports Riley (racing green) and then bought my partner out. No great scope for use except trips to the other side of the Rock i.e. Catalan Bay for beach parties, one of which included Vivien Leigh and B Lillie. Also trips to pick up Wrens from the Wrennery, had so many in the Riley once that the under-slung battery was ripped off going over a slightly raised track. However got the dockyard to mend the damage. Cannot remember what happened to the car when I left.

Within his records he also includes the following reports:

GILBRALTAR 1943

For information from HDML 1235
To: N.O.I.C. Gilbraltar

During the past few weeks the building of what appears to be two small gun batteries have been noticed in progress on the Spanish coast. The approximate position being (a) 047 Rocadillo Tower 13 cables. (b) 092 Rocadillo 9 cables. (a) Appears to be built of stone from the outside but it was also noticed that steel sheets from a derelict hulk nearby were being placed in the inside. (b) Is surrounded by boarding.

And the following amplification on an incident with a fishing boat off Punta Majorca:

At approximately 10.30 on 27 September a small fishing boat *Anita* was seen under the stern of an American merchant ship. On approaching to investigate *Anita* made off towards the shore using sail and oars. I closed her and told her to come alongside but she altered course away, the same thing happened again. This continual avoiding action naturally made me suspicious of boat and occupants so I drew up alongside them and caught hold of their mast, again they tried to get away and in so doing their boat capsized displaying several cartons of American cigarettes, which floated away.

The boat was recovered and towed with its crew to the Security Police Waterport where they made a statement. The only damage caused to the boat was a slight break in the beading on the gunwhale, and apart from losing two oars, rudder and tiller they appear to having nothing on which to claim. *Anita's* sails were in perfect condition. The three occupants of *Anita* were well looked after and re-clothed with roll necked sweaters, trousers and underclothes.

Norman stayed in touch with many of his wartime colleagues and in his papers there was this fragment of a letter from Alan.

… On the July patrol you entrusted me with the watch and turned in. Some of the 5 lb TNT charges we dropped brought up a number of stunned fish and your lads produced a net to catch some, for which purpose I stopped engines – which brought you, I am afraid, up from your slumbers! On the October patrol I relieved your coxswain for the morning watch and brought 1235 into harbour in a stiff breeze and you came on deck and berthed the vessel. On Nov 13th, I see, I stood the morning watch again, dropping the TNT charges but got no fish! You fellows seemed to develop some confidence in me, for I see that over a period of nine months I was watch keeper on 46 patrols – in the HDs and the 18s and I can only suppose that your long suffering colleagues welcomed the relief I could give them from watch keeping!

Have you found the 'call of the sea' getting you afloat since the war? I have always found it a strong call – the call of the 'running tide'! For some years I was a dinghy sailor. On retirement from the Rank in 1971 I made a cruise as purser in the STA Schooner *Malcolm Miller*, in 1973 in the *Sir Winston Churchill* and in 1974 in the *Miller* again. Wonderful experiences … But ere I bore you completely I must belay. I am sure if we met we could reminisce for hours about CFB Gib. They were, now we can fortunately look back having survived the war, happy times – with the tougher experiences largely forgotten.

Will always be pleased to hear from you

Alan

P.S. forgot to mention – my wife and I, on a cruise, 1980, visited Gibraltar. We sought out C.F.B. – but what a disappointment: a derelict embankment of oily polluted water with one abandoned derelict cabin cruiser. Perhaps by now the opportunity has been taken to make our old base a decent, attractive marina.

At the beginning of February 1944 the 20-year-old Roy Hussey was on his way back to England from just over two years combat service, and Norman, coming up to his 25th birthday, was also going home, having served for a little short of four years.

FEBRUARY 1944
Left Gibraltar for UK with Tommy Tucker and I think it was on this occasion with Bill Bailey and Crabb, arriving at Tilbury on a destroyer. We missed the last train to London so were put up in a hotel for the night where we started to look for a bit of night life … found it in a dance hall where news soon got around that some famous Frogmen had arrived, soon we were all busy signing autographs, as for partner – no problem. Next day returned home on leave where I got my 2-seater Morris 8, which was chocked up at Stoate & Sons Temple Mills, Bristol, working again. Soon after I was told that a new B type M.L. was being built at Toughs, Teddington and that I would be given Command when it was ready. Drove up to see it twice but I do not think it would have been ready for D-Day so I was switched to one which was ready at Leigh-on-Sea, namely M.L. 909.

Norman was not only respected by his crew on ML 909 but also liked – a trick difficult to pull off. Their post-war reunions, initially in Portsmouth and subsequently at the United Services Club in Shaftesbury Avenue, London, were well attended (In a letter dated 9 November 1998 Mike Rosher, one of the crew, wrote there were still at least six 'still on deck') until gradually one by one they passed on. There is however one survivor at 84 years of age, Frank (Yorkie) Kay, whom I had the privilege of meeting in March 2010. I asked Frank how they addressed Norman, was it Boss, Skipper, Captain or what? He looked up in surprise and replied 'No, we all called him Norman!'

In a letter to Norman dated 21 April 1984 Frank wrote: 'One reads about happy ships but 909 was without equal, and one which I was happy and privileged to have sailed on.'

Frank volunteered for the Navy when he was 17. He told me all his friends were involved and he wanted to do his bit, so he said to his boss that his call up papers had arrived and that he would be leaving. He was employed as an apprentice tinplate worker, a reserved occupation, manufacturing Jerrycans. When his boss told him not to worry, he would soon put a stop to that, Frank asked him not to (remember there were no call up papers, Frank had volunteered) and so he was wished good luck and off he went to Plymouth.

There he volunteered for a variety of jobs, including training for submarines and to be trained as a Japanese interpreter. Fortunately for ML 909, neither of these was taken up and he was eventually selected as a gunner (and as we shall see a very good one). He was sent to HMS *St Christopher* at Fort William (now the Highland Hotel) where he learned his gunnery skills ploughing up and down Loch Linnhe shooting at drogues towed by aircraft 'I was glad I was at my end of proceedings rather than being the pilot of those aeroplanes,' he told me.

Rockets attached to the bridge of ML 909.

His next drafting was to be operational on MTB 354, which was flotilla leader under a New Zealand CO. By his accounts that was a first class job for the teenage Frank. The CO was an excellent leader, after action he would order tin mugs of rum all round. His idea was to loosen tongues to see whether what they had just done could be improved upon next time. Frank recalls:

> At the first of these sessions the mess deck was sitting around with their tin mugs when the captain noticed that I didn't have any grog. The Quartermaster in charge of the rum ration explained that I was under age, but he got pretty short shrift 'Guns is doing the same job as the rest of us – fill him up.'
>
> I suppose because we were the flotilla leader we were often given experimental arms to trial. The skipper was always keen to hear my views and he really wanted to hear what I thought, not a sanitised version. On one occasion we had what was called a Holman Projectile fitted to the bow deck. The idea was to launch a projectile from the deck with a cable attached. When the cable reached its full height a parachute deployed, the idea was that an aircraft should fly into the cable, this would release a further parachute from the deck end of the cable such that the aeroplane would be dragging this length of cable with parachutes attached each end and hopefully crash as a result. The weapon was pretty useless in practice. The gunner had to scramble as best he could along the bucking deck to the launching tube, drop this cannon ball-like thing down the spout rather like a mortar bomb and up would shoot the cable. The cable was not that long – I can't remember exactly how long but probably not much more that the 70 foot length of the MTB. Of course if we were moving – which we would be if we under attack, then the cable would quickly stream aft. The skipper asked my views and what with all that and the difficulty of loading the charge, the idea was quickly abandoned – at least as far as MTB 354 was concerned.

This was an adaptation of the PACs (Parachute and Cable) devices used with some success on the ground to protect, in particular, airfields. At Kenley airfield, for example, the launchers were sited at sixty-foot intervals outside the northern perimeter track and were arranged to be fired in salvoes of nine. The devices had a 500-foot cable.

On another occasion we were issued this new American ammunition, I think it was called Grazenosed Fused ammunition. These were bullets that exploded if they so much as touched a piece of tissue paper in their flight. Well my gun was the 20mm Oerlikon cannon and I was confident in my shooting ability, I was not scoring like I knew I could and began to think about this ammunition. When the skipper did his usual of asking my opinion – I told him it was useless – he challenged me and told me it couldn't be as this was the very latest stuff. 'Well' I replied 'No doubt it's excellent for the Flying Fortresses but on this ship it's useless, take me out for a night shoot and I'll show you.' So we set out and I opened fire – you could see in the spray the sky lit up with flashes, what was happening was the bullets were being exploded in the spray and not reaching their target – another idea gracefully declined.

There was another armament which I didn't think much of, that was the addition of rockets – they were stored alongside the bridge. I am sure these might have been effective on larger vessels but the pitching and rolling motion of our small ships made them virtually useless except perhaps as star shell launchers. Unlike the Holman Projector and Grazenosed ammunition however, these stayed.

As with many things connected to the Services there is an instruction or rule telling you how to do it. For example there were King's Rules and Admiralty Instructions on loading ammunition. Well, those instructions might be useful if you followed their aiming instructions as well. Admiralty instructions were to aim at the engine room to disable the target ship – perhaps dating from the days of sail, I don't know. But for me sat there pretty exposed behind my gun shield – and I was very conscious of how exposed we were as I had seen our W/T operator killed by a flying splinter of wood – that didn't seem a good idea so I always shot at the gun crews first – once they were out of action you could do what you liked with the ship. As a consequence I loaded less armour piercing ammunition. The types we used were; HE (high explosive), HEI (high explosive incendiary) HET (high explosive tracer) AP (armour piercing). I can tell you your thumb and whole hand was aching by the time you had loaded the boxes. They were sprung fed so although it wasn't too bad when you started, the spring got stiffer and stiffer the more you loaded.

After his spell on an MTB 354 Frank was drafted to ML 909. Travelling to Leigh-on-Sea where ML 909 was moored and waiting, Frank was standing at Colchester station and got into conversation with a RNVR officer. It soon became apparent that they were both bound for the same vessel. The officer was Norman Stoate. They were the first to arrive on board and so the young Frank had the pick of the bunks aft and selected the Oerlikon gun just by the funnel as his post – so he could keep warm, a good plan, as after D-Day they were bound for the North and Baltic seas in the cold winter of 1944 and spring of 1945.

APRIL 1944

24th   Commissioned M.L.909, brand new ship and crew, at Leigh-on-Sea. 1st Lieutenant Bert Gillett, Sub lieutenant, ex policeman, grand fellow.

26th   First trip out, to Tilbury for compass swinging.

MAY 1944

1st   Took ship to Brightlingsea for 'working up', getting everybody used to the ship, gun practice, damage control, first aid etc.

8th   Started physical training exercises in the mornings. Continue 'working up.'

22nd   Finish 'working up' and proceed to Harwich and join the 33rd M.L. Flotilla. Secure
          at Felixstowe.

28th   Proceed to sea to blow up wreck, dropped five depth charges – not successful.

29th   Set out again to blow up wreck but again not successful, torpedo party eventually
          blew it up with demolition charges. Good practice for setting and dropping charges.

33 ML Flotilla

CO   1st Lieutenant
Bill Kelly   Graham Baldray

ML 909
Norman Stoate   Bert Gillett

Benny Goodman
Jack Spratt (PGR)
? Roberts
Johnny Bick
Humphrey Massey
Bill Sanders
David Tinker
Dick Jenkyns

By June 1944 ML 909's complement is listed as:

A.P. Askew	A.A.3
P.R. Barnes	A.B. S/D
F.W. Cox	O/tel
A.L. Gillett	S/Lt. RNVR
L.F. Graves	A.B. A.A.3
J.T. Hardy	A.B.
C.A. Honneyball	A.A.3
R. Hughes	P.O./MM
F.J. Kay	A.A.3
L.J. Lawson	Sto I
W.S. Lavers	Sto II
H. Mills	O.S
G.F. Northcott	L/Sea Coxn
M. Rosher	A.B.
D. Rushworth	O/Tel
B. Sloan	A.B.
N.R. Stoate	Lt. RNVR
R.B. Turnball	O.S

MLs had a relatively small crew, living on top of each other, each with defined roles and
dependent upon each other. To that extent life was not unlike the pilots in a squadron with a
blurring of rank in favour of respect for the job done. Norman stayed in touch with a good
many of the ship's company for many years after the war.

Laurie Graves in his Kapok boiler suit. Frank was gunner of the 3 pounder on the foredeck, which would have been a very cold and wet job. (Frank Kay)

S.–325. (Established—April, 1938).

MONTHLY LOG OF

H.M Motor Torpedo Boat "No. 907 ."

Month of *June* 19—

Lt N. R. Stoate Commanding Officer

Approved,

_____ Commanding Officer of Flotilla

N.L. 496/38.

2277(a) 51456/D9036 7M bks 4/43 2P 10/705/1

S.–325.

Log book. (Norman Stoate)

For a while Norman's own notes run out but he fills the gap by using those of another of the ship's company, Laurie F Graves. Laurie was another of the ship's gunners (the others being Frank Kay, Askew and Honneyball), Laurie conveniently lived not far from Queenbury wharf where ML909 moored up pretty frequently and enjoyed an unusually large number of nights home.

Norman, his crew and the 33rd ML Flotilla were being readied for the momentous events that were about to unfold in the joint services assault on the beaches of Normandy. Norman reproduces extracts from the logbook of H.M.M.L. 909 for the month of June 1944: '2nd at Felixstowe 0900 – 10 cwts coal taken aboard.'

The coal was to fuel the solid fuel heater on board. Later we shall learn about a horrendous accident at Ostend harbour. Meanwhile Frank Kay refers to the awful event:

> After we had broken away from the blazing vessels at Ostend we picked up five people who had been blown into the water. When I took two of them below I smelt the distinctive smell of petrol – we used 100 octane – very volatile stuff. These chaps were soaked in it, so I told them to get their clothes off and threw those overboard as I was terrified the vapour might ignite from the solid fuel heater. I got the guys to soak in a tub. I lent one of them my padded boiler suit – never got that back.

From 909's log book for June 1944, the days leading up to D-Day:

3rd	at Felixstowe
1200	Hands to dinner. Make and Mend.
4th	at Felixstowe
0700	Hands called.
0730	Breakfast
0810	Harbour Stations.
0820	Slipped moorings to proceed on Operation *Neptune*
0830	Operation postponed due to weather.
0840	Secured a/s quay Felixstowe dock. Usual routine.
5th	Felixstowe to Le Havre
0630	Hands called.
0845	Harbour stations.
0850	Slipped moorings and proceeded on escort duties with L.3 group Operation *Neptune*.
1036	Course S 84 E formed up with convoy. Station astern.
2255	Course S 50 W.
6th	
0210	Outer gate busy abeam. L.C.A. [Landing Craft Assault] found abandoned in position 50 32N 00 16W. Passed L.B.V. [Landing Barge Vehicle] abandoned.

Frank Kay:

> When we came to these stragglers and ships that had been abandoned, being the young-est and fittest Norman would say 'Guns' – we were called by our duty on board so the torpedo man was Torps, wireless operator Sparks, gunner Guns etc – 'Guns slip aboard and secure tow so I'd jump aboard – not too bad in that direction as we were the larger vessel but difficult on occasions getting back – to secure the towing lines. The LCA mentioned in the log was filled with dead and seriously wounded. Those landing craft were mostly timber except for the ramp so there was very little protection for the soldiers on board so

we towed it to the hospital ship that was anchored a fair way out to sea, hopefully out of range of the 88s.

| 1653 | E3 buoy abeam convoy reformed |
| 1930 | through swept channel to landing area. Rounded up all straggling L.C.Ts [Landing Craft Tanks] and led them into Juno area. |

Frank Kay:

The way we dealt with the stragglers – and there were dozens of them – that were powerless or sometimes rudderless because the cox'n had been killed, was for me to jump over to them and secure lines fore and aft so they were rafted up alongside us and we drove them onto the beaches and then smartly went astern for the next one – that was when getting back on board 909 was most difficult for me.

On one occasion I remember a German fighter flying up the whole length of the beach with virtually the whole fleet blazing away at it – without apparently a scratch.

| 2330 | Entered Baie de la Seine when a stick of bombs landed alongside. |
| 2400 | Left convoy to contact S.O. of escort. |

7th
0200	Secured to stern of M.M.S. 226 [Motor Mine Sweeper – American-built in timber for magnetic mine sweeping duties]
0445	Forward fairlead and guardrails carried away owing to rough weather.
1600	Proceeded with escort and convoy to Isle of Wight area.
	Instructed to assist L.B.V. 47 (see report). Took in tow Juno area.

Frank Kay:

It was mayhem, then we were ordered to take in tow this fuel barge, filled with aviation fuel. Again from the bridge it was 'Guns, slip aboard,' over I went. To my amazement there was nobody, the ship had been abandoned.

Now you couldn't just take barges and landing craft anywhere, The beaches were all colour coded – red and blue and yellow and so on. There were Beachmasters who were trying to keep some form of order so that landing craft didn't foul each other on the way in or out.

By some stroke of luck we managed to find the right spot for the barge. But I can tell you we did not raft this one – no, we joined as many warps together as we could find to keep our distance, that was probably why the lines parted – we were sailing through unswept waters and if that barge had gone up we'd've certainly joined it.

| 1910 | Tow parted. |
| 1930 | Tow secured. |

8th
0900	Towed L.B.V. to depot ship. Juno area.
1630	Closed K472 for orders.
1700	Fuelled ship. 1500 gallons. Took in tow L.B.E. (Landing Barge Emergency Supply) 22. Towed to Land area. No engine or rudder.
2200	Anchored. Bearings Courseulles Church S50W. Berniers Church S10W, St Aubin Church S27W

9th   Weighed anchor. Joined convoy of coaster to Tilbury. 9 knots …

12th
0805   Slipped and proceeded to Southend.
0915   Secured to stern of 141.
2040   Slipped moorings.
2140   Proceeded in convoy E.T.C.S. to Portsmouth. [Convoys ETC, FTC and ETM with
         suffix numbers were all convoys sailing from England to the Normandy beaches to
         supply the beachhead and advancing troops.]

13th
2015   Left main convoy proceeded with 4 ships to Portsmouth.
2350   Secured at petrol pier Aslar.

14th
0355   Slipped moorings, proceeded to St Helens Road to form convoy.
0730   Commenced passage to Thames.

15th
0530   Dover harbour abeam.
0100   Secured at No.13 berth Queenborough. [Docking on the Isle of Sheppy.]
0400   To fuelling jetty 1100 gals.

16th
0100   12cwts of coal taken on board. Harbour routine.

17th
0800   Clean ship for Captain's rounds.
0900   250 gals fresh water taken aboard.
1400   Slipped moorings secured to stern HMS *Avondale* [a destroyer escort] at Southend.

18th
0700   Slipped mustered convoy E.T.C. 13.
1115   Passed weather report from K513 to Commodore of convoy. Told to pick up body in
         sea, unable to, body too decomposed.
2255   Engaged enemy robot aircraft, V1, flying towards coast. Told to pick up body in sea.
         Unable to, body too decomposed. Opened fire with all guns on V1 which crashed
         into the sea and exploded.

Frank Kay:

All the thanks we got for having shot down that V1 was a roasting from the convoy commander complaining that it might have come down on one of his ships. It actually came down
near Tilbury Harbour – no doubt saving many lives.

The V1 was about half the size of a Spitfire and very fast, so to bring one down is testament
indeed to 909's gunnery skills. To keep his hand in Frank Kay told me if they passed a sunken
ship he would ask permission to shoot the masts off.
   The V-2s were a good deal larger rocket powered ballistic missiles. Their one-ton war heads
caused considerable damage and as we shall see in Jack Stoate's story, the most effective way to
stop them was to to destroy their launch sites.

Norman Stoate on his 'perch'. (Frank Kay)

19th
1310   Nab tower abeam.
1445   Refuelled 870 gals.
1530   Secured No. 11 berth petrol pier Gosport.
1800   Shifted berth to 23 Trot secured as M.L.291.

20th
1940   Slipped proceeded to St Helens Road convoy F.T.C. 13 to Thames. Took station on Starboard beam.

21st
2145   [Norman] One ship in convoy was being a bit slow. I was told to look after her and see if I could get her to go a bit faster. A huge puff of smoke appeared from her funnel. This must have been seen by the Germans who sent over a volley of shells. One exploded on starboard bow, the shrapnel damaging where I was sitting minutes before. Quickly laid smoke.

Frank Kay:

That was a memorable occasion, there was Norman speaking through the megaphone to this merchantman, 'Could we squeeze a couple of knots more out of the old girl?' Now Norman had a favourite perch on the bridge not far from the gas-operated Vickers .303 machine gun. All of a sudden there was a huge plume of smoke as the merchantman tried for those extra knots, the German shore batteries ranged on it and shells were coming over at us. Norman had left his perch for some reason and when things had settled down a little he returned to find the Vickers gun destroyed and a piece of hot shrapnel the size of a dinner plate where he usually sat, had he not moved it would certainly have cut him in half.

22nd

0500	Left convoy at B2 buoy.
0600	Secured Berth 13 Queenborough.
1300	1st Lieutenant A.L. Gillett discharged to hospital.
1400	Slipped to fuel 600 gals.
1530	Secured Queenborough No.16 berth. Temporary 1st Lieutenant taken on …

26th

0700	Call hands. Harbour routine.
1955	Start up, slip and proceed to Southend pier.
2040	Proceed with convoy ETM 18 to Portsmouth. 18 knots. Very rough.

27th

0414	Convoy stopped while ETM convoy passes through Goodwins.
0845	Received signal from Corvette to close up rear of convoy.
1351	Closing M.L. 113 at rear of convoy.
1413	E.A. [enemy aircraft] abeam left convoy, proceeded to Portsmouth harbour, secure alongside fuelling jetty and fuel.
1710	Secure alongside No.12 berth.

28th

0700	Call hands, Harbour routine.
14.15	Immediate notice.
14.30	Receive sailing orders proceed.
1557	Nab Tower abeam.
1700	Stopped awaiting convoy.
1800	Buttoned on to convoy E.T.M.
2220	Changed W/T to 1700 kcs.

Juno Beach stretched from Saint-Aubin-sur-Mer on the east to Courseulles-sur-Mer on the west. The 3rd Canadian Division was placed under the command of the British I Corps for the initial phase of the invasion, and did not come under Canadian command again until July 1944 and the establishment of II Canadian Corps headquarters in Normandy. Despite its being assigned to the Canadians, significant British forces were also present at Juno Beach, where the naval component of the invasion force was known as Force J. Later in 1944 Norman was asked to report upon his doings on and around Juno Beach to Lieutenant Commander Kelly RNVR, the Commanding Officer of Flotilla 33.

REPORT ON THE OPERATIONS OF HMML 909

7th, 8th, 9th JUNE 1944

From: Commanding Officer HMML 909
Date: 26 November 1944
To: Lt Comdr. W. Kelly RNVR (S.O.33rd M.L. Flotilla)

At 1620 on 7 June a fast convoy was formed in the Juno area, setting sail for the Thames. After 1½ hours sailing we passed LBV47 full of aviation fuel who semaphored a signal saying she was out of control in a non swept channel. The senior officer of the convoy instructed me to go to her assistance and tow her to Juno beach area. Speed of advance approx 4 knots. On the way we were challenged and lit up by the star shells of the destroyer screen. 0230 anchored in Seine Bay, weighing at daylight and towed LBV to fuelling depot, great difficulty in finding

By the KING'S Order the name of
Ty. Lieutenant Norman Roberts Stoate,
R.N.V.R.,
was published in the London Gazette on
6 March, 1945,
as mentioned in a Despatch for distinguished service.
I am charged to record
His Majesty's high appreciation.

First Lord of the Admiralty

Gazetted, 6 March 1945.
(Norman Stoate)

it, nobody seemed to know, but was welcomed with open arms when I arrived as supplies were desperate. Secured to MMS 2233. Slipped at 1630 and closed to K4/2, took Capt N.S. to Depot ship for conference. Was instructed to tow LBE 22 who had neither screws nor rudder to the beaches. Finally secured at 2245, air raid 2315, assisted by making smoke. Received orders from Capt N.S. following morning 9th to lead in a Flotilla of Minesweepers. Sailed at 1225 with convoy of Coasters for Tilbury.

Norman was not to know at the time, but this resulted in his being gazetted as Mentioned in Dispatches in the London Gazette of the 6 March 1945. The citation read 'For skilled leadership and initiative while protecting the British assault area'.

Norman picks up his diary again for July 1944. ML 909 was engaged in convoy escort duties from the Thames Estuary to Portsmouth and shoots down her second V1 flying bomb. The diary includes extracts from L.F. Graves' diary (the crew member who lived near Queenbury wharf).

9th   Slip with convoy to Thames, usual flak. V.I. shot down, shared with two other ships …

18th   7th convoy to Portsmouth, best trip yet, very hot …

From now, L.F. Graves diary.

26th   Arrive Thames.

27th   0750 hour engine routine.

28th   9th convoy to Portsmouth, flying bombs about.

31st   Came across four damaged Liberty ships, one sank later 0600 hours. Escorted others
        to Dungeness.

If the construction of the Fairmile MLs was to give a clue about future manufacturing processes, the construction of Liberty ships would provide the whole story. Liberty ships, though
British in conception, were built in the United States. They were 7000-ton cargo ships purchased for the US Fleet for lend lease to Britain to replace its sunk tonnage. The ships were
made assembly-line style, from prefabricated sections, which were then welded together. The
average build time was around 42 days and by 1943, three new Liberty ships were being completed every day.

AUGUST

2nd   3 pounder gun found to be defective. [Frank Kay told me there was a defect in the
           breach, but in fact this gun was not used much.]

3rd   10th convoy.

4th   Still at sea, baking hot day.

9th   11th convoy to Portsmouth.

10th   Fog deadly at night. Met convoy coming the other way. Told all hands to come on
           upper deck with life jackets. Not very popular at about 0200 hrs when the watch
           below were sound asleep, but ships were everywhere and we could have easily been
           hit.

11th   Tied up to Merchant ship, still thick fog.

15th   Trot boat at tower off Margate.

19th   12th convoy to Portsmouth. A.A. shells off Dover. Weather very rough.

22nd   Still at sea, longest trip for some time.

23rd   Routine maintenance, crew went on leave, four of us left. A good quiet time.

28th   All crew back by noon.

29th   13th convoy to Portsmouth. Flying bomb exploded overhead. Nasty night.

31st   Very rough journey. Saw flashes of German guns at Calais, while off Beachy Head.

On 19 September there is a diary reference to Arnhem. Following the triumph of the D-Day
landings in France the advance had become bogged down with slow and costly progress
through the heavily and skilfully defended Normandy fields and hedgerows.

As the Allies pushed through France and Belgium nearer to Germany's borders, German
resistance stiffened further. Montgomery believed that a powerful, narrow thrust deep into
German lines would be more effective than an advance on a broad front, which had become
difficult to supply from the few ports controlled by the Allies. The result was Operation
Market Garden, the largest airborne landing ever undertaken. Thirty thousand British and
American airborne troops dropped by parachute and in gliders were flown behind enemy
lines landing near the Dutch towns of Eindhoven, Nijmegen and Arnhem, to capture the
eight key bridges that spanned the network of canals and rivers on the Dutch/German
border and over which the advancing British armour were supposed to push through to
Germany. As with earlier airborne assaults seen by both Allied and Axis forces, notably in

Sicily and Crete, there was an inherent risk of troop separation and the separation of those troops from their armaments. Both happened on Operation *Market Garden*. The Parachute Division would leave behind nearly 1,500 dead, and more than 6,500 prisoners, many badly wounded. Operation *Market Garden* failed. It would be another four months before the Allies crossed the Rhine again.

Meanwhile ML 909 was ploughing back and forth on convoy escort duties. Frank Kay told me what a boring duty this was, grinding along at about 7 knots with nothing much to do it seemed, but things would be livening up again in due course.

OCTOBER 1944

5th   Ashore at Gosport. Up to Porchester Hill. Saw film 'Song of Bernadette'

9th   Arrive back at Queenborough.

11th   Home by 5 pm. Tried for extension of leave as Maurice home … no luck!

16th   18th convoy. Took shelter in Dover as sea very rough. Dover looking very bedraggled.

17th   Still too rough.

18th   Back at Queenborough. Big row over night order book, 7 day leave rota cancelled as punishment.

When I asked Frank Kay what this was about he told me: 'The night order book was instructions on what was to happen on the following day. On this occasion there was to be a VIP visit and the crew were to be dressed in No1s. Some wit had overwritten 'bullshit' in the night order book – Hence the disciplinary action.'

November's diary is continued by Laurie Graves, who records the loss of a friend on board ML 916, which on 10 November hit a mine in the Scheldt estuary outside Antwerp, where Norman and ML909 were bound in January 1945.

As early as September 1944, the Allies were acutely aware of the urgency to clear both banks of the Scheldt estuary in order to open the port of Antwerp to Allied shipping, thus easing logistical burdens in their supply lines stretching hundreds of miles from Normandy eastward to the Siegfried Line. Since the Allied forces had landed in Normandy, the British Second Army had pushed forward into the Low Countries and captured Brussels and Antwerp, the latter with its port still intact. But the advance halted with the British in possession of Antwerp, while the Germans still controlled its seaward access, the Scheldt Estuary.

Nothing could be done about these matters during September, however, because most of the already strained Allied resources were allocated to Operation *Market Garden*. In the meantime, German forces in the Scheldt were able to plan a defence.

The Battle of the Scheldt was a series of military operations to determine control of the entrance to the port of Antwerp. The hard-fought battles took place from October 2nd 1944 to November 8th 1944.

When Laurie Graves' friend was killed on 10 November, the fighting was over but the business of clearing German mines was underway. Indeed it was an another three weeks before the first ship carrying Allied supplies was able to unload in Antwerp (on 29 November) due to the necessity of de-mining the harbours.

In early October, after *Market Garden* had failed, Allied forces led by the First Canadian Army set out to bring the Antwerp ports under control. The well-established German defenders staged an effective delaying action making good use of the waterlogged terrain. This largely forgotten battle proved to be especially gruelling and costly.

It took five weeks of difficult fighting for the First Canadian Army, bolstered by attached troops from Britain, Belgium, The Netherlands, Norway and Poland, to take the Scheldt, after numerous amphibious assaults, canal crossings, and fighting over open ground. Both land and water were mined, and the Germans defended their retreating line with artillery and snipers. Later on Norman's Brother Donald (Jack) will describe the German use of snipers by its retreating army from the point of view of a Royal Marine.

The final phase would be the capture of Walcheren Island, which had been heavily fortified. As part of the Atlantic Wall, Walcheren Island was considered to be the strongest concentration of defences the Nazis had ever constructed.

Heavy batteries on the western and southern coasts defended both the island and the Scheldt estuary, and the coastline had been fortified against amphibious assaults. A landward-facing defensive perimeter had been built around the town of Vlissingen to further defend the port facilities should an Allied landing on Walcheren succeed. The only land approach was the Sloedam—a long, narrow causeway from South Beveland, little more than a raised two-lane road. To make matters more difficult, the flats that surrounded this causeway were too saturated with sea water for movement on foot, but had too little water for an assault in storm boats.

To hamper German defence, the island's dykes were breached by attacks from RAF Bomber Command: on 3 October at Westcapelle, with severe loss of civilian life; on 7 October in two places, west and east of Vlissingen; and on 11 October at Veere. This flooded the central part of the island, forcing the German defenders onto the high ground around the outside and in the towns, but it also allowed the use of amphibious vehicles. The island was attacked from three directions: across the causeway from the east, across the Scheldt from the south, and by sea from the west.

After a heavy naval bombardment of Westkapelle by the Royal Navy, troops of 4th Special Service Brigade (41, 47, and 48 Royal Marine Commando and 10 Inter Allied Commando, the latter consisting mainly of Belgian and Norwegian troops) attacked. They were supported by specialised armoured vehicles (amphibious transports, mine-clearing tanks, bulldozers, etc), which were landed on both sides of the gap in the sea dyke. Large landing craft as well as amphibious vehicles brought men and tanks ashore. Heavy fighting ensued before the ruins of the town were captured. Some of the troops moved south-eastward, toward Vlissingen, while the main force went north-east to clear the northern half of Walcheren and link up with the Canadian troops who had established a bridgehead on the eastern part of the island. Fierce resistance was again offered by some of the German troops defending this area, and that fighting continued until 7 November.

The Allies finally cleared the port areas on 8 November, but at a cost of 12,873 Allied casualties (killed, wounded, or missing), half of them Canadians.

2nd   20th convoy. Nice trip.

3rd   Saw film in Gosport 'White Cliffs of Dover'

5th   Visited friends on Isle of Wight.

8th   After 4 days bad weather left with M.L. 588 for Dover.

10th   Departed suddenly for Southend. Heard M.L. 916 being hit by mine in the Scheldt estuary, had friend on board.

11th   Job was to escort tug towing a big drum of ocean cable from Dungeness to France I.E. Operation *Pluto*, (Pipe Line Under The Ocean) pipe carrying oil. Rather boring, speed only 3 knots.

12th   21st convoy but turned back after 17 hrs.

16th   22nd convoy.

17th   Worst beam sea ever experienced off Selsey Bill. Whole gale blowing on arrival at
        Gosport at 0700 hrs.

25th   [Christmas Day.] Left for Gillingham slips, 17 days leave from 1400 hrs. Pay etc on
        board and very convenient for 'Rabbits.'

'Rabbits' is Naval slang for articles taken, or intended to be taken, ashore privately. Originally
'rabbits' were things taken ashore improperly (i.e. theft or smuggling – the name arose from
the ease with which tobacco, etc, could be concealed in the inside of a dead rabbit) but with
the passage of time the application of the word has spread to anything taken ashore; an air of
impropriety nevertheless still hangs over the word. Hence the derivation of the phrase 'Tuck its
ears in,' said to crew seen going ashore with a parcel.

26th   Entered harbour 0540 hrs. Skipper and Jimmy down for dinner, it was his turkey.
        Finished orgy at 1600 hrs. Everybody pretty well away. Two of us stayed aboard for
        the evening.

Norman explains the turkey:

I brought the turkey back from leave in a tea chest, Pop got the turkey from the country
somewhere. It was kept on board on the bridge, fed, watered, came on convoy patrol, woke
everybody up in harbour with its gobble, gobble. 'Jumped ship' in Sheerness dockyard but
with the help of the dockyard workers and the crew we recaptured it. One poor WREN on
leaving the ship after attending to the W.T. (Wireless Transmitter) was in tears at the thought
of what was in store for the bird, which was eventually dealt with by 1st Lt. Bert Gillett.

And Frank Kay:

Well that turkey … it was not only the WREN who was upset, that turkey was a pet, it would
follow you about with its gobble, gobble, gobble. We loved it. When it came to be dispatched
no-one wanted to do the job, so 'Jimmy the One' Bert Gillett the ex-Nottingham policeman,
got the job. He stood on its neck for what seemed like ages with the bird flapping like mad. I
offered to get a revolver and shoot it but that offer was declined. Eventually it became still, was
roasted up and set at the head of the table on the mess deck with officers invited. Well, no-one
really had the stomach to eat it, but in deference to Norman we did.

28th   At sea.

30th   In at 0530. Water discovered coming in at dinnertime. Frank Kay was playing darts
        with others and his dart fell in the bilges, when they lifted the mess deck floor they
        found water was lapping the deck. Started pumping. Must have been noise heard
        when at sea last night, probably scraped submerged wreck.

Again Frank Kay offers: 'The fault was actually Norman's – he had cut a corner coming back
into port – it was not a submerged wreck but a rock!'

31st   Boat put on slips, 9ft gash in bottom, at least a 3 weeks job but danger of being paid off.

In January 1945 ML 909 was dispatched to the European mainland.

1st   5 days leave apiece in 3 watches.

2nd   News of Jimmy's draft. [The second in command or 1st Lieutenant on board was commonly known in RN slang as 'Jimmy the One', so this would have referred to Sub Lieutenant Bert Gillett.]

3rd   Leave apparently to be curtailed. Merry hell on Mess deck.

4th   Order reversed, there is some leave.

7th   Snow fell pm, saw 'Dear Octopus.'

8th   Home on 5 days leave.

14th   Returned to Queenborough.

15th   Expected last visit home, going to Ostend.

19th   Once more at home, this time with Rose.

20th   Left for Ostend, nasty stern sea.

21st   Not very impressed by first glimpses.

22nd   Out on patrol just outside harbour for 24 hrs. Jerry reconnaissance planes over at night. Coldest night at sea.

24th   On patrol, swapped cigarettes for a bucket of fish, fresh herrings from Belgium smack. Threw first 100lbs charge on suspected midget sub.

25th   Ice forming over harbour.

27th   Patrol cut short at 0830 owing to bad weather.

29th   Several charges failed to go off while trying to blow up wreck.

In February 1945 ML 909 is moored up in Ostend, when disaster strikes. This was no 'heroic action' but there were many acts of individual heroism. As with many accidents it was not one factor but a combination of factors that caused a massive explosion and the loss of virtually an entire Small Ship flotilla and many lives. Not unnaturally it was fairly well hushed up at the time but there was a Board of Inquiry and much of what follows is taken from its report.

Norman's 26th birthday was on 14 February 1945, but there were no celebrations. On that fateful day the Creek or Crique, a part of Ostend harbour, was crowded with shipping including two LSTs (Landing Ship Tanks) but notably with the timber-built Small Ship class of the ML MTB and Dog Boat type. The MTBs were there to harass German E- boats laying mines and attacking shipping off the Belgian and French coasts.

Amongst the MTBs were the nine ships of the Canadian Flotilla 29. They were packed into the 'knuckle' – a finger of water bordered by timber piles, jetties and a lock entrance. They were arranged in 'trots', rafts of three and four ships tied up side to side. The first of the trots was lettered A and the last actually in the knuckle 'finger' was trot D. ML 909 was in trot E, she had a stern line to trot D and had fairly good access to the open water of the main harbour.

A few of Flotilla 29's ships (notably MTB 464) had been having trouble with water in their petrol tanks. The Petty Officer Motor Mechanic of MTB 464 reported the problem to his 'Jimmy the One' who in turn claimed to have reported it on to the CFMU (Coastal Forces Mobile Unit) the mobile maintenance unit, which had been stationed in Ostend for around six months. Nothing was done to alleviate the water problem so the M/M set about dealing with it himself, as they were to be on patrol at 1730.

The problem was not uncommon and was often dealt with by onboard crew using a small volume pump such as a semi rotary or plunger type to expel the water. There were however precautions, such as advising adjoining vessels and posting a proper lookout to observe the pumping. On this occasion the M/M could not properly use the smaller volume types and so coupled up the bilge pump – a vastly more powerful pump than was commonly used – and started to clear the water. This, so the Inquiry was informed, was not uncommon.

The outlet from the bilge pump was only 6 inches from the water line and by the time the M/M had noticed the pump was venting petrol, the colour of which the Board of Inquiry noted was not dissimilar from the harbour water, and had gone to turn the pump off there were gallons of 100 octane petrol floating in the confined area of the 'Knuckle' where 15 MTBs were tightly moored together.

A returning MTB first noted the smell of petrol at around 1330. It was smelt by others but not reported. At 1400 hundred hours it was ignited. The Board of Inquiry never discovered the cause of the ignition – perhaps it was a fag end spun into the water. There was a blue flame tracking across the water followed two minutes later by the first explosion, MTB 465 had disintegrated, closely followed by MTB 462.

The fire spread extremely rapidly throughout the creek area; 'There were a number of violent explosions accompanied by flying debris as well as the explosions of rockets and ammunition and the burning of depth charges and torpedo warheads, which, in a chilling understatement, the B.o.I. noted 'considerably hampered the fire fighting, salvage of MTBs and rescue operations'.

It was estimated that there were some 40 men in the water, either having jumped or having been blown overboard. These men used life belts or scrambled on to Carly Floats thrown by other MTBs and MLs or were picked up by the ships from trots E and F, of which ML 909 was one. She picked up five.

Frank Kay, Norman and the rest of 909's compliment were on board, rafted up in trot E. Frank remembers talking over the stern rail to a sailor on board MTB 798 immediately before the first explosion – then suddenly the man was headless.

The MTB immediately to their outside slipped and moved ahead, as she was proceeding down harbour the commanding officer Lieutenant Galbraith RNVR was killed on his bridge by flying debris.

Norman meanwhile had started engines and was trying to move ahead but was held by the stern line near where Frank was standing. Norman sent Able Seaman Sloan with an axe for Frank to cut the line, which by this time was as tight as a banjo string. The axe head bounced off so Frank told Sloan to return to the bridge to get the ship put astern so he could slip the line in the normal way. Sloan was felled by a flying scrubbing brush on his way back (he was not seriously injured) and the plan was put into action, they slipped the line and five survivors were taken on board, as was a flying gun shield that had landed on the foredeck.

The toll was five officers and 59 ratings killed or missing and five officers and 60 ratings wounded, in addition to which there were civilian casualties.

One of the only pieces of good fortune noted by the B.o.I. was 'The handling of casualties was extremely effective and this was facilitated by the presence of three ambulance trains parked in the station south of the Maritime Building and a total of eleven Medical Officers (Two Naval and nine Army Medical Corps) were on the scene within ten minutes of the first explosion.'

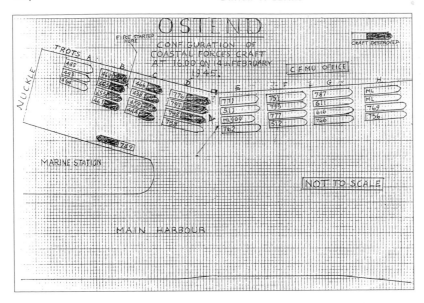

Sketch plan from the Court of Inquiry after the disaster at Ostend. (Frank Kay)

There is a section tucked in at the end of the B.o.I. report titled 'Damage to Wharves and Buildings' and within this section, apart from commenting upon compensation claims is the note: 'Glass windows in the Cathedral were broken as well those in houses over quite a large area. It appears that the population of Ostend have endured at least three explosions and evidently that which occurred on 14 February seems to have caused little comment or complaint.'

The Inquiry was critical of many procedures and people. The Naval Officer in charge of Ostend Harbour came away pretty well unscathed – not so the Commanding Officer of the CFMU who was censured.

There were many others however, who were singled out for their outstanding courage. One of these was Lieutenant I.A.H. Quarrie RNVR, Commander of MTB 776. His vessel was the innermost one on trot D, the trot immediately to the stern of 909. The Inquiry noted 'He was indefatigable in his efforts to get his boat and possibly the whole trot away.' The Inquiry report continued:

He did not hear the first fire alarm as he was in the bathroom when his quartermaster gave the alarm. He was knocked down by the first explosion and coming on deck found the fire had reached 791. Lieutenant Quarrie went to his bridge and rang down 'Start Main Engines' but got no response and he therefore let go all berthing ropes from MTB 776 to the jetty and proceeded to MTB 791 to find engine crew personnel with the idea of taking all four boats clear of the fire. He could find no-one on board, however, so he endeavoured to start the engines himself until he remembered that 791 was carrying out a maintenance. He then proceeded to 758 where he found sub lieutenant Whiteside and Able Seaman Burroughs. They were unsuccessful in starting the engines of MTB 758. By this time fires had started out on MTBs 758 and 776 but these were mainly extinguished by these three persons. The tragic part was that had Lieutenant Quarrie gone down aft in MTB 798 he would have found the Petty Officer Motor Mechanic who had stuck to his ship and a few minutes later was able to start all four engines.

Also mentioned was Lieutenant Fletcher RNVR, commander of MTB 798, to which 909 was berthed. He came to Quarrie's aid, went to start his engines but was blown overboard. The other two commanding officers in the four-ship trot D were less favourably viewed by the Board '… both were in the wardroom of MTB 791 … and proceeded ashore.'

Eventually the four-ship trot made it away from the knuckle and beached by one of the LSTs. The day was a long one. Four hours after the first explosion at 1800 the fires in the Creek and CFMU area were extinguished. The fires on Lieutenant Quarrie's trot at 2 LST were extinguished by 2210, but broke out again at 0040. A further explosion occurred there at 0110 and the subsequent fire extinguished at 0400 on 15 February.

Of the eight craft forming the 29th Flotilla only three remained, the flotilla was disbanded and surviving boats joined other flotillas. Under a section entitled 'Comments on Specific points' the report noted:

To berth these heavily armed, petrol driven and therefore highly inflammable boats safely in any harbour would be difficult and require such an amount of dispersion as to be administratively inconvenient. The real solution is to construct Diesel boats which are neither so potentially dangerous to their crews nor need so much maintenance. It is understood the Germans use Diesel-driven boats which are faster than our own.

To continue with Laurie Graves' log; but one must bear in mind these terrible events, as the memory will linger on with the crew.

1st   Too rough to go out.

3rd   Visited Bruges.

8th   Routine on board giving rise to trouble. Everyone is generally fed up. Coxswain not really up to his job. Got Jimmy (No.1) to look at Mess Deck. Earlier rising recommended.

10th   Sea too rough again.

14th   Awful explosion in harbour (Ostend) Canadian M.T.B.s pumping out bilges contaminated with petrol, cigarette thrown overboard, set alight to harbour. Debris flying everywhere, torpedoes exploding, our loud hailer direction pole was cut in half just missing my head. Put to sea immediately but just as we got a few yards out spotted five sailors swimming away in the icy water, ordered scrambling net to be lowered and picked up survivors, flak still flying around, one of the crew getting a slight cut on his leg. Survivors taken down below, change of clothing and hot drink, they soon recovered. Continued out to sea. 'Graves.' 13 boats destroyed, approx 100 killed, Military Policeman on dock gates decapitated, windows of St Peter & Paul Cathedral shattered. We were very lucky, being tied up only two boats lengths away.

15th   Out in bad fog. Watches eased for nighttime.

16th   Demolition in harbour delayed our re-entry.

17th   Duty boat job. M.T.B. sinking. One of our engines conked out.

18th   Bought album of photos taken by German sailors during their occupation. E boats & armed trawlers.

19th   Engine trouble being repaired, worst luck!

20th   Cylinder head changed after two days work, but engine exploded after start-up. [Causing a fire which was quickly put out, but everybody very jumpy!]

21st   After much suspense left Ostend for Queenborough. Good going for one engine
            only, but sea very flat.

23rd   Home for all night. Dockyard for engine repair and tons of stores to come on board.

24th   Home at 2.30 pm.

25th   Leave until Tuesday.

28th   Left for Ostend.

1st   Buzz about a Rhine job.

Frank Kay:

We started out up the Rhine but we didn't get far, as the retreating Germans had blown up
the lock gates. It was an eerie experience though, we could see the dead soldiers – German
and Allied, still on the banks of the Rhine. If we had been involved in any action we wouldn't
have stood much of a chance in a timber boat with all that petrol on board. We were issued
with an early type of flack jacket, they were like a smock and were as heavy as lead. You
couldn't do a thing with them on and had we needed to abandon ship we would have sunk
like a stone, so like quite a few 'good ideas', we didn't use them.

4th   Left Ostend for U.K. Fairly rough trip. Was seasick for first time in two-and-a-half
            years. Both engines out, water in fuel.

5th   Home by 5.30 pm after defuelling.

6th   At Queenborough. Buzz of slipping to Thames and leave. De-ammunitioned ship.
            Panic again over fire started in engine room. Nearly all crew ran for it up to the jetty.
            Skipper severely cautioned us. Probably memory of Ostend explosion three weeks
            previous.

Norman adds a note of his own:

Base staff had been messing around with the engine and got petrol in the sump, on start up a
spark must have ignited the fumes causing a mass of flame but motor mechanic Hughes and
stoker Lawson, both long-standing crew members, put fire out with extinguishers – a very
brave effort. Recommended them to the Captain of the base who formally acknowledged
both for their bravery. Cannot say the same about most of the others who got a good dressing
down, which I have heard afterwards, sunk in. Admittedly they had gone through a bit just
lately but there was no excuse for abandoning ship, without orders to do so.

According to Frank Kay, what Norman omits to record is that the reason he knew it was
Hughes and Lawson who put out the fire was that he, Norman, did the job with them.

7th   Left for Westminster Bridge Pier. Some crew went on 7 days leave from here.

8th   Arrive at Teddington 0930, four of us left on board. Nobody knows much about us
            here.

9th   Visited Uncle Bert at Surbiton.

10th   Home early by 1500 hrs until mid-night tomorrow.

11th   Returned to Teddington 2300 hrs.

14th   Left Teddington. Spent P.M. in Oxford Street, then went on leave.

Norman adds a further note; 'Took 909 up the Thames, secured alongside Westminster Pier, stopped for the night then continued on to Toughs of Teddington. Not too sure what happened at Toughs but think we had another skin put on below the water line to cope with the ice in the Baltic.'

23rd   Felt rather under the weather, getting ammunition on board did not improve matters.

24th   Home by 1515 hrs.

28th   Home at 1645 hrs.

29th   Made Leading Seaman. Very thankful really, especially just before leaving for the Rhine.

30th   Departed Queenborough 0700 hrs entered Antwerp Docks 0200 hrs.

31st   Moved into Strasborg Dock. Ashore, very good R.N.B. (Royal Naval Base)

1st   Easter Sunday, High Mass in Cathedral very ceremonial.

2nd   Duty boat.

3rd   Football, drew 5-5 against M.L. 597.

4th   Improvised cricket match. Tried to collect rugby team.

6th   'Patrick the Great' film, wangled in without ticket.

8th   With party to Brussels. Lovely hot day for city tour. Life seems almost normal. Guides available, cinemas open. Canteen grub first class and ice cream gorgeous. Shops full of everything. Returned on very crowded train 2200 hrs.

10th   Ashore early to visit Antwerp zoo.

Frank Kay:

Our time in Antwerp was memorable for two reasons; firstly just as Norman met up with his brother in Brunsbuttle and had him on board so by chance did I meet up with my father. He was on a salvage boat – LC9 – and there it was in Antwerp. I went on board and asked if there was a chap called George Kay on board and there he was. The other event was memorable in the sense that high jinks can sometimes lead to tragedy. Not too far from our berth was a barrel-shaped barge and Norman mentioned it was filled with schnapps. It was guarded by one of the Royal Marines in Antwerp at the time, so we thought it would be rather fun to get him tipsy on some of our rum and grab some schnapps. Well the plan went well and we attacked the barrel with an axe and filled saucepans and a tin bath with the stuff. The next morning the Marine was found dead. He had shot himself – out of depression, by accident or in fear of his dereliction of duty – we never found out.

ML 909 was detailed with graves at sea duty and I had the job of stitching him in a bolt of canvas weighted at the bottom so he slid into the sea at attention. There is a code when doing this job. The last stitch has to go through the corpse's nose to make sure it really was a corpse. I really struggled to get the needle through and none of the others would help me.

11th   Day full of surprises, Bradford [CO HMS *Gadfly*] was supposed to have inspected us. Skipper told us that the Rhine job was off.

12th   Duty boat on our last night here, however slipped ashore on duty to buy a few things out of Docks.

13th   Left Antwerp 0700, River Scheldt. A few more wrecks at mouth, arrived Queenborough 1900 hrs.

14th   Home by 1430. Lift all the way.

15th   Home by 1615.

17th   After sudden decision sailed for Ramsgate at 1400 hrs. Fuelled before proceeding to Dover.

18th   Left at 0600 to escort tug towing a PLUTO cable drum to Boulogne, very flat sea.

19th   Did a sub for Mickey (Rosher) hoping to get Saturday. Now in Ramsgate again.

20th   Ashore in Ramsgate, cafes etc. opening for holiday season.

22nd   24 hr patrol of 4 miles between Dover and Folkestone. Monotonous job, first 4 hr watch for some time.

23rd   Home by 1615, hitch hike.

27th   Very cold night at sea. Tons of fish.

28th   Home by 1600 hrs.

30th   Blizzard at 0800.

1st   Messing around all afternoon with fuelling and asdics

4th   Surrender of German troops in N.W. Europe.

6th   Left for Queenborough, home by 1515.

7th   Into Sheerness dockyard for putting on Y guns (all boats). [Depth Charge launchers]

8th   Home by 2000. Very sober celebrations [for V.E. Day]. Floodlit buildings and bonfires. Back on board at 0500.

9th   Sailed at 0500 for Immingham, arrived 0730. Just missed escorting E boat back.

10th   Typhus inoculation.

12th   Visit aunts and uncles at Alford.

14th   Big surprise first thing this morning. Relief arrived for me from *Hornet*. [Coastal Forces Base, Portsmouth]. Started draft routine. Played football against 595 in Cup Final. Had to sleep in base.

15th   Left Grimsby 0905 train after collecting Burberry and gas mask from 908.

Lawrie Graves ends his diary:

I got home 51 times for either midnight or all-night leave for the 12 months I was aboard 909, a record I would think, normal leave was on top of this.

These notes are un-edited but I would like to mention the 6 March episode. Panic had obviously got amongst the crew. My conscience pricked as I was climbing up the jetty wall and duly returned to the boat. We were lucky not to have been on a serious charge of desertion. You [Norman] must have been in a terrible plight.

In one of those strange coincidences of war Norman records meeting up with his younger brother Donald (Jack) Stoate in Brunsbuttel.

Back again across the North Sea to Ostend, then worked our way up the coast to Antwerp, Imuiden, Cuxhaven, Brunsbuttel [entrance to Kiel Canal]. We were met by the Royal Marines, happened to ask if a fellow called Stoate was amongst them ... And he was. Jack was amongst other things the entertainment officer of the Company or Battalion, he came on board for a meal, he also put us in touch with the Burgomaster who supplied us with shotguns and radios which the Germans had handed in. Jack also gave us two cars for the flotilla. Proceeded through the Kiel Canal to Flensburg, HMS *Cadfly*, shore-based establishment. We were reported to be the first warships through the canal since the war ended.

Frank Kay:

Norman's reference to shotguns and radios wasn't just casual, arms and radios had to be handed in, but Norman seemed to be fanatical about these radios, there were stacks of them

ML 909 off Holland. Note the bicycle on deck.

Lubeck 1945. Left to right, ' Sparks'
Rogers, Everet 'Flags' Rule, and Frank
'Yorkie' Kay. (Norman Stoate)

in the wardroom. I told him they wouldn't work in England because of the different electrical
supply, but that didn't seem to worry him at all.

Jack, my father, was rather keener on the ordnance side of things and apart from the shotgun
and .22 rifle that ended up with Norman after the war we had one particularly fine Browning
9mm automatic pistol on the farm. My father eventually consigned it, along with a couple of
other less interesting pistols, to the bottom of the Solent.

Flotilla 33 was now detailed up the Kiel Canal to emerge at Kiel in the Baltic where they
carried out Bay and Baltic patrol duties, calling in at Ekenforde about two and half hours sailing time from Kiel, Lubec, Travemunde and other ports on the Baltic coast.

Frank Kay:

It was a strange time, it was about May/June 1945, there was no military action as such. We
had some involvement in taking soldiers with SS tattooed on their arm for internment on one
of the islands. In spite of this the Germans seemed keen to have us on their soil as the alternative would have been Russian occupation. We had a fair amount of leisure time, Norman
even strapped a bicycle to the railing of 909 so we could get about in the port areas. He would
also organise shooting parties and go over the estuary from Lubec to the Russian side with
cigarettes and return with fresh meat and eggs for us. Sometimes we would do similar trades
with the Danish fishermen, but you only had to lob a depth charge over the side and you'd
have plenty of fish.

So although the war was not over yet, both the military and civilian Germans – particularly the civilians – were friendly. I struck up with a German lady who had a beautiful little seven-year-old daughter who spoke perfect English – sentence construction, intonation and all. I suspected her mother was English but she denied it and only spoke in German to me, so I learned to get by in that language. The little girl, they lived at Lubec, wanted me to be her Dad and take her back to England with me.

At that time there were non-fraternisation orders, the sanctions were quite harsh – three months in prison and a dishonourable discharge I think. Well, Norman had already lost Petrie, a fairly recent crew member for this, and one day he called me to the bridge. There he showed me a signal that I was to report back to England. We were in Kiel at the time, the town had been severely bombed – it was a wasteland and there I was, set ashore.

I had nothing, no pass, nothing. Even getting past the port area guard was a nightmare. My next task was to find transport. I stopped a German couple to ask the way to the barnhoff, the railway station, and they walked me there even carrying my kit bag. There I found a train with some liberated PoWs on board and so arrived eventually at Cuxhaven, from there I found passage on a ship to Tilbury.

So there I was back in England but with no English money. In those days if you were in uniform it was not hard to jump on a train, so that's what I did arriving at Gosport where I thought someone must know something. No-one did so it was suggested I went on to Plymouth. There thankfully a Regular CPO [Chief Petty Officer] took me in hand and found me a job clearing mines off Wareham and that's where I stayed until I was demobbed.

Of course I realise now that Norman probably rigged that signal for my own good. I was very young and was getting in too deep but at the time we didn't part on the best of terms, and I often wonder what became of that little girl and her mum.

Norman, in note form takes up the thread again:

One of the first jobs I was given with 909 at Kiel was to escort a landing craft and be in charge of loading it with small boats of all types which had to be given up by the Germans living on the small islands and the mainland, these had usually been assembled at certain points by the Burgomaster of the area. One yacht I thought was far too good to be thrown up on the L.C. [Landing Craft] so I towed it astern and on the return presented it (not mine to present) to the Kiel Yacht Club.

Invited to a Russian Music Hall show; all told not to whistle our appreciation as this means just the opposite. Also visited Denmark by car and occasionally put into their Baltic Ports.

Commander of HMS *Cadfly* (our base ship) C.G. Bradford summoned all ships officers for a 'pep' talk, said that one of his officers was driving about in an un-officer-like car and he was to get rid of it. I changed it for a large Buick limousine! He also said that one of his officers had arranged a soccer match against the German staff and that this must be cancelled as this was fraternising, so again I had to oblige. A little later, about July I think it was, the non-fraternisation ban was lifted. Social life consisted of visits to other boats, soccer matches, Ballet Rambert entertained us! Visits to Denmark. I also organised occasional shoots with volunteer crews as beaters, have since learnt that they thoroughly enjoyed these. Also took out the Buick limousine, with large sunshine roof, at night with Jack Spratt and Johnny Bick, one driving and two guns through the sunshine roof and we would shoot the odd deer or two in the headlights. Luckily there was a peacetime butcher in the flotilla who cut up the deer and distributed them amongst the boats – very welcome.

Frank Kay said those shooting parties were great fun, although he remembered one occasion when they were out: 'A little muntjac deer came out of the trees towards us, the little thing was damned near tame, Norman told me to hold it whilst he shot it, I couldn't do that but he shot it anyway and it was eaten on board.' Norman:

Norman Stoate in Baltic overcoat.
(Geoffrey Stoate)

One thing we did have to be careful of was, the Germans would stretch piano wire across
the road, from tree to tree about windscreen height, mainly against the army in open jeeps,
hoping to decapitate them or us.

In September 1945 Norman was home on leave.

Motored from Flensburg with Jackie Spratt and Johnnie Bick through Germany into Holland,
spent the next night at a small army camp at Xanten in one of the officer's tents, very cold, fortunately he had a bottle of whisky. Cracked the ice for shaving the next morning. Continued
on through Holland into Belgium, Antwerp, Ghent and onto Calais to cross over to England.
Left car at Calais but when we came back it had been stolen; managed to get another car and
so back to Flensburg, to resume duties.

January 1946:

Took M.L. 909 home for paying off, went via Cuxhaven, Imuiden across North Sea to
England. Had a farewell party in a pub and said goodbye to boat and crew. Asked H.M. Navy
for ship's bell if 909 was to be scrapped, as I commissioned the ship from new and was the sole
'owner'. I had to pay for it but the bell arrived and it has been in the family ever since.

On 19 February 1946, five days after his 27th birthday Norman wrote:

Received my release from HMS *Pembroke* [Royal Naval Barracks at Chatham], was given 13
days foreign service leave and 56 days resettlement leave to 29 April 1946 when I officially left
the Navy.

9

FROM GLOUCESTERSHIRE
TO THE LOW COUNTRIES

Jack Stoate, the farmer, resigns from the Home Guard to volunteer into the Royal Marines where by chance he meets his brother Norman at the south end of the Kiel Canal, in Brunsbuttle. His wife-to-be Betty Hussey joins the Women's Land Army and Jack's younger brother Geoffrey volunteers for the Royal Observer Corps.

Arthur Donald Stoate – Jack – my father, was born on 9 April 1921 and died just before his 80th birthday on 5 March 2001. He came immediately after Norman and ahead of Geoffrey. His school career was not distinguished and having been encouraged to leave Badminton school Bristol (which at that time took boys and girls) he eventually ended up with his brothers at Clifton College. The circumstances of his removal from Badminton always remained an annoyance to my father and in a sense are a clue to his character. One of his cousins told me he was expelled for sticking another boy's head down a lavatory pan. The reasons however may vindicate the action. The boy concerned was allegedly an inveterate bully and my father, whose sensibilities were offended by injustice and unfair behaviour, took his own independent action. Those two qualities of independence and that sense of justice and fair play governed much of what he passed on to his children.

Formal discipline and Clifton College did not suit him greatly either, although, in spite of his slight figure, he liked boxing. (One can perhaps see in this an early leaning towards volunteering for the Royal Marines).

After Jack left Clifton College in 1937, his father sent him to a farm near Yeovil to receive practical training in agriculture and following that in 1938 installed him as manager of Henfield Farm, near Mangotsfield to the north of Bristol.

His father, Leonard, a businessman of considerable acumen and owner of Henfield and other farms, had some difficulty in leaving his son to get on with the job, and the farm workers understandably had confused loyalties. Though it could not have been too problematical as he remained at Henfield Farm until he volunteered to join the Royal Marines in May 1943.

Leonard Stoate was a staunch Methodist with whom I stayed many times as a young boy and whom I visited often when he retired to Bournemouth. Towards the end of his life his eyesight failed badly, but that did not prevent him from playing his favourite card game of Canasta.

Leonard was a generous and charitable giver, he bought, equipped and gave the community in Watchet its library and in similar mannner set up a home for the elderly in Minehead. He was a lovely man but he did not acquire his wealth by not having a sharp and competitive spirit – he preferred to win rather than lose. Those games of cards were a truly wonderful education in guile and tact. I tried to ensure his victory by sneaking glimpses of his cards without him knowing so that he could make his melds.

On the subject of money he had a homespun philosophy that perhaps should be spread more widely. 'Edward,' he told me as young boy, 'money is all about lakes and rivers – the trick is to be the lake.' I mention this to put a story into context.

One day Leonard was paying a visit to Henfield Farm, the men were busy cutting grass to make silage. Leonard had bought an experimental clamp made up of a type of weld-mesh and fabric to receive the grass which was coming in from a field opposite the main farm entrance, transported to the farmyard by horse and a two-wheeled cart. Now, as Tim Hussey retold, the horse was an old grey mare, she was blind in one eye and a somewhat wilful creature. Leonard insisted on taking the reins and was making for the gateway out of the field on to Henfield Lane. Tim, though only some 15 years old at the time, was an experienced farm hand and suggested that he should perhaps take over. Leonard declined and the horse and cart proceeded towards the gate with the old gardener perched up on top of the pile of freshly cut grass. The mare approached the gate, saw 'home' out of the corner of her good eye, snorted and shot out of the gateway, in so doing the cart struck the right-hand gatepost ripping off the wheel, it slewed and lost its second wheel and landed with a crunch on to its axles. The gardener was thrown off the top onto Leonard who was dislodged from his perch onto the ground. The knowing winks and nods from the assembled on lookers can be well imagined.

Farming was a 'reserved occupation', excused conscription. Like many others however, Jack was unhappy about this and he joined the LDV, later called the Home Guard, on 30 May 1941.

In 1938, his local watering hole became the 'The Beaufort Arms', affectionately known as 'The Folly,' at that time a country inn. The Folly was run by Nellie Hussey, her eldest child was Roy Hussey's older sister Betty; and so my mother and father met. The locals with their distinctive South Gloucestershire burr were intrigued by this good-looking young man with a public school accent. Being friendly but not knowing his name they addressed him as Jack and that name stuck for the rest of his life.

After her father's death on 12 March 1932 Betty had left the Folly to live with her grandparents at Littlewell farm, at Coxley near Wells and then at the age of 15, in 1935, moved to London where her aunt on her father's side of the family helped her to find work in Green and Edwards, a department store in Finchley High Street, where she doubled as a model and seamstress in the gown department.

By 1941 she was back at the Folly and on 3 February 1942 she joined the Women's Land Army. It was not hard to get into the WLA, the official minimum age was 17 but some lied and became Land Girls at 16 or even younger. Life then changed and gave many new Land Girls a rude awakening. Betty would have filled out the necessary form and sent it to Winterbourne Park, where the local WLA Secretary was the Hon Mrs W.R.S. Bathurst. She would have been interviewed to see if she was suitable, then given a superficial medical examination and enrolled.

When researching at the National archives in Kew I was helped to find her WLA index card. Her card shows that Betty Hussey – present occupation clerk – was accepted on 3 February 1942 (No WLA 64195). There is a note of her change of name to Stoate after she married my father in January 1944. On 13 May 1944 her card records 'resigned (health)'. I pondered this for a moment and then realised she would have been two months pregnant with my elder brother Tony.

A former Devon farmer told me that Land Girls were encouraged to resign if pregnant as the work was too arduous. In any event the parting was presumably on good terms as my mother retained her uniform and good service badge (which in the event of resignation was supposed to be handed back) in a drawer under her bed until she died of cancer aged only 52, in 1972.

Memories can be short, and the history of the Women's Land Army proves it. Despite praise in 1918 for the WLA from politicians and farmers alike after the near disastrous food

1942   W.L.A.

Land. Betty

Betty Stoate (nee Hussey) in Land Army uniform. (Author)

shortages the year before, by the time it seemed inevitable that Britain was facing war again, its re-establishment was met with suspicion and derision. Before the Second World War; Britain imported about 60% of its food; now there was a recognition that it needed to grow more of its own. Above all, this meant growing more wheat and potatoes.

The amount of land used for growing crops increased by 50% during the war, mainly by using pasture and marshland. Between May and September 1939, farmers were paid £2 per acre of grassland that they ploughed up, for what was known as the Battle for Wheat. WLA Director the doughty Lady Denman, married to the former Governor-General of Australia, said in 1939: 'The Land Army fights in the fields. It is in the fields of Britain that the most critical battle of the war may well be fought and won.' The aim was to have two million acres of grassland ploughed in time for the 1940 harvest. The target was reached in April that year.

Alongside the policy for increased food production, there was a realisation that there was a shortfall of around 50,000 agricultural workers, following decades of migration to urban factory work, recruitment into the forces and then general conscription. It was to fill this gap that the second WLA was reborn.

Lady Denman used her experience from the previous conflict to good effect. She set up systems for recruitment, enlisting, training, placements and welfare of Land Girls. She was also outstandingly successful in recruiting the titled and well-connected to the cause. The list of County Chairmen is out of Debretts. To give just a flavour: Derbyshire, Her Grace the Dutchess of Devonshire; Devonshire, the Countess Fortescue; Kent, the Lady Cornwallis. For Gloucestershire, Betty's county, the Secretary was The Hon. Mrs. W.R.S Bathhurst, Winterbourne Park. Telephone, Winterbourne 71.

There is little doubt that the WLA achieved its goal so successfully through the great vision and organisational skills of the determined and resourceful Lady Denman, and the hard work, dedication and cheerfulness of thousands of girls who met the challenge. Lady Denman's home, Balcombe Place in Sussex, became the WLA headquarters. Each district had its own WLA representative to ensure the Land Girls were being treated well and were working effectively.

The second WLA was officially formed on June 1st 1939 and recruitment got underway. The first two groups of Land Girls were trained before war was declared. Initially, women were asked to volunteer for the WLA. However, in December 1941 the government passed the National Service Act, which allowed the conscription of women into the armed forces or for vital war work. At first only single women between 20 and 30 and widows without children

Women's Land Army handbook.
(Author)

were called up, but later the age limit was expanded to include women between 19 and 43. Women could choose whether to enter the armed forces or work in farming or industry. By 1943 there were some 90,000 young women, the 'Land Girls', employed in agriculture.

Lady Denman produced a booklet, *Land Girl, A Manual For Volunteers in the Women's Land Army*. It makes interesting reading. Acceptance into the WLA was not to be taken lightly. The terms were very strict, the work was hard and resignations were frowned upon. The short manual is precise and proscriptive.

Every member of the Women's Land Army, either placed in training or in employment, is provided free of charge with a smart uniform. This uniform consists of:

a)   A serviceable rainproof mackintosh
b)   A Khaki overall coat
c)   Two fawn shirts with turn-down collar
d)   A pair of corduroy breeches
e)   A pair of dungarees
f)   A green knitted pullover
g)   Three pairs of fawn stockings
h)   A pair of heavy brown shoes
i)   A pair of rubber gum boots
j)   A brown felt hat
k)   A green armlet with red royal crown on it
l)   A badge of the 'button-hole' type to wear in civilian clothes.

What to take with you

In addition to the uniform, be sure to take with you:

a) Two complete sets of underclothes (at least)
b) Two complete sets of night clothes (at least)
c) A pair of house slippers
d) Another pair of walking-out shoes
e) One or two frocks for changing into in the evening
f) A woolly scarf to put round the head early in the morning
g) Woolly gloves
h) A bicycle, if you possess one
i) Ordinary toilet requisites

The manual details uniform replacement rules – how additional uniform items may be purchased – and their price.

For work the Land Girls wore laced brown brogue shoes, baggy brown corduroy breeches and knee length fawn socks. A green, V-necked, long-sleeved ribbed jumper was worn over a fawn aertex shirt, with the WLA tie for formal wear. On their heads they wore brown felt pork-pie-style hats. A three-quarter length waterproof brown overcoat finished the outfit. Brown dungarees, a matching jacket and wellington boots were also issued for work clothes. The WLA badge depicted a wheat sheaf as a symbol of their work.

The following section covered employment issues including pay and holidays and includes a paragraph on resignations.

A volunteer will only resign for health or urgent private reasons, and on doing so she must hand in her uniform, and, if in a position to do so, she should refund the cost of her training and equipment.

Resignations, naturally, are not welcome, for it is expected that girls who take up this vital and very important work of feeding the nation will not resign.

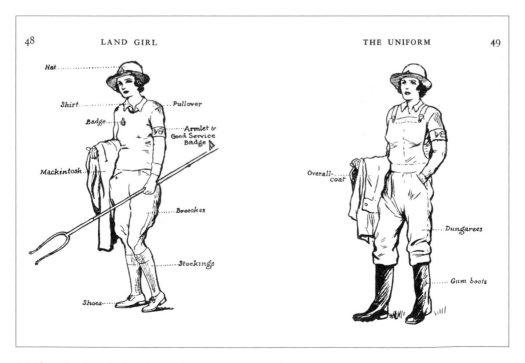

'Uniforms' as described in the Land Army manual. (Author)

Most Land Girls had been barmaids, waitresses, maids, hairdressers, mill workers and so forth before joining the WLA. Some had joined straight from school. Few had ever worked the land and many had not lived in the countryside. More than a third of the girls came from London and the industrial cities of the north. They did not always understand what was required of them, despite their introductory training.

The reality of being a Land Girl was far from that depicted on the glamorous recruitment posters. Not only were there new skills to learn and knowledge to acquire, but the work was arduous. In 1939, the farming community of Britain initially greeted the idea of a Women's Land Army with scorn. In 1939, it was the view of those who worked the land that it was no place for a decent woman. Farm machinery was made for and operated by fit men used to the physical requirements of the job. Many of these girls, however, proved how useful they could be – even beating local men in horse-ploughing competitions and when it was disbanded in 1950, the National Farmers Union was one of the loudest complainers.

Whilst the *Land Army Manual* could give the girls advice about adapting to their new life-styles, the reality would have been a shock for the city girls in particular. The hours were long: morning milking usually started at 4 o'clock. They were expected to work 48 hours a week in winter and 50 hours a week in summer, but most girls worked many more, especially during the harvest when they worked during all the daylight hours, 7.30 am to 9.30 pm. In winter it was cold work and it was perhaps not surprising that farmers at first doubted whether the girls could do the job.

The Land Girls did everything that had to be done on the land. They planted and harvested wheat; they milked cows and delivered the milk by pony and trap to local houses; they picked sprouts and fruit; dug potatoes; tended flocks of sheep; looked after pigs and poultry; they ploughed fields and dug ditches. There were even some 1000 specialists who were trained in rat-catching, a very useful job – a rat could eat about 50kg of food in a year. And there was the Timber Corps, chopping down trees and running sawmills – the so called Lumber Jills.

At the outbreak of war, the average wage for a male agricultural worker was 38 shillings a week, well below the national average wage of 80 shillings a week. Thanks to Lady Denman, Land Girls were awarded a minimum wage, but this was less than their male counterparts would receive. They earned not less than 32 shillings a week, The Manual stated 'If the County wage rates are higher, higher wages are paid to the volunteer. In some Counties, for instance, these rates are as high as 38 shillings.'

At the start of the war most of the Land girls lived in with their host employer or in cottages with the families of other workers but it was not unusual for hostels to be set up to house a local group. If the volunteer was billeted in the farm house she had to receive a minimum of 16 shillings per week in addition to free board and lodging. As the wages were paid directly by the farmer, rather than by the state, however, it was sometimes difficult to ensure that everyone was paid properly.

As the war progressed, mobile gangs of Land Girls were set up to work on different farms. They lived in hostels, which were typically vacant country houses, YWCA hostels and schools, where they were looked after by a warden and where conditions tended to be more comfortable than in billets. There could be anything between 6 and 100 girls in these hostels.

One problem that was acknowledged by the organisation was loneliness. It was probably not too bad if there were a group of girls working together but a singleton posting must have been very hard. Lady Denman had foreseen this and the County Committees and support staff that she set up ensured that the girls had somebody to talk to about any concerns that they had. On the subject of welfare there is a paragraph on parties that seems quaint by today's standards:

> There is no reason at all why little parties should not be arranged for a few girls in any town or village. Sometimes the girls themselves arrange these and perhaps pay a visit to the local cinema together, or meet for a game of cards or good gossip round the fire.

Betty Hussey in Land Girl uniform astride
Jack's Velocette at the rear of the Folly Inn,
Mangotsfield, Bristol.

Group at rear of 16 Queen Street Wells.
Left to right, Auntie Edwina, Roy Hussey's
girlfriend Madge Jefferies, Jean Crokes
(Edwina's daughter, later to be Betty's
bridesmaid) and Betty Hussey. (Author)

As for holidays, the Manual states 'There are no special Women's Land Army regulations about holidays, with or without pay, but where a member of the Army has worked for six months at least 20 miles from her home she becomes entitled to a free home journey at the expense of the Women's Land Army.'

It was left up to individual farmers to decide when a girl could take time off and Betty Hussey was fortunate in her employers. She worked with a group of girls for the Pearce family who had combined their farms around Tytherington, near Wootton under Edge, in south Gloucestershire, not too far from her home or her boyfriend, my father, who was the proud owner of a 350 cc Velocette motorcycle.

Betty's first farm was just down the road from the Folly. It was owned by the McGowan family. Dot Wilcox (nee Wembridge) was there with Betty and described the hard and tedious work they put in hand hoeing and thinning mangolds.

> For a townie like me – I was a clerk at Imperial Tobacco before call-up – the house at Tytherington without running water or electricity and with a two holer at the end of the garden was something of a shock. The farm was mainly dairy, owned by the Pearces, a good family to work for. There were machines to milk the cows but we found moving those churns about very hard going.

At Mill Farm, Tytherington, the Pearces were not mean in granting holiday time, as is shown by the messages on a number of postcards from that time. One, sent from Perranporth, Cornwall, is highly evocative of the times. Did someone mention health and safety?

> Dear Mother, this beautiful spot has been our trip for today and we are sitting on the beach. It's a grand place, utterly wild and almost deserted. RAF and army have chained partitions on the beach for shooting practice.

Towards the rear of the WLA Manual there are some quotes from farmers and Land Girls. Mr. H.M., Cheltenham:

> We have two permanent workers on this farm, and I take my hat off to them both. They have never complained, nor once hesitated to tackle any job given them to do, and are always on time no matter what the weather.

An Isle of Ely farmer:

> You might like to know the kind of work which my land girl does:
> Drives away manure cart etc
> Harrows in with one horse behind a drill
> Loads straw when at litter-cart
> Hold sacks when putting up corn
> When chaff-cutting pushes the straw to the feeder
> Takes chaff when threshing
> Took quite a lot of beet, and always earned her money and a little more at £2 per acre
> Takes up mangolds very well.

A Women's Land Army Volunteer in East Sussex:

> I have been here over a year now, and am getting more and more interested in my work, and am given more responsible jobs … I am doing work which I like but would never have done but for the war. I suppose I am helping my country, but I am certainly enjoying myself too.

A Volunteer in Soham, Cambs:

> I love working here. I have also learnt to milk, although I confess I still like looking after the pigs best. It's good to see them grow so quickly … I now have to work a steamer to cook potatoes for the pigs. I cook 15cwt a day. I manage the boiler very well. This is another job I have learnt. I also have lovely lodgings and am very happy.

The Volunteer's manual was written by W.E. Shirwell-Cooper who was the Principal of The Horticultural Education and Advisory Bureau and Late Horticultural Superintendent of the Swanley Horticultural College for Women. The rear pages are packed with tables, charts and formulae for lotions and potions for the dressing and efficacious growing of all manner of crops.

When peace came many girls who had given up full-time work in factories, in hotels and in service to join the Land Army, despite Lady Denman's best efforts, and unlike servicemen and women, had no help to find peacetime work at the end of the war. This caused considerable distress. In fact Lady Denman was so incensed by the situation that she resigned as Director of the WLA in 1945 in protest. Needless to say, there were girls who stayed on the land; either as farmhands, or because they married men they met while they were in the WLA, but most eventually found work elsewhere. Betty, as we shall see, was one of those who stayed on the land.

On 19 January 1944, my parents were married; a rather poorly constructed press article reads as follows:

> Bells Ring out
> Bristol Lieut. Weds at Westerleigh
>
> Church bells were pealed at Westerleigh today for a wedding for the first time since the outbreak of war. The wedding was that of Lieut. D. Stoate RN [sic] son of Mr and Mrs A Stoate [sic] of Redrock, Stoke Hill, Bristol and Miss Betty Hussey daughter of Mrs Hussey and the late Mr H Hussey of the Beaufort Arms Hotel, Westerleigh Rd Mangotsfield.
> Mr Stoate is a member of the well-known milling family, and Miss Hussey is sister of Flt-Lieut. Roy Hussey DFM DFC.

After they were married they lived at first at Heath Walk, Downend and later moved to Cleave Wood Rd, Downend, Bristol.

Returning to 1941, life for Jack on Henfield Farm continued. In May 1941, nine months before Betty joined the WLA, aged nineteen he volunteered for the Local Defence Volunteers, the 12 Gloucestershire (City of Bristol) Battalion Home Guard. He was put in Number 1 platoon Bristol East Double Company, at Page Park, Staple Hill, Bristol.

The Home Guard was not formed in preparation for war but very much as a result of it. Furthermore it was not instigated by government or officialdom but as a result of freelance action by a few and the will of many. It started life as the Local Defence Volunteers, LDV or more colloquially (Look, Duck and Vanish). The LDV was barely an organisation, more a collection of local groups often run by former First World War military personnel. Some that emerged during the early part of 1940 were clearly managed better than others. But over the period of a few months, this rag tag group was armed, uniformed and trained.

After Britain declared war, a Spanish Civil War International Brigade veteran, the extraordinary Tom Wintringham, started a civilian organised training area in Osterly Park, West London, He gave training in guerrilla tactics, the manufacture and use of Molotov cocktails and the like. To this the Home Guard undoubtedly owes its training origins.

Using the Home Guard Manual they were taught basic field craft, how to survive in the open, how to destroy tanks, ambush the invaders, use weapons of varying sorts, make booby-traps, read maps and send signals. The fledgling volunteer was turned into a useful soldier.

Westerleigh Church, January 1944. Left to right, Geoffrey Stoate, Jack Stoate, Betty Stoate and Jean Crokes. (Author)

Local groups were largely armed with whatever they could lay their hands on. When Winston Churchill became Prime Minister in May 1940 he was made aware of the ramshackle force. He concluded that part of the reason for the generally low morale in the units lay in its name – branding is not a new concept. He determined, against some cabinet opposition as arm bands and other matter had already been printed under its old name, to call it the 'Home Guard'. This change came on 22 July 1940 when the call went out for 500,000 volunteers of men aged between 17 and 65 who were not in military service but wished to defend their country from invasion. Such was the ground swell that some 1.5m volunteers came forward to their local police stations for enrolment.

It should not be overlooked that at the time the LDV was becoming the Home Guard, the government and military were faced with the failure of the British Expeditionary Force's support of France and its withdrawal from Dunkirk, dispirited and having left much of its hardware behind on the beaches. The imperative was to ensure the re-equipping of the front line forces in terms of uniforms and armament. The Home Guard therefore had to make do with whatever was left. This included First World War weaponry, such as the American M1917 rifle, which had a calibre different but very similar to the British Lee Enfield .303 rifle. Later in the war before the Home Guard was stood down in December 1944, it became reasonably well equipped, but the reputation of 'pitch forks and shot guns' remained.

Following a public appeal 20,000 firearms of all sorts were handed to in to assist. Even then only one in ten were armed with a firearm, some of which had been 'liberated' from museums. By the autumn of 1940 khaki battle dress began to arrive with steel helmets and greatcoats. Armbands still continued to be used.

At Well House Farm near the village of Eversley where I was brought up there was only one other house in sight. It was called Well House and at that time we were all part of Lord Brocket's Bramshill Estate. The tenants at Well House were General and Mrs Lucas (not the General Lucas familiar from the Italian campaign in the latter stages of the War). General Lucas, late of the Royal Horse Artillery had a role with the War Department in Whitehall during the

Jack Stoate in the Home Guard on his own cherished 350cc Velocette motorcycle; and on parade. (Author)

war. Following the death of the General and later his wife, after the house had been cleared out my father and I went round to have a little look and in the loft we found General Lucas's First World War service Webley .455 revolver in immaculate condition, still in its tan flap style holster, a Browning .32 calibre automatic pistol complete with firearms certificate (issued to Mrs Lucas for her defence when the General was away) and some rounds of 12 bore cartridges that had a single large lead ball at the end wrapped round with waxed string. These my father immediately recognised as ammunition issued to the Home Guard for use in 12 bore shotguns. The waxed string was to permit the ball to exit down a choked barrel without splitting it. A fearsome piece of ordnance!

The Lucas's had a wonderful Scottish live-in housekeeper called Daisy (I never knew her by anything other than Daisy), one of those incredible band of women of the Air Transport Auxiliary (ATA) who, during the Second World War, flew aeroplanes from the factories to operational airfields. She was paid almost nothing at Well House for years of devoted service and when Mrs Lucas died she quietly packed her bags and went to live in New Zealand – if only I knew then what I know now.

Through the Lord Lieutenants (The King's representative) in each county the War Office laid down the logistical and administrative foundations of the Home Guard. It would operate in pre-defined military areas already used by the regular army, leaving it to local General Staff Officers to divide these areas into smaller zones.

This did not mean that the volunteers and those commanding them sang from the same hymn sheet. Many local 'commanders' having served in the First World War did not see the need for training other than that which they devised themselves. The War Office saw the force as a type of armed constabulary whose role was to observe enemy troop movement and report back to the regular army. In contrast, many of the volunteers were looking for a more offensive role, attacking and harassing German forces. The question of uniforms was also not to be ignored. In the event of a German invasion armed civilians would not be able to claim rights under the Geneva Convention. In short they could be summarily executed.

The expected invasion never came of course, but the Home Guard performed a valuable role in escorting shot-down enemy airmen to custody and guarding airfields, munition factories and 5000 miles of British coastline, freeing regular forces to undertake frontline duties. They also performed the role of sky watching for potential paratroop invasion. They developed a simple code system, for example 'Cromwell' signified a paratroop invasion was imminent and 'Oliver' that landings were underway. Additionally, the Home Guard arranged to use church bells as a call to arms for the rest of the volunteer force. This led to a series of complex rules governing who had keys to bell towers, and the ringing of church bells was forbidden at all other times. Thus the newspaper article on Jack and Betty's wedding on 19 January 1944 had made special reference to the bells at Westerleigh Church.

Individual commanders, including Tom Wintringham, made their own arrangements regarding training; after September 1940, however, the army began to take charge of training at Osterly Park and the Home Guard became increasingly 'regularised'. It was not until 1943, however, that they became a properly trained and equipped force, by which time Jack had joined the Royal Marines.

From April 1942, Home Guard Anti-aircraft units were formed and by 1944 these units had taken over many A-A batteries, operating light and heavy guns as well as some of the Z-batteries, firing 2-inch rockets supplementing traditional anti-aircraft guns. Tom Wintringham himself, who resigned in April 1941, was never allowed to join the Home Guard because of a policy barring membership to communists.

On 8 April 1942, the day before his 21st birthday, Jack was formally discharged from the Home Guard 'in consequence of joining the Forces'. He was not required to volunteer for active service, but a combination of farming and the Home Guard, whilst being satisfactory so far as it went, was not sufficient for him. His brothers were represented in the Air Force,

Army and Navy, so in order to cut his own swathe, on 17 March 1942 he volunteered fo the Royal Marines.

His initial training was undertaken at Lympstone on the Exe estuary in Devon. His drill history sheet is sparsely completed, but notes that he undertook parade, Table 'A', physical and bayonet training from April to July 1942 as a Marine in C Company; no doubt he was on the receiving end of the Royal Marine sergeant's mantra of mind over matter – 'I don't mind and you don't matter!'

In September 1943 Leonard Stoate asked his sons to write for him on a single quarto sheet a brief resumé of their activities to date. Jack's is in some ways more revealing than his service record. For confidentiality reasons Jack was not able to pass on the nature of his various Special Courses. The next paragraph takes its information from that quarto sheet following which we turn to his service records.

Having completed initial training at Lympstone he was posted in May 1942 to 2nd Battalion RM at Dunblane in Scotland. In June he moved to Haverfordwest, he had one day's leave in July when he was recalled to Lympstone to attend a Selection Board. From there he became an Officer Cadet and was posted to Brown Down near Gosport. He had four days leave in August and from thence to Thurlestone, Devon. Following his commissioning in November, he went to Kidwelli to 2nd Royal Marine Anti-tank Battery. In December he was posted to Bournemouth and then to Ilkley on a Special Course. In May he was posted to Plymouth. On 13 May he was commissioned 1st Lieutenant. June 1943 saw him posted to Wimbourne, then in July to Larkhill for another Special Course, followed immediately by another at Bournemouth. In August he was transferred to No 1 Royal Marine Anti-tank Corps. In September, back in his natural element he 'took a group of 22 men, with a sergeant, for three weeks farming near Winchester.' One assumes there was a harvest panic on and 'bootnecks' can turn their hand to anything! At the end of September he was transferred again, this time to Support Craft Battery.

From his service record, we can see that having completed his Initial Training his command-ing officer signed him off as 'Suited by personality and intelligence to be trained with a view to being commissioned' and on 12 November 1942 he was posted in order to take up his promo-tion as Temporary 2nd Lieutenant RM at HQ RM Division Artillery. His general character is noted as 'Very Good'.

His new unit was the OCTU (Officer Cadet Training Unit) at Thurlestone, Devon, this period included a three-week spell at Ilkley in Yorkshire with a Royal Artillery unit – a county he was to re-visit in January 1945 training in 30 Battalion RM.

The next year and a half saw him being moved around quite frequently but still on the HBL (Home Based Ledger). From November 1942 to two days before his 22nd birthday, on 7 April 1943, he was attached to the Artillery Division. On 13 May 1943 he was promoted to Temporary Lieutenant at 13 shillings per day.

June 1943 saw him back in Plymouth for a three-week disciplinary course then to the School of Artillery at Larkhill in Wiltshire and a 14-day aircraft recognition course in July before joining the 1st Royal Marine Anti-tank Battery. By November 1943 he had been appointed Company Adjutant and credited with a special allowance of two and six a day for the responsibility – so the one who kicked against discipline was now responsible for it – not the first or last time that ploy has been used.

He later told us that the most important words he learned at this time were 'Carry on Sergeant Major.' He like many others knew very little about service life and it was far better to leave matters to the regulars.

On 19 January 1944 he and Betty Hussey were married. His pay was increased by a further eight shillings and sixpence as Married Allowance.

By April 1944, two months before D-Day, part of the RM had been broken up and the Divisional Artillery had been formed into what eventually became known as the RM Armoured Support Group, specially formed for Operation *Neptune* – so still in reserve. Montgomery had conceived the idea that on D-day the coastal and beach defences should be bombarded during

Jack Stoate as 2nd Lieutenant Royal
Marines, 1943. (Geoffrey Stoate)

the run-in by guns mounted in the landing craft; this was to be the task of the RM Armoured
Support Group. The original plan was for the men to remain afloat but fortunately for Jack the
gun and the landing craft never met up and anyway, on 3 June 1944, three days before D-Day,
he was sent to the RMSAS (Royal Marine Small Arms School) near Lee on Solent on temporary attachment for platoon weapons training.

Jack was a proficient handler of small arms and shotguns and he told us children that he
remembered the Thompson machine gun as a pretty inaccurate weapon but that the Bren gun
was too accurate – what he meant was that in skilled hands the Bren could put two bullets
through the same hole – a waste of ammunition.

Following RMSAS he returned to the Royal Marine Transport Group on 17 June. Then
back to Lympstone Depot until the end of 1944. So Operation *Neptune* had come and gone
and Jack had still not left England's shores – but that was shortly to change.

30 Battalion Royal Marines was formed in January 1945. It was part of the 116th Infantry
Brigade Royal Marines and began to form on 15 January and that day Jack became a part of it.

The Royal Marines are a service apart, in that they 'pop up' in all theatres of war performing
functions as varied as bandsmen, naval and army gunners, aircraft pilots and fulfilling transport,
infantry and tank roles and it is for this reason that Jack's training was so intense and varied,
from gunnery to transport and small arms. 30 Battalion was organised as a normal infantry battalion. D-Day had come and gone, likewise the fighting through Normandy and through the
autumn of 1944 the battles at Arnhem, the Scheldt estuary and in the Ardennes, all of which
put considerable strain on infantry manpower – particularly British and Empire manpower.

The lack of British infantry is part of a wider picture and to see it we need to return to 1942
and North Africa. Operation *Torch* by 12 May 1943 had successfully expelled the Axis forces
from North Africa using both American and British command chains and forces. After initial
setbacks, at Tobruk in October 1942 Montgomery had succeeded at El Alamein and liked the
applause. But it was here that the seeds of political tension between high ranking personalities

were sown, nearly two years before 30 Battalion RM had to be hastily formed in January 1945. Field Marshal Alan Brooke, superior officer, close friend and admirer of Montgomery wrote:

> Montgomery requires a lot of education to make him see the whole situation outside the Eighth Army orbit. A difficult mixture to handle; brilliant commander and trainer of men but liable to commit untold errors due to lack of tact, lack of appreciation of other people's outlook. It is most depressing that the Americans do not like him and it will always be a difficult matter to have him fighting in close proximity to them. He wants guiding and watching continually.

Montgomery's greatest moment must surely have been his victory at El Alamein followed by the triumphant advance of his Eighth Army into Tunisia in early 1943. Once in Tunisia he had to co-operate both with the British First Army and the US Army. For the first time his over-cautious approach began to show and his arrogance alienated the American generals.

As Tunisia fell, Roosevelt and Churchill were deciding upon an Allied invasion of Sicily later that year, code-named Operation *Husky*. Montgomery expected to be in sole charge of the Allied armies in Sicily. Eisenhower, however, Supreme Commander of the Allied forces in North Africa, was against this and Churchill agreed. As a result Montgomery was left in command of the British Eighth Army and General George Patton had a separate command, the US Seventh Army. Both were to be in General Alexander's 15th Army Group with Eisenhower, headquartered in Algiers, in overall command of Allied forces. From the start Eisenhower and Alexander made it plain that Patton and Montgomery were to be on an equal footing. To Montgomery, who had so enjoyed being in sole command in North Africa, this seemed like a step down.

The planning for Operation *Husky*, in Montgomery's words, was a mess. Eisenhower's staff had produced seven different plans and were about to produce an eighth. Montgomery had not been consulted. When this eighth plan was shown to Montgomery he turned it down flat as essentially it divided the British and American landings into two separate areas, The American 7th Army, commanded by Patton at the north-west corner at Palermo and the British Eighth Army commanded by Montgomery in the south east around Syracuse and Gela.

The big lesson learned at Gallipoli and Dieppe was that amphibious landings operations are the most difficult form of military action. They should never be undertaken except as a last resort. Such operations will be a failure if opposed by an enemy of the character of the Germans in strength unless they are covered by an overwhelmingly superior air force.

Montgomery was insistent that the two armies should be concentrated in the south east, in order to ensure that the airfields around Gela should be captured and held. This plan was adopted but Patton was not best pleased, as he had set his heart on acting independently and resented Montgomery's interference.

In 1943 there were 350,000 Italian and 50,000 German troops on Sicily, the German 15th Panzer Division had nearly 100 tanks and the Hermann Goering Division was on its way; German morale was high.

On the Allied side more troops and ships took part in the Sicilian invasion than in the initial Normandy assault. 2500 naval vessels carried 115,000 British and Commonwealth and 66,000 American assault troops. The British landings were to be preceded by airborne assaults with the British First Airborne Division landing in gliders and the US 82nd Airborne parachuting in.

Although the seaborne operations were successful, the airborne landings were disastrous. On the night of 9 July 1943 1200 men of the British Air Landing Brigade were flown to Sicily in 144 gliders. The American pilots of the towing aircraft were inexperienced and many of them loosed their gliders far too early; 69 gliders (nearly half) fell into the sea, 56 were scattered along the southern coast and only 12 gliders with around 100 men landed on the target, the Ponte Grande near Syracuse. Eight officers and 65 men held the bridge until they were relieved, but the proportion of casualties amongst the scarce, highly trained elite troops was huge.

Although Montgomery had captured Syracuse the German armour held up his advance to the airfields at Catania and he badly needed Primosole Bridge. 1900 parachutists in 126 Dakotas piloted by Americans, together with 19 gliders carrying antitank guns, dropped at the same time as the Germans dropped their redoubtable Fourth Parachute Regiment into almost the same zone. Of the British only 250 of all ranks could be assembled after landing. They captured the bridge but after removing mines and detonators ran out of ammunition and were forced to leave it to the Germans.

When it came to encircling Mount Etna the Allies failed to fight as one, with the result that the Eighth Army suffered some 12,000 casualties and the Americans 7,500. The delay enabled the Germans, in spite of the Allies now having control of the air and the Royal Navy dominating the seas, to evacuate some 60,000 men and 10,000 vehicles across the straits of Messina before before the fall of Messina on 17 August 1943.

Even the taking of Messina wrankled Montgomery as by the time his forward troops arrived at the City, General Patton's men were already in evidence. So with his laurels tarnished if not stolen during the 38 days of *Husky,* Montgomery now set his sights of becoming the 'overlord' of the Allied assault into Italy. In this again he was to be disappointed, he was to remain as land commander of the Eighth Army whilst the American 5th Army was to be commanded by the enthusiastic but inexperienced General Mark Clark. In 1940 Clark held the rank of Lieutenant Colonel. His proximity to Eisenhower and his prominence in the negotiations with the French command in North Africa was no doubt instrumental in ensuring his meteoric rise in rank to General – the youngest American ever promoted to that rank – in command of an entire Army by 1943.

Montgomery landed in Collabra in the toe of Italy – Operation *Baytown* – whilst Clark assaulted the beaches south of Salerno in Operation *Avalanche*, the Peaches Beaches referred to by Roy Hussey (and as we shall see, Tom Stoate). A massive creeping artillery barrage reminiscent of the First World War preceded Montgomery's landings. There was in fact negligible opposition to the landing and on 3 September a chain of fishing villages in the small town of San Giovanni and shortly thereafter the large town of Reggio were swiftly occupied. Four hours later Allied fighters were using the airdrome at Reggio.

By this time Roy Hussey and 72 Squadron were in Casala in the north of Sicily, having moved there from Malta by way of Comiso to Pachino and Panebianco. It was from Casala that the Squadron flew air cover over the British invasion beaches on 4 and 5 September. On 6 September they moved again to Falcone from where they flew to give air cover to the Salerno landings on 'Peaches Beaches' from 12–25 September using slipper tanks – the 90-gallon long range tanks. From then on Roy Hussey and 72 Squadron remained in support of General Mark Clark's 5th Army whereas, as we shall see, the Squadron and Wing with which Tom Stoate served supported the British Eighth Army.

Montgomery now had the toe of Italy to himself and proceeded northwards at a fairly leisurely pace. Had he been responsible for *Avalanche* as well as *Baytown* he would surely have had his troops moving swiftly northwards up the approach roads from the toe to the Salerno beaches to secure the south flank of *Avalanche*. Now he concentrated on building up his supplies in preparation for a German counterattack which would never come.

There was a dit in circulation about this time. One day an Australian fighter pilot was shot down quite near Montgomery's HQ. Montgomery saw the parachute open and detailed someone to fetch him back for lunch. Now Montgomery had decided to rewrite the principles of war – at least to introduce his new principle of war – the first and greatest principle of war – which is 'Win the battle first.' Monty was very proud of this and about half way through lunch he turned to the Australian and said ' Now, do you know what the first and greatest principle of war is?' 'Well I don't know much about the principles of war but I should say it's got to be stop frigging about!'

As ever anxious to portray himself in the best light, on 4 September 1943 Montgomery signalled Churchill, somewhat disingenuously; 'We have advanced a long way and very quickly.

It had to be done in order to help the 5th Army but it is a great strain on my administration, which had to be switched from the toe to heel during the operation and which is now stretched to the limit.'

On the way northwards, Eighth Army intelligence uncovered the Germans preparing defensive positions at Termoli behind the Biferno River and in a brilliant pre-emptive strike Montgomery successfully pushed them back. With Termoli now in Eighth Army hands, the Foggia airfields already captured by the Eighth Army were now safe from counter-attack and became operational for both strategic and operational airforces.

On 14 December Brooke visited Montgomery and let it be known that Churchill was unhappy with the Eighth Army's progress. Montgomery in turn was not happy with the Italian campaign. It was not being run to his liking, he was trailing northwards up the Adriatic coast not in a glory zone and he was already angling for his next move – Commander Allied ground forces for the assault on northern Europe.

On Christmas Eve 1943, his wish came true; Montgomery received a coded signal for his eyes only that he was to command the invasion. On the 31st he flew from the Adriatic coast of Italy to Marrakech in Morocco for a meeting with Churchill and Eisenhower, who had just been chosen as Supreme Commander for the invasion.

Lieutenant-General Frederick Morgan, Chief of Staff to the Supreme Allied Commander had been working on the invasion plan since March 1943. On being invited by Churchill to read the plan, Montgomery, like Eisenhower, was unhappy with it. Overnight Montgomery produced the outline of a different plan showing the invasion beaches spread out over a much wider area to dissipate the enemy defences and Morgan's recommended three divisions increased to five.

Montgomery's plans for five divisions for *Overlord* produced a demand for an extra 72 LCIs, 47 LSTs and 144 LCTs (Landing Craft Infantry, Landing Ship Tanks and Landing Craft Tanks). By postponing D-Day from 1 May to 1 June it was just possible to accumulate the necessary landing craft in time, partly by removing them from *Anvil,* the proposed landing in the south of France, which was, thereby, postponed and subsequently named Operation *Dragoon.*

In a strategy meeting at St Paul's School, London, Montgomery emphasised rather too strongly that he would command the US troops during the invasion. At that time there was harmony between the British and the Americans, and the American General Bradley, in a friendly way, encouraged Montgomery to tone down his remarks, which Montgomery did, but American high command had been pricked.

Montgomery's strategy was for the 1st US Army to assault astride the Carentan Estuary to capture Cherbourg, then develop operations towards St Lô to tie in with the advance of the British Army.

The Second British Army was to assault to the west of the river Orne to develop operations to the South and East in order to secure airfields and to protect the extreme flank of the US Army whilst the latter was capturing Cherbourg.

The First Canadian Army was to land after the Second British Army and take over from it the left or northern sector of the lodgement area. Troops of the Second British army in the area so taken would come under come under command of the First Canadian Army.

The Third US Army was to land after First US Army and was to have the tasks of clearing Brittany then covering the south flank of the lodgement area while First US Army was directed northeast with a view to operations towards Paris.

Coming up to D-Day the weather had been poor – Norman Stoate's log showed the operation being postponed on 4 June and on 7 June the forward guard rail on ML909 being wrenched away owing to rough weather. However a clear spell was predicted as possible for 24 hours from late on 5 June. Eisenhower told the conference that the invasion would go ahead as planned on 6 June.

Montgomery predicted that Rommel would try and hold Caen, Bayeux and Carentan and he emphasised the menacing minefields and hidden obstacles. This meant the invasion forces needed to touch down on the beaches 30 minutes before the incoming tide reached the obstacles while the latter were still exposed and therefore less effective.

On D-Day itself traffic congestion on the beaches was far greater than anticipated and Montgomery's armoured thrust could not be made in strength. A small detachment of Canadian tanks did reach the outskirts of Caen but by the evening they had to withdraw for lack of support. He did not mean at this stage to risk the sacrifice of his British Divisions in a desperate effort to break out of the Caen sector. He knew only too well that, although more US divisions were available, the British and Canadian reserves of manpower were too low for such losses and that no fresh British divisions could ever be raised because of the country's already daunting commitments.

Nevertheless, the success of the British assaults – by nightfall on D-Day British troops had advanced up to six miles inland – was a triumph for the detailed Allied planning, of which Montgomery had been chief architect.

The landings for the American Divisions were considerably tougher, but as we shall see, Montgomery's strategy drew in the German armour to the British, Canadian and Polish Divisions and Bradley and Patton achieved all their objectives. On Omaha Beach US 29th and First Infantry Divisions faced near defeat, out of 35 amphibious tanks only five arrived safely because of the high seas.

For hours the American troops on Omaha were pinned down by accurate observed fire and at one stage were on the point of being evacuated. By mid afternoon after considerable naval and air support had been committed, troops crossed the shingle in single file because of the almost impossible task of clearing wide tracks across the minefields by hand under observed fire.

On D-Day alone 75,000 British and Canadians and 57,000 Americans had landed but within a week of the landing vehicles and stores were lagging far behind schedule, at around 75 per cent of target. It was these convoys that Norman Stoate, as part of ML Flotilla 33, had been escorting.

The liberating Allied Armies needed to break out of their beachheads and Montgomery's plan for Operation *Goodwood,* the break out of the Caen/Falaise area, was firstly to overrun the German defences and capture airfields and secondly to draw German armour away from the American Divisions. The Americans in turn would liberate the Cherbourg peninsula, then Brittany and its ports and finally St Lô and Paris (the latter surrendered on 25 August 1944). The American operation was code-named Operation *Cobra.*

The first element of *Goodwood* was not successful in the time frame Montgomery had in mind. Montgomery, not unreasonably, reported positive projections on the battle as the second leg of his objective was working to plan. Eisenhower and his advisers at SHAEF, however, did not share Montgomery's optimism, which they considered to be quite unjustified. Both Tedder and Portal agreed that Montgomery was the cause of the failure. Bradley, however, preferred to look on *Goodwood* as a preliminary to *Cobra* and considered the two operations should be judged as one.

Although the campaign in Normandy ended in triumph for Montgomery, it was intensely frustrating. Both of the Canadian frontal attacks on the main German armour in Falaise were repulsed with heavy losses. His biggest error in generalship was his failure to send fresh British divisions to reinforce the Canadian and Polish forces during the battle for Falaise and it rankled with him that he never got the glamour of his longed-for breakout by the Second Army into the open country beyond Caen.

In contrast, Bradley had enjoyed the glory of the capture of Cherbourg; and the spectacular breakout beyond St Lô so brilliantly exploited by Patton's Third Army was a major contribution to victory. Bradley, whose relations with Montgomery were good throughout the Normandy campaign, appreciated that the latter's master plan had succeeded. And he wrote 'Montgomery bossed the USA First Army with wisdom, tolerance and restraint. I could not have wanted a more tolerant or judicious commander.' Sadly however, fierce disputes between the two generals would flare up before Hitler was defeated.

The US government had always made it clear that Eisenhower must take over personal charge of land operations in Europe once the assault and breakout phases were over. On 1 September SHAEF (Supreme Headquarters Allied Expeditionary Forces) became operational at Grandville and Eisenhower, not Montgomery, was now in full charge of the land battle.

Neither Montgomery nor Brooke realised that for political reasons it was no longer possible for Eisenhower to give a British general overall command of the American troops since by now they so greatly outnumbered the British; but Montgomery continually put the Supreme Commander under pressure in an effort to force him to change his mind, not only on command but also on Montgomery's plan for his 21st Army to cross the Rhine north of the Ruhr and to press on to Berlin.

Eisenhower had realised there were merits in Montgomery's plan and SHAEF administration kept on emphasising the need to capture Dutch ports nearer to Germany. Churchill had repeatedly impressed upon him the paramount need to overrun the V-bomb launching sites, which were mostly based in Holland. Having been in London himself Eisenhower was acutely conscious of the dire threat to Britain from the V-bombs. There was no effective defence against the V-2s and Allied intelligence had learned from Ultra and other sources that these were about to be launched against London.

On 29 August the Supreme Commander told Montgomery that he would issue a directive giving 21st Army Group the task of pushing on to Antwerp and thence eastward to the Ruhr, Bradley's principal offensive mission being to support the British commander. Montgomery would also be given First Airborne Army (consisting of one British and two US airborne divisions). This directive was later watered down to Bradley having to support Montgomery's flank.

Montgomery now appointed General Horrocks as commander XXX Corps. Horrocks was still not fully recovered from wounds he had received earlier but he lived up to Montgomery's expectations; by the night of 3 September 1944 British tanks rumbled into Brussels. On the next day 11th Armoured Division triumphantly entered Antwerp before the Germans could demolish the electrically operated sluice gates and cranes in the harbour, pausing there for four days.

Although the town of Antwerp and its harbour were now liberated; as we saw in Norman Stoate's story, it could not be used by the Allied forces because the entrance was blocked by the German defence line along the Scheldt Estuary and its sea entrance at Walcheren.

This should have been the moment to clear the 65-mile Scheldt estuary and to destroy the defeated German 15th Army to the west of Antwerp without heavy casualties. Montgomery, however, gambled on his conviction that German resistance was crumbling so fast that the Allies could win the war without using Antwerp as a port of entry for supplies. In the event, no Allied ship entered Antwerp until 27 November 1944, by which time the mistake was only too apparent.

Montgomery was bent on bypassing German 15th Army and shooting straight on over the Rhine. Hurrying eastwards he might have been successful if he had continued on 4 September but the three-day halt after that date gave the Germans their chance. By his heady advance from the Seine to Brussels and Antwerp in four days, Montgomery had proved that British armour could move as fast as the Americans, but the pause at Antwerp was to prove costly.

Having pushed north through Normandy and south via Alsace the Allied armies were ranging up to the Rhine, Montgomery's 21st Army north of the Ruhr had taken Brussels and Antwerp. To the south of the Ruhr were the American armies led by Bradley and Patton.

Eisenhower was incessantly being pressed by Montgomery that he be appointed overall land commander and for his army to have precedence over supplies so that he could force his 'finger' across the Rhine through to Berlin and encircle the Ruhr and thus take the German industrial heartland. With regard to manpower and supplies, for a while he was successful. Eisenhower put the American 9th Army along with the British 21st Army under Montgomery's command. With regard to land command Montgomery was irritating the entire American high command and even some of the British staff at SHAEF.

For his part, on 7 December 1944 Montgomery wrote to Brooke of Eisenhower: 'If you want the War to end within a reasonable period you have to get Eisenhower's hand off the tiller. I regret to say he just does not know what he is doing …'

Montgomery now faced major strategic considerations, in his eyes they were all equal militarily; from his own memoirs the first option was to clear the island of Walcheren and the South Beveland Isthmus and thus free up the port of Antwerp; the second was to use airborne troops to obtain a bridgehead over the Rhine at Wessel; and the third to obtain a bridgehead at Arnhem.

In the first he reasoned he would be heading in the wrong direction and involved in an unrewarding hard slog, unlikely to enhance his reputation. Once Antwerp had opened and the supplies landed there he considered they would probably be used to support a triumphant USA drive to Berlin with the 21st Army group's part in the final stages of the war being unglamorous.

In the second he would have had to share the Rhine bridgehead with the Americans who, because of their great numbers, would have received most of the glory for the final battles of the war on German soil.

If he were to undertake the third option successfully it would be hailed as a dazzling and daring operation and Eisenhower would have been forced to give him all the help in troops and supplies he needed for his push to Berlin. On top of this there was another by-product from the third option, namely that if British troops saved London from further punishment by capturing the V-2 launching sites in Holland, this would put the seal on his reputation.

From the very moment that his troops reached Antwerp Montgomery failed to appreciate the absolute necessity of opening the port. On his own admission from this single error stemmed a host of others. Montgomery was about to make the two worst military decisions of his career. Having decided upon an airborne operation to secure a Rhine bridgehead instead of opening up Antwerp, he compounded the error by going for the Arnhem option for Operation *Market Garden* instead of Wessel. Eisenhower backed these wrong decisions. Montgomery wrote in his memoirs:

> I admit a bad mistake. I underestimated the difficulties of opening up the approaches to Antwerp. I reckoned the Canadian army could do it while we were going for the Ruhr. I was wrong.

It was, it seems, Montgomery's extreme anxiety for the final glory to be his that caused the disaster at Arnhem. That is not to say that strategically and tactically his plan was wrong, what Brooke and even Churchill did not grasp was that at this stage of the war Britain and its empire were the junior partners to the Americans. Eisenhower had the task of balancing all these massive egos.

Montgomery was firmly established as a brilliantly successful commander in the field. In the final analysis the decision to execute *Market Garden* rested with him. Eisenhower was hardly likely to contradict Montgomery following his success in Normandy and the subsequent swift advances.

Part of the mistake was that neither Montgomery nor Eisenhower showed a proper understanding of the true significance of the escape of the German 15th Army from Normandy and of the threat it posed to any further Allied advance through Holland to the Rhine. Throughout September 1944 SHAEF intelligence reports were overoptimistic about the end of the war and gave no prominence to the menace of the German 15th Army in Holland, where Jack Stoate was headed, nor to the impossibility of opening Antwerp unless more divisions were directed to the battle of the Scheldt. It is instructive to compare Allied optimism with a very stiff directive that Himmler issued on 10 September 1944.

> Certain unreliable elements appear to believe the war will over for them as soon as they surrender to the enemy.

I want to contradict this belief and emphasise that every deserter will be prosecuted and will find his just punishment. What is more his ignominious conduct will entail the most severe consequences for his family. Upon exposure of the circumstances of desertion they will be shot.

Before final victory in Europe the Allies were to suffer substantial losses opening up the port of Antwerp in the Scheldt Estuary and were about to suffer at Arnhem and in the Ardennes – the Battle of the Bulge – where the American 101st Airborne Division fought so courageously at Bastogne.

The Canadian Corps Commander Simonds (the same inexperienced Canadians that Norman Stoate and ML909 helped to land on Juno Beach, who had taken severe losses at Caen but who had fought so well up though the Low Countries) originally thought he could take the Breskens pocket in three days. In fact it took three weeks, so stiff was the enemy's resistance.

When *Market Garden* began both Montgomery and Eisenhower were euphoric about an early end, however, they were unaware at the beginning of September that new parachute regiments were training and re-equipping in Germany. On 4 September Hitler ordered the establishment of a new army, the First Parachute Army. It was positioned on the Albert Canal in Belgium with its western flank held by those elements of the 15th Army already emerging from the North Scheldt Peninsula. It was this hastily assembled force that was to partially rob Montgomery of success at Arnhem.

Market Garden was not purely Montgomery's baby; it was also heavily promoted by the Airborne Corps. They were a very expensive organization that wanted to be used. Montgomery wanted to overturn his reputation for excessive caution and make sure he undertook the main attack over the Rhine himself, not sharing with the Americans.

His system of command was to formulate strategy, use his tried and tested planning team to deal with the tactical detail and whilst that was in train to use the time to visit the troops to heighten morale. This formula had worked well. For *Market Garden* there were two major differences. Firstly, as the Allied First Airborne Army was a SHAEF strategic reserve and not part of 21st Army group he had little influence on the detailed operational plan. The plan was flawed in many ways – not least of which was inadequate radio communication and the splitting of the Airborne Forces at Arnhem – Montgomery should have sent more senior staff officers from the 21st Army group to take part in the planning. This he failed to do and the inexperienced airborne planners let him down badly.

Secondly, although Montgomery knew of the reported Panzer strength at Arnhem on 10 September he did not heed his intelligence officers' warnings and he would not change his mind. This was out of character as he was usually very careful to minimise casualties, with his philosophy of 'metal not flesh'.

After the war Montgomery claimed that 'full success' at Arnhem was thwarted because of bad weather preventing the build-up of forces. This ignores the point that by sending the First Airborne into drop zones eight miles from the objective, not only was the fighting force halved on landing but it was in fact reduced even more because half of the initial force successfully landed had to stay eight miles from Arnhem bridge to guard the descent of the second lift. Once Montgomery had agreed to lift on successive days instead of all on a single day, he ruined his chances of victory. Out of some 10,000 men of the first Airborne Division landed near Arnhem only about 700 reached the bridge that was the focus of the whole operation.

Another major avoidable problem related to XXX Corps, Horrock's relief force. Here the traffic congestion was much worse than it need have been because it was never realised that the road verges had not been mined by the Germans. Two additional traffic lanes could have been used if the verges had been driven over.

Life is full of 'ifs' but if the gliders had come down closer to Nijmegen and Arnhem bridges (as was proposed in *Market Garden* plan 1 and as took place earlier at Benouville Bridge at Caen (now renamed Pegasus Bridge), the airborne forces would have stood every chance of capturing the bridges and there is no reason why the ground troops should not have linked up with them in time. The lesson had already been read but not learned that it is a tactical mistake to make the dropping zone too far from the objective and to split forces.

That Arnhem was 90 per cent successful as claimed by Montgomery in his memoirs seems to stretch credulity. British First Airborne Division casualties were appalling. The Nijmegen bridgehead taken and held could not be exploited until March 1945, six months later, thus leaving the Allies with a deep salient to defend.

Jack Stoate with part of 30 battalion RM was sent forward later as attachment to forward Army units in the Nijmegen area, to give them experience in the line. Jack said being in the line was rather like a rest cure after the strenuous training the Battalion had undergone and most men showed a keenness to get up there as soon as possible.

Although by March 1945 Eisenhower had quietly decided that Berlin was no longer 'the main prize', in September 1944 this was not the case and he emphasised that he would give Montgomery priority in supplies and that Bradley would support 21st Army group on the right. He did however make it clear that he still intended to push a double front into Germany, one in the north and the other in the centre towards Leipzig, this decision was dependent upon the port of Antwerp being open to supply that double front.

The banks of the Scheldt estuary, which could so easily have been taken immediately after Antwerp fell on 4 September 1944, were not tackled until the end of that month. By that time Montgomery was so heavily involved in the Nijmegen bridgehead that he just could not spare extra divisions. The banks leading into Antwerp were 50 miles long and were heavily defended.

To Montgomery it was not an interesting military operation; it lacked glamour and did not appeal to his vanity. He was too intelligent, too clear minded, however, not to understand that he had insufficient troops to clear Antwerp and to continue with offensive operations from the Nijmegen salient. He knew it would be a battle of attrition with very heavy casualties – in the end nearly 13,000, mainly Canadians.

Some of the blame must also lie with Eisenhower for in spite of his acknowledging the paramount importance of the Scheldt he was still sending extra supplies and troops to Patton in the South.

Because of *Market Garden* the opportunity for a timely clearance of the Scheldt and the opening up of the port of Antwerp as an early forward supply line had been irrevocably lost and the infantry paid a heavy price. Montgomery said later that he regretted that in his 3 September directive, he had put clearing the channel to Antwerp at the bottom of the agenda for the Canadian troops.

Meanwhile, Hitler was finding extra manpower for the war and for the manufacture of arms by an intensive combing out of able-bodied Germans and by unscrupulous use of slave labour from occupied countries. Even 12- to 14-year-olds were taken out of school to dig fortifications and his new battalions had a significant proportion of schoolboys.

On 16 December he unexpectedly launched two giant Panzer armies comprising over half a million men at the weakest point in the American sector of the Allied line in the Ardennes, progessing as far as Dinant.

A great number of troops from the US 1st and 9th Armies had been cut off from Bradley by the bulge of the German attack and Eisenhower had little option but to put Montgomery in charge of all the northern sector, including parts of the American Armies.

On 23 December Montgomery noted: 'I will not write my views on what has gone on here. I do not know of any ink that would stand it. Personally I am enjoying a very interesting battle but we ought to be in tears at the tragedy of this whole thing.' Calmly and methodically the British commander and his staff set about restoring the situation.

The Americans had wanted to Montgomery to snip off the bulge at its widest place, however Montgomery demurred and successfully cut off the German advance through the junction at Houfalize. By February 1945 the German forces were back in their original positions having lost an estimated 125,000 men killed, wounded or taken prisoner.

The last straw for theAmericans came at a press conference Montgomery held on 7 January 1945. Montgomery had produced a very good briefing note, but it was his crowing attitude in the discussions which did so much harm.

It was manifestly patronising of him to say the battle which cost many American lives and produced the crisis of the campaign was 'one of the most interesting … battles I've ever handled.' Both Eisenhower in Versailles and Marshall in Washington now made no secret of the fact that they both distrusted and disliked Montgomery. The self-seeking press briefing was like the bridge at Arnhem, a step too far, and Eisenhower was determined to clip Montgomery's wings.

Oblivious to this, Montgomery continued his incessant pressure on Eisenhower to give him the role of Land Commander. Eisenhower, however, continued to control events at SHAEF and even many of the British staff there, including Tedder, were ranging against Montgomery.

In the US there were fresh divisions and reserves of trained men, in Britain after five years of austerity and complete mobilization, the people were sick and tired of war. Following the fighting in Normandy and the battle through the Pas de Calais, Dunkirk and the losses at Arnhem, the Scheldt and in Belgium, there was a shortage of infantry from British and Empire sources and numbers needed to be replaced.

Montgomery might also have sensed that Eisenhower was about to take the American 9th Army away from his command. It was clear there was to be no shortcut to victory and more British infantry was needed from somewhere. Jack Stoate and The Royal Marines were to provide part of the answer.

On 15 January, a week after the press briefing, 30th Battalion RM, a unit of some 700 men in five companies, forming part of the 116th Infantry Brigade (Royal Marines), began to assemble at Dalditch, near Plymouth. The officers – including Jack Stoate – NCOs and key personnel arrived first, to be joined within a week by the remainder of the Battalion, most of whom were from landing craft or from M.N.B.D/O. (Mobile Naval Base Defence Organisation) I and II.

Few of these men had been in the field since their initial training and the task of re-training in the limited time at their disposal was formidable. To assist, instructors were loaned from the R.M.I.T.C. (Royal Marine Infantry Training Centre), Dalditch. With only a few days to organise the men into companies and platoons, it was planned to proceed directly to Yorkshire to carry out field training up to platoon level. The advance party went on ahead and reported that conditions were so bad, because of heavy falls of snow and the lack of water from frozen pipes, that it was advisable to delay the move of the main body.

It was known that they would be departing overseas before very long and the opportunity was used to send the men on embarkation leave. Companies, already working at high pressure in order to get their organisation going in such a short space of time, found themselves strained to the utmost to cope with this new situation.

The first few days of February 1945 found them at their new location in Yorkshire, the Battalion being split into three camps, an arrangement necessary for some reason or another but not helpful in achieving quick results in training. To add to their difficulties, they arrived during a freak spell of weather, with heavy falls of snow completely cutting off their communications. Telephones were even not laid to their camps. Living conditions were most uncomfortable. It was intensely cold and there was an acute shortage of water caused by frozen pipes. This long spell of freak weather, however, ended as abruptly as it had begun and before long the roads were clear and conditions improved considerably, enabling training to accelerate.

In Germany command was falling apart, with an attempted assassination attempt on Hitler in July 1944, Lyons had been taken in September and the Germans had been driven out of Greece by late 1944. The Third Reich was not yet finished, however, and both Roosevelt and Churchill were seeking as prominent a role as possible for their respective nation's armies in the final victory. These roles would be of great importance in gaining votes in the postwar elections. Though there woul be no 'Khaki' election victory for Churchill, as there had been for Lloyd George in 1918.

For 30 Battalion, mobilisation started on 1 February and had to be completed by the 14th. The advance party of the Battalion was to leave for N.W. Europe on the 13th.

Just as Norman Stoate in the RNVR had been at Roedean School to receive his training in torpedos and mines, so 30 Battalion RM on 13 February used Ampleforth school as a location to first form up and march as a Battalion. They also produced a rugby team to play a team from Ampleforth made up of masters and pupils. Afterwards they were addressed by their CO, Lieutenant-Colonel T K Walker, who announced they would be shortly embarking for the fight. After so much training this was generally greeted with high spirits – they were to be in at the kill.

The Battalion practised forming up for convoy and on 14 February it moved to Tilbury by road and rail. The crossing over the North Sea was not marred by any accident and except for distant gunfire and reported E-boat activity, was uneventful. Jack and certain other officers were sent on a course of instruction and followed on a little later. Jack disembarked on 9 April 1945, his 23rd birthday.

The bulk of 30 Battalion disembarked in February at Ostend and remained at a transit camp, where the organisation for the reception and accommodation was extremely good. My father told me it was difficult to realise that only a few miles away German troops were still resisting bitterly in Dunkirk. After a brief stay at Ostend the Battalion moved off in convoy, passing through the Belgian towns of Ghent and Antwerp, on its way to the coastal town of Bergen-op-Zoom, some thirty miles across the Dutch frontier.

In Belgium, some months had elapsed since the First and Second Armies had passed through and life had returned to a fairly normal state. On the whole the Belgians did not suffer in the same way as did the Dutch. Although, on the road from Brussels to Antwerp not too far from the route taken by 30 Battalion, was the Gestapo prison, Breendonk. It must have made an impression upon some of the men, as my father spoke of it.

In the inner courtyard there was a row of bullet-damaged posts against which the prisoners were strapped to be shot. Inside there were the cells with just room for a little wooden bed of planks. There were no windows, just a central alleyway before the doors of the cells. These were the cells occupied by the special political prisoners. There were also great wooden barns for the other prisoners where they lived without heat and practically no ventilation. Sanitation was primitive.

There were also the special rooms where interrogations were carried out. There were all sorts of methods of making people talk. Generally, Jack was told, the women held out longer than the men. There was a steam chamber where the victims were slowly roasted. In another room there were pads which were clamped on to various parts of the anatomy and electric currents passed through, gradually getting stronger and stronger. In another room victims of either sex were stripped and their hands tied behind their backs. They would be either beaten with a leather whip or branded with a red hot iron on forehead, breasts and abdomen. All this on a starvation diet designed to break down the victim's resistance.

Before the Allied Armies liberated Belgium, patriots had captured many of the Gestapo. They were kept as their prisoners had been until the English took over and Jack told us that they were treated to a dose of their own medicine in the meantime.

Jack said that Belgium showed little sign of the destruction of war, but as they entered Holland they saw more and more signs of bombing and the effects of shell and mortar fire. Jack was moved by the wild enthusiasm of the Dutch people as they passed through. The Dutch had suffered greatly. At the time Antwerp was the chief target for the V-1 weapon. Just outside Antwerp, Jack's Battalion narrowly escaped disaster from a flying bomb that crashed into a field nearby.

Later on after the surrender of Hamburg, Jack had a role with the Dutch police to intern Dutch civilians who had collaborated with the German occupation forces. Bitterness ran high

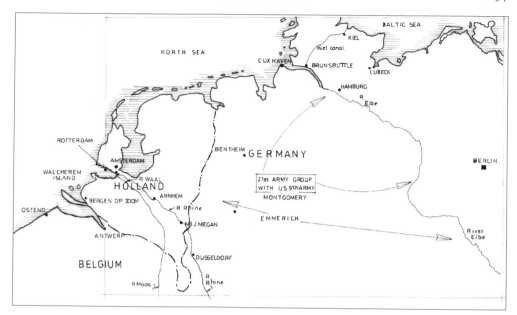

Sketch map of north-west Europe.

and this was more for their own protection than for any other reason. My father told us a story which brings these events sharply into focus. He had discovered that the police officer responsible to him for bringing in these people, whilst armed, had no ammunition for his weapon. Jack therefore arranged for some to be issued. On the following day the officer reported that the group he had been escorting had tried to escape and that they were all now dead. My father had to inspect the corpses crumpled in a ditch. He was told afterwards that the lack of ammunition was not accidental and it became clear that the group had been murdered by the police officer.

On the larger canvas, in the early stages of the campaign Eisenhower had made every effort not to be over-nationalistic in matters of command, but by March 1945 he had become anti-British and prodded by his Chief of Staff General Marshall back in the USA he was ready to snub both Churchill and Montgomery. The final role for Montgomery in the 21st Army's liberation of Europe was to be modest and it was in this lesser role that Jack Stoate and 30 Battalion Royal Marines would lend a hand.

The Supreme Commander's intention was that Montgomery should 'cross the Elbe without delay, drive to the Baltic coast, loop back and seal off the Danish peninsula.' The British forces now were downgraded to occupying Holland and Denmark and would also forego the coveted prize of Berlin. The American 9th Army was to be removed from Montgomery's command.

In spite of his frustrations, as long as he had a job to do, Montgomery was not one to worry for long about past grievances. He was elated by the rapid advances of his divisions and by the coming defeat of Germany. He was not to enjoy his long-planned advance over the Hanover Plains to Berlin but he happily pushed his divisions forward via Bremen and Hamburg and on towards the Elbe. His main objective was to reach the neck of the Danish peninsula before the Russians, since the occupation of Denmark by Soviet troops would have had dire political consequences.

General Bill Simpson, Commander of the American 9th Army, wanted to go on to Berlin. He was less anti-Montgomery than the other US commanders and stated when his 9th Army crossed Elbe on 12 April, only 48 miles from Berlin, that he could have been there in a day and a half because the German resistance was non-existent.

Meanwhile, 30 Battalion RM had made its way up to Bergen-op-Zoom where it was accommodated in a seminary until suitable training areas could be found. The Battalion remained there until 6 April, to fit them for their future task. Some specialist instructors from the Army were attached and they got down to some hard training. Signal exercises were held by Brigade H.Q. T.E.W.T.s (Tactical Exercises Without Troops) were run for officers, and everyone was practised in Battalion moves, which were likely to be often and at short notice in the near future.

Keen rivalry was set up by inter-company football competitions and competitive spirit was introduced in the training. Much emphasis was laid on the firing of all weapons and competitive patrolling.

The Battalion was encouraged by the stories of those returning from the forward units, they felt ready, and their wish was to be fulfilled. They had thought that they would initially pause at a concentration area, but instead on 5 April the reconnaissance group moved to the Nijmegen Salient and on 7 April the Battalion followed moving in without further delay, taking over some of the positions during daylight hours and the more forward ones by night.

The relief was accomplished successfully, in spite of the fact that none in the Battalion had had previous experience of such a task. This was a quiet sector of the front and the main purpose of their being there was to gain more experience and to relieve more experienced troops for the great offensive, which was already on the way into Germany proper.

The Battalion area was vast and difficult to control and even section posts were not in every case mutually supporting. Their main task was to contain the enemy and to prevent his patrols from infiltrating through the Battalion's lines and sabotaging in the rear. Mostly the days were quiet, except for occasional shelling, but when the night fell firing broke out all along the front and interceptor patrols were frequently sent across the river to harass enemy positions with artillery and mortar fire.

Whilst lack of sleep was a problem, the weather was favourable and civilians still carried out their daily toil close to Battalion positions, making life fairly bearable. In fact, for Jack the greatest difficulty was the apparent normality of life. The placid Dutch villagers almost ignored the danger of possible enemy attack and there was a great temptation to relax. Furthermore, the men had seldom eaten so well, for there was much growing in the gardens close at hand.

Nevertheless everyone realised that this period was would not last forever and it was important to learn all they could whilst they had the opportunity. In the first few days it was found that the men were 'trigger happy' and that the faintest suspicion of an enemy in the darkness would cause intense fire to be put down. My father admitted to being one of those jumpy at night. Whilst patrolling in the darkness, one night, he heard some something; in his peripheral vision he sensed rather than saw a movement and let fly, only to find he had shot a cow! So one thought twice about approaching a section post without having given previous warning!

Another common problem was enemy sniping in daylight, so the men moved with caution. The removal of snipers was by no means straightforward. They usually positioned themselves in high buildings or even industrial chimneys. Jack told us it was a near perfect way to demonstrate the use of one type of ammunition above another. If Amour Piercing rounds were used they would tend to remove a brick or two from the sniper's hiding place but if High Explosive was used it was not sufficiently accurate. So as often as not it was an infantry job to do the clearance.

During one night at this time the carriers had a short, sharp firefight with a strong enemy patrol which had worked round to the rear of the forward positions and was making its way across the stretch of marsh land that separated the forward and reserve positions. The fight resulted in one of the carrier's crew being killed.

Incidents of this nature occurred from time to time but chiefly it was a question of waiting and watching. Companies were changed around to bring them into reserve for a spell and for use as a mobile reserve. In the meantime the news of the progress of Allied troops across the

Rhine was immensely cheering and made them impatient to cross the Maas, and once again they were not disappointed.

On Sunday, 22 April, the Battalion was ordered to attack across the Maas and secure the Island of Alem and the stretch of land east of the island, between the Rivers Maas and Waal, so making contact with a Belgian Brigade on their right. On the night of 21 April a patrol led by Lieut. F. R. Bell went across to the island to remain there for 24 hours and wireless back information on enemy movements. The first knowledge that they were to attack was on the morning of the 22nd and in the early hours of the 23rd the first troops were crossing the river.

The first part of the plan was to capture the island with a two-company attack, 'X' Company on the right and 'A' Company on the left, clearing a stretch of land east of the Island of Alem later that day, using one company and keeping one company in reserve. The 3-inch mortars kept up harassing fire on the enemy positions whilst the artillery hit them from farther back.

The first Companies did not meet with strong opposition, but German Schu mines had been laid liberally in many places, which caused some casualties. Shortly after landing. 'A' and 'X' Companies had successfully secured their objectives by dawn. After this phase of the attack 'A' Company's task was to occupy the town of Kerkdriel, which had been reported as having few enemy in it. After entering the town, however, it was quickly discovered that the enemy were there in some strength and the troops after several hours of severe fighting were finally withdrawn because an attack by another formation on 'A' Company's left had proved unsuccessful.

In the meantime 'X' Company had established themselves in the town of Alem. Jack told the story of how a Corporal went to ring the church bells to celebrate the town's liberation, but for some reason instead of pulling the bell-rope, he climbed to the top of the church tower where to his horror, he found a booby trap which, had he pulled the rope, would have blown the church and himself to kingdom come.

Later on that day, 'B' Company made a fresh crossing of the river to extend the flank north-eastwards from the island. As the boats were being paddled across, Spandau and rifle fire spattered around them, causing no casualties at first, but soon after the platoons landed, fire became more accurate and they were less fortunate. The first objective of this Company was to take a fort which held a commanding position overlooking the river. The two forward platoons assisted each other with fire and closed to within assaulting distance. Just prior to the assault going in, the air was rent by a terrific explosion as the centre of the fort blew sky-high. Many of the enemy were in the fort at the time and were killed by the explosion and no further opposition was met, except for small arms fire from the far bank of the River Waal. Contact with the Belgians was made in the village of Heerewarden and they were acclaimed wildly by the Dutch townsfolk.

The Battalion remained in their newly won positions until the morning of 25 April 1945, when they learned, to some disappointment, that they were to withdraw to their original positions on the Maas. This was deemed advisable, as the Dutch, who were to have attacked on the Battalion's left flank, were repulsed and failed to make contact at Kerkdriel. With their left flank exposed, the Royal Marines would have found great difficulty in holding their new positions and so began the withdrawal at 1400 hrs. By 1600 hrs. they had completely withdrawn and taken up their original positions. Nevertheless, the increasingly good news of the progress of the Allied armies in Germany softened their disappointment and shortly they would be on the move again.

When the 21st Army group with US Airborne Corps crossed the Elbe, German resistance collapsed altogether. On 24 April Jodl told the German commanders in the west that the fight against the Bolsheviks was now the only thing that mattered and that the loss of territory to the Western Allies was of secondary importance. This order prompted immediate surrender negotiations from the German commander of the Hamburg Garrison, which gave up to the British without a fight on 3 May 1945. On the day before, a British armoured column had entered Lubeck without opposition and also on 2 May another column with US troops in support entered Wismar a few hours before the Russians. Montgomery's army had saved Denmark from Soviet occupation in the nick of time.

On 2 May 30 Battalion were relieved by an R.A. Regiment and moved back to Vaught, where they concentrated for the night. With news full of fresh Allied gains, it was understood that Germany's end might come any day. At Vaught they were told that they were to be sent to the Hamburg area. Once again, the orders were at short notice, and on 3 May, the day that the Hamburg Garrison surrendered, they found themselves on a journey that took the next three days.

The column passed through Nijmegen and entered that part of Germany near the Reichswald forest that seems like a kind of salient into Holland. As they crossed the frontier Jack saw a sign that read 'Civilisation Ends Here.' After five and half years of war the Allies were at last advancing into Germany. They passed through Cleves, very battered and war scarred, the few civilians staring at them glassily. The column rumbled on towards the Rhine, which they crossed at Emmerich. Here the devastation was frightening. Jack said not one building was undamaged, many not much more than rubble. There were no signs of life of any kind. He said there was something about the city that was not of this world; even the voices of his own men were subdued, it was a city of the dead.

They stopped the first night at Bentheim and continued on early next morning when the countryside now became more varied and interesting. In parts the Germans seemed little affected by the war and en route they heard rumours of an armistice, but most of the men were still a little sceptical.

The second night found them in Vorverden (just east of the Elbe), and the following day they entered Hamburg, which had fallen two days previously. Here the town was a shambles. The result of what was behind those cryptic remarks of the B.B.C. announcers, when they said that our bombers were 'over Hamburg' during the night.

On 3 June, the General Officer Commanding Royal Marines (today Commandant General RM) honoured them with a visit and they learned that the necessity for using Royal Marines as infantrymen of the line was at an end and that the Brigade was to be disbanded. This meant a return to England and leave, but for Jack the prospect of further action had not passed.

Before embarkation for England Jack was handed something of a sinecure for a couple of weeks. He was handed the keys to a car, given a projector and some films and his job was to travel organising the film shows for the troops. It was during this period that he met up with his brother Norman Stoate in Brunsbuttel. At that moment, Jack was being moved on with no apparent successor, so he had little compunction in handing over the car, projector and other 'liberated items' to his brother.

Montgomery wrote the following note about the North West Europe Campaign for his log:

And so the campaign in northwest Europe is finished. I'm glad. It's been a tough business. When I review the campaign as a whole I am amazed at the mistakes we made.

The organisation for command was always faulty. The Supreme Commander (Eisenhower) had no firm ideas as to how to conduct the war and was blown about by the wind all over the place; at that particular business he was quite useless.

The Deputy Supreme Commander (Tedder) was completely ineffective; none of the army commanders would see him and they growled if ever he appeared on the horizon.

The staff at SHAEF were completely out of their depth most of the time and yet we won.

The point to understand is if we had run the show properly the war could've been finished by Christmas 1944. The blame for this must rest with the Americans.

To balance this it is merely necessary to say one thing, i.e. if the Americans had not come along and lent a hand we would never have won the war at all.

Jack returned to England on 26 June to go on a Motor Transport course, following which he was moved from Portsmouth to Plymouth in expectation of embarkation to the Far East.

Fortunately, VJ day came on 15 August 1945 and he was sent back to Chatham Division for release on 31 October 1945.

On 19 January 1944, my parent's wedding day, my father's best man was Geoffrey Stoate, the youngest of the Stoate brothers. Geoffrey Llewellyn Stoate (the Welsh middle name was chosen by his mother, a Swansea girl) was born on New Year's Eve 1924. Geoffrey, like his brothers, was educated at Clifton College but only until it was evacuated to Cornwall during the war, when he was sent to Monkton Combe School near Bath.

Schooling completed, Geoffrey would very much have liked to have joined his brothers in the armed services, but it was not to be. The call up papers duly arrived in 1943 but he had been plagued by chronic asthma since childhood and the medical board said a firm no.

By this time Geoffrey had embarked upon his chosen career in law at Bristol University, but he looked for something he could do at the same time for the war effort. He spotted an announcement that new members were required for the Royal Observer Corps and this seemed to fit the bill admirably.

Although its roots go back to the First World War the Observer Corps' formal organisation dates from 1925, when the formation of an RAF command concerning the air defence of Great Britain led to the provision of an air raid reporting system. It comprised representatives from the Air Ministry, Home Office and the General Post Office. The idea was to provide for the visual detection, identification, tracking and reporting of aircraft over Great Britain, and was eventually to become known as the Observer Corps. As the whole of Great Britain would be covered, cooperation was required amongst the RAF, the Army, the Police Forces and the General Post Office. (The GPO being responsible at that time for the national telecommunications system).

In 1929 the control of the Observer Corps passed from the County Police Forces to the Air Ministry, although Chief Constables retained responsibility for personnel and recruitment matters. By 1939, practically the whole of Great Britain was covered with observation posts, with the western parts of Wales and Scotland together with England's West Country being included during 1940.

In 1935, when the potential threat from Germany was apparent, the joint Air Ministry and War Office Committee created a new continuous 26-mile wide defended zone running from Portsmouth in the south, east of London up to the Tees in the north.

The full implementation of this scheme took some years and included moving bomber squadrons northwards with fighter squadrons filling the empty stations in the south. It also involved the extension of the Observer Corps network to new regions. By 1937 the politicians accepted in principle the necessity to provide better home defence on the ground by way of more anti-aircraft guns and barrage balloons in more locations; however, this understanding 'in principle' did not translate into very much in the way of concrete investment.

As part of this acceptance the Air Ministry and Home Office between them saw to the expansion of the Observer Corps, whilst Civil Defence, the provision of shelters attracting volunteers as air raid wardens and auxiliary firemen, became the responsibility of local authorities.

Hitler's invasion of Czechoslovakia initiated the mobilisation of the Royal Navy, part of the AAF (Auxiliary Air Force), the Observer Corps and Anti Aircraft Units, the distribution of gas masks to the regions, the announcement of makeshift plans for the evacuation of the big cities and the hasty digging of shelter trenches (soon to be waterlogged) in the London parks.

At the end of September 1938 the political crisis which culminated in the Munich Agreement had led to the Observer Corps being mobilised for a period of one week. This single act proved to be invaluable as it highlighted a number of organisational and technical shortcomings, and provided the impetus for the development of solutions.

Whilst high-quality Royal Navy binoculars were issued to observers, at this stage the only uniform items handed out were steel helmets bearing the stencilled letters 'O C', together with armbands bearing the same, similar to those issued to the Local Defence Volunteers.

Geoffrey Stoate in Royal Observer Corps uniform. (Geoffrey Stoate)

King 4 Group. Geoffrey Stoate is third from right, second row. (Geoffrey Stoate)

Geoffrey, having been accepted for the Corps, was allocated to a post in the Bristol Group entitled King 4 – that is to say it was a member of a group of four posts in and around Bristol, all linked by telephone with each other and the Bristol Headquarters. King 4 post was situated at Almondsbury, on the northern outskirts of Bristol and not far from the Bristol Aircraft Works and the RAF Station at Filton, where Geoffrey's eldest brother Tom served during the bombing attacks of 1940, at the start of a highly active RAF career we shall look at shortly.

Observation Posts often consisted of nothing more than a wooden garden shed located next to a telegraph pole, this arrangement enabling a telecommunications link to be established with a control centre, often via a manual switchboard at the local telephone exchange.

These 'garden shed' style observation posts were eventually replaced by more substantial brick-built structures, protected by sandbags. Often having being constructed by Observer Corps personnel themselves, no two posts were identical. They were usually located in open playing fields, hilltops or cliff edges and, particularly in urban areas, on the rooftops of public buildings and factories. Geoffrey remembers:

> Our post was on the top of a turret of a large house and like all the posts was open to the elements at all times and in all conditions. This was essential for the deployment of the tracking device and for the visual and auditory detection of all aircraft, both friendly and hostile. Usually three or four observers were on duty and thankfully there was an undercover room where those who were not on watch could relax and brew up a cup of tea.

From 3 September 1939, observation posts and control centres were manned continuously until 12 May 1945, four days after VE Day when it was confirmed that the Luftwaffe had ceased combat operations.

We hear today of 'friendly fire' and have heard it mentioned a few times in Roy Hussey's story. In the early days of 1939 aircraft recognition was not yet the highly prized skill it was to become in the Observer Corps. Other armed services regarded accurate aircraft identification as being nigh on impossible. The Observers realised that there existed a chronic skills deficiency and the profile of aircraft recognition was raised from within the ranks of the Observer Corps.

> Our periods of duty on Post were interspersed with training sessions. I remember filing into the Odeon cinema in Bristol where silhouettes of aircraft from different angles were displayed on the screen for a second or two and each had to be identified and written down by the Observers.

This aircraft recognition training material described by Geoffrey, consisting of aircraft silhouettes and other data, was introduced almost entirely under the auspices of the unofficial Observer Corps Club. Only much later did this skill obtain official recognition, eventually spreading throughout the armed forces. In Roy Hussey's tin box were two looseleaf files packed with the the silhouettes of different aircraft which he would have had to have learned to identify during his training. The skill, however, was still sadly lacking at the time of what became known as the Battle of Barking Creek.

On 6 September 1939, three days after the declaration of war, 151 Squadron flying Hurricanes was mistaken by ground radar and Observers as enemy aircraft. As a result ground fire from anti-aircraft batteries opened up and 56 Squadron set off in pursuit, shooting down two Hurricanes and killing one pilot. It was largely down to Squadron Leader E.M. Donaldson of 151 Squadron, one of the three well-known Donaldson brothers in the RAF in the Second World War, who ordered 151 Squadron not to retaliate, that greater loss was avoided. One of the pilots involved in this tragedy was the South African, 'Sailor' Malan, the famous brother of George Malan, one of Roy Hussey's colleagues in 72 Squadron. At the court of inquiry Malan was absolved of any wrongdoing.

Aircraft recognition silhouette for Me 110. From Roy Hussey's tin box.

By 1940 the Command structure of Home Defence was improving. Dowding, head of Fighter Command, was also head of Anti-Aircraft Command, which included static defences and the issuing of public air-raid warnings. The anti-aircraft guns defended the cities, dockyards, airfields and special targets such as the Rolls-Royce plant in Derby and the Supermarine plant at Southampton. The AA Command was under the direct command of Lieutenant-General Sir Frederick (Tim) Pile. It seems that Dowding and Pile, both headquartered at Stanmore, got on famously. Pile was the only officer to hold the same major command during the whole war and by mid 1940 he deployed about 1700 guns (of the 2200 approved in 1938). Some of these were old 3-inch pieces supplementing the more modern 3.7s and 4.5s.

By mid 1940 there were 31 Observer Corps Groups in Britain, each containing 30 to 50 posts. It was manned entirely by volunteers, the Corps had acquired a morale and enthusiasm unsurpassed by any other civilian service. To be fair, in July 1940 at the beginning of the Battle of Britain, the standard of competence in many places was not high, though rapidly improving.

In recognition of their role during the Battle of Britain, the Observer Corps was granted the 'Royal' title in April 1941 and it became a uniformed civil defence organisation administered by Fighter Command. During that same year, in a change from the policy of the old Observer Corps, the ROC undertook to recruit women personnel for the first time. The management of communication was the sole domain of the women of the Auxiliary Air Force (WAAF) known as Clerks Special Duties, or more simply 'plotters'.

The volunteer aspect is underlined by the fact that despite the uniform and the reporting chain up to Dowding, the ROC remained a civil defence unit and was never one of the armed forces. The Seaborne Observers are the only members of the ROC whose service during the Second World War entitles them to wear the HM Armed Forces Veterans Badge, as that Division was on temporary attachment to the Royal Navy. Nevertheless, the 30,000 or so members of the Royal Observer Corps, women as well as men and mostly part-time, were as essential to the Battle as the RAF's own radar stations.

The ROC complemented and at times replaced the Chain Home defensive radar system by undertaking an inland aircraft tracking and reporting function. The Chain Home radar system provided predominantly coastal, long-range, tracking and reporting. Once inland, the movements of German aircraft were visually tracked and reported by the Royal Observer Corps.

I had hoped to be one of those chosen to be seaborne on D-Day, but wasn't, either because my health was unreliable or possibly because my aircraft recognition abilities were not up to the exceptionally high standard required for this job. Were it not for this, maybe Norman and I would have been close to each other on that day. Mind you, in the back of my mind I was dreading the possibility that a mistake in a split-second decision might lead to friendly casualties.

Not surprisingly aircraft flying at great heights or in cloudy conditions often made accurate recognition difficult if not impossible. However, enemy low-level attacks, most notably undertaken by the 9th Staffel led by Hauptman Joachim Roth flying Dorniers at under 100 feet, were below radar trace. In August 1940 when RAF Kenley was attacked, it was the Observer Corps who reported the nine aeroplanes skimming in over Beachy head.

They were tracked through by other Observer Corps groups but regrettably the AA gunners at Kenley, although alerted and ready, had not reckoned on the extreme low level of the Dorniers and were unable to bring their guns to bear in the time available.

The airfield was plastered but the German crews paid fairly dearly, everything opened up at them including the PACs, the Parachute and Cable devices as on Norman Stoate's ML.

The headquarters of each ROC Group operated from a Control Centre, responsible for between 30 and 40 Observation Posts, each of which would be some 10–20 km from its neighbour. By 1945 there were 40 Centres covering Great Britain, controlling in total more than 1,500 posts.

During the period from July to October 1940, the whole Observer Corps was at full stretch operating 24 hours a day, 7 days a week, plotting enemy aircraft and passing this essential

Sketch map of air group defences, August 1940.

ROYAL OBSERVER CORPS

CERTIFICATE OF WAR SERVICE

This certificate is awarded by the Air Council as an expression of their high appreciation of the war services rendered to the Royal Air Force by Observer G.L.STOATE, *as a member of the Royal Observer Corps*

SECRETARY OF STATE FOR AIR

JANUARY 1946

A thank you to Geoffrey, The Royal Observer Corps were 'civilians in uniform'. (Geoffrey Stoate)

information to RAF Fighter Command Groups and Sector Controls. ROC personnel were deployed in two specific roles: Those in Class A were required to undertake 56 hours duty per week, while Class B personnel undertook up to 24 hours duty per week.

As the Battle of Britain faded in October 1940 so the Blitz campaign commenced. Again, the Observer Corps provided vital information that enabled timely air-raid warnings to be issued, thereby saving countless lives. The Blitz itself continued until early in the summer of 1941 and bombing continued, albeit on a reduced scale, until March 1945.

The ROC's methods could in some senses be considerd quite crude but like many uncomplicated systems it worked well in practice. In order to monitor aircraft, observers used a simple but effective mechanical tracking device. Where the approximate height of an aircraft is known it becomes possible, by using a horizontal bearing and a vertical angle taken from a known point, to calculate the approximate position of that aircraft. Geoffrey remembers:

> Our report consisted of the number and type of aircraft and their height and bearing. This enabled the plotters to maintain a continuous trace. At busy times, with four Posts giving reports, it was quite difficult to get immediate attention from the plotters, but if the situation appeared urgent the use of the phrase <u>Red</u> King 4 took priority over others.

Posts were equipped with a mechanical sighting height adjuster positioned over a map grid. After setting the instrument with the aircraft's approximate height, the observer would align a sighting bar with the aircraft. This bar was mechanically connected to a vertical pointer that would indicate the approximate position of the aircraft on the map grid. Observers would report the map co-ordinates, height, time, sector clock code and number of aircraft for each sighting to the aircraft plotters located at the Centre. The WAAF plotters, positioned around a large table map, would wear headsets to enable a constant communications link to be maintained with their allocated cluster of Posts, usually three in number and so the progress of enemy aircraft would be plotted across the country and AA or fighter interception coordinated.

The plotting table consisted of a large map with grid squares and posts being marked. Counters were placed on the map at the reported aircraft's position, each counter indicating the height and number of aircraft, and a colour-coded system was used to indicate the time of observation in 5-minute segments. The table was surrounded by plotters, responsible for communicating with their allocated cluster of Posts. Over time, the track of aircraft could be traced, with the system of colour coding enabling the extrapolation of tracks and the removal of time expired (historical) data.

From 1943 onwards, long-range boards were introduced into centre operations rooms, with 'tellers' communicating with neighbouring ROC groups in order to hand over details of inbound and outbound aircraft tracks as they were plotted on their map.

The Observer Corps formed the cornerstone of Air Marshall Dowding's air defence system for Britain. In a dispatch marking his appreciation following the Battle of Britain Dowding wrote:

> It is important to note that at this time they (the Observer Corps) constituted the whole means of tracking enemy raids once they had crossed the coastline. Their work throughout was quite invaluable. Without it the air-raid warning systems could not have been operated and inland interceptions would rarely have been made.

10

BACK TO AFRICA AND ITALY

Dr Tom Stoate takes up his duties with the RAF. Stationed at Filton, he sees his home city of Bristol heavily bombed and is then posted to Africa, in which theatre he remains on front-line duties for the next two-and-half years.

Perhaps we should review the progress of the family. David Stoate had joined the Honourable Artillery Company in 1940 and had trained in India to receive his commission. Serving briefly in Singapore he had become a prisoner of war under appalling circumstances after Singapore was overrun by the Japanese in December 1941/January 1942. Norman Stoate was an Ordinary Seaman and then Able Seaman on HMS *Eagle* in the Indian Ocean and in the Eastern Mediterranean until May 1941, after which he received his commission and served on the small ships based in Gibraltar; following which he commanded ML 909 in Home Waters. Jack, my father, had been managing his father's farm and after joining the Home Guard in May 1941 gave all that up in March 1942 to volunteer into the Royal Marines, Geoffrey, after completing his law studies volunteered into the Royal Observer Corps. My mother having left her job in London had returned to South Gloucestershire and in February 1942 had volunteered into the Women's Land Army. Her brother Roy Hussey, after exaggerating his age, had joined the RAFVR and after flying training in America during late 1941 and early 1942 had joined 72 Squadron, part of 324 Wing and was heavily engaged in Africa as part of the Operation *Torch*, the Algerian/Tunisian landings. It is to that theatre via South Africa, in 1941, that we now return to follow Tom Stoate.

Tom Stoate was the quietest, most reserved and eldest of the Stoate brothers. He was born on 21 October 1914 and along with his brothers was educated at Clifton College, Bristol. Like his youngest brother Geoffrey he was academically gifted and went up to Caius College, Cambridge where he studied medicine.

He never married and in spite of producing a number of books, all that he left behind him at his death in 1997 by way of notes or stories of his five-and-a-half years of wartime service as a doctor in the RAF is a similar quarto sheet to to the one in Jack Stoate's story.

His service records reveal that as well as spells on permanent Stations he served on frontline duties as Medical Officer. We see him in Cyrenaica, that part of modern Libya that adjoins Egypt with 94 Squadron and in Sicily and Italy with the Boston-equipped night operation 114 and 18 Squadrons, part of 326 Wing (later 232 Wing). Later he was promoted to Senior Medical Officer with 239 Wing, flying Kittyhawk and Mustang fighter-bombers, also in Sicily and Italy. We can therefore track his movements fairly accurately. Although being in the same theatre of war as Roy Hussey, so far as records show 239 Wing and 324 Wing, of which 72 Squadron formed part, never shared the same base at the same time. Tom's service was almost entirely to the east of Roy, supporting the British Eighth Army in Egypt and Cyrenaica and up the Adriatic side of Italy, whereas Roy, in 72 Squadron, was fighting in Tunisia and then mostly supporting the American 5th Army on the Mediterranean side of Italy. What follows is necessarily a reconstruction of how some aspects of Tom's life might have been as a squadron doctor but maybe it is not too far removed from reality.

After Tom came down from Cambridge his first job was as a Junior Houseman in the Westminster Hospital, London, he then became a House Physician in the Royal Berkshire Hospital Reading, the same hospital that brought Douglas Bader back from the brink of death after his flying accident in 1931.

After war was declared, Tom was called up and joined the RAF on 9 July 1940 when the Battle of Britain was in its early stages. He undertook a very brief course at Halton, Near Wendover, Buckinghamshire, for training into Service ways. There was, and no doubt still is, a form for everything – and in triplicate!

Halton was a centre of excellence for RAF engineering apprentices; it was a permanent camp with fine amenities – cinema, swimming pool, dances and plenty of entertainment. It was also the site of Princess Mary's hospital. Princess Mary's was opened in 1927 as a large military hospital and as an institute for pathology and tropical medicine, It became the first AeroMed unit, meaning it could accept patients flown in by air, and it is likely that later, when Tom was serving with frontline squadrons, some of his casualties were flown in to Princess Mary's.

His first operational posting, with the rank of Flying Officer on 19 July 1940, was as Medical Officer at RAF Filton near his home in Bristol. Filton was home to the Filton Sector of 10 Group RAF Operations Room and Staff. Whilst it did not have a defensive fighter squadron attached to defend the airfield, 236 Squadron with Bristol Blenheim twin-engined fighters, flying defensive sweeps over the Channel, was based there; as was 935 (County of Glamorgan) Barrage Balloon Unit (Auxiliary Air Force), which provided part of the site's defence with 2 Flights of 8 barrage balloons. A month before Tom's posting a lone German bomber attacked the Bristol Aircraft works at Filton. As a result during August 1940 the barrage balloons were increased to 24. On 3 July, nearby Whittocks End was bombed, the only casualties were a pig, five ducks, two rabbits and a hayrick. Things would get worse.

On 22–23 August more than 400 bombs fell in and around Filton. The main target was of course the Bristol aircraft factory, which was very badly damaged. Just before mid-day on 25 September 1940, 57 Heinkel 111 bombers with a Messerschmitt Bf 110 fighter escort dropped 300 bombs. 160 of them hit the aircraft factory, 6 of these scored a direct hit on one of the air raid shelters and 5 other shelters were seriously damaged. Over 200 people were killed or injured. Eight enemy aircraft were shot down. In the unlikely event that Tom was unsure about the grislier aspects of war this baptism of fire would surely have educated him very early on in his service carreer, as he was smack in the middle of this action.

After the event, it seemed that Luftwaffe reconnaissance planes had determined that there were no fighter aircraft stationed at Filton. Subsequently 504 (County of Nottingham) Squadron (Auxiliary Air Force) was moved in from 26 September 1940, flying Hawker Hurricane Mk1 fighters. On 27 September the Luftwaffe was punished severely when it revisited.

The evacuation of the British Expeditionary Forces from Dunkirk, the Battle of Britain and the Blitz had left Britain bloodied but unbowed. The possibility of re-opening a front in northern Europe was discarded and for the several reasons which we have already noted, a second front in North Africa was decided upon and it was to this theatre that Tom was bound.

Tom, aged 25, set sail from Gourock, on the Clyde, arriving on 8 February 1941 at overseas station East London, some two hours south of Durban, South Africa.

This stretch of ocean was quite heavily populated by the Stoate family at this time. Just one month after Tom had landed on the African East coast; in March 1941 two of his brothers had

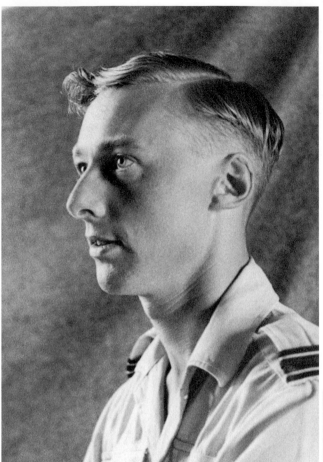

Tom Stoate in uniform. (Geoffrey Stoate)

Kittyhawk in North Africa. (Author)

sailed by, David in the *Highland Chieftan* on his way to India to receive his commission and Norman in the *Christian Huggens* sailing back to England to train for his.

When Britain declared war on Germany, the South African United Party (a political coalition) split. J.B.M. Hertzog wanted South Africa to remain neutral, but the venerated General Smuts argued for joining the British war effort. Smuts's faction narrowly won the crucial parliamentary debate and Hertzog and his followers left the coalition, many rejoining the National Party maintained since 1934. Smuts became prime minister, and South Africa declared war on Germany.

South Africa made significant contributions to the Allied war effort; some 135,000 white South Africans fought in the East and North African and Italian campaigns, including those in 5 SAAF squadron who formed part of 239 Wing in which Tom was also to serve.

As we saw in Roy Hussey's story, many pilots and navigators did their flying training abroad. Some, like Roy Hussey, were sent to the USA, others to Canada, Rhodesia and South Africa. The RAF Base at East London housed amongst others 41 Air Training School.

Large bodies of men were being drafted into the North African theatre of war by way of South Africa, then on to North Africa by Sierra Leone or the Gold Coast or travelling the other way, up the east coast of Africa, which was the way both Norman and David Stoate journeyed.

The men passing through East London had to be fully immunised. For Tom, the doctor, this would have meant turning up each man's record. If he had not been vaccinated within five years or inoculated against typhoid or against tetanus within a year, he would have the omission rectified.

Apart from the actual bookwork of making lists there was considerable thought needed. Vaccination may have meant that a man needed a day or so off duty in a week's time. The inoculation against typhoid may have meant a day off straight away, possibly another in ten days time, after the second dose. By contrast an anti tetanus jab fortunately creates no side effects. Thus all a man might have needed if he had all three at once, was a day off immediately, another in about a week and a third in about ten days.

Treatments, of course, had to be staggered so that the whole of a section was not put out of action at once. Sufficient pilots and ground crew had to be kept fit, with everyone immunised in the shortest time possible. If a squadron were to be suddenly transferred and all the personnel not ready, those in high places were apt to ask questions. So Tom would check the men over and vaccinate as appropriate.

Unlike the more leisurely pace of civilian practice, in the services a queue was formed with the required part of the body exposed, be it arm, leg, thigh, abdomen or foot. One assistant cleaned the selected spot, another prepared the instrument, the MO did the actual deed and the third put on the pad while a clerk registered the names. The average rate was about four per minute.

On 17 July 1942, after 14 months at East London, Tom was posted to 21 P.T.C. (Personnel Transit Unit) and on 4 August, with the rank of Flight Lieutenant back-dated to 10 July 1941, he arrived at 94 Squadron Middle East Command, an operational squadron flying Hurricane Mark I and IIcs based at El Gamil near Port Said. Tom had a seven-day handover period with his predecessor Flt/Lt Hicks, who departed on 8 August.

In the same way that Roy Hussey's logbook seemed to lose its sparkle when he was posted back to England and ultimately 19 Squadron, the Operational Record Book of 94 Squadron seems flat and demoralised – maybe not too surprisingly.

94 Squadron, flying Hurricane fighters, had had a torrid time earlier in 1942. In the opening months it had had a succession of new COs. On 15 January 1942 the ORB records 'a disastrous day'. On a seven-aircraft sortie, six were destroyed, leaving the Squadron with only five service-able machines. In February the Squadron converted to Curtiss Kittyhawks.

A deadly problem cropped up for Kittyhawk pilots: under the high-g forces of dog-fighting and severe dust conditions their six .50 calibre guns would often jam. They would get in a few bursts and then nothing, so in the middle of a dog-fight they could be left without guns. No doubt, many Kittyhawks and pilots were lost because of this problem, which apparently was never completely fixed.

On 15 February 1942, when Rommel was in the process of recapturing Tobruk – an objective he successfully completed in June 1942 – one month to the day after the January disaster, the Squadron carried out a raid over Martuba, west of Tobruk, and of the five aircraft taking part only one returned. Four pilots including its new Squadron Leader, E.M. Mason, were killed. The squadron was withdrawn from operational duties for 'Intensive Training'.

In one of those apparently unfathomable military decisions, having completed its retraining in Kittyhawks in May 1942 the Squadron was ordered to hand these over to 2 SAAF squadron, whereupon it was re-equipped with Mark 1 Hurricanes and was detailed for defensive duties. This was the case when Tom joined, in August 1942. Hopefully not as an example of general capability, the ORB records on 27 July 1942 that one pilot 'Fired at 1 mile range, height of optimism – right idea.'

August 1942 in this theatre of war was an important period; Rommel had advanced the Axis forces into Egypt once again and was expecting Montgomery, who now had assumed command of the Eighth Army from Auchinleck, to counter-attack. Montgomery however declined at this stage. He deferred action for a month whilst he built up his supplies and troops. It was partly the passage of these two elements that 94 Squadron was patrolling. In October and November the Battle of El Alamein was fought, with Rommel being expelled from Egypt, then Cyrenaica and finally Tunisia and North Africa altogether.

Before we start to examine in more detail what 94 Squadron was up to when Tom joined we should perhaps look at what were the duties of a front line squadron MO. Tom was later to serve with 18 Squadron and buried in 18 Squadron's records there is an excellent Medical Officer's report of conditions at King's Cross, Souk-el-Khemis, Tunisia, in May 1942. It might be remembered in Roy Hussey's story that 72 Squadron was at Souk-el-Khemis in January 1943 when Jimmy Corbin and Roy Hussey were suffering from the 'Dysentery' caused by a surfeit of rough wine stored in petrol tins. The airstrips at Souk-el-Khemis were named after the London mainline train stations, 72 Squadron was based at Waterloo and Euston whilst six months earlier 18 Squadron had been at King's Cross.

Exerpts of the camp report give an interesting insight into the conditions under which the Desert Air Force fought in the dark days of 1942 and improving ones of 1943.

18 Squadron Operations Record Book month of May 1942

Part I
Monthly hygiene report RAF King's Cross – [Souk-el-Khemis]

I Supplies the same as the last month, and purification by direct dosage has been continued. Horrocks and Chloratex cases which are on order have not yet been received

II Throughout the month salvaged British type rations have been in use, supplemented by local purchase. There was definitely insufficient variety, and food of this type is not considered suitable for this type of climate. This was no fault of the cooks, however, as the standard of cooking and service has always been high.

III Accommodation has been adequate and marquees for communal purposes are now on order and are expected shortly.

IV The disposal of all waste matter was continued along the lines of the previous month. A large grease trap was erected at the cookhouse, which proved adequate for their purposes.

V Bathing and ablution arrangements were the same as last month. By way of an experiment a small squadron laundry, run by two ACs and ACHs was started but did not prove very successful as difficulty was experienced in the heating of water and also difficulty in obtaining sufficient soap.

VI Portable box type disinfectant is still available when required in sick quarters but supplies of AL 63 have now been exhausted. In our present locality there does not appear to be any danger of typhus.

VII Full issue of tropical kit has not been possible owing to difficulty in obtaining supplies. It is considered essential that all squadron personnel should receive an issue of solar topees as the majority of work is in the open.

VIII Since the conclusion of this campaign work has been considerably reduced and two entertainments via an open air film show and an open air concert were arranged. Also half of the squadron had a week's leave in La Calle, but so far it has not been possible to arrange a similar rest camp for the other half of the squadron. The morale of the squadron has dropped considerably since the cessation of hostilities in North Africa. This can be largely attributed to the wholesale exchange of flying personnel which has recently taken place.

IX Antimalarial equipment is still not been received by the squadron, in spite of repeated applications. The use of anti-malaria medications and repellants are the only measures possible and have been carried out methodically.

X No further lectures on hygiene and antimalarial measures have been given during this month.

XI One NCO and three Airmen and are available as an anti-malarial squad. This NCO also supervised two Arab labourers who were employed on sanitary duties. This arrangement was found to be satisfactory.

Part II
Sick Quarters diary:

The entire month was spent at RAF Station King's Cross [Souk-el-Khemis]. Units under the medical charge were 18 Squadron 4341LA RAFR, number 10 MTLRU, RAF 39LLA RA, 1st AFS [Army] 230 Company PC [Army] and 132 company PC [Army], also for a short time the sick quarters were responsible for TBF detachment, No. 326 Wing detachment and 109 RSU attachment. At the peak the total strength of units for which we were responsible totaled approximately 1000 …

Part III
Unit medical occurrences of historical interest

a) There was a moderate epidemic of enteritis, which began on the 12th of this month amongst personnel of the 1st AFS [army] and which reached its peak on the 22nd when 40 members of the squadron were confined to bed. Towards the end of the month, the attacks appeared to subside considerably, although there were still a few fresh cases daily. The outbreak was general in the whole area, and seemed to coincide with a large increase in the number of flies.

b) There was only one flying accident during this month. On the 14th of this month 581014

Warrant Officer Brown JA NAV/B sustained a fractured neck and second metatarsal of the right foot, when the nose wheel of Boston AL 775 collapsed when landing at Tunis aerodrome. This Warrant Officer was admitted direct to 1 CCS.

c) A number of crews were granted seven days leave, which they were entitled to spend at Constantine, Tobaka or Tunis. Accommodation and living conditions are satisfactory, and there are separate messes for officers and NCOs. Owing to the heat, flying clothes have been largely discarded. After operations, the Nav/B has frequently complained of headaches, which is being attributed to the extreme heat and glare in the nose of the Boston aircraft.

d) It has been found that the two-way Higginson syringe supplied in the Z1 equipment is unsatisfactory for aural syringe. An improved aural syringe has been constructed from a douche can rubber tubing and glass nozzle. This is operated from a height of approximately 6 feet and it is found extremely satisfactory. Enamel trays borrowed from the photographic section have been used for the storage of bandages, dressings and surgical instruments, in the crash room and dressing room …

f) The springing of the floors in the ambulances is found to be rather harsh and the rear doors on account of their weight seem to suffer from 'drop' and become difficult to close. Also it is thought that the vehicle is unnecessarily large and unwieldy and a lighter type of vehicle such as the American units employ would be more suitable. The addition of an aural syringe and aural probe to the existing Z1 equipment would be appreciated. Also there is great difficulty in obtaining replacement batteries for the auroscope.

Signed: K. O' Brian.

On an ordinary RAF station the Senior Medical Officer had the softest quarters in the whole place. He had his own little flat in Sick Quarters with heating and bathroom. No doubt Tom would have had a comfortable billet at East London, so it might have taken him a little while to get used to a camp bed, washing in the open in a canvas basin and the presence of bedfellows such as earwigs and spiders and of course the torments of the climate, one of the worst of which was the desert sandstorm. A neighbour of mine described one:

> A gale of wind got up blowing several tents down and the sand got in everywhere, the weather got hotter and hotter until putting your face outside was like meeting a blast furnace. Visibility was down to a yard and later you couldn't see your hand held out in front of your face. It was like the thickest London fog only it was comprised of a fast moving cloud of sand. If you went out it stung your legs and arms and blinded you. If you stayed inside it seemed as thick. The tent of one of the officers blew down and some of his things were recovered later about half a mile away. We ate sand, breathed sand, swallowed sand; even the toilet paper had become sand paper. The temperature had been 104°F with a 60 mph gale. The first experience was not uninteresting, but repetition made it monotonous and very tiring.

The condition and health of the Squadron was to a degree a product of diet and living conditions so apart from the obvious medical duties Tom would also have had a hand in determining how the 'tented village' was set out and erected.

Imagine trying to find a new site for an airfield. It must not be surrounded by army camps and be too obvious a target, there must be room for the proper dispersal of aircraft, machines were much too scarce to risk being wiped out by a raid. So the desert would be searched for miles for a level patch half a mile each way. If the desert were a flat sandy waste it would have been easier but it is undulating and rocky and distances are deceptive. A small hillock four hundred yards away may look like a high hill half a mile away. Doubtless what might have seemed

Desert sandstorm. (Author)

like a good spot is found and then rejected for one reason or another, then eventually one last hope might prove to be just right. A stretch of flat sand about a mile-and-a-half long with scope for a runway in two directions. Here at last, the prospect of a really healthy camp.

As we saw with 72 Squadron's disastrous return with its new Mark IX Spitfires on 25 February 1943, the desert was fickle, it was by no means unremitting sun and heat, it had another side – torrential rain and fierce winds. All hands would be on deck erecting medical tents on muddy ground in wind and pouring rain, handling compo ration boxes – and there would have been a lot of these, as one box fed only 14 men for one day – snatching meals at odd times. Eventually the tent poles, fastened together after a great struggle, were raised. There it was like a great sail and a gust of wind could blow it down again with men buried beneath. Eventually up it would go again, this time firmly anchored and gradually its desired shape would appear.

The tent then had to be divided into compartments. A cord was tied across from one pole to another with the smaller division becoming the dressing area. Another cord stretched between the poles and carried on to the door to divide the medical inspection room and the waiting room. Blankets would be hung over the cords and sewn there for security and so the 'walls' were complete. Once set up, the medical quarters would have to be scrubbed down in order to make them hygienic.

A second marquee might have been erected for an office or a second ward. With the addition of a few slabs of concrete as a path, the SSQ (Station Sick Quarters), which were situated a little way from the main part of the rest of the camp, were complete.

Tom would walk down to the airfield for sick parade in the morning. After sick parade – and there would have been relatively few sick as most of the men picked for overseas duties were on the whole fit – there would be various visits to people sick in billets and maybe visits to outlying hospitals for Medical Boards. This last came about through regular liaison with the RAMC (Royal Army Medical Corps) hospitals. Where possible, visits were made there two or three times a week to see squadron patients, do the Medical Boards and get to know everyone. Fortunately, the Germans did not seem to deliberately bomb hospitals, of course there was the odd accident but nothing obviously planned.

Tom Stoate off the strip in Cyrenaica
but not far; note the windsock in the
background. (Geoffrey Stoate)

The RAMC hospitals – even their tented ones – were different from SSQs as they had operating theatres and a surgical team; their duties and resources were different. Even the RAMC
Field Surgical Units had a surgeon, an anaesthetist, a couple of operating room assistants, two
orderlies and probably three drivers. They also came equipped with their own lorries and a
lightweight truck so that they could move in response to an emergency very quickly. As in
any walk of life, sometimes individuals were less careful than they should have been. In the
RAMC unit at La Calle (the airfield where Roy Hussey so skilfully force landed his new
Mark IX Spitfire when returning from Gibraltar in that desert hail storm) the tattered clothes
of a seriously wounded patient were thrown into the incinerator only for there to be a sizable
explosion – the clothes having contained a hand grenade.

After a period of intensive action the RAMC hospital would see the wounded come in by
the hundreds. Some might already have had primary surgery, others not. Sights were often
gruesome and sometimes heartbreaking; but such was the pace that attendance was needed for
48 hours at a stretch and such emotions could not be entertained. It was not that compassion
was missing, on the contrary the disgraceful waste of life and the maiming of thousands of
young lives must have seemed an outrage to Tom and his colleagues.

Tom may not have met, but he would certainly have heard of, 'Five table Clarke'. Major
Ruscoe Clarke was known of in medical circles the length and breadth of Tunisia and Algeria
on account of his unusual method of operating. His operating theatre was a large marquee
housing five operating tables. Major Clarke and another officer, Captain Faux, would operate
on two patients on two of the tables with two teams of assistants while two dressers would be
attending to two patients who had already been operated on. These would be being dressed
before going on to the wards. The fifth table would hold a patient who was being cleaned up in
preparation for an operation. Rather like the 'just in time' manufacturing methods of building

MLs and Liberty ships described earlier, Major Clarke followed a similar methodology in his operating theatre. It was by all accounts very effective for dealing with a rush of casualties, as was often experienced in RAMC units, if a little brutal sounding.

The desert conditions presented another difficulty for the medics; the heat affected the X-ray tent. As soon as the tropical films were lifted out of the ice-cooled water after development was complete, the emulsion began to melt. So there were only a few seconds to inspect them to look for fractures and metallic bodies before all features merged and disappeared.

The same temperature conditions of course prevailed on the airfield. In the Station Sick Quarters the clinical thermometers had to be stored in water. A patient's temperature would record very high if not read at once. When the outside temperature reached 120°F the thermometers had to be kept in a fridge or they would have broken.

Ignoring for a moment casualties arising from air attacks on the airfield and the losses and wounded on sorties, illness was not very prevalent. There were two main troubles, sores and 'gypy tummy'. Sores were more a nuisance than deadly. There were septic sores with a variety of germs found in them that developed into ulcers, chiefly on the legs and arms. Treatment was varied and usually prolonged. Every MO would have had his favourite routine. One method was to use a saturated saline dressing to clean the ulcer and then gradually reduce the saline to normal. Elastoplast alone was very effective, but impossible to get in sufficient quantities.

Gypy tummy was a mild form of dysentery, which generally knocked the patient out for two or three days. There was no special treatment, except rest. Most people got an attack on arrival and were then fairly free, with care. There was a theory that diet had little to do with this (except as we saw in the case of Roy Hussey and Jimmy Corbin). The greater cause was thought to be chill, either during the afternoon nap or during the night. It was sometimes so hot that people just lay on their beds without anything on and any draught caused a chill of the abdominal wall. If a towel was laid across, it absorbed moisture and prevented chilling from speedy evaporation.

The job of Medical Officer also included important outside jobs, including sanitation, which of course was key. This was a wide remit involving the ventilation, cleanliness and mosquito proofing of living quarters, the size, cleanliness, organisation, disposal of waste, ventilation, bench space, lighting, dish washing and disposal of water in the kitchens, and even the provision of fire fighting buckets to those areas. On the subject of water, it was necessary to ensure supplies were adequate and clean, organising not only sterilisation where necessary but also proper disposal in all areas, but particularly the ablution area where washing facilities had to have antiseptic treatments to duckboards and so forth.

The careful management of waste, both human and general, was an essential duty. Latrines needed to be adequately ventilated, have flyproof seats, be properly cleaned and be located at the correct distance from the camp. Toilet paper needed to be provided and buckets emptied and sterilised. On the wider aspect of waste, rubbish bins with properly fitting lids were required and incinerators had to be set up and their use properly controlled.

An old Bedouin in charge of a donkey and cart was found at every camp, the cart loaded with 40-gallon oil drums. Seen up-wind it might have been a picturesque and colourful sight. But our Beduin formed the sanitary squad. His job was go around the camp collecting the refuse into the drums, emptying the latrines and generally keeping the camp tidy. The contents of the drums would be taken about a mile down-wind from the camp and buried in pits about 8 ft deep with plenty of oil and creosol. The inevitable sometimes occurred – the cart overturned and the resulting big stink was dealt with by pouring petrol over the area and firing it.

Sanitary duties were not to be underestimated, the 300 or so men of the Squadron were living in less than ideal circumstances but each had a role in ensuring the pilots and aircrew were effective in combat. Everyone therefore needed to be fit and healthy.

On Tom's typical round, a medical orderly with a notebook would accompany him. First, the sergeants mess. The kitchen might be dirty, there might be butter left on the table not covered with muslin and there might be refuse lying about outside –a reprimand for the cook. Justice, however would be tempered with mercy as the cooks really tried very hard to disguise the sameness of the rations. There might be a small slice of bread per meal with bully beef or M&V (meat and veg.) as the meat ration. There was, however, a reasonable quantity of fresh fruit, peaches, pears, plums, figs and grapes, which made for some variation as 'bully' and 'hard tack' became very monotonous. As for the M&V concoctions, neither the meat nor the veg. would have been very exciting. It had a special flavour which could not be disguised in spite of the efforts of the cooks to hide it. Nevertheless, it was amazing what one could put up with when really hungry. In spite of the sameness, most food was eaten and grumbles waned as it was real-ised that the conditions were unavoidable. Hunger makes a grand sauce.

Next, the sergeants latrine. Quite in order but there is a broken seat so the carpenter must be instructed to make repairs. The officer's kitchen is dirty. Then off to the YMCA tent. Followed by the NAAFI. Here the native manager needs a thorough nagging. He is a slacker so is threat-ened with the loss of his job. He has a battered old drum without a lid for his waste refuse, a perfect fly breeding ground. Also two dustbins for water storage. Tom points out to him that old petrol tins are the proper things in which to store water, then he can use his dustbins with their lids for storing refuse.

The men's dining area comes next. The inner fly-proof screens, obtained after many months work, are useless as they are tied open. There are dishes of uncovered butter on the tables and the tables themselves are dirty. Flies are swarming all over the place. The kitchens are fairly clean but generally there is usually something to grouse about. Tom is not being finicky, stand-ards need to be maintained.

On to the tailor's and barber's shop, both run by natives. Scattered about the tents are remains of empty tins and other havens for germs. Inside it is nearly as bad. The tailor is inherently untidy, the barber will not keep the shaving brushes in carbolic and his clippers and scissors are dirty. More forcible gesticulation, though does little good as it will be as bad next week. A fine is the only thing that has any effect. These low standards were the cause of most of Tom's work. Dirt and flies were constant enemies. Wherever there were Arabs or Egyptians, the trouble was the same. Their sanitary habits were fine in the middle of the desert away from habitation but the perma-nency of the Squadron's living quarters meant that any lapse from European standards produced countless swarms of flies, which were the harbingers of disease and illness amongst the men.

Next comes the Dhobie – the washer man – lumps of soap are being left on the clothes and anyway they are not clean. He is, of course, handicapped by shortage of water, but the point must still be made. Then on to the main pits which are generally in excellent order as the natives have done this job for a long time. Next he wanders round the flights. The defined areas such as equipment and transport are easy but when he passes round the out-of-the-way areas between the flights he has to keep a very sharp look out.

Sanitation, of course, was only part of Tom's job, another was the actual treatment of ill health. The desert housed some interesting creatures, centipedes about a foot long, scorpions some six to nine inches and spiders about the size of a saucer, but far more troublesome than these was the tiny sand fly. Aesthetically, the sand fly is a lovely little insect. Its wings are semi-transparent and covered with down, it is only just visible to the naked eye, especially when one is searching inside of a mosquito net with a candle. The only way to spot it is to bang the net, when the swift flying hop gives the intruder away. The unprotected human body holds a pecu-liar attraction for this little pest, who bites viciously and raises a lump bigger than itself with an after-irritation hard to bear. In addition, it is the source of a nasty fever that knocks the victim out. There is a sudden onset with temperatures up to 105 degrees, which completely incapaci-tates the victim. It was no good trying to be tough, one had to give in. When I spoke to Daryl Briggs, who was the dispatch rider for 72 Squadron, he said those sand fly bites were the worst problem in the desert. He remembered one airman covered in bumps all over his face which were not only irritating but also made shaving almost impossible. Fortunately, the fever did not last long, a week generally saw the patient quite fit without complications. One attack did seem to give some sort of immunity, as locals were very rarely severely affected.

An Arab donkey cart.
(Norman Stoate)

Signposts in both German
and Italian point to former
Axis offices, Tobruk, Libya.
(Library of Congress)

After the reversals in early 1942, as we have seen from the activities of Roy Hussey and 72 Squadron in Operation *Torch,* in early 1943 the Allies were beginning to push the Axis forces back; the port of Biserta fell to the Allies on 7 May 1943, Tunis fell on 9 May and Tunisia on 12 May. Front line squadrons were impermanently based under canvas, mobility was the watchword. Everything had to be kept in such condition that the whole squadron could be moved at a moment's notice and established elsewhere quickly.

What comprises a fighter squadron is a moveable feast. In theory, it should comprise 26–28 pilots with 21 aircraft, 16 operational and 5 in reserve, such that at all times 12 pilots with operational aircraft are in readiness. Supporting this front end were some 250-300 ground personnel – fitters, riggers armourers, instrument repairers, cooks and a whole infrastructure that set out to make the Squadron a self-contained unit. In the circumstances of 1942/3, these ideal arrangements did not exist. Pilots and aircraft were constantly being lost, spares were not freely available and the climatic and living conditions militated against efficient maintenance of machine and body, the latter of course the Squadron doctor's remit.

Through the latter part of 1942 the Allied strategy of starving the Axis of equipment by constant attacks upon their supply lines was beginning to take effect. By the end of the year, the German and Italian forces were being driven back and consequently the forward RAF squadrons were constantly on the move. Everyone was busy clearing, sorting, and packing up. It would not have been easy moving a squadron in the desert or indeed in the mud of Italy during 1944/5, particularly if it had become semi-permanent. The planning of the new camp and layout of the cooking and sanitary arrangements occupied a good deal of an MO's time. Ideally the new site would be practically fly-free, but whilst it might have been possible to keep the living areas and food clean with netting, it would have been another matter to keep the whole area clear.

Perversely, flies were not just enemies, they were also allies, or at least in larvae form they were, in the treatment of burns. The patient would be exposed to flies, covered with nothing more than a layer of gauze. The flies would lay their eggs in the suppurating burns and the resulting maggots fed on the pus. The results were quite spectacular. The maggots eating away all of the putrification left the burns quite clean. This form of treatment avoided sepsis, which was the curse of burns.

Ground crew who remained on the airfield were by no means 'behind the lines'. Enemy attacks were constant and aggressive. Raids at night were nearly always under moonlight. Although attacks by the Luftwaffe were more accurate and intensive than those of the Italians, the latter dropped nasty little devices called thermos bombs – usually from a high altitude.

Thermos bombs were about the size of a thermos flask and similar in shape. They did not explode on impact, but just lay there until the sand blew over and covered them. There were two types; one exploded when picked up or rolled over and the second went off with the vibration of a heavy step close by. Everyone was warned but inevitably there were some casualties. Tom no doubt treated Arabs who had picked one up, with feet or hands blown off and one side of the body peppered with little pieces, as if a shot gun had been fired at them from a distance.

During daylight raids, whilst previously they had sheltered in slit trenches, now more as a morale booster than an effective defence, rifles were issued to a good part of the ground crew. Some now became quite expert in allowing sufficient deflection for low flying aircraft. It must have been quite a show with a hundred or so rifles blazing away.

During those raids the trajectory of bombs had to be calculated; a stick of bombs might seem to be lazily falling towards a particular spot. Nine times out of ten, however, they would miss that spot by 100 yards. It was easy to run into an explosion, rather than away from it. It was a variation on the theme of the constant mental calculation the pilots undertook each time they fired, before the advent of giro-sights, to estimate deflection – Roy Hussey's 'Angle off'.

My ground crew neighbour told me about an Egyptian manned aircraft battery at the airfield where he was serving.

If a friendly aircraft came over they were only restrained with difficulty from firing. If, however it was an enemy they had all sorts of excuses. First of all they never fired after 8.oopm even if an enemy aircraft came over, which they did several times, so low that their outline could be seen in the moonlight, so low that we could see the red glow of their exhausts. There was no firing from our battery – oh no. Their commanding officer would explain this by pleading that he could not fire after dark, as the aircraft would see the flashes of the guns, and in 10 minutes they would be hurt.

94 Squadron flew Hurricanes, four of which were called the MacRobert Hurricanes, given in memory of Lady MacRobert's son who was killed whilst serving with 94 Squadron in 1941. They were individually named 'The Lady', 'The Sir Alasdair', 'The Sir Roderick', and the 'Sir Iain.' The handover of those aeroplanes, on 19 September 1942, was quite a day, with Air Commodore Wann, the AOC of 212 Group, arriving in a Lancaster and the whole squadron, including Tom, on parade with 127 Squadron taking over their flying duties during the parade.

In the summer of 1942 the desert conflict was fierce, with the tide of fortune flowing back and forth. 94 Squadron's duties were defensive, in the main carrying out shipping patrols, flying over the constant stream of convoys supplying Allied forces, in particular the needs of Montgomery building up his Eighth Army in preparation for El Alamein and also restocking the island fortress of Malta. The Operational Record Book usually recorded 'mission successfully completed without incident.' There was the occasional scramble but usually without contact being made with the 'bogey'.

In October there was a most unfortunate incident. Two pilots were scrambled, who intercepted and shot down the 'bogey' which crashed into the sea. The 'bogey' was in fact a friendly DC 3 of USAAF. Doubtless Tom would have been involved in debriefing the two. Less than 14 days later one of them flying as section number two was himself lost when attacking a JU88; the ORB leaves one wondering whether his death was the result of excessive zeal resulting from the earlier incident.

These obscure pointers to stress are found from time to time. In February 1943 a pilot was recorded as having returned early with fuel tank problems; a few days later he force landed and hitch hiked back to base after encountering instrument failure. Two weeks later he was recorded as having left the Squadron for a course at Higher Control School at SAAF base depot. Were the apparent technical faults a cry for help? Perhaps Tom was involved in giving the pilot a break from the constant pressure of operational flying.

In December 1942 Tobruk had been relieved and the Squadron made a six-day journey to Martuba (the airfield that was in Axis control in January 1942 when the Squadron lost nearly half its aircraft) via Mena, Amrya, El Darba, Sidi Barrani and Gambut, the large complex about 30 miles east of Tobruk.

The winter weather was not good and on many days the aerodrome was unserviceable. In March 1943 there was a lucky miss when Sgt Hyrons landed on the slippery surface, couldn't stop and struck the flight office tent, damaging the starboard leg fairing of his machine. The tent was ripped to pieces but luckily the NCOs and airmen had time to get out.

At the end of March the Squadron moved again, this time to Cyrene, some 30 minutes flight from Martuba. On 3 April the aerodrome being unserviceable. B flight was removed up to Apollonia and for the rest of April A and B flights alternated between Cyrene and Apollonia.

Wherever you are there is always an expert close at hand. Squadron Leader Birkett of 16 sector was a well-known authority on the ruins of Cyrene and on 24 April 94 Squadron was treated to a talk on that subject.

Savoia was the next move and on 14 May Tom took 14 days leave, returning on the 24th. In June the Squadron started night flying practice on moonlit nights, an activity Tom came to know intimately when he was transferred to 114 and 18 Squadrons flying night operations in twin-engined Bostons. The officers and men of 16 Sector put on *A Midsummer's Night Dream* in the amphitheatre of Cyrene on 22 June. June was not without some rather more worrying drama: on the 14th an Italian aeroplane was seen to drop about 20 parachutists. Some were rounded up fairly promptly, dressed, as the ORB noted, 'In exaggerated plus fours'. On the 19th two were thought to be still at large, one dressed in British army uniform. A sniper dressed in Arab clothes was also seen close to the airfield.

The ORB records that life away from the front line was also dangerous. On 15 July one of the pilots on his way to a new posting was killed when his Wellington transport plane crashed. A few days after Tom left the Squadron there was another accident due to the slippery condition of the runway when a pilot lost control and crashed on landing suffering burns to his face; a fire tender crewman was hit between the shoulders by flying debris and was admitted to hospital.

On 9 July 1943 the ORB indicates how existing technology was being pushed to its limits. The Hurricanes escorting a Liberator fully bombed and flying on three engines only had difficulty keeping up. Earlier, on 19 April, the ORB describes a Hurricane opening fire when climbing up to a 'bogey' at 32,000 ft and the aircraft practically stalling on the recoil of its guns.

A few months later Tom was to join 114 Squadron, part of 236 Wing flying Bostons and Baltimores, posted to Sicily and Italy. Such was the Allies' command of the skies at that time that these obsolescent aircraft were able to fly with little chance of air attack – the danger was the thick and very accurate enemy flak, particularly from the 88s, which were effective up to 15,000 feet.

Tom left 94 Squadron on 18 July 1943 for medical duties at Helwan, Cairo. Just after he left, on 23 July, Crete was attacked by the Allies and 94 Squadron had the dual role of convoy escort and 'heartily attacking ground targets'. These were tasks for which the Hurricanes were ideally suited.

The RAF station at Helwan, (16 miles from RAF Heliopolis, which had the style and status of a permanent RAF Station in Egypt – an elegantly planted and favoured post) had a base hospital. No1 General Hospital Helwan was the main base hospital in Egypt. It was very busy in 1942, before, during and after El Alamein, when casualties were over 900. One of the advantages of Helwan was that like RAF Halton, Tom's initial training centre, it was an AeroMed unit with the landing strip close at hand so that the wounded could be admitted very quickly. Later in 1942, after Tom had left for front line duties, the hospital was inundated with an epidemic of serious cases of jaundice. Extra tents were erected in fields around the hospital to cope. At Helwan Tom would have treated severe trauma cases, fractures and burns, as well as those ailments that don't let up just because there's a war on, such as appendicitis.

Tom arrived too late to visit the Cairo museum and see the marvellous Tutenkhamen exhibits and spectacular jewellery wing; it was closed in spring 1940 for the duration. Tom might have had time to visit the pyramids – but he must surely have visited the Egyptian State Fever Hospital in Cairo and experienced the distinctive smell of typhus. A sense of smell was vitally important to a squadron doctor based in the desert, living under canvas.

Tom was still at RAF Helwan when the invasion of Italy by the American 5th Army and British Eighth Army commenced on 3 September 1943, three years after war had been declared. Italy had surrendered on the 8th. 114 Squadron was moving to Sicily and the appendix to the ORB sets out the Movement Order, which included a medical section written by Tom's predecessor:

23 7 43

Move to Sicily

Standing Orders during move to Sicily and for initial stages of stay on aerodrome.

Medical

The risk of malignant malaria dysentery and sand fly fever is very great indeed.

The following rules will be strictly observed:

i) Mosquito nets will be used to the fullest and they will be kept in good repair
ii) After 1900 hours long trousers will be used and shirt sleeves will be turned down
iii) Guards and others who must be out for long periods after dark will use anti-mosquito cream on all exposed parts
iv) All ranks except aircrew will consume four tablets of Mepracine per week (one tablet every Monday, Tuesday, Thursday and Friday)
v) All aircrew will consume one quinine tablet per day. Strict discipline must be maintained in disposal of waste products including night soil. On beaches and in transit out hole sanitation will be carried out. Immediately on arrival at destination buckets will be put into use, night urinal buckets will be set up and deep trenches dug for disposal of contents. The ground will not be fouled.

During August, 114 Squadron, flying from Gela in Sicily, had been bombing the Reggio area in the sole of Italy in preparation for Operation *Baytown,* the Eighth Army's invasion of Italy. In September they were bombing the Naples area and Salerno beaches south of Naples in support of the American 5th Army. 114 Squadron's Form 540, the monthly report to Group HQ records the Squadron's move from Gela to Comiso and to Gerbini.

Medical history form 540 for the month of August 1943.

A The advance party of the squadron arrived at Gela on 1 August 1943. Site selected for the squadron was within 150 yards of a stagnant stream. This produced, on inspection, a very large number of mosquito larvae both of the Ampholine and Culcine type. No suitable pumps or oil were available for spraying purposes. Finally the stream was sprayed with diesel oil by means of stirrup pumps.

This proved very effective and no live larvae were detected on daily inspection up to the day the squadron left for Comiso. No medical cases of particular interest occurred during this first week.

B. On arrival at Comiso, the camp very well sighted in olive groves and upon the hillside. The mosquitoes were scarce and there was no trouble with bites. The squadron operated from here during the moon period doing armed road reconnaissance. The morale of the squadron which had been definitely low at Gela began to improve under the pleasanter living conditions at Comiso.

C. On 21 August 1943 the squadron left Comiso for Gerbini. Conditions here were not so good as at Comiso. The whole squadron has had a lecture on both VD and malaria during the course of the month. Frequent reminders of anti-malarial precautions appear in DROs.

Signed
GW Bellis Flt. Lt.
Officer in medical charge

This was one of F/Lt Bellis' last reports; 17 September 1943 was a very sad day for 114 Squadron. Five officers were killed in a flying accident. The squadron ORB shows that the aircraft was last seen flying on one engine but that the cause of the crash was not determined. One of the officers was Flt/Lt G.W. Bellis, Doctor. 114 Squadron was in urgent need of a replacement Medical Officer with frontline squadron experience and on 23 September 1943 Tom Stoate, still with the rank of Flight Lieutenant, was posted to Gerbini from where the Squadron was flying their Boston IIIB light bombers on night raids over Italy.

Bostons in flight. (Author)

The Douglas Boston aircraft with its distinctive high mounted wing and glazed nose was a highly effective light bomber/light attack and night fighter aircraft. Its initial role was coastal surveillance, however, it soon changed to ground attack missions, often at tree top height. In this role the aircraft was configured with four .50 cal cannons and four .303 machine guns in the nose in a fixed firing position, plus a mid upper gunner operated twin .303 machine guns, and two fixed rear firing .50 cal cannons. The Boston usually carried a crew of two, a pilot and gunner, but sometimes carried a spare gunner in the rear compartment. It had an impressive top speed of 260 knots.

Test pilots at RAF Boscombe Down summed it up: 'Has no vices and is very easy to takeoff and land … The aeroplane represents a definite advantage in the design of flying controls … extremely pleasant to fly and manoeuvre.' Ex-pilots often considered it their favourite aircraft of its type due to the ability to toss it around like a fighter. In all its variants some 7500 Bostons were built.

So Tom was about to say goodbye to North Africa and from Sicily join in the assault on and conquest of Italy.

The founder of the RAF, Lord Trenchard, said that all land battles are confusion and muddle and the job of airmen is to accentuate that confusion and muddle to a point where it gets beyond an enemy's capacity to control. This happened in Italy, but though there was a final victory, this campaign above all others showed that the underdog can survive, hold ground and even inflict massive damage, despite being completely dominated from the air.

Allied strategy for the Italian campaign had two aims – the elimination of Italy from the war and containment of the maximum number of German divisions. By March 1944 General Alexander's forces were holding down 23 German divisions including many of Hitler's finest – notably the Herman Goering Division. There were three tasks: to keep enemy aircraft out of the air, to assist the army in close support and interdiction and to support the strategic air offensive against the enemy war machine. Experience was to demonstrate what air power could and could not do.

Relative ground dispositions varied throughout the Italian campaign, but there was never any doubt about who was superior in the air. On the eve of the invasion of mainland Italy, the Allied air forces totalled 3127, of which 1390 were fighters and fighter bombers, 461 heavy bombers, 162 medium night bombers, 703 medium and light day bombers and 406 transports.

The German forces were commanded by the immensely tough and able Field Marshal Albert Kesselring – 'Smiling Albert'. Kesselring was reputed to smile, if not whistle, under all difficulties and was held in very high regard by his troops. There was a story that when he was carrying out one of his frequent tours to the frontline his vehicle was in collision with a motorised gun emerging from a side road and he was injured. The report wryly observed: 'The Field Marshal is doing well but the gun has had to be scrapped!'

Chronologically, the invasion and victory was a sequel to the conquest of Sicily but in strategic terms the two events are widely separated. The fall of Sicily might be said to mark the end of the opening stage of the Second World War. The invasion of mainland Italy initiated a new, offensive phase, which climaxed in the final defeat of Germany. In just one campaign in 1944 the US 5th Army sustained 32,000 fatalities – just short of the number of American servicemen killed during the entire Korean War.

At Cambrai on 20 November 1917, 1003 guns of the 3rd Army opened fire at zero hour with a single crash. Then a line of 378 fighting tanks under an umbrella of 289 aircraft led forward eight divisions to attack German positions. Such joint air and land cooperation restored surprise and precision to the battlefield and in so doing signalled the beginning of the end of the hellish war of attrition that had been the story of the First World War. The trouble was that by 1939 the RAF had largely forgotten how to support the Army and Navy and all the lessons had to be relearned in the Second World War.

A major architect of such cooperation or 'jointery' was Air Chief Marshal Sir Arthur Tedder, a former army officer and fighter squadron commander who by early 1943 had become air C-in-C for the whole Mediterranean theatre.

By early July 1943 the Axis had about 775 operational combat aircraft within range of Sicily and 63 more bombers on the point of arriving. Three quarters of the 434 aircraft on the island were fighters and fighter bombers. The Allies with their 267 available squadrons in the Mediterranean – 146 American 121 British – had clear air superiority.

ACM Tedder's experience in pursuit of Rommel across the desert had convinced him of two things – the paramount importance of air security and the need for the early capture of enemy airfields to maintain the momentum of an assault. At its best there was a comradely synergy in all this. The air would help the army, whereupon the army must help the air by seizing the airfields it needed.

As Malta was within single-seat fighter range of southern Sicily, some 600 front-line aircraft plus radar and control links were positioned in Malta and Gozo by June 1943 under the energetic direction of ACM Sir Keith Park, the battle group commander of 11 Group during the Battle of Britain.

Tedder had briefed General Alexander, C-in C Middle East Army, that single-engine fighters operating out of Malta or Tunis could only provide an air defence umbrella over the southern half of Sicily. They could not effectively operate over the main Sicilian port of Messina from Malta alone. Alexander listened carefully as Tedder pointed out that the Comiso-Gela airfield, inland from the south coast, had been developed into a first-class airbase and that unless it could be captured the Air Force would labour under an intolerable handicap.

By June 1943 the Axis powers had 19 principal airfields in Sicily, plus a dozen newly constructed strips of lesser importance and in Tedder's words ' A crescendo of attacks based at Gerbini on the enemy's airfields was launched.' The Gerbini complex in the east, home to most of the Luftwaffe fighters, was thereafter given special attention by the RAF and Allied air forces' Cyrenaica-based heavies.

Thus was the Luftwaffe bombed out of Sicily. 740 axis aircraft were lost defending Sicilian skies while 584 damaged or destroyed aircraft were abandoned on the ground including 280 Bf109s, 70 FW190s and 80 Ju88s. Before an assault on Sicily could be effectively launched, however, the small island of Pantelleria athwart the narrows between Tunisia and Sicily needed to be neutralised.

Pantellaria was a volcanic rock pock-marked by 100 or so gun emplacements supporting an aerodrome with underground hangers and powerful radar apparatus. Its 42.5 miles were defended by some 10,000 men well provisioned with sufficient though not ample supplies of water.

The island functioned chiefly as a gigantic spyglass to keep Rome informed of every movement in the narrow straits, on the north African coast, and in the air above. To mount an invasion of Sicily without first knocking out Pantelleria would allow the enemy to know everything. To leave its 80 aircraft unmolested was to invite attacks on formations bombing in support of the landing on Sicily. Between 8 and 9 May, a few days before the Tunisian surrender, therefore, a formidable three-day air attack was made and the island surrendered without an Allied combat casualty.

Although the Allies had supremacy in the skies it did not mean that their aircrews had free rein to fly without losses. They remained vulnerable to enemy fighters, ground fire (including friendly fire) and mechanical failure and the wounded needed to be treated and cared for. The friendly fire casualties in the heat of battle were one of the saddest aspects of the war over Italy and Lance Bombadier Spike Milligan's throwaway words were horribly true. 'It was a mixed day of planes, one moment Jerry, then the RAF, then Jerry. The Ack-Ack boys took no chances and fired at the lot.'

In the desert of Cyrenaica, Tom's use of marked air ambulances had been commonplace. As the Allied frontline squadrons gradually gained supremacy in the air, so the use of ordinary transport planes became more widespread, particularly after the fall of Sicily and the Italian surrender in the autumn of 1943. Indeed throughout 1944 the evacuation of no fewer than 121,889 allied patients and casualties was undertaken.

Sketch map
of Italy.

In the early days of the use of transport aeroplanes for the evacuation of wounded the usual proviso was that ambulances with the wounded on board would have to be on the airstrip before the transport aeroplanes arrived, thereby minimising the risk of their being destroyed on the ground by enemy fighters. This was a small price to pay and transport by air was used as often as possible as it saved the seriously wounded long and uncomfortable journeys by ambulance over rough roads in stages to a base hospital.

The main purpose of air evacuation was to improve the combat efficiency of the armed forces by rapidly relieving units of non-effective personnel. A secondary purpose was to reduce the number of medical units and staff from the front line, not least because such units and their personnel themselves had to to be supplied. So the use of transport aircraft was a virtuous circle. The aircraft were cargoed up on journeys out and back, the wounded received better and faster treatment, saving lives and reducing the incidence of permanent disabilities and supply lines were relieved. A further benefit to the airlifting of wounded is that the morale of the fighting units is lifted in the knowledge that excellent medical facilities are available within a matter of hours, rather than days.

The Second World War was the first occasion that air evacuation of the wounded was undertaken on a large scale and Tom Stoate naturally became skilled in operating the system. Where possible, Divisional Clearing Stations would be located as close as feasible to the landing fields and the sighting of the landing fields in relation to the combat areas was also carefully considered. Sometimes it was necessary to use a relay system using a small aeroplane to the main landing strip and then onward by larger aeroplane.

A group of DC3 Dakotas in Italy, 1943. From Roy's tin box.

There were no aircraft specifically designed as air ambulances but larger transport aircraft such as the Dakotas could be converted by the use of factory fitted webbing straps and stanchions to take up to 40 recumbent men. Loading time was about eight minutes, provided everything was properly set up on the ground first. In general, there was some provision for medication on board but none for food, so the Medical Officers had to make their own arrangements for their patients on the ground before take off.

Up to 650 patients could be removed to a rear zone 3500 miles away by the use of 20 transport aircraft in less than 48 hours; yet to hospitalise this number of patients would require several train-loads of equipment initially and many tons of supplies each week. A large number of surgeons, physicians, nurses, orderlies and enlisted men would also be necessary. That is not to say however, that there were no hospitals at or near the front. The 100th British General Hospital on the scrubland overlooking the beaches at Jeanne D'Arc, about six miles from Philippeville, was a 1200-bed unit under canvas. At Djidjelli there was a much smaller unit of 100 beds set up in what had been a small hotel. In Tunis the hospital was housed in the ancient amphitheatre. There were large hospitals in Cairo where Tom had been stationed after leaving 94 Squadron.

Gradually there emerged an order of priority for the air evacuation of patients; The first category was men for whom essential medical treatment was not available locally, followed by casualties for whom air evacuation was a military necessity, and so on down to patients suffering from certain diseases which could only be improved by treatment other than that available locally. In the event that there was adequate space in the aircraft there was no class of patient who could not be air lifted away, provided the patients did not have conditions that would make air travel inadvisable; such as severe shock, recent major operative procedures – particularly abdominal – head injuries, severe anaemia due to haemorrhage, or marked elevation of the diaphragm due to severe intra-abdominal pressure.

The air evacuation of casualties must have been an exacting and intriguing job. Tom must have felt as if he was really achieving some good. There was the forward service which brought the wounded back from the front lines to a base hospital, from there, if necessary, they could be flown back to the UK, including St Mary's Hospital at Halton where Tom was inducted into the military way. His first posting at Filton, Bristol, received a great many of the American wounded from Omaha Beach on and immediately after D-day, who were transferred from there to nearby Frenchay Hospital.

In dealing with these patients Tom would have had to handle multiple cases. The information would have been sketchy – Is it 4 cases or 10? How was the transport to be set up? How were the patients getting to the strip? What were the conditions? Deep burn on leg – not too good; burns on face and neck; multiple burns all over, broken leg; Were there adequate supplies of plaster? Initially of course the job was to get the cases to SSQ (Station Sick Quarters) and from there to relevant destinations.

Aircraft did not follow a timetable, casualty numbers were usually uncertain. But at least the wounded were on their way home, despite any delays. It must have been a strange sensation flying with a load of stretcher cases. The noise, vibration and lack of room would have made any care difficult, but most of the casualties would have been fairly well doped up before the journey began. Previously it would have taken an age to get the wounded back to a base hospital. Now they were immediately treated at the advanced posts then airlifted back to a base hospital or even back to England, tucked up in bed and treated by the best the same day. Tom could not have expected much more.

The loss of experienced aircrew either wounded or killed of course increased the pressure on those remaining. 114 Squadron ORB for 29 September indicates how highly valued experience was by the operational squadrons:

> No operations. Today was used for training new crews. It is not quite understood what these crews are taught at OTU (Operations Training Unit) as when they reach the squadron they have neither experience in night flying nor in formation flying and until trained are useless for day and night operations.

The Luftwaffe fared even worse, they did not operate a 'tour and rest' system, old hands were worn out by months of unbroken operations, the youngsters lacked experience and were inadequately trained and by this time were flying equipment mostly inferior and certainly fewer in number than that of the Allies.

On 4 October 1943, 114 Squadron had movement orders from Gerbini in Sicily to Italy. On the 6th the orders were cancelled but the camp was held in 12 hours readiness. On the 7th the advance party comprising 11 aircraft and 5 crews departed for Brindisi, the remainder staying at Gerbini for the time being.

114 Squadron records do not disclose whether Tom was with the advance party or the bulk of the Squadron following. We have seen that the duties of a frontline squadron doctor included the setting up and sanitation of the camps. 114 Squadron was bound for Brindisi on the Italian mainland and Brindisi turned out to be wet and boggy.

The ORB reports that aircraft dispersal was closer than the usual 100 yards between aircraft, the view seems to have been that the greater risk to aircraft damage lay in getting bogged down in the mud rather than from attack. In the appendices to the ORB there is a report by the then MO that brings the conditions that frontline squadrons were enduring in the Italian winter of 1943/4 into stark relief.

Camp Inspection

I General
Owing to the extremely heavy rain and low-lying situation of this camp site the ground over the whole area is completely waterlogged.

Drainage ditches are plentiful but there are practically no falls, so the water tends to stand in the runs and the soil being of clay consistency allows next to no seepage.

The result is although in the rare dry spells a certain amount of water drains or seeps away, it is more than replenished in the wet spells and the day is fast approaching when the site will be flooded. That is not merely supposition, it is borne out by the local farmers who not only say that it floods, but keep a boat each. This seems highly significant.

II Officers' Site
Very muddy with water standing in all foot marks as well as drainage ditches. Several tents were in such bad condition that their lower portions are in shreds and have to be helped out by anything procurable, corrugated iron, old ration boxes etc …

III Airmen's site
The amount of mud on the site must be seen to be believed, being 8 inches deep in places and 4 to 6 inches average. All drainage ditches are nearly overflowing. Under these circumstances it is quite impossible to have decent conditions inside the tents, some of which are no better than quagmires.

Every effort has been made by individuals to better these conditions but it is a losing battle with the weather. The Nissen hut with brick walls and homemade stove, and brick floors throughout the dining tents greatly helps and the original cookhouse hand made of timber and floored with gravel is a very creditable effort on the part of its builders. Before its erection the cooks had to work in the mud which was fluid and came half way up their gumboots.

The greatest ingenuity has been shown by many airmen in such matters as drainage around the tents, so far with signs of success, but the sub soil water is now only 4 inches from the surface and if any more heavy rain occurs, which one gathers is a certainty – no drainage system will be of any use and several inches of water will appear in every tent.

The latrine buckets are housed in a US tent which serves to protect users from a large percentage of the rain which would otherwise add to the discomfort of using these. They are on a brick base to prevent them from becoming permanent fixtures in the mud. Seepage pits for urine would be of no use as nature would fill them with water far faster than man so buckets are used. The sanitary squad remove all excrement at a considerable distance from the camp.

IV The non-commissioned officer's site
This is much the worst on the camp despite strenuous efforts on the part of the occupants to improve it.

It consists entirely of deep glutinous mud both outside and inside the tents. On arrival a number of noncommissioned officers in a praiseworthy attempt to make themselves comfortable, dug the floors of their tents down two or 3 feet. At the time this seemed a good idea, and to prevent surface water running in, they banked the edges and ditched round them.

The surface water stayed out to quite an extent, but since then the subsoil water has risen and the conditions under which they are now living differs only in minor degree to the conditions outside their tents, and in some cases are much worse. This is because of the ground conditions, the ground outside is still just above water, but the lowered floors of the tents are below site water level.

Herewith notes of conditions of particular tents, nine of which on the far side of the site are not dug in. Tent numbered L. 31 abandoned because of 6 inches of water throughout had insufficient occupants to keep it bailed out. Tent labeled W/U. had to be bailed out this morning so was inches deep in water. Occupants were sitting on their beds with their feet in the water up to their ankles. Any bedclothes which accidentally touch the floor have of course to be wrung out.

I know at least one warrant officer who sits all night in the mess (nissen hut) preferring the relatively small quantity of mud in it to the large quantity of water in his tent.

It will be appreciated that these conditions are leading and will continue to lead, gathering momentum daily, to a serious falling off in morale, health and efficiency of the men.

Whilst conditions are very bad in the airmen's site they are absolutely abominable in the noncommissioned officers', most of whom are air crew.

FOR HOT CLIMATES

AVOID MALARIA
   Wear mosquito boots, long-sleeved shirts
     and slacks from sunset to sunrise.
   Sleep under a mosquito net.
   Aircrew take a quinine tablet daily, others
     take mepacrine.

AVOID DYSENTERY
   Keep flies off your food.
   Eat and drink only in messes and authorised
     restaurants.
   Practise latrine discipline (use sand, close
     lid).
   Drink no casual water.
   Keep your belly covered when resting.

AVOID V.D.
   Beware of native women and " controlled "
     and " supervised " houses.
   Excess of alcohol increases V.D. risk.

AVOID SUNSTROKE
   Wear suitable head covering in the sun.
   Avoid thirst.
   Take extra salt when sweating (up to a
     tablespoonful a day).
   Sunbathe for not more than five minutes at
     first.

DO NOT DRINK ALCOHOL BEFORE
SUNDOWN.

WASH FREQUENTLY AND DRY
YOURSELF THOROUGHLY.

REPORT ANYTHING WRONG AT ONCE
TO YOUR M.O.—headache, earache, rash
or anything.

GET LOCAL " GEN " FROM THE M.O.
ON THE SPOT.

CARRY YOUR INOCULATION CERTI-
FICATES.

               Transport Command, R.A.F.

(65157-2) Wt. 37577/M.2181 5,000 12/43 Hw. G.371

Medical guidance for hot climate postings. (Author)

Already far too many are suffering from colds, fibrositis (muscular rheumatism) sore throats and it is a source of some surprise to me that as yet there has been no pneumonia. This is not an alarmist remark. The conditions could hardly be more perfect for the production of serious illness.

A number of the newly arrived aircrew have not even yet got gumboots or beds and it will be seen that billets are <u>urgently</u> needed.

Malaria was an illness that was best prevented rather than cured. Considerable care was taken therefore in taking adequate anti-mosquito and anti-larval measures using nets, sprayers, dusters and flit guns, including the use of oil and paris green as insecticides in the breeding areas. (Paris green was a particularly nasty chemical containing amongst other metals, arsenic, lead and copper, it was sprayed extensively in Italy, Sardinia and Sicily in an effort to combat malarial mosquitoes.)

Prophylactic measures would, of course, include quinine. In this regard, as in many others, Tom had to demonstrate the judgment of Solomon and it was at times difficult to combine strategy with hygiene. As far as malaria was concerned 10 grains of quinine would keep malaria at bay, but pilots would not have been able to fly with 10 grains on board. For ground crew mepracine was issued at the rate of two tablets per day for one week and one per day thereafter. There was also the issue and correct use of protective clothing and mosquito boots. Even the hours of working would have a part in the control of mosquito infection as would the timing of the use of the flit gun – early morning and early evening. Serving men not using protective clothing could be subject to disciplinary measures as the resulting illness could be considered self-induced in the same way as the contraction of venereal diseases.

Tony 'Red' Weller, a colleague of Roy Hussey in 72 Squadron, remembered that such was the prevalence of malaria (he had to be rested away from the Squadron because of an attack) that the forces began to think that the Germans were deliberately infecting watercourses with mosquito lavae.

Apart from the treatment of malaria there was also dysentery, infectious hepatitis, typhus as well as the usual complaints of civilian life –appendicitis, intestinal obstructions, abscesses of all sorts – also non-urgent elective operations for chronic wound conditions, delayed union of fractures etc. For the majority of these last the Squadron facilities in terms of equipment and surgical capability would not have been appropriate so the patient would have been transported to a base hospital, sometimes by wheeled transport and at other times by air.

A further and most important part of Tom's duty was to gather knowledge about his people; squadron morale was a key component in its effectiveness. Tom's knowledge was largely obtained by his living amongst the personnel.

Tom might be sitting in the mess reading, censoring letters, playing bridge or taking part in some party or another, but all the time he would be using his experience to gain impressions. Is so-and-so drinking more than usual? That one seems a bit down, a third unnaturally festive. Is it anything to do with the job? Has he had bad news from home? Does he want a rest? Does he need a quiet peptalk over a pint of beer? It might be thought that a squadron MO had little to do. The job, however, was 24/7 if properly undertaken. It was also without doubt very interesting and absorbing.

There might have been another benefit to being an 'invisible man' in the mess. After a raid, all the crew would roll in and report results. 'Any fighters?' 'What about flak?' Did you see anything?' Reports would be given of explosions, direct hits on targets, flares etc. A crew cannot usually see the result of its own bombs – they have to rely on the reports of the others – all the reports were correlated into a complete sanitised picture of the raid and written up. Sitting in a tent on an up-turned petrol tin, it would have seemed very much more immediate and real.

114 Squadron was part of 326 Wing which included 18 Squadron also flying Bostons. Sharing Brindisi airfield was 232 Wing flying Martin Baltimores. In due course 114 Squadron was to come under the administrative and operational control of 232 Wing.

On 17 October 1943 the remainder of 114 Squadron arrived at Brindisi having travelled the 400 miles from Sicily including the ferry crossing from Messina to the Italian mainland.

There were 50-odd rivers on both flanks north of Salerno and the Germans used them all to make the conflict more like the First World War trenches than the wide-ranging battles fought in North Africa or Russia. The Germans constantly retreated to the next ridge but it was said at the time that they always seemed to take the ridge with them. The central Italian terrain generated all manner of tunnels, bridges, viaducts, and embankments and it was against these that the RAF Tactical Command was directed in Operation *Strangle*. The bulk of this interdiction effort fell to the medium bombers and fighter bombers with which Tom was to serve for the whole of the remainder of his operational service up to the end of February 1945.

The air forces of the whole theatre were under Mediterranean Air Command, beneath that came Northwest African Air Force and under that, Northwest African Tactical Air Force and it was beneath this again, to Desert Air Force, that Tom's Wing reported.

The Eighth Army under General Montgomery was moving north past Foggia, which had fallen at the end of September, well supported by the bombing efforts of 114 Squadron who were detailed to destroy enemy strongholds previously pinpointed. These included a special target at Penna Point to act as a diversion while the Army made a landing farther north.

Montgomery's army was conducting itself in a way that had served it so well in North Africa, including the system for describing battlefield targets that the infantry wanted the Desert Air Force to attack. This task fell to ground-based air liaison officers at all wing and group HQs and with the mobile operations room. When a target had been accepted by DAF and Army Area HQs, the air liaison officer briefed the squadrons detailed to carry out the operation.

Such an arrangement worked fine over sandy deserts, but in the much more rugged and closer-combat Italian theatre, faster and more precise responses were needed. The answer was a mobile observation post in a lorry or jeep with a trailer situated with the forward troops at Brigade HQ and in direct VHF communication with aircraft already airborne in cab-rank formation.

The cab-rank system comprised 6, 12 or 18 aircraft flying, probably in line astern, for 20 minutes or so in radio contact with the mobile squadron post or command base. If the pilots heard nothing they attacked a pre-determined target. If they received a request to attack a specific target, one or more of the 'cab-rank' would peel off for action. In due course the horses for courses principle was learned; for example, an attack by a squadron of fighter bombers on some narrow bridges and pontoons was usually more likely to bring success than ordering up a formation of mediums.

The cab-rank system was a very successful system but it needed a large number of aircraft to sustain 'ranking' and it would have been unworkable if the Luftwaffe had been able to dispute the presence of Allied aircraft over the battlefield.

The plain around Foggia – the only large mass of level ground in Italy south of the Po Valley – was now set to become the Allies' terrestrial aircraft carrier and it was there that Tom and 114 Squadron were bound. The plain of Apulio was less affected by winter weather than East Anglian bases and the use by the Allies of the Foggia airfields extended Allied bomber range by some 400 miles. All southern Germany would be within comfortable range, two of the largest German aircraft factories could be reached, half the German fighters currently facing the UK would have to be moved down south and bombers flying from Italy would enjoy an alpine shield against the German warning system. Henceforward, from Lincolnshire and Foggia strategic Allied bomber spokes would radiate outwards over every part of the Reich. To Kesselring, the loss of the Apulian airfields was a terrible blow.

The inaugural Foggia-mounted Strategic Air Force operation on 1 October 1943 was a re-run against the aircraft factories of Wiener Neustadt but from now on it was possible to bomb not only southern Germany but also all of the Balkan Peninsula, the industrial areas of Silesia, the factories of Czechoslovakia, the oil fields of Romania and closer at hand Yugoslavia ('Yugoland'). Thirty-one plants producing around 44% of German crude and synthetic oil were less than 600 miles from Foggia, which was just one reason why the intelligence staffs now considered that 'qualitatively', more of the important targets were now closer to Italian bases than the UK.

To General Alexander the presence at Foggia of the Strategic Air Force was more of a liability than an asset. They were engaged in carrying out the strategic bombing programme which had no direct relation to the military operation for which he was responsible. The problem of supplying heavy bombardment groups stationed at Foggia put a severe strain on the supply service and on shipping, and their maintenance requirements were nearly as great as those of the Eighth Army.

On 26 October 1943, a few days after Tom's 28th birthday, the Squadron, still based at Brindisi, was under movement orders again, this time to go to Foggia 3. This was soon changed to Foggia 1. At the same time 114 Squadron came under 232 Wing for operations but remained under 236 Wing for administration. Both Wings were directed by Desert Air Force but under the overall command of NWAAF (North West African Air Force).

The following extract from the Movement Order gives a feel of how the Squadron were expected to conduct themselves and how Command viewed the conquered nation.

114 Squadron Movement Order No 8 Brindisi to Foggia October 1943

e) Personnel; remembering that they are in a conquered country should by their good behaviour and general smart appearance show their obvious superiority to a nation whose lack of discipline and general scruffiness contributed greatly to the unenviable condition in which they find themselves today

f) Shirts will not be removed while travelling in lorries and personnel will keep themselves shaved and as clean as possible.

In the previous month the Squadron had moved 500 miles but had nevertheless managed 18 nights of operational flying putting up an average of 8 aircraft a night. The winter weather was still a major problem for effective bombing although on 8/9 November they successfully bombed the Formta area from 6000 feet, dropped flares for a naval bombardment of Gaeta Head and on 27 November dropped 29,000 leaflets.

For Tom there was a minor change, he was transferred, Operational Officer Echelon, on 23 November 1943 from 114 Squadron to 18 Squadron (the same 18 Squadron that Roy Hussey had escorted in December 1942 over Tunisia) also flying Bostons, with whom 114 Squadron were sharing an operations room in any event. At the time Tom was moving, 114 Squadron received the welcome news that 4 DFCs and 2 DFMs had been awarded.

There is a recurrent reference in both 114 and 18 Squadrons' ORBs to transport targets – road and rail, to disrupt the German supply lines – the tactical interdiction role. We will shortly see in detail just how successful the Allied Tactical Air Forces were in this regard. General Westphal travelled to Germany to tell Hitler in person that it was impossible to bring the necessary artillery allocations to the front owing to the daily severance of rail communications in Italy by bombing attacks. But still Kesselring, partly by force of character and brilliant leadership, had his troops yielding every inch at a cost to the Allies.

Unfortunately, the inability to operate at night in bad weather meant that Allied capacity to damage railways was never decisively greater than the ability of the Germans to repair them. The cloak of darkness saved the German forces from destruction time and time again.

On 3 December 1943 the ORB records the weather had improved and 18 Squadron bombed a train. Later in December, the targets changed from Italy to Yugoslavia and the towns of Split and Sibenik, which were occupied by the Germans. On 15/16 December the ORB reports a searchlight from the island of Huar shining on to the German-occupied mainland at Dubrovnik. It was assumed that patriots had captured the light to help the Allied bombers. On the same day the Squadron moved from the flats of Foggia to the main aerodrome.

1944 brought a change to the bombing tactics and daylight raids were undertaken. On 16 January the Squadron bombed targets for the American 5th Army and a special target for the British Eighth Army. So Tom was one of the few people in the campaign who was involved in the support of both the British Eighth Army and the American 5th. The returning aircraft landed at Pomigliano a little closer to the 5th Army, partly on account of the continuing bad weather.

By the middle of February 1944 the Squadron was based at Marcianise but was using Pomigliano and Celone as satellite strips. On the nights of 15 and 16 February the Roman Catholic monstery that towered over Monte Cassino became the target. The objective was the maximum destruction of its walls and buildings. It is unclear whether the Abbey was or was not being used by the Germans, but there is no doubt that after the bombing the ruins certainly were used to very great advantage by German troops.

On 19 February 1944 – more or less as Roy Hussey became tour-expired and was being posted back to England – the Bostons were detailed with bombing a tank concentration ahead of the Eighth Army. The ORB notes that the tanks were very close to the Allied front line and very careful time and distance navigation from a fixed point was required to avoid a 'friendly fire' incident. On the same day the rest of the Squadron moved up to Marcianise from Foggia.

A job that sometimes fell to the MO would be to go out into the wilds to collect the remains of one or more of his own people. No such journey was necessary in early March 1944, when 18 Squadron experienced a sad day; they lost one of their best crews when their aeroplane crashed on take off. Tom would certainly have had to deal with the bodies, some or all of whom would have been his friends. One of the roughest jobs for an MO was to go through the personal items found in the pockets of a dead serviceman. It must have needed the wisdom of Solomon to know which of the sometimes mangled letters, girls' photos and note books to hand over to relations and which to destroy.

Operation *Strangle* was paying off. April 1944 saw further advances and so the ORB notes a welcome change of operation from armed recce. The Germans had resorted to using the sea and small ships for transport and the Squadron was detailed to attack shipping or in default, bomb San Stefano harbour as a 'standard target'.

The Allied Armies were pushing northward, notwithstanding a five-mile exclusion from Rome. Allied forces were still being subjected to artillery fire from that city. The squadron was being urged to 'maximum sustained effort'. 178 sorties were flown in March 1944 but even greater efforts were to follow, with 270 in May, when the Squadron became fully under 232 Wing, resulting in a shortage of replacement aircraft.

In June the Americans were ordered to take Rome, not it is said, that it was tactically necessary. Indeed, for the prosecution of the advance it has been argued that it would have been better to have kept the retreating German army on the move, but Roosevelt in particular wanted to announce the falling of the first Axis capital city to the Allies. In the same way as the prevarications in northern Europe postponed the final outcome, so it is argued did this politically driven delay.

By June the Allies had taken Rome and passed well beyond and the Squadron was moved to La Banca, where the ORB notes the runways were u/s in bad weather. Behind the German 'Gothic line' the harbours at Senigalia and Rimini became the targets, weather permitting.

During June and July when the Squadron achieved 207 sorties, it was given a few Boston A20 Gs to try. The verdict was that they were not as good as the IIIbs they already had – principally because the navigator was located in the rear rather than in the nose. The ORB notes that these aircraft were only any use on moonlit nights and that the 4.5 inch machine guns fitted to the nose but depressed by 12 degrees were useless, as the pilot could not see his target. The A20 Gs were therefore returned to the Americans.

Perversely, the A-20G, delivered from February 1943, which received such poor comments from 114 Squadron would be the most produced of all the series – 2850 were built. The glazed nose was replaced by a solid nose containing four 20mm (.79in) Hispano cannons and two .50in Browning machine guns, making the aircraft slightly longer than previous versions. After the first batch of 250, the unreliable cannon were replaced by more reliable machine guns. It seems from the ORB that it was this last version with machine guns in the nose that 114 Squadron was trying out.

On 19 July 1944 the Squadron moved northwards again to Cecina, opposite Corsica on the Mediterranean coast. On 18 August 1944 when the south of France was invaded in Operation *Dragoon*, 18 Squadron was detailed to draw enemy flak from the invasion forces. They then proceeded on an armed recce along the roads Digne–Nice–Cannes. That August Winston Churchill visited the Squadron on his way to inspect the American 5th Army. For Tom, after some 12 months, his time with 236 and 232 Wings was nearly over and on 26 September 1944, coming up to his 30th birthday and with the then acting rank of Squadron Leader, he was transferred to 239 Wing. They were flying Mustangs and the Curtis P-40, known as the Kittyhawk to the RAF and Warhawk to the USAAF. Tom was still on front line duties – very much so.

Unlike 232 Wing, which was equipped with light bombers/night fighters, 239 Wing comprising, initially, four and later six squadrons, was a fighter bomber Wing. Tom remained with the Wing for six months until 2 March 1945.

239 Wing was formed on 24 April 1942. Before Tom joined it had been in Tunisia and Libya. By September 1943 however, it was based at Grottaglie airfield near Taranto in the heel of Italy. 'Based' is a deceptive term, as in the six months between September 1944 and March 1945 when Tom left, it had moved 12 times, moving with the Eighth Army up the Adriatic side of Italy, including flying from Melini in Sicily, Crete and Fano. When Tom left it was flying from Cervia – a former Fascist holiday camp, north of Rimini.

Kittyhawk pilots were sometimes known as the triple threat men: to get maximum value from their time in the air, they dropped bombs on their way to the target, did their time providing air defence cover and strafed the enemy on the way back. The Wing's record is astonishing. Their role was close support to the army or tactical bombing.

The RAF defines the term close air support as 'The immediate availability of aircraft to attack and destroy, in response to army requests, targets engaging or being engaged by the forward troops, thereby improving the tactical situation of the moment.'

It has to be said that pilots were never overly fond of this activity. To find and hit well camouflaged, relatively small tanks and guns was far from easy whilst hurtling along, jinking to keep clear of solid ground and ever mindful that a thousand and one guns of all calibres, many of which were on your own side, were about to be let loose.

Form 540 is a roundup of a Wing's monthly activities. It includes not only medical and operational matters but also personnel numbers and details of consumables in some detail. Rounds of ammunition used are expressed to the actual number, not rounded up or down.

Extracts from the Wing's Form 540 report for March 1945, although out of chronological context, give a very clear idea of the Wing's activities in interdiction or tactical bombing.

260 Squadron became operational with rocket projectiles and carried out thier first operation on the 20th … Once again no close support was undertaken, the bulk of the work being done on armed recces and attacks on communications; in the latter category bridges and rail diversions stand very high … 99 missions, over 1000 sorties were flown against 35 bridges and rail diversions. About one third of them were broken but the diversions are very speedily repaired; others were also hit but were of too tough construction. A shortage of 1000 lb bombs has necessitated attacks with 500 pounders and the latter have frequently proved to be of insufficient weight to crack the bridge though the railway tracks have been rendered temporarily u/s. In almost every case where the bridge itself has been missed approaches and tracks were cratered necessitating repairs before the line could be reused. Probably the most difficult bridge target was the centre span of PADOVA North. This was originally a three span bridge and the two outside ones were broken some time ago. Persistent reconnaissance had revealed that the wily Hun had turned it into a 'night operational' bridge by hauling temporary bridging into position at night so that it could be used while, in the day time it still appeared u/s. The removal of the centre span would effectively prevent this, so on March 7th 450 and 250 Squadrons were assigned to the job of doing it while 3 Squadron kept the flak quiet. The latter succeeded admirably in their task but unluckily F/Lt. HODGKINSON was hit and had to bail out near CORBOLA. 450 Squadron who were first to go in were impeded by a large cloud but this had drifted south by the time 250 were ready to go in … Another excellent feat was the breaking of BROD railway bridge by 3 and 112 Squadrons, a job which was undertaken at the special request of B.A.F. who had never been able to hit it. The road bridge a little further east was also attacked but, though temporarily rendered impassable, it was not broken. Credit for breaking the rail bridge is due to 3 Squadron and 112 Squadron took a three-quarter bite out of the road bridge.

On 21 March 1945 the Wing took part in Operation *Bowler,* the attack on Venice, so called because the Air Vice Marshal in charge told his crews that if they messed up and were not precise in the attacks he would be 'bowler hatted', i.e. retired. The whole Wing took part.

It is the first occasion that all the squadrons of the Wing have operated on a single target at the same time and the first occasion that Venice has been attacked during this war. The target was the S.W. docks of Venice where there was the 3,500-ton merchantman *Otto Leonhardt,* the largest active cargo vessel remaining to the enemy in Adriatic waters. In addition to the shipping there were also warehouses, stores and rolling stock on the quays. The operation was so-named because, had there been some error of judgment whereby any of the historic and artistic buildings in the town were damaged, it was thought that several officers of the DAF HQ and maybe Wing would be hurriedly presented with bowler hats.

The attack was carried out by 250 Squadron, led by Wing Commander Flying, 450, 5, and 112 Squadrons in that order while 3 Squadron attacked flak positions on a small island S.W. of the docks. There is no doubt that the hun was caught with his pants right round his ankles. Accustomed he has been for many months to seeing gaggles of aircraft passing him as he lies out on the Lido, he no doubt expected the same thing would happen and they would pass by to harass his brethren further north. As no.3 Squadron went in, bodies were seen madly rushing to their positions and the Leader's bomb was seen by 5 Leader to fall slap into an 88 gun post at the same moment as its crew arrived. Action Photographs of 260's efforts also show the crews out of position and, the next moment, the effects of a rocket explosion envelope them in decent obscurity.

Two squadrons of Thunderbolts of 79 Group with 40 lb fragmentation bombs and rockets also did invaluable work and kept the flak quiet along the LITORALE di LIDO … It was a complete success achieved for the loss of one Kittyhawk, the pilot of which bailed out over the sea and was rescued by Catalina after only 30 minutes in the water … The operation is perhaps best summed up in the gracefully worded signal sent by A.O.C. Desert Air Force:

FULL PHOTOGRAPHIC COVER HAS NOW BEEN RECEIVED OF THE RESULTS OF THE ATTACK AGAINST VENICE HARBOUR INSTALLATIONS ON MARCH 21ST. THE RESULTS ACHIEVED ARE EXCELLENT AND THE MAXIMUM AMOUNT OF MILITARY DAMAGE HAS BEEN DONE BY A COMPARATIVELY SMALL FORCE. BOMBING WAS MOST ACCURATE AND NO APPARENT DAMAGE HAS BEEN DONE TO ANY OF THE CULTURAL MONUMENTS WHICH WERE IN CLOSE PROXIMITY TO THE TARGET.

THE ANTI-FLAK ATTACKS WERE WELL TIMED AND ACCURATELY DELIVERED. THANKS TO THIS AND TO THE A/SEA MEASURE, WE DID NOT LOSE A PILOT IN THIS MOST SUCCESSFUL OPERATION.

MY BEST CONGRATULATIONS TO ALL THOSE WHO TOOK PART IN THIS NEATLY EXECUTED OPERATION

The highly dynamic action in Italy was the cause of many tragic incidents of friendly fire, The theoretical answer was to establish a demarcation line immediately in front of friendly forces, known as the close cooperation line, but as the location of this line could change as often as ten times daily, the scope for someone not getting the news in time was large. Troops were supplied with canisters of yellow smoke with which to identify themselves to friendly aircraft but that did not stop some strafing P-40s from inflicting over 100 casualties in just one incident during the advance on Rome.

The aim was to establish a bombline, in front of which aircraft could operate freely on any target that might present itself. The bombline was marked by blobs of white smoke made and maintained by artillery smoke shells. These were about a mile apart extending across the whole front as nearly in line as the natural features of the ground would allow. The bombline would be 3000 yards in front of the forward troops and would move forward as a whole on a timed programme lifting about every 15 minutes. The effectiveness of the air strikes would be reported by a flying controller based on the ground who would also be responsible for controlling the aircraft engaged on the attack.

August 1944 was the last MO's report of Tom's predecessor at 239 Wing.

It was expected that in the month of August that there would have been a rise in the sickness rate due to malaria and fly-borne diseases. It is therefore extremely gratifying that it turned out to be the reverse with a marked decrease in the sickness rate.

The total number admitted to hospital or Wing Sick Quarters were 81 compared with 110 for July. There were no cases of primary malaria, the fly-borne diseases showed a decrease, the number of cases of B. dysentery was 1, compared with 6 for July. Gastro-enteritis cases were numbered 4, compared with 6 for July & 11 for June.

The decrease in fly-borne diseases corresponded with the supply of anti-fly netting arriving on this Wing and the fly-proofing of kitchens etc.

There has been a marked decrease in the mosquitoes, which shows that the steps taken by the Army and RAF against them have been very successful.

W. Hopkin-Jones S/Ldr
Senior Medical Officer
239 Wing RAF

The weather in September continued to be trying as expressed in the monthly medical report for September, which Tom had written by his subordinate whilst he got his feet under the table:

There have been occasional spells of heavy rain during the month, some of the squadron sites have been under water, indicating that the sites themselves are unsuitable for winter conditions … It is considered that either billets will have to be found or the squadron sites moved to higher ground, or adjacent to permanent roads. None of the squadron ambulances have four wheel drive, and to enable them to operate at any period of the day or night it is considered necessary that they have chains at the earliest possible moment.

The total number admitted to hospital or Wing Sick Quarters during the month of September was 63 compared with 81 for the month of August.

Considering the extensive operations of this Wing, and the consequent number of working hours this entails on both pilots and ground personnel the health of this Wing can be considered excellent.'

H. Kenyz F/Lt.
For Senior Medical Officer

On 9 September shortly before Tom arrived the wing's 'bag' is recorded in the ORB as:

1x 2000 ton steamer
1 JU88 in sky
1 Motor transport destroyed
19 Enemy aircraft on the ground
2 Rail trucks damaged
13 locomotives destroyed
3 rail trucks destroyed
1 locomotive damaged
3 Motor transport damaged

This was not exceptional, after Tom had arrived, on 30 September 1944 the bag was:

16 Locomotives destroyed
30 rail trucks ditto
17 Motor transport flamers
2 DRS destroyed
5 Me109s destroyed on ground

On 30 May 1943, 239 Wing had caught about 200 vehicles at Subiaco, stationary and nose to tail. They first blocked both ends of the line with bombs and then strafed the column, accounting for 200 vehicles. The total motor transport claims by the crews of the Tactical Air Force over the last six days of May 1943 were 1,148 destroyed and 766 damaged. In December 1944 the ORB notes 200 locomotives destroyed that month.

This was not a risk-free 'turkey shoot', the decorations list each month was impressive. The following extract is from 27 May 1944:

John Cassons exemplified courage. He strafed enemy transport near Altari then flew top cover. Cassons R/Td my leg's pretty well shot off. He was so calm they thought it was his oleo leg [landing gear strut]. In fact a cannon shell had hit his left thigh shattering the bone and hitting his right arm and damaging the ulna nerve of his left arm. On landing he didn't ask for emergency landing and waited his turn. He died shortly after landing.

Cassons was awarded the Conspicuous Gallantry Medal.

Later, in the winter, when flying on a mission over Yugoslavia S/L Nash (CO 3 SAAF Squadron) had trouble finding the target owing to cloud ceiling at 3000 feet. S/L Nash dived through the cloud, located and fixed the target, returned to his squadron led them into attack then returned above the cloud base again to guide in two other squadrons to the attack area.

There was another aspect of life that would have concerned Tom as Senior Medical Officer. After Italy had surrendered some men long deprived of female company, not surprisingly, wanted to marry Italian women. On occasions it was sometimes contrived to arrange a posting as a 'cooling off' period, but all potential brides were submitted to strict medical examination to exclude all physical diseases including venereal infection, before permission to marry was granted. The reverse was not also instituted and on occasion it was the innocent bride who became infected.

VD was rife in Sicily and Italy, it had reached epidemic proportions because so many armies had passed through. Tom would have given lectures on the nature of the illness, its avoidance and treatment. Almost every village and town had huge notice boards in English warning servicemen that all female inhabitants they were likely to encounter were already infected and would transmit the disease to them. Men were warned that as with sunburn, the contraction of the disease was a self-inflicted injury and liable to disciplinary action unless it could be proved that the man had taken full precautions against it, for example taking condoms, which were available from a special centre and leaving a numbered slip of paper, which could be referred back to if the need arose. Such was the incidence notwithstanding all efforts that some hospitals had permanent VD specialists.

The matter of leave and Rest and Recuperation raised its head. The Wing reports for October include an appendix by the Group Captain Commanding 239 Wing, regarding leave arrangements:

In an attempt to alleviate the strain imposed on personnel by a long period of sustained, intensive operations and to maintain a high morale during the winter, the problem of leave facilities for O.R.s was tackled in earnest … A deputation … explored the possibilities of establishing a centre in Florence and found what they considered to be a well nigh ideal place …

The hotel restaurant had been in disuse for some considerable period and there were other domestic difficulties to be solved. With the experience of last winter's leave hotels ventures at Amalfi and Naples to draw on howeve,r it was felt that all obstacles could be surmounted … The proprietor was more than agreeable to a private financial arrangement and all that remained was to obtain the authority of the military authorities … Approach was made to Florence Command by the deputation and it was requested by Command that application … be submitted in writing with the backing of Desert Air Force.

The full case was, therefore, immediately submitted to Headquarters Desert Air Force, stressing Wing Headquarters' willingness to implement the proposed scheme in its entirety without external assistance. After an interval of about a week another Wing representative armed with Desert Air Force's written blessing of the project hurried to Florence hoping to 'clinch the deal.' He found the American forces in possession! Appeals to various authorities in Florence either to release the hotel or make available an alternative were fruitless. Florence was Fifth Army, it seemed, and there was little or no concern about units associated with the Eighth. A dismal end to a promising venture.

Group Captain, Commanding
No. 239 Wing D.A.F.

By October 1944 5 SAAF had joined the wing and 112 Squadron RAF were to say goodbye to their Kittyhawks as they converted to P-51 Mustangs. On 4 October the 79th American Fighter Group arrived from Corsica with '52 P-47 Thunderbolts, many DC3s several Fortresses and Liberators'.

Of all the Allied fighter types pressed into service as fighter-bombers, many think the P-47 Thunderbolt was the most suited. Weighing almost 7 tons (three times more than a fully laden FW 190) it could roll with amazing agility, was faster at all altitudes than either the FW 190 or the Me 109 and it had no peer when plunged into a dive. It was easy to fly in formation and easy to land. It provided a stable gun platform and unlike most of its contemporaries, the cockpit was roomy and comfortable.

As the new arrivals appeared, the airfield at Fano where the Wing was now based was chaos, on one or two occasions aircraft were seen hurtling down the runway in opposite directions; but there were no crashes. One Mustang was written off when a bomb fell off and rendered the flaps useless.

The base had already housed squadrons of the RAF, RAAF and SAAF but the addition of the American group added a little spice, as shown in the ORB for 7 October.

Wing supported the Eighth Army. 2 bridges at Savio were to be destroyed. One was definitely hit and the other obscured by mud and smoke of bombing. Incidentally both these bridges had been attacked earlier in the day by the Thunderbolts of 79th Group who claimed to have destroyed them both. 260 Squadron saw that both appeared undamaged so that the Americans either indulged in wishful thinking or attacked the wrong targets.

By November the Wing was attacking targets in Yugoslavia. The ORB of 22 November 1944 records:

A Lysander was escorted on a special job by six Mustangs of 3 SAAF squadron who had converted from Kittyhawks. It is regrettable to have to record that a XIIth USAAF Mustang cut in between Squadron Leader Nash DFC and the Lysander and made a quite unprovoked attack from very close range and shot the Lysander down in flames – no-one was seen to get out.

This incident comes up several times in the ORB, including the reference to S/L Nash being ordered as witness to a US Court Martial – presumably of the pilot concerned.

On 29/30 November Tom was extremely busy dealing with another tragedy. A 'hang-up bomb' fell off a returning aircraft and landed on the town of Fano. The medical team worked hard all through the night. Leading Aircraftsman Rowley and many civilians were killed. Again, this incident re-appears as the circumstances are investigated at various Boards of Inquiry.

November 1944

The whole Wing is now in billets. Careful attention has been given to the prevention of over-crowding, particularly in view of the occurrence of a case of cerebro-spinal meningitis within the Wing. The minimum space per person is about 50 feet.

Venereal Disease is slightly on the increase probably owing to increased opportunities on moving into billets in a town. As a whole however the health of the Wing continues to be good. The total number admitted to hospital or Wing sick quarters during the month was 59 compared with 63 last month.

TL Stoate
Squadron Leader
Senior medical officer
Headquarters 239 wing

On the positive side, Tom would no doubt have been pleased to learn that the camp at Fano scored highly in the comfort stakes. The November ORB records:

All personnel appreciate the 'winter billets' instead of waterlogged tents and will assuredly benefit by living n a civilised manner … Group Captain Easton DSO DFC inspected all billets and found them in excellent order and the occupants quite happy in their unaccus-tomed surroundings.

In December the ORB notes the Medical Officer checked billets to see each man had a mini-mum area of 36 square feet.

Appendix A to Form 540 –December 1944

The health of the Wing continues to be good, with no epidemics and very little preventable disease.

The blankets of all personnel of Wing Headquarters and the squadrons have been changed for newly washed and disinfected ones by arrangement with an Army Mobile Laundry.

Volunteers to act as blood donors have been called for from Wing Headquarters and all the squadrons and a panel of about 50 group O(4) donors has been formed. Twenty were supplied to 59th General Hospital, at their request, during the month.

In an echo of Roy's last job with 19 Squadron, the ORB for December includes the follow-ing; escorting the strategic air force bombers would not have been high on the wish list of the fighter boys:

The extremely uninteresting job of escorting medium bombers reared its ugly head during the month; it was not made any simpler by the fact that the bombers strayed all over the sky as well as frequently making a mess up of the rendezvous.

As the campaign proceeded and the Wing moved northwards life in Italy was no more com-fortable or secure. The 7 December ORB notes 'Landscape inundated as far as the eye could see as Jerry had upset the gentle flow of the river Po.' It was, however, this river that finally did for the courageous German defence, as the German General Von Senger pointed out:

It was the bombing of the River Po crossings that finished us. We could have withdrawn suc-cessfully with normal rearguard action despite the heavy pressure but owing to the destruction of the ferries and river crossings we lost all our equipment. North of the river we were no longer an army.

It was not just the water that caused difficulties, on 4 December the American interpreter for 79th Group was beaten up by the Italians and on the 22nd a number of vehicles were sabotaged. Accordingly, the guard was doubled to 100 around the airfield. Accidents continued to be a part of life; on the 17th a Mustang crashed on takeoff and ploughed into and killed a number of a group of American airmen working in dispersals. Always on the move the Wing was about to shift again and on 17 December the ORB notes:

> S/L Stoate (SMO) … started off at first light on a recce of the Ravenna airfield area … The prospective site was surveyed. Owing to the fact that the Hun was only 400 yards away at the time, it was thought advisable not to fix too definitely on any of the buildings for billeting purposes in case they were no longer standing and only a pile of rubble when the time came to use them.

It is often good value to look at an ORB for Christmas, for 239 Wing, Christmas Day 1944 reads: 'With singular lack of tact and consideration, the clerk of the weather decided to send a spell of fine weather, which seriously impeded the seasonal celebrations during daylight.' As for New Year: 'A large percentage of the unit are Scotsmen or Northerners and consequently the old year was seen out and the new one seen in with quite a bang!!!!'

With customary changes of plan, it now seemed that the Wing was to move not to Ravenna but Rimini. Members of the Squadron, very likely including Tom as Senior MO, were told to go up and see about billets they were to take over from 324 Wing (72 Squadron formed part of this Wing having seen action up the western side of Italy, then the south of France and now back to Italy, but Roy Hussey had left about a year earlier). The ORB notes: '324 only have 4 squadrons and are already under canvas so how are we with 6 squadrons going to fit into that space?' In the event the next stop was Cervia.

On 12 January 1945 rockets were fitted to the Mustangs with the comment 'Wizard', so the experimental work Roy Hussey carried out at the Air Fighting Development Unit in 1944 was now being applied in anger in the Italian as well as northern Europe theatres.

Making a further connection, this time with Jack Stoate's progress through Belgium on the way to the Elbe at Hamburg and the comments made about the Gestapo Headquaters at Breendonk, the ORB for 18 January 1945 notes: 'Gestapo Headquarters in Rosa Nr Bassons attacked by 2 Kittyhawk squadrons.'

On 26 January Wing Commander Westlake returned after having damaged his knee in a forced landing and being hospitalised.

The Form 540 report for January 1945 recorded 'an even lower scale of effort than did December.' Everything is relative, some 50 tons of bombs were still dropped, 7000 rounds of ammunition expended and 7000 miles flown, including 59 close support missions and 53 rail interdiction missions. The author of the report includes this exchange:

> No combat with enemy aircraft occurred but on one occasion a pilot of 260 Squadron, intending to rejoin his squadron above cloud after bombing started to join up with 3 Me109s. Having recognised them as hostile he was about to open fire when remembering his 'Tee Em' [the mirror], he looked behind and saw a fourth Me109 on his tail so he hastily took cover in cloud. His leader who was below cloud heard frantic cries of 'Help, help; I'm surrounded by Messerschmitts.' To which the Leader dourly replied; 'What is your call sign, clot?' and was told it was Blue 2. After about five minutes of silence Leader called up 'Hello Blue 2, have you been shot down yet? Blue 2 replied, 'No, I'm in a cloud.' The adventure ended happily.

Tom was shortly to leave 239 Wing tour expired but not before the Rimini site had been declared inappropriate and he had sorted out the next camp at Cervia. His successor S/L Jones was enthusiastic: 'We now prepare for ground and air supremacy over the mosquito and hope a well co-ordinated anti-malarial campaign will prevent the crescendo of the war being compli-cated by malaria.' As to Cervia, the ORB notes:

> The Wing moved to Cervia which is an excellent site amongst pine trees and is also mainly sand. The men were all for tent life this place previously being a modern fascists holiday resort. Chalets are in abundance and some of these are being used as operations room and flying control, and being only 50 yards away from no. 22 MFH (Mobile Field Hospital) has been a terrific help, injured pilots being able to have blood transfusions within a short time of land-ing. This has happened recently.
>
> In conclusion I should like to say that this is a near perfect a Wing layout as we have seen under field conditions.
>
> GH Westlake
> Wing Commander Flying
> 239 Wing DAF

So just as his younger brother Jack in 30 battalion RM was about to embark overseas for the first time for action in North West Europe so Tom's time to leave 239 Wing had come. The ORB notes on 11 February 1945: 'Second tour expired party leave for embarkation. S/L TL Stoate on boat waiting expectantly.'

Having completed four years service overseas, two-and-a-half years of which was on front line duties, Tom arrived back in England on 13 March 1945 and finished his war service with a number of short postings including 1 PDC (Personnel Dispatch Centre), HQ CCU (Costal Command Unit), 56 PTC (Personnel Transit Centre) 5 ACMB, (Air Crew Medical Board) 1 CMB (based co-incidentally at RAF Halton, where Tom did his induction - the Central Medical Board was where one might have gone to obtain permission to fly again after an illness), 9 PDC and finally 100 PDC from where, on 26 January 1946, a year after he had left front line duties, he received his Class 'A' release, although his last day's service is noted as 11 May 1946.

Hippocrates wrote that 'War is the only proper school for the surgeon' and 'The finest pabu-lum [nourishment] of a young surgeon is the blood of warriors.' Tom was a physician not a surgeon but in the same the way that tiredness comes to seasoned pilots, their lives lived so violently during their combats that ten years of experience was squeezed into the space of two or three, Tom probably underwent a similar form of overload with medicine. After the war he gave up doctoring in favour of farming. Although he remained with the RAFVR until 2 July 1959, when he was gazetted as having relinquished his commission.

11

CARRYING ON

The family after the war

It is hard to know how to round off this narrative, neither people nor wars last forever. I have taken the title of this final chapter from the letter my grandmother, Nellie Hussey, Roy Hussey's mother, sent to her sister Epps after Roy was killed:' Nothing will ever be the same again, we just carry on.'

When writing this book I sent copies of the sections to various members of my family, not only for their interest but also to get a response from time to time. One of my younger brothers, Tom, who flies and maintains aeroplanes, and is married to Sabine, a German lady, reacted to Roy Hussey's story in such a way that I thought it was worth reproducing:

Hi Eddy,

Read your transcript on Roy Hussey over the weekend. I found it very interesting although you couldn't help shedding a few tears on some of the sad times they went through. It just goes to show what do we really know about our family.

I just didn't realise he was such a great and talented pilot. Over five hundred hours of combat flying is quite remarkable and he was so young at the time. It makes me think of the sacrifices they made to have the world we live in today, it just goes to show the young kids today don't have a clue how lucky they are. Although with his experience in flying warplanes, how could he make such a fundamental mistake of letting the speed drop off on an approach to land? It's one thing I am very conscious of because as soon as you start lowering the undercarriage and flaps etc the drag becomes very noticeable and soon your speed has dropped off to the stall. Fighter planes are built to be unstable for better response in roll etc, so at 800–1000 feet you stand no chance of recovery.

All the best
Tom.

Jack Stoate on Symphonic Poem and Tony Stoate on Topsy. (Author)

The author on Topsy at Well House Farm. (Author)

Nellie Hussey outside the Folly. in the late 1970s. (Author)

PS Sabine wants to take it on holiday to read. I don't think she will be impressed with the mention of bombing Dortmund, her home town!

In researching for this book I have been constantly impressed by the modesty of those Second World War veterans I have been able to meet and for the most part how they found their experiences enjoyable – the innate optimism of youth. Brother Tom's words must surely echo in many households today. How little we know about that generation in our families and how little time there is to speak to those who can add the colour of first-hand memories of those days.

Roy Hussey, of course did not survive to reap any reward for his sacrifice, and in a sense, having spoken to his brother, Tim, and several men who served with him, we should not grieve too much. As Tim Hussey says, flying was all he ever wanted to do and he had that wish. That is not a unique reaction amongst the fighter pilots who have been kind enough to share their experiences with me.

Far darker, to me, would be the thought of incarceration without any clue as when or if one might be released. That would be a real spirit breaker, Yet David Stoate reflects on how those four birthdays showed him man's kindness to his fellow man and the real value of friendship and duty. The trick must be to look forward, not back. The list of men's singles champions in the pavilion of the Beaufort Road Tennis Club in Bristol for 1952 inlcudes David Stoate as winner. After the war, in 1948, he married Patricia Hardy, whom he met in 1947, and had two children, Pamela and Kenneth. Today my uncle, at the age of 94, plays golf and bridge at local clubs. So the brother who suffered by far the worst privations certainly 'carried on'.

Maybe if there had not been political fiddling, or if Operation *Market Garden* had gone better for the Allies, it might have been Montgomery and Bradley entering Berlin at the end of 1944, rather than the Russians who first hoisted their flag over the ruins of the Reichstag building. In that event my father Jack Stoate would almost certainly have never left these shores in the Royal Marines – but then he would never have met up with his brother Norman in Brundbuttle either; and the family know what pleasure that gave them both.

So what did this family of pre-war millers and farmers, the doctor and aspiring lawyer do when the war was over? David went back to Spillers who sent him overseas to Canada and later on in his career to Rhodesia.

After demob at the end of the war my father was offered by his father the manager's job on what was by all accounts, a lovely farm, called Petherton Park near North Petherton, Somerset. It had an old manor farmhouse (albeit in poor condition as it had been requisitioned during the war) and a few hundred acres of very fertile land. Like many others, however, he had broken free of paternal ties and wanted to do his own thing. Wanting literally to plough his own furrow he took a lease of 125 acres of rather poor land at Well house Farm in Eversley from the Lord Brocket Estate. There he and Betty had four other children, me, Susan and the twins Tom and Roland, my elder brother Tony having been born earlier in December 1944.

Sadly, as earlier mentioned Betty died at 52. My father remarried, adopted his new wife Ann's twin boy and girl, Nigel and Louise and lived to just before his 80th birthday.

Norman bought Cann Mills near Shaftesbury in 1947. In 1954 the mill was pretty well burned down and Norman turned up at Well House Farm with his Bedford Lorry to borrow the hammer mill and mixer that his brother Jack was happy to spare from the farm granary. The mill was rebuilt and one of his two sons Michael (a fifth generation Stoate miller) still works the overshot water wheel powered stones. The other son, Christopher, inherited Norman and Jean's interest in wildlife and nature and how they need not be incompatible with profitable estate management.

I remember with pleasure Norman's visits to Well House Farm. Eventually he met and married Jean Humphry, a stunning brunette. He (as well as the rest of us I might add) was captivated by her.

After he died, Jean told me she had found his war diary which had gone missing; she explained that she knew he had one but that neither of them had been able to locate it for many years. At some stage he had had his original hand-written notes typed up, but even this version is not in a perfect condition.

Tom settled down to farming 140 acres of fertile land at Lower Court Farm Almondsbury, near Bristol, ultimately putting it all down to cider apple orchards. His death, in 1996, car-ries a little 'dit' of its own. He had been suffering with cancer and said to his neighbours that if one morning they were to see the curtains drawn later than usual in the morning they were to come in. Well, some time later the inevitable happened and they entered to find a propped up Tom, cold in bed with a half filled nightcap tumbler still clutched in his lifeless hand resting on his chest. A dignified end.

Geoffrey rose to become Senior Partner of a firm of solicitors in Parkstone near Poole. He is our family historian and with his warm chuckle a wise counsellor to boot. In 1950 He married Joy Evans and produced five children. He and Joy now live in Somerset close to the Stoate family roots, looking across the countryside to Watchet where William Stoate started his first flour mill.

The connection between the Stoate and Hussey families did not stop when my parents married in January 1944. In 1950 the Radford family who were connected to the Husseys by marriage, were

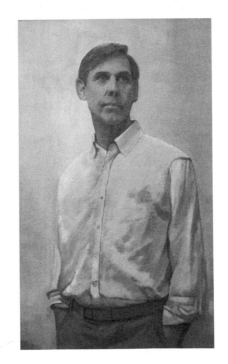

Portrait of the author by David Fallow.

looking to sell the somewhat run down Whitehouse Farm in that part of north Bristol now called Emmerson Green. White House Farm was an easy walk along Folly Brook from The Folly Inn and close to Henfield Farm, owned by Leonard Stoate. Tim Hussey longed to buy the farm but had no money and was unable to raise a mortgage.

My parents went to Leonard to see if he could help, only to find he too had plans for the Radford's property. Leonard generously stood back and lent Tim the money he needed to secure the farm and his future with his wife Paddy and their two sons, Stuart and Chris.

I am part of that generation born in the two decades following the Second World War. We are almost certainly the luckiest people in history, we are the richest, most powerful and most secure generation the world has seen.

Our parents scrimped and sacrificed through the depression of the early thirties and suffered the deprivations of the Second World War. In contrast we have basked in handsome benefits, cheap holidays, mostly secure employment, women's liberation and the consumer driven shopping revolution.

For more than half a century we have been living it up, borrowing and spending in the sure knowledge that money would not run out. But now the cost of that spree is becoming unpleasantly apparent. Like Roy's 'end of term' party at AFDU – what a party and what a mess.

What makes it particularly disturbing is the way in which my generation seems to have cast our own progeny to the winds. Historically the ethic was for one generation to leave things better for the next. They were merely caretakers or custodians. It is to be hoped that at some stage a sense of duty and loyalty will re-emerge, for when all fails the most effective and basic welfare system of all is the family. This is a story about families; and duty.

Roy Hussey's grave.

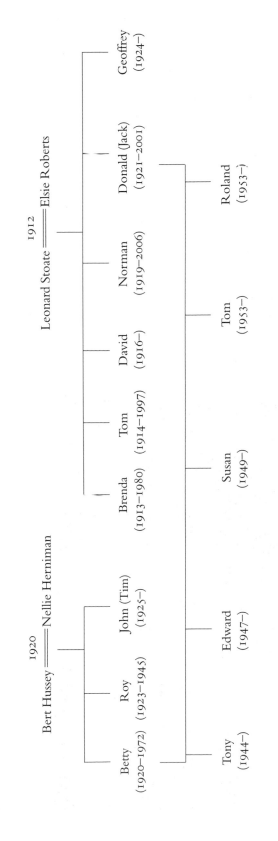

Hussey/Stoate Family Tree

Bert Hussey $=\!\!=\!\!=$ Nellie Herniman
1920

Betty (1920–1972)　Roy (1923–1945)　John (Tim) (1925–)

Tony (1944–)　Edward (1947–)

Leonard Stoate $=\!\!=\!\!=$ Elsie Roberts
1912

Brenda (1913–1980)　Tom (1914–1997)　David (1916–)　Norman (1919–2006)　Donald (Jack) (1921–2001)　Geoffrey (1924–)

Susan (1949–)　Tom (1953–)　Roland (1953–?)

For Roy Hussey C.G.M., D.F.C., R.A.F. (Killed January 1945)

Who knows Roy Hussey? The thrush, the thrush
With his quivering song in the blackberry bush.

"Will he shout with us, anon, anon,
"As in summers gone, in summers gone?"

No, not this year will he whistle and call.
We shall not hear his voice at all.

"Tell me then, is our Roy grown rich
"That he leaves his fellows by Folly ditch?"

"Or is he ailing as it would seem
"That he leaps not over by Folly stream?"

"I've sung in the orchard merrily,
"But never a note to answer me."

"And I peer each evening from out the hedge
"But there's only shadows on Folly bridge."

"Only green shades and a yellow sky
"And Folly idly lisping by,"

"And the willows dark on the grasses still
"And the dwindling road on the silent hill."

"Say, is it told within your book
"Why he no more lingers by Folly brook?"

I've spelt and searched, but it's not told there
And it's not told rightly anywhere

Why he should leave this lovely land –
That we shall never understand.

I only know that two abide
Watching the fading countryside;

Two in England and one away,
And summer brings never a summer day.

Terence Packer (friend of Roy Hussey)

Dedicated to the Crew of HMML 909

Cox'n Northcott is a Scot
All out for games and fun
And when he's told to do a job
It's always being done

The Motor Mac, a broader Scot
Who lives up, up the line
And when you give a job to him
He never has the time

Ldg Seaman Wood comes next
An efficient man is he
In fact he's just resigned his job
He's now an ex-flunky

Next comes the Asdic Rating
By name Ldg Seaman Bland
A recent addition to the crew
But quite an oldish hand

Graves we pick at random
He doesn't often moan
The only reason we can think,
He's always going home

Able Seaman F.J. Kay
A keen young kind of guy
For when we come close to a wreck
He tries to catch my eye

Rosher is a good ship's cook
But what gives me the pip
When any little thing goes wrong
He doesn't fail to drip

Next comes Sparker Rushworth
A lad just from his teens
Who keeps well hidden down below
And thrives on tinned baked beans

Askew is a gunner
A willing lad to keep
But I think you'll all agree with me
He does so like his sleep

Rule is next upon our list
In his hands a new aldis
But after a night out his
Reading is as poor as piss

Sloan another Scotsman
A quiet lad we think,
We sometimes wish we were like him
And never took to drink

Lavers is a Stoker
Looking somewhat grave
Early in the morning
Always needs a shave

Lawson is a Stoker too
He does not look so glum
The funny thing about it
He is Stoker One

Rogers is a Sparker
Oh so hail and hearty
Nothing much is said of him
Care and maintenance party

Mills an Able Seaman
A dapper sort of lad
But oh when he's on look out
He does look very sad

Stanley is a new one
A good lad I believe
No sooner does he come on board
Then he shoots off again on leave

And so this is the ending
The story is unfurled
The best thing is about it
It's the best crew in the world.

Norman Stoate

BIBLIOGRAPHY

Barker, Ralph, *Down in the Drink* (Pan)
Bolitho, Hector, *Combat Report* (B.T. Batsford)
Brookes Andrew, *Air War over Italy* (Ian Allan Publishing)
Burns, Michael G., *Bader the Man and his Men* (Cassell)
Carver, Michael, *Dilemmas of the Desert War* (Spellmount)
Coast, John, *Railroad of Death* (Hyperion Press)
Corbin, Jimmy, *Last of the Ten Fighter Boys* (Sutton Publishing)
Darlow, Steve, *Five of the Few* (Grub Street)
Docherty, Tom, *Swift to Battle* (Pen & Sword)
Farrish, Greggs, *Algiers to Anzio* (Woodfield)
Glancy, Jonathan, *Spitfire* (Atlantic Books)
Hardie, Robert, *The Burma Siam Railway* (Imperial War Museum)
Hough, Richard & Denis Richards, *The Battle of* Britain (Hodder and Stoughton)
Jenkins, C.A., *Days of a Dogsbody* (George G Harrap)
Lamb, Richard, *Montgomery in Europe 1943–1945* (Buchan & Enright)
Macintyre, Donald, *The Battle for the Mediterranean* (Pan)
Mansfield, Angus, *Barney Barnfather* (The History Press)
Mansfield, Angus, *Spitfire Saga: Rodney Scrase DFC* (The History Press)
Shankland, Peter & Antony Hunter, *Malta Convoy* (Fortuna)
Rolf, Mel, *Hell on Earth* (Grub Street)
Shewell-Cooper, W.E., *Land Girl* (English Universities Press)
Shores, Christopher, Hans Ring & William N. Hess, *Fighters over Tunisia* (Neville Spearman)
Squire, H.F., *Middle East Scrapbook* (Pentland Press)
Warner, Oliver, *The British Navy* (Thames and Hudson)
Wellum, Geoffrey, *First Light* (Penguin)

INDEX